CHAPLIN

CHAPLIN

The Tramp's Odyssey

SIMON LOUVISH

faber and faber

First published in 2009
by Faber and Faber Ltd
Bloomsbury House 74–77 Great Russell Street London WC1B 3DA

Typeset by RefineCatch Limited, Bungay, Suffolk
Printed in England by CPI Mackays, Chatham ME5 8TD

A CIP record for this book
is available from the British Library

ISBN 978-0-571-23768-5

2 4 6 8 10 9 7 5 3 1

Contents

CONTENTS

List of Illustrations

PROLOGUE

Charles Chaplin, behind the camera.

The King in Exile

In Charles Chaplin's last but one film, and the last in which he starred, *A King in New York*, released in 1957, the ex-Tramp plays the ruler of an imaginary European kingdom, who is deposed by a popular revolution. The people swarm through the palace gates, carrying an effigy of the King stuck on a pole, but when they break into the King's chambers they are all empty, and in the vault where his money was kept a row of great steel doors are unlocked and open – the King has fled with all the loot. In the next scene, Pan American Airways deposits the dapper King, with his Balkan-style fur hat, at New York's airport, where he is met by his faithful ambassador and faithless prime minister and a crowd of pressmen, who follow him into the immigration hall. In the hall, as his fingerprints are being taken by uniformed officials, the deposed King delivers a short little speech, to a newsman's question:

'Your majesty – won't you say a few words to the American people?'

The King replies, as his fingers are dipped in ink one by one:

'I am deeply moved by your warm friendship and hospitality. This big-hearted nation has already demonstrated its noble generosity to those who come to seek a refuge from tyranny. Thank you.'

At the time, it seemed to many viewers of the film that, amusing as the scene was, it may have been a clumsy way of venting Chaplin's fury at the country to which he had contributed so much over forty years and which had then, in the red heat of the anti-Communist witch-hunts, set a barrier to his return to the US and declared him an unwanted visitor while he was aboard a ship travelling to England in 1952. Now, more than fifty years later, when we view the new 'normalities' of fortress America's suspicion of every tourist, presenting our right and left index fingers at the immigration booths, we might regard Chaplin as more prescient than most. For the Englishman who had travelled to North America aboard the steamer *Cairnrona* in September 1910 with a troupe of Fred Karno's Speechless Comedians, and had become within five years an American and a universal symbol, it was a bitter irony – that decades of success should be crowned with so curt and churlish a rejection.

The exiled King Shahdov, unaware at first that his loot has been looted in turn by his treacherous PM, sets off, in the company of his ambassador Jaume, to see the town, enthusing: 'Ah, Jaume! If you only knew what it means to breathe this free air! This wonderful, wonderful America! Its youth! Its genius! Its vitality! The glamour of it all – New York!' as he opens the window curtain upon a stock shot of the Empire State Building. Since the film was shot in England, Chaplin's New York is a contrived fantasy, a studio-built, futuristic metropolis of skewed nightmares and distorting satire. Borne along a downtown crowd to the warbling strains of a voice crooning 'When I think of a million dollars – tears come to my eyes . . .', Shahdov and Jaume seek refuge in a movie theatre, where the films are preceded by a rock 'n' roll band belting out its licks to a horde of youngsters bopping robotically in the aisle. Pushing through hysterical girls – 'She bit me! Completely insane!' – the two foreigners settle in the front row to be regaled by a succession of widescreen horrors: the 'Coming Attractions' feature a cold-blooded killer ('You'll love him – he'll creep into your heart!') and *Man or Woman*, a perhaps unconscious reprise of Ed Wood's little-known *Glen or Glenda*, with the woman speaking in a man's voice and vice versa, 'inspired' by a Danish sex-change sensation. The main feature's shoot-out Western ranges across the huge Cinemascope screen, so that after a few neck-twisting right-to-left head turns King Shahdov decides to leave the theatre.

The *New York Times* reported on Chaplin's new film sourly on its release in September 1957:

LONDON, Sept. 10 – Charles Chaplin was here today beating the drums for his latest motion picture, 'A King in New York,' which will have its world premiere here Thursday.

Reviewers for the London newspapers saw the picture today at a special preview . . . An American who attended the preview and who has seen most of Mr. Chaplin's films summed up the judgment by saying: 'It isn't funny.'

The *Times* of London found 'A King in New York' disappointing. The *Daily Telegraph* said it was 'the work of a very bitter man.' The *Daily Mail* found it 'a lumpish mixture of subtle slapstick and clumsy political satire.' But the *News Chronicle* reviewer said the picture 'nails more genuine lies in its 105-minute duration than any 105 pictures I have seen in the past year.'

Mr. Chaplin uses his eighty-first picture to ridicule many aspects of American life, from television commercials to the House Committee on Un-American Activities. There are no arrangements at present for it to be shown in the United States.

Mr. Chaplin left the United States in 1952. The Attorney General announced that he would not be permitted to return without a hearing on charges of 'moral turpitude and Communist sympathies.'

Chaplin's departure from America had been an unusual instance of the use of immigration laws to proscribe a world-famous person. Technically, Chaplin was not prevented from re-entering the United States in 1952. The newly appointed Attorney General, James P. McGranery, had merely 'ordered authorities of the Immigration and Naturalization Service to determine whether the famous comedian should be readmitted'. When he returned, the *New York Times* reported on 20 September, 'he will have to satisfy the requirements of law imposed on any new immigrant'. That is, he would be required, if he returned by ship, to disembark offshore at Ellis Island and face an interrogation 'to satisfy the authorities that he is of good health, sound mind and good morals'.

In a strange echo, this was the same procedure that had been waived for his mother, when Chaplin had arranged for her transfer from England to Los Angeles to live in old-age comfort in 1921. At that time, Chaplin's fame enabled him to pull favours to evade the rules which would have refused her admission on the grounds of her poor mental state. In 1925, her permission to stay was revoked by immigration officials and preparations were made to arrange for her to live in Vancouver, but in the event, Chaplin's clout enabled her to stay until her death in Glendale in 1928.

In the charged atmosphere of Cold War paranoia, Chaplin's continuing decision not to seek US citizenship was proof of his un-American status. Chaplin had endured two years in the 1940s embroiled in a paternity suit by a young actress who had been a one-time lover, Joan Barry, including a lurid and sensational court case in which his 'moral turpitude' was mixed with allegations of his 'socialist' and 'Communist' views. A decade later sex and socialism remained a heady brew for the guardians of America's gates at a time of US–Soviet rivalry, the leaking of atom bomb secrets and the threat of a nuclear Armageddon. When in 1947 the House Un-American Activities Committee had requested him to come to Washington to appear before them, he sent them a telegram stating: 'While you are preparing your engraved subpoena I will give you a hint where I stand. I am not a Communist. I am a peacemonger.' In a great news scrum on 12 April that year in New York, called to introduce his latest film, *Monsieur Verdoux*, Chaplin told the press that he had never become an American citizen because 'I am not a nationalist.'

Chaplin cast himself a decade later as King Shahdov to highlight the absurdity of a king being accused of Communism, imagining his final confrontation with the House Un-American Activities Committee as the King, having got his finger stuck in a fire hose in his hotel elevator, drags it along to soak the stern senators in a great wishful-thinking denouement. Shahdov has come to America, not just to escape the wrath of his own people, but to bring the American people his plans for a peaceful use of atomic energy and his 'hopes of revolutionizing modern life and bringing about a utopia'. His fate is alike absurd and self-induced, as his faith in a better future is undermined by his own shortcomings, his frosty royal marriage and his innate conservative and patrician identity.

The most poignant part of *A King in New York* is the relationship between the exiled King and a small boy, Rupert, who is in a 'model' reform school after his parents have been arrested as Communists who have defied the Committee. Chaplin cast his own son, Michael, in this role, and coached him through his finger-wagging diatribe at his father-king, presenting a basic version of Chaplin's own personal creed 'out of the mouth of babes': 'I dislike all forms of government,' rants the boy, who has been introduced at the home to Shahdov as the editor of the house magazine on 'current events':

Politics are rules imposed upon the people . . . they have become weapons of political despots . . . they have every man in a straitjacket and without a passport he can't move a toe . . . to leave a country is like breaking out of jail and to enter a country is like going through the eye of a needle! And free speech! Does that exist? And free enterprise – today it's all monopolies . . . today the whole world will blow up because of too much power! If civilization is to survive, we must combat power until the dignity and peace of man are restored!

Rupert's fate, however, is to be defeated, and he escapes the home when he is pressured by government agents to save his parents by providing names of their friends. Despite Shahdov's kindness in taking him in, he is returned to his guardians, and is last met by the King as a cowed, weeping child, having given in to power. Chaplin wraps up the film by a *deus ex machina*: newspaper headlines reveal, despite the hosing, that KING SHAHDOV PROVES FRIENDLY WITNESS, followed by the ultra-absurd KING CLEARED OF COMMUNISM, so that Shahdov can fly out of New York to rejoin his glacial queen in Paris.

Along the way, Chaplin unfolds more satirical swipes at the commercialization of American life, as Shahdov falls foul of a ruse by an attractive TV journalist, appearing to endorse certain products at a society party that is secretly filmed by a concealed live camera. Television screens in the bathroom may have seemed a clumsy artifice to the critics, in those innocent early 1950s. Realizing he is bankrupt, Shahdov soon succumbs, and even accepts a facelift so he may better advertise 'Royal Crown Whisky'. Ever mindful of his past, Chaplin slips in some slapstick painter-and-stooge-with-paint-bucket routine that was old hat in Mack Sennett days. On sawbones' orders to keep his new face set, Shahdov dissolves in laughter and ruins his cosmetic surgery. Slapstick moments slip in at other points in the plot, when Shahdov has to mime the short life of the sturgeon for a waiter when ordering caviar under an ear-splitting jazz band, or using the plate and his hand to invoke turtle soup. In the final, drawn-out hosepipe-on-the-finger gag, old Keystone lives briefly once again.

Chaplin knows well, as we do, that Shahdov is still Charlie the Tramp, grown older, shorn of his old clothes and toothbrush moustache, the mask of the eternal vagrant who had last been seen in his traditional form in *Modern Times*, in 1936. In *The Great Dictator* of 1940 he split into the two sides of his personality – the light and the dark: the Jewish barber and the deranged ruler Adenoid Hynkel. In one of history's inevitable ironies, Adolf Hitler's toothbrush moustache had seemed to challenge Charlie's, and the dictator's ranting – which appeared clownish and eccentric to the citizens of western democracies – meant, as Chaplin understood quite well, that Charlie the Tramp had to run and hide, and take on new disguises. He was to emerge, with a different moustache, and different attire, as Monsieur Verdoux, the serial wife-killer of a decaying and decadent Europe, and then as his unmasked self, the English clown Calvero, before his final bow as Shahdov. And then, with one further, ill-fated film, *A Countess from Hong Kong*, starring Sophia Loren and Marlon Brando, in 1967, he was gone, his ghost appearing in a brief scene aboard an ocean liner at the tag-end of the cast list, as 'An Old Steward'. This last film was full of Chaplins, his sons and daughters – Sydney, Geraldine, Victoria, Josephine – but the tramp-clown had departed.

History has, as we know, been kind to Charles Chaplin, whose Tramp creation has now stood the test of time for over ninety years, and will within a few years gain his centenary. Their reputation, both creator and creation, has waxed and waned over the decades. Perceived as the world's most famous screen person in the 1920s, Chaplin was nevertheless damaged at home by the American government's hostility in the wake of the Second World War, although his star remained ascendant abroad. The British, the French, the Germans, Russians, folk the world over from Chile to China recognized and adored the 'little fellow', who sailed through life's troubles kicking against all the odds. Later, in the 1960s, when film fans became more analytical and stern about their movie heroes, Charlie was devalued, often placed as a poor second to the apparently more cerebral antics of Buster Keaton, or the homely genius of Harold Lloyd. But his films continued to be recycled as TV staples, and books proliferated, in a host of languages, around the world. Of books on Chaplin there appears to be no end, and in the age of media studies and archival restorations, Chaplin has climbed back to the top of the comedy tree. The image of the Tramp has remained so familiar that there are now conflicts and disputes over its use in a wide range of advertising campaigns, from lotteries to computers. In the world of commerce, as King Shahdov discovered quickly, recognition is all, and the merit of that recognition counts for little, or nothing, as time flies on.

So why another book? In biographical terms, David Robinson's magisterial tome, *Chaplin: His Life and Art*, first published in 1985, remains the most comprehensive of the many lives of Chaplin the Creator, the Man behind the Mask – his childhood, early life, his later loves and marriages, the circumstances, twists and turns of his life as a producer, director, star of his own films. Film historians and archivists have excavated his archaeological layers in projects such as Kevin Brownlow's presentation of the 'Unknown Chaplin', while archival work by the British Film Institute, various national archives and, in particular, the central Chaplin archive in Bologna have made sure every piece of evidence of his long life and work is preserved. Chaplin's own *My Autobiography*, of 1964, remains a classic. Most recently, the indefatigable fan and historian A. J. Marriot has delved into the details of the pre-film Chaplin to correct past misconceptions and complete the definitive record of his stage life to 1913, in *Chaplin, Stage by Stage*. Biography seems to be sated.

Still, there remains, I think, more mileage in the tale of this most iconic of screen artists – whose image is known even in places where his films were never shown, and among people who never saw him on the screen – that can provide a different and fascinating journey. In all the unravelling of the 'man behind the mask' there should now be room for a return, full cycle, to the initial view of Charlie when he first burst upon the world: the mask before the man.

Charles Chaplin was unique in that, as a screen actor, he only ever played one role – albeit with some alter egos – that of his own creation, the Tramp, who had pre-existed in embryo before that much vaunted and fabled spur-of-the-moment in which, in his own account, he came across the costume, cane and boots in Mack Sennett's prop department. Many other comedians settled on an image, like Lloyd's 'glasses character', Stan Laurel and Oliver Hardy's perennials, the Marx Brothers, W. C. Fields and Mae West, but none parlayed this mask into as powerful an image of humanity's response to the challenges of society, authority, the sheer orneriness of life and the material universe as Charlie. This character, larger than life and perhaps more real than his creator, deserves a biography of his own.

And so this is a tale more of Charlie than of Chaplin. It assumes that the reader is by now reasonably familiar with the blow-by-blow accounts of the embattled producer, husband and father, or can turn to other accounts for those oft-told details. Here is another kind of double, or rather triple history: that of the Tramp himself, his origins and travails, the way he saw himself, and the way his fans saw him, in different periods and places, from the moment in which he seemed to spring, fully grown, into the world's affections, during a few months in 1915. It is the story of a myth, and how that myth became a part of the twentieth century's self-perception, how we see ourselves reflected in an imaginary person, an artist's fabrication. It is not, like many modern tales, one of 'celebrity', that latest bubble of fantasized identity with someone who is famous just for being famous, but that of fame that was achieved by effort, craft, thought, creative endeavour and a genuine insight into things that were important to vast numbers of people at certain historical moments. It is also a social history, first of an England that made the man who made the mask out of his stinging briar-patch, and then of an America at a time of change, transformation and crisis, that recognized in this foreign interloper a deeper truth about its own underlying harshness, brutality, corroding greed, and the raw energy of its capacity to rise above its faults.

When Attorney General McGranery decided that Charles Chaplin could be judged to be an alien plant on American soil, he was firing a shot in a long internal war of a certain view of the City on the Hill, pristine and joke-free, untainted by the musty quarrels of Europe and her ugly revolutionary terrors that were potentially importable by dangerous immigrants, be they anarchist Italians, Catholics, Jews or Muslims in our own day. In the wake of the decision, liberals and 'patriots' rallied to the defence or denunciation of the man behind the 'little fellow'. In the *American Legion Magazine* in December 1952, Victor Lasky attacked Chaplin's refusal to become an American citizen. Lasky wrote, in a long article entitled 'Whose Little Man':

He wonders why he's being 'persecuted' because he has retained his British citizenship. Other English actors have made films in Hollywood, people like Ronald Colman, Basil Rathbone, Herbert Marshall, Sir Cedric Hardwicke, Stewart Granger, Cary Grant, and no one seems to be particularly interested whether they took out American citizenship papers. On the other hand, their deeds and words have not had an anti-American flavor . . .

Lasky, while admitting that Chaplin was not likely ever to have been an actual member of the rigidly disciplined Communist Party itself, counted up Chaplin's political offences: lending his name and prestige to the Communists, sponsoring their fronted peace conferences, calling the Russians 'comrades', calling for wartime 'second front' aid to Russia while shunning the support actors gave US troops during the war, failing to visit war fronts and entertain soldiers – 'he never paid a visit to the Hollywood Canteen, sponsored by the motion picture industry to give servicemen a good time . . . For the communists,' Lasky continued, 'Chaplin has been a remarkable lucky find. He is their most important "catch" anywhere in the world.' Lasky noted that:

. . . as far back as 1921, Chaplin was sounding off to the press on problems of the day much in the manner of a university president . . . That same year, Chaplin took a trip to Europe. But before he left, he granted a shipboard interview to reporters. 'Mr. Chaplin,' asked one reporter, 'are you a Bolshevik?' Chaplin replied in his usual circuitous manner, 'I am an artist. I am interested in life. Bolshevism is a new and challenging phase of life. Therefore I must be interested in it.'

Chaplin was considered, in this onslaught of right-wing polemic and opinion well into the mid-1950s, to be the most dangerous kind of subversive, a member of the elite who espoused extreme left-wing views, an opinion-leader who could mislead good and honest patriots and the many many fans of his movies, innocent followers of the beloved Tramp.

But was it true that Chaplin had always been a subversive? Was Charlie himself, behind the baggy pants, the battered bowler and cane and shabby shoes, a revolutionary dupe, an Enemy of the People, a snake in the all-American grass? And what other secrets, and hidden agendas, might be found under the clown's careless mask?

PART ONE

The Immigrant

Synopsis

Part One: On board the ship

Among a shipload of immigrants rolling over the high ocean waves towards America, Charlie is one of the steerage passengers, who bed down as best they can on the deck. Meals are served over one great table on which the soup plates slide with the roll of the ship from side to side and spoon to spoon. The passengers include a rough crowd of card-sharpers from whom Charlie manages to win a sizeable wad of cash. On board is also the Girl (Edna Purviance) and her mother, who is robbed of all their savings while sleeping. Charlie consoles her, and, when she is not looking, puts the money he has won in her purse. In an afterthought, he takes back one note for himself, and is caught by the eagle-eyed purser. Threatened with the brig, he is saved by the Girl's intervention, as she discovers Charlie's kindness.

All crowd to the ship's side as the heartwarming sight of the Statue of Liberty comes into view – Arrival in the Land of Liberty! But the immigration officers rush to corral the passengers behind a thick rope, as one by one they are summoned to the officers' desk.

Part Two: Ashore

In a shabby street, Charlie the Tramp shuffles up to the doorway of a cafe, wistfully thinking of an unaffordable meal. His eye catches a coin on the pavement; he grabs it and rushes in. The cafe is dominated by the rough waiters, chief among them Charlie's regular foil, the massive and fearsome Eric Campbell. Charlie orders a meal, and then notices the Girl sitting disconsolate and alone. He brings her over and orders another plate of beans for her. Another diner, meanwhile, is roughed up by the waiters and thrown out violently – he was short of a dime. Charlie reaches in his pocket and finds to his horror that his only coin has fallen out. It is there, on the floor, and a fearful dance ensues as he tries to reach for it and Eric the waiter keeps inadvertantly stepping on it. Finally he retrieves the coin. A large flamboyant bearded man bustles up and is taken with the Girl. He introduces himself: I am an artist. He wants to paint the Girl's portrait. A few deft moves with the bill being argued between the Artist and Charlie end with success – the waiter is paid, and Charlie's life is saved. Charlie pulls the bashful Girl towards a Registry Office to be married . . .

Caught in a Cabaret

Once upon a time there was Fred Karno. And Dan Leno, and George Robey, and Arthur Roberts, and Albert Chevalier, and Little Tich, and a host of performers, great and struggling, who made the British music halls. 'An entertainment of the People, for the People, by the People,' as described by W. MacQueen Pope: 'Larger than life . . . it ignored half tones, it went out for highlights all the time . . .' In this, the music hall derived from the wider tradition of the English satirical theatre, born from the ebullient echoes of Shakespeare and Ben Jonson, revived in John Gay's *The Beggar's Opera*, the eighteenth-century play which prompted the imposition of censorship upon the English stage. But comedy continued to flourish, married into the Italian *commedia dell'arte* and its stock characters of Harlequin, Pantaloon and Pulcinello, who in turn morphed into the English big-nosed Punch, and, on the London stage, into the King of Clowns Joey Grimaldi in the era of the French Revolution and the Napoleonic wars. Grimaldi satirized everything, from the quintessentially English John Bull, through European classics like Baron Munchausen and Don Quixote to everyday London types: the modern fops, dandies, fashionable fools, street vendors, fish-women, bakers, piemen, lovers and tramps, caught in the eternal evil of gin – the booze-soaked undertone of John Bull's bulldog roar.

From the somewhat crazed world of Regency England, with its wide-open divides of rich and poor, its parliamentary circus pitting Whigs against Tories, its mad cartoonists such as Gilray and Rowlandson lampooning the Powerful up to and including the Regent Prince of Wales – whom they portrayed as an obese and dissolute lout – with images of politicians farting money and generals carving up the plum-pudding world, Grimaldi's freakshow of the Industrial Revolution gave way to Victorian Britain: the era of empire building, bold technological and scientific change, and political reform driven by continuing pressure and rebellion from below.

The music halls became Britain's safety valve, the topsy-turvy fantasies of the world turned upside down – beggars become rich men, rich men beggared, men dressed as women and women as men – but it was also a medium of mass entertainment not only for the battered working class but for the new middle classes, belonging to 'an era of prosperity, and the people who welcomed it and supported it . . . the sons and daughters of Beef, Beer and Peace'.

If it was Charles Dickens who best portrayed, in magazines and books, the stresses and strains of early Victorian England – the cruelties of industry and exploitation, along with the gallery of characters of all walks of life, orphans, beggars, thieves, humble and unhumble clerks, young ladies born into a rough patriarchy, virtuous men, ambitious men, villains, busybodies, widows lax or prudish, young men on the make and older men already well or badly made, dreamers and eccentrics – it was the music halls that would represent the breath of the streets and the dreams of 'ordinary' men and women on the stage. The diminutive Dan Leno, ex-'Champion clog-dancer of the world', would follow Grimaldi in donning variously the garb of the Cobbler, the Railway Guard, the Fireman, Shop-walker, the Unemployed, the Hen-pecked Husband or the 'Chattering Wife'. George Robey sang comic songs and delivered his rambling patter dressed in a black clergyman-like collarless coat, an ill-fitting bowler hat on his head and twirling a flexible cane. 'Let there be merriment by all means,' he said to the cheering audience, but, damping them down nevertheless, 'kindly temper your hilarity with a modicum of reserve.'

'Little Tich,' born Harry Relph, in Kent, who never grew beyond four feet tall and had six fingers on each hand and, it was said, six toes below, had begun his stage life playing a black-faced minstrel character and starred with his own singular songs and patter from the later 1880s. Emphasizing his distinct physique, he added a pair of elongated shoes to his costume, more than two feet long, on which he performed his 'big foot' dance. Another star of the halls, Albert Chevalier, sang cockney 'coster' songs, inaugurating the 'pearly king' costume that would become a London staple, warbling 'Knock 'em in the Old Kent Road'. Great women stars, like Vesta Tilley and Vesta Victoria, played with audience expectations of gender by performing in slick male attire.

These were the headliners who would dominate the halls when the nineteenth century rattled towards the turn of the twentieth, as the British Empire reached its zenith, one quarter of the world was pink in the atlas and the Old Queen was approaching her seventh decade on the throne. But beside these famous names there was a host of smaller fry eking out a living on the British variety stage. Two of them were a married couple, Charles and Hannah Chaplin, resident at 57 Brandon Street, in Walworth, London, just south of the New Kent Road, at the time of their marriage in June 1885. Charles was twenty-two years old and his bride was twenty.

David Robinson has traced Chaplin's family back to one Shadrach Chaplin, born 1786, the village bootmaker of Great Finborough, Suffolk. In true Biblical form, Shadrach indeed gave birth to Shadrach II, Meshach and Abednego, as well as three daughters. The lineage passes down, in Suffolk, towards our hero's grandfather, Spencer Chaplin, a butcher by trade. This was not a theatrical family, but both Charles and young Hannah Hill grew up in the golden age of the halls. 1861 saw the opening of two major theatres in the West End, the Oxford and the London Pavilion. In 1878 there were 347 halls in London with a seating capacity that ranged from the top three, which could hold fifteen or twenty thousand people each, to six theatres with a capacity of between two and three thousand, thirteen that could hold up to fifteen hundred each, and fifty-three with up to seven hundred seats. The best of these were true palaces of entertainment, and they would be joined through the turn of the century by some of the great halls still extant in London, from the Empire, Leicester Square, opened in 1887, to the Hippodrome of 1900 just up the road, and the 1905 Coliseum nearby. The mid-sized halls were dotted all over the city, from the Paragon in Mile End Road to the Shepherd's Bush Empire, the Middlesex in Drury Lane, Gatti's Palace and the Canterbury on Westminster Bridge Road, the Grand, Clapham Junction, and many many more. There were hundreds of smaller venues for variety acts in public houses, 'harmonic meeting places' and other concert rooms. All one needed was a modicum of talent for song, dance, some sort of physical dexterity or a novelty or some trained animals, or just some gumption and get up and go to find a job entertaining around town and further afield, up and down the land. And for those with even more get up and go, there were foreign tours to the growing variety circuits of the continent, to Paris, Berlin, Madrid, Milan, Vienna, and across the ocean to the United States.

Charles Chaplin of Walworth was primarily a singer of comic songs of ordinary life, about errant husbands and nagging wives, and men about town looking for good times, with titles like 'Eh! Boys?' and 'Oui, Tray

Bong! or My Pal Jones'. Promotional song sheets show him as a raffish chap, with shiny top hat and coat or light breezy jacket, with vignettes of bottles of champagne and cognac and a panel of three revellers out for the night with the words: 'Off to the Moulin Rouge'. These songs, which, the sheet tells us, 'may be sung in public without licence, except at Music Halls', appear to have been part of a publicity spin-off for his trip to the United States, which took place in 1890, although he returned pretty soon. This absence enabled Hannah to pursue a romance, and more than a romance, with a fellow actor of Charles's, Leo Dryden, aka George Dryden Wheeler, with whom she had a son, George, in 1892.

This affair did not, of course, feature in the official biographies that her second son, Charles Spencer, concocted in future years. Charles himself appeared on 16 April 1889 (or possibly the 15th, as documented), a baby brother to Hannah's first son, Sidney (later spelled Sydney) John, born on 16 March 1885, three months before her marriage.

Evidence excavated by David Robinson suggests strongly that neither Charles nor Hannah Chaplin went on stage before their marriage, and yet they pursued separate lives in the theatre. Hannah took on a professional stage name, Lillie (or Lily) Harley ('a refined and talented artist'), although she later appeared also as Lily Chaplin, 'Serio and Dancer'. Early photographs show a greater resemblance between the son and his mother than to his father. Neither father nor mother was poor when they married, and clearly it was the circumstances that broke up their marriage which brought their children into dire straits.

The difficult, 'Dickensian' childhood of Charles and Sydney has become the stuff of legend, sifted by biographers, and addressed by Chaplin himself several times, beginning with the earliest years when his fame began to spread across the world. In 1916, just over two years after he accepted an offer from Mack Sennett to join his Keystone Comedy studio, the Bobbs-Merrill company published a book, *Charlie Chaplin's Own Story* – 'Being the faithful recital of a romantic career, beginning with early recollections of boyhood in London and closing with the signing of his latest motion-picture contract.' This was a narrative ghostwritten by a *San Francisco Bulletin* writer, Rose Wilder Lane, deriving from interviews Chaplin had given her in 1915. On receiving the book Chaplin threatened to sue, and the book was withdrawn from publication. The text was republished in 1985 by Chaplinologist Harry M. Geduld.

David Robinson has published chapter and verse of the exchange of letters and telegrams between Chaplin's lawyer, Nathan Burkan, the editors at Bobbs-Merrill and Mrs Lane herself, who admitted she had submitted the book without proper clearance from its subject-cum-'author'. The book is full of errors of fact and detail (misspelling of Karno as Carno, Bodie as Body and so forth), but it could not have been written without Chaplin having told Mrs Lane his row of porkies in the first place. The lies and tall tales reflect what Chaplin told other early newspaper writers at the time, and show him constructing his myth at the earliest opportunity, including the easily refuted claim that he had been born while his parents were on tour in 'a little town in France', elsewhere named as Fontainebleau. Mrs Lane wrote, on Chaplin's behalf: 'I do not know my mother's real name. She came of a good respected family in London, and when she was sixteen she ran away and married my father, a music-hall actor. She never heard from her own people again.' That last part appeared to be true. 'She had a beautiful sweet voice but she hated the stage and the life. Sometimes at night she came into my bed and cried herself to sleep with her arms around me.'

Lane/Chaplin related the day when Charlie was five years old, playing with Sydney in their room, 'when my mother came in, staggering. I thought she was drunk. I had seen so many persons drunk it was commonplace to me, but seeing my mother that way was horrible. I opened my mouth and screamed in terror . . .' The kids put their mother to bed, and 'after a long time the door opened and I saw my father's boots walk in. I heard him swearing. The boots came over and stood by the bed. I smelled whisky . . .'

Of his father, the semi-fictional Charlie told, via Mrs Lane:

My father was a great, dark, handsome man. He would put me upon his shoulder to bring me out, and I did not like it, because his rough prickly cheek hurt me. Then he would set me upon the table in my nightgown, with the bright light hurting my eyes, and everyone would laugh and tell me to sing for the drops of wine in their glasses. I always did, and the party applauded and laughed and called for more. I could mimic every one I had ever seen and sing all the songs I had heard.

It seems unlikely that Mrs Lane made all this up, though she clearly was writing through the fog of bad memory. Charlie's gift for mimicry, however, rings very true, and would be fully confirmed in his teenage impersonations of such stage luminaries as Herbert Beerbohm Tree and the mercurial 'Doctor' Walford Bodie, the electrical savant who cured cripples and the infirm by strapping them to his electric chair. Five decades later, and with the hindsight of age, as well as some proper research, Chaplin presented his childhood in *My Autobiography* in a more convincing light, though that account too airbrushed Hannah's lover, Leo Dryden, and his half-brother George out of the tale. In the later version Dryden was replaced by an alleged sweetheart with whom Hannah had run off to Africa when she was aged eighteen, before she met Charles Senior. This was, it appears, the tale she told her children, but no biographer has verified it so far.

The later account describes moments when Hannah would act out historical, Biblical or Christian tales and plays, from Nell Gwyn to the martyred heroine of *The Sign of the Cross*, and the story of Jesus and the woman about to be stoned, to whose accusers he said, 'He who is without sin among you, let him first cast a stone at her.' 'Like all of us,' she told her son, 'He too suffered doubt.' As her estranged husband's absences precipitated the poverty into which she sank with her children, she clung on to dignity and appearances, keeping her sons as well clothed as she could. She was suing Chaplin Senior for his children's maintenance but, Chaplin wrote, 'Father's payments of ten shillings a week had completely stopped.' In 1893, David Robinson recounts, 'Dryden entered her lodgings and snatched away their six-month-old son. The baby was to vanish from the lives of the Chaplins for almost thirty years.' This shock was followed by the descent of her own mother, Charlie's Grandma, Mary Ann Hill, into alcoholic delirium and eventual consignment to the London County Asylum. When Charlie was six, and Sydney aged ten, Hannah herself became ill and, while she was in the Lambeth Infirmary, Sydney was first taken to the Lambeth Workhouse. Less than one year later Hannah was hospitalized again, and both Chaplin boys were placed in the Workhouse, and then in the Poor Law School in Hanwell, West London, in June 1896.

It is no wonder at all that, in the sunny climes of Los Angeles, California, Charles Chaplin skewed this melancholy tale of booze, deprivation and parental strife into something more befitting the kind of tale his American fans might easily digest, in the mode of Oliver Twist or David Copperfield, and then waxed wroth when some inadvertent home truths among the blarney found their way into an unauthorized memoir. In his earliest encounters with the press, in January and February 1915, immediately after his switch from Mack Sennett to the Chicago-based Essanay company, an aspiring interviewer for *Photoplay* magazine, E. V. Whitcomb, found that 'the funniest thing about this extremely funny man is his violet-like reluctance to talk about Charlie Chaplin':

'There's nothing worth talking about,' he says. 'I am no one – just a plain fellow . . . There is absolutely nothing interesting about me. I have no fads, no automobiles – I am just myself. But, if you insist, I will be very glad to talk to you.'

A lad about twenty-five years of age, a very lovable lad, with a delicate sensitive face and with his hair painstakingly wetted and smoothed down . . . all apology for having kept me waiting . . . We talked for nearly two hours and I have tried to put down here exactly what he said in the way he said it.

'I have always worked hard since my father died, when I was seven years old. My mother was a wonderful woman, highly cultivated, yet life was very hard on her. We were so poor, she used to sew little blouses by hand, trying to earn enough to keep us. That was in England – she died there . . . I have never had a day's schooling in my life; my mother taught us what she could, but after she died, I was an apprentice to a company of traveling acrobats, jugglers and show people . . . I have never had a home worth the name . . .'

Three lies in only one paragraph! Charles Chaplin Senior had indeed died, but in 1901, aged thirty-eight, when Charles Junior was twelve years old, and after practically a decade of abandoning his children and avoiding his maintenance payments. Hannah Chaplin had been declared insane and committed to the Cane Hill Asylum in May 1903, though she was discharged for the New Year of 1904 and rejoined her sons. She had been readmitted in 1905 and remained at Cane Hill until September 1912, three weeks before her son Charles embarked on his second Karno tour to America.

Charlie fantasized further in that first *Photoplay* article, telling the gullible Whitcomb: 'I came to New York with my brother Sidney, while I was still a boy, he is four years older than I am, and is the only relative I have in the world. You have no idea how terribly lonely we were when we arrived in this country. Sid was out hunting for work and I sat looking out of the window of the shabby little boarding-house bedroom. The Times Tower loomed into the sky and I sat there with my head on the window sill and cried . . . The world has never seemed so big nor so lonely since then.'

In fact, as we know well, he arrived in New York – via Montreal, and the SS *Cairnrona* – in 1910, with a couple of dozen jovial performers and their manager, as one of the leading men of the Karno troupe, having, as witnessed by fellow trouper Stanley Jefferson (later Stan Laurel), leaned over the railings of the ship as it rolled up the St Lawrence River: 'America! I am coming to conquer you! Every man, woman and child shall have my name on their lips – Charles Spencer Chaplin!' But the modest Englishman appeared more attractive. Within a few weeks he was moderating his shaggy tramp tale for another interviewer, Victor Eubank of *Motion Picture* magazine, in March 1915:

When I asked Mr. Chaplin for a history of his life, he came nearest to grinning of any time I was talking with him.

'There is little to tell,' he said. 'I was born in a suburb of London twenty-five years ago. I went on the stage because there seemed nothing else to do. In fact, I don't know anything else. Both my father and mother are on the stage, and so were all my ancestors as far back as I can trace the family tree. I was practically born on the stage.

'I started my stage career at the age of seven, when I did some clog-dancing in a London theater. Then I appeared in "Rags to Riches," an anglicized American production. Later I left the stage to attend the Hern Boys' College, near London, where I stayed for two years before the lure of the footlights took me back to the stage again.'

'Rags to Riches' was of course the perfect metaphor for the self-made performer, although the methodical chronicler A. J. Marriot has established that Charlie featured in it only as a gleam in the eye and possibly in a set of rehearsals, since he was listed as about to appear in a show of that name on Boxing Day (26 December) 1904. The advance notice lists 'Master Charlie Chaplin as Ned Nimble', but he never actually appeared in the act, as he was employed instead for a new season of *Sherlock Holmes*, the play he had first appeared in in July 1903. But by the summer of 1915, in America, Chaplin was already honing the tale he would tell, and more or less stick to, properly to link the story of Chaplin, the actor, to the burgeoning fable of his creation, the inimitable character the world was falling in love with, the truer-than-real-life Charlie, the Tramp.

2

The Kid

In 1883, the Reverend Andrew Mearns published a pamphlet entitled *The Bitter Cry of Outcast London*, in which he wrote:

Whilst we have been building our churches and solacing ourselves with religion and dreaming that the millennium was coming, the poor have been growing poorer, the wretched more miserable, and the immoral more corrupt . . . [In their homes] you have to ascend rotten staircases, which threaten to give way beneath every step . . . You have to grope your way along dark and filthy passages swarming with vermin. Then, if you are not driven back by the intolerable stench, you may gain admittance to the dens in which these thousands of beings who belong, as much as you, to the race for whom Christ died, herd together. Have you pitied the poor creatures who sleep under railway arches, in carts or casks, or under any shelter which they can find in the open air? You will see that they are to be envied in comparison with those whose lot it is to seek refuge here . . .

The plight of the urban poor, which Mearns likened to the conditions 'of the middle passage of the slave ship', galvanized the rectitude of the Victorian reformers, who were as concerned about social unrest as about their moral duties. The crusading journalist W. T. Stead, who revealed Mearns's litany of horrors in no less an organ than the *Pall Mall Gazette*, urged the enforcement of existing laws on the duties of tenement landlords. The same date, 1883, saw the foundation of the Fabian Society, the parent of the twentieth century's Labour Party, and other socialist agitation, not to speak of the legacy of Karl Marx, who died in London in the very same year. Charles Booth,? founder of the ← *false, it was. William Booth.* Salvation Army, began the investigations that would lead to his series of reports on London's poor, which would expose for the first time the bare statistical facts. The census of 1891 provided him with the raw material for a borough-by-borough account of London's poverty, and the degree of overcrowding counted by the number of persons per room. Out of a population of over four million, about twelve per cent lived three or more persons to a room. Although Booth expected to find the poorest populations in East London, Hackney and Tower Hamlets, his researches exposed 'historic poverty-stricken Southwark', round about the London bridges southwards, where even greater destitution could be recorded.

The condition of children in particular exercised the reformers. 'The child-misery that one beholds is the most heart-rending and appalling element,' Mearns had written:

. . . many of them have never seen a green field, and do not know what it is to go beyond the streets immediately around them . . . Here is a filthy attic, containing only a broken chair, a battered saucepan and a few rags. On a dirty sack in the centre of the room sits a neglected, ragged, bare-legged little baby girl of four. Her father is a militiaman, and is away. Her mother is out all day and comes home late at night more or less drunk . . . This is the kind of sight which may be seen in a Christian land where it is criminal to ill-treat a horse . . .

Many good Victorian gentlemen in positions of power were puzzled – in a manner not unfamiliar in our own times – that the great surge of national prosperity that had transformed the country's industry and infrastructure had not equally transformed the condition of the urban poor. Various hard-fought reforms, like the Factory and Workshops Act of 1878, the Employers' Liability Act of 1880, and the Education Act of 1870, which should have ensured that all children between the ages of five and twelve went to school, were not as effective as they should have been. The moralists were as appalled by the behaviour of the poor as by its social causes: the wages of poverty were exploitation, brothels and drunks. In one area of the Euston Road, Mearns wrote, there was one pub for every hundred people. And as for crime:

A child seven years old is known easily to make 10s. 6d. a week by thieving, but what can he earn by such work as match-box making, for which 24d. a gross is paid, the maker having to find his own fire for drying the boxes, and his own paste and string? Before he can gain as much as the young thief he must make 56 gross of match-boxes a week, or 1,296 a day.

Little Charles Chaplin and his brother Sydney were in fact lucky, because their parents, although losing their grip, had not been born into these generations of grinding poverty, but emerged from the more established artisan class. Hannah, left most of the time on her own to cope with her two boys, was fighting a battle that was by no means lost, in a state where social reform had established some safety nets. The Victorian workhouses, where the inmates would rise at six in the morning, breakfast briefly and work till six p.m. with one hour for lunch and lights out at seven or eight in the evening, enforced strict rules enjoining silence at work, abstention from alcohol, smoking, stealing, quarrelling, fighting or getting up from a meal before grace was said. The forbidding nature of these institutions is recorded in many gloomy photographs of the gaunt houses and the dining tables where masses of men and women sat separately, though these were places where children as well as adults were provided with proper meals and beds away from the squalid tenements and streets. The School at Hanwell, moreover, was out in the country, Hanwell being, in Chaplin's own words: 'beautiful in those days, with lanes of horse-chestnut trees, ripening wheat fields and heavy-laden orchards'. The boys were lonely and miserable without their mother, and 'we slept in different ward blocks, so we seldom saw each other.' Institutional reform could be as daunting an experience as the hazards it was installed to avert.

'Although at Hanwell we were well looked after,' Chaplin wrote in *My Autobiography*, 'sadness was in the air; it was in those country lanes through which we walked, a hundred of us two abreast. How I disliked those walks, and the villages through which we passed, the locals staring at us! We were known as inmates of the "booby hatch", a slang term for workhouse.'

It was also, and more commonly, a name for the insane asylum, where Hannah would end up in the autumn of 1897, and where the doctors reported her bouts of violence, shouting and incoherent singing, and wild changes of mood. She would be discharged a year later and resume her efforts to keep herself and her sons afloat, moving from one address to another in search of an affordable berth. In 1899, the social reformers were still reporting:

. . . The story of Lambeth in the last ten years is a story of worsement. The fairly comfortable have left or are leaving. The poor remain and additional poor are coming in. The effect of cheap trams and cheap railway fares is most marked in this area. Brixton and Stockwell have claimed the mechanic and artisan, while the labourer remains and his ranks are reinforced by displacements in Westminster across the river.

But Hannah and her sons were still trapped in this sinkhole.

What intimations of this life Chaplin had revealed to Mrs Rose Wilder Lane were mutated by her into a strange melange of impressions supposedly described in his own words:

It was a cold wet evening in the beginning of winter and the rain struck chilly through my thin clothes as I walked, wondering where I could find shelter. Probably in America a homeless, hungry child of eleven would find friends, but in London I was only one of thousands as wretched as I . . . I slept that night in Covent Garden market, cuddled close to the back of a coster's donkey, which was warm, but caused me great alarm at intervals by wheezing loudly and making as if to turn upon me . . .

'The strange, eerie chill of the morning, while the gas lamps in the streets were still showing dimly through the fog,' was a suitable setting for the origins of the Tramp, the Little Fellow who had already affected the audiences of Chaplin's early films. But Mrs Lane's claim that she was merely elaborating on Chaplin's own account is made more credible by separate tales Chaplin told other newspaper and magazine writers, in the summer of 1915, about his pre-American life. Consistency was not a virtue. He told the *San Francisco Chronicle*, which began a seven-part, lengthy story of his life on 4 July: 'Merrie England was the land of my birth,' while telling Harry C. Carr of *Photoplay* magazine, also in July: 'My brother Syd was four years old when I was born. That interesting event happened at Fontainebleau, France. My father and mother were touring the continent at the time with a vaudeville company. I was born at a hotel on April 16, 1889. As soon as my mother was able to travel, we returned to London.'

Meeting the expectations of myth, Chaplin repeated to all comers that he was the proper scion of a stage family – to *Photoplay*:

The very first thing I can remember is being shoved out on the stage to sing a song. I could not have been over five or six years old at the time. My mother was taken suddenly sick and I was sent to take her place in the vaudeville bill. I sang an old coster song called 'Jack Jones.'

It must have been about this time that my father died. My mother was never very strong and, what with the shock of my father's death and all, she was unable to work for a while. My brother Syd and I were sent to the poorhouse.

English people have a great horror of the poorhouse; but I don't remember it as a very dreadful place. To tell you the truth, I don't remember much about it. I have just a vague idea of what it was like.

The strongest recollection I have of this period of my life is of creeping off by myself at the poorhouse and pretending I was a very rich and grand person.

My brother Syd was always a wide-awake, lively, vigorous young person. But I was always delicate and rather sickly as a child. I was of a dreamy, imaginative disposition. I was always pretending I was somebody else, and the worst I ever gave myself in these daydreams and games of 'pretend' was a seat in Parliament for life and an income of a million pounds.

There is an obvious disconnection between Chaplin's bad memory at the age of twenty-six and his much improved recollections of 1964, aged seventy-five! For his San Francisco interviewer in 1915 he gave another version of that childhood blur:

My early life was far from humorous. It was one of struggles with a bitter world. It is a wonder that as a boy I did not have my sense of humour erased by experience . . . My family was a theatrical one . . . All my early training was of a theatrical kind. I could jig, do the buck and wing and the sailor's hornpipe almost as soon as I could toddle across the floor. I could sing ballads and musical ditties when other children of my age were stumbling and stuttering through fragments of 'Mother Goose.'

At the age of 7 I made my debut under the spotlight. I became No. 8 of the 'Eight Lancashire Lads.' We were all young, apt and agile, and the act proved a favorite with the English vaudeville public. We appeared in Eton jackets, in sailor suits and in other adult and juvenile costumes.

Here we are coming closer to fact. A. J. Marriot, tracking Chaplin's first stage appearances, suggests his debut may have been with his mother, who was appearing as Lily Chaplin, at Aldershot in the spring of 1896. Charlie had been at school – the Addington Street School – since October 1895. His first paid performances were, however, undoubtedly with the Eight Lancashire Lads, an established child act that he joined late in 1898, aged nine.

Chaplin told *American* magazine in November 1918 that he had learned most of his craft from his mother. In particular, mime: 'She was one of the greatest pantomime artists I have ever seen. She would sit for hours at a window, looking down at the people on the street and illustrating with her hands, eyes, and facial expression just what was going on below . . . And it was through watching and listening to her that I learned not only how to express my emotions with my hands and face, but also how to observe and to study people . . .'

Observation, of course, lies at the heart of every comedian's (or any actor's) work and Chaplin proved to be the grand master of the art, right to his antics in *A King in New York*. There can be little doubt that his mother must have inspired and coached him too in his further great love and talent, music. As he told *Photoplay*: 'Music, even in my

KIND NEIGHBOR KEEPING FROM DOING MURDER

BY EAR!

WHEN A MERE CHILD HE PLAYED THE CELLO, VIOLIN AND PIANO.

poorhouse days, was always a passion with me. I never was able to take lessons of any kind, but I loved to hear music and could play any kind of instrument I could lay my hands on. Even now, I can play the piano, 'cello or violin by ear.'

One wonders whether there is some unsung teacher who gave the small boy music lessons, lurking in lost history. There were certainly other teachers remembered – or mythologized, and imagined in vintage cartoon form, over the heading: 'HIS EARLIEST RECOLLECTION OF SCHOOL WAS OF BEING RAPPED ON THE LEFT HAND BY THE TEACHER.' The abuse, Chaplin said, was to discourage him from left-handedness, and the result was dexterity with both, another useful gift. In *My Autobiography*, Chaplin recalled more standard lessons: 'History, poetry and science ... some of the subjects were prosaic and dull, especially arithmetic ... History was a record of wickedness and violence, a continual succession of regicides and kings murdering their

Earliest recollections of school as seen in 1915.

wives, brothers and nephews; geography merely maps; poetry nothing more than exercising memory. Education bewildered me with knowledge and facts in which I was only mildly interested . . .'

Perhaps so, but the evidence of his work suggests that the boy took in more than he admitted to in the fantasy clouds of his later mythology. Education, even at primary level, was more rigorous in British schools then than now, as a perusal of the school exams of 1898 recently exposed today's woeful comparison. It was not just the smacking teacher's cane but the quality and quantity of the curriculum that was effective. The essential difference was between those who were schooled and those whom destitution left ignorant and even illiterate. When Chaplin writes about the kings and queens, the maps and poets et cetera, this means his schooling went beyond the five-to-ten age group, and, as David Robinson discovered, his mother made sure he went to school even outside London, when on tour, whenever possible.

Chaplin's talents did not come from nothing, and the young Charlie was clearly an omnivore, taking in each and every experience and storing it for use, even when he appeared to many early witnesses, nurses or neighbours, who contributed to later articles, as just another frisky boy with a dog: 'A mischievous boy, always up to monkey tricks, tripping himself up, climbing up fences, and falling down.' (This from A. J. Marriot, via a Mrs Harriet Tricks, reminiscing in *The Star* in 1921.)

While Charlie was too young to think of earning, Sydney, eleven going on twelve, began training for sea-service aboard an old moored warship, the *Exmouth*, learning 'seamanship, gunnery and first aid', as well as how to play the bugle. It would be five years, however, before he actually went to sea, in 1901, making a total of seven voyages as a steward.

By that time, Charlie had been a paid actor for more than two years. His first gig was, as expected, wrapped in further flimflam in early accounts. Chaplin told *Photoplay*:

I don't remember when I began regularly as a professional, but I remember that I was already working on the stage when I had a narrow escape from drowning. I remember that I was on tour with a show called 'The Four Yorkshire Lads.' It seems to me I could not have been much over five or six years old, but I suppose I must have been a year or two older. Two or three boys of the company were throwing sticks into the River Thames and I slipped into the stream. I can remember how I felt as I slipped down the river on the current. I knew that I was drowning, when I felt a big, shaggy body in the water near me . . . and was dragged ashore by a big black woolly dog which belonged to a policeman on duty along the river. If it hadn't been for that dog, there wouldn't have been any Charlie Chaplin on the screen.

And opposite is the *Photoplay* picture to prove it.

David Robinson quotes a 'romantic account' of Chaplin's first foot on the stage given by him to the *Glasgow Weekly Herald* in 1921:

One day I was giving an exhibition of the ordinary street Arab's contortions, the kind so common to the London streets, when I saw a man watching me intently. 'The boy is a born actor!' I heard him say, and then to me: 'Would you like to be an actor?' I scarcely knew what an actor was in those days, though my mother and father had both been connected with the music hall stage for years. But anything that promised work . . . was welcome, and I listened to the tempter with the result that a few days later I was making my appearances in London suburban music halls with the variety artists known as the Eight Lancashire Lads . . .

Saved from a watery end.

This tempter was the act's manager, William Jackson, who became Charlie's first proper stage mentor. A. J. Marriot verifies Chaplin's later account that Jackson had known his father, and it was Charles Senior who, in a rare positive interruption of his attempts to avoid payments and responsibility for his sons' welfare, made the crucial contact, probably in Manchester, over the yuletide period of 1898. The Eight Lancashire Lads were appearing at the Tivoli, while Charles Senior was at the nearby Theatre Royal. The Lads were losing a kid dancer, and Charlie was picked up to close the gap. (A. J., thorough as ever, clinches the fact, as he found that Chaplin *père* and Jackson were near neighbours at Kennington Road.)

One of Chaplin's main objections to Rose Wilder Lane's phantasms of his early life was her mutation of manager William Jackson into the Simon Legree of London theatrical life, bawling out the boys and always reaching for his cane, as she related – in Charlie's voice – of this character, 'Hawkins': 'I lived in terror of him – a terror that colored everything during the day and at night made my dreams horrible. The other boys were afraid of him too.' Did Mrs Lane make this up out of whole cloth? Perhaps, or perhaps Charles was in a particularly fanciful mode of 'memory' on that day:

In the evenings we were marched out before him to music-halls. These music-halls were very different from the ones my mother sang in. They were large rooms, with rough wooden benches and tables arranged around a square in the center, where we danced. The air was thick with tobacco smoke and heavy with the smell of ale and stout, and the ugly bearded faces of hundreds of men staring at us confused me sometimes so that I could hardly dance . . .

This strange description bore, of course, no resemblance to the actual music halls in which the Eight Lancashire Lads performed, but it does bear a close resemblance to the ambience of Mack Sennett Keystone comedies, replete with smoky taverns, tobacco smoke thick as industrial waste and men with a variety of false whiskers hawking into spittoons. It is an early memory, then, not of Chaplin's own life, but that of Charlie, the Tramp . . .

A. J. Marriot's chronicle of Chaplin's stage appearances provides a definitive record, and shows the halls and venues at which the Eight Lancashire Lads performed. It now seems clear that Charles Junior was in rehearsals with the troupe during their eight-week stint at Manchester's Royal Theatre as part of the seasonal pantomime of *Babes in the Woods*. Charles Chaplin first appeared in the act when it went on the road in its own right, playing Portsmouth before arriving at the Oxford in London in April: 'The Eight Lancashire Lads won hearty approval with their smart clog dancing.'

This now moribund form of galumphing in wooden-soled shoes has died out in the British Isles, and is best described as a European tap dance. The Oxford, of course, was no smoke-ridden dive but the queen of music halls, rebuilt after two fires in 1868 and 1871 to the highest standard: 'A splendid promenade . . . a new stage of much larger proportions than the old . . . In point of colour and decoration the Oxford may vie with any building in the kingdom. The prevailing tint is light blue. . . the relievo ornaments white, with stencilled decorations upon the walls, and choice salmon tints filling up the spaces. . .' A programme reprinted by Marriot, of 9 April 1899, reveals the staggering brevity of the acts that had to crowd the three hours between 7.15 and 11.15 p.m. – twenty-eight acts in all, each appearing for between five and ten minutes! Even headliners like Eugene Stratton, the McNaughtons, Bransby Williams and George Robey rated only ten minutes each, the same time as the Eight Lancashire Lads, who appeared just before Robey. The show closed with 'Hamlet by Bransby Williams: Impersonating well-known Actors and Variety Celebrities as it is done and might be done', an act that made a strong impression on young Charles and prompted him to copy it later, impersonating the maestro Williams himself as well as the 'electricity king' Walford Bodie.

The Eight Lancashire Lads were, therefore, a standard act, playing at the best venues, and appearing on a tough weekly schedule along with all the greats of music hall: Robey, Dan Leno, Harry Randall, Will Evans (whose nephew Fred was 'Pimple', the earliest comedy clown of British movies), Vesta Victoria, et cetera, et cetera, et cetera. Sometimes, as on 9 June 1900, they would do as many acts did, rushing from one hall to another to perform on the same night, on that date at the Canterbury and the Paragon, Mile End. At the Paragon, as often elsewhere, they shared the bill with the no longer novel moving pictures, the 'Gibbons Bio-Tableaux', showing the latest films of the Boer War in South Africa, scenes from Pretoria, Johannesburg and Bloemfontein. For this was an era not of 'Beer, Beef and Peace', but of beer, beef and war, with the music halls reverberating to patriotic songs that may echo as ambivalently in our own day as then:

> They said old England was worked out – our Empire couldn't last,
> Our army was degenerate, our fighting days were past!
> In the kennel of the nations the bull-dog stands alone,
> But our gallant boys have shown still we know to hold our own!
> Let them read how British soldiers smiled into the face of death!
> And, dying, cheered their comrades on with every gasp of failing breath!

And thus was England's twentieth century born . . .

3

The Face on the Bar-room Floor

Twas a balmy summer evening and a goodly crowd was there,
Which well nigh filled Joe's bar-room, on the corner of the square,
And as songs and witty stories came thru the open door,
A vagabond crept slowly in and posed upon the floor.

'Where did it come from?' some one said. 'The wind has blown it in.'
'What does it want?' another cried. 'Some whisky, rum or gin?'
'Here, Toby sic' him, if your stomach's equal to the work,
I wouldn't touch him with a fork, he's filthy as a Turk . . .'

Synopsis (*The Face on the Bar-room Floor*, Keystone, 1914):

Based on the poem by H. A. D'Arcy: A tramp wanders into a bar
full of drinkers and loafers. Handed a glass by a sailor, he proceeds to tell the barflies his tale: Flash back to the tramp as a
painter in his studio, painting a smug moustached swell. The
artist's model, a svelte young girl, flirts with the swell. The painter
pleads his love with the girl by his picture of her as a figure on a
classical pedestal. The swell and the girl, however, go off together
and stick a note on the portrait. When the painter finds the note
he reads it: 'Good bye, you great big hunk of man, and remember
not to fall over your feet. Yours that was, Itsy-Bitsy Madeline.'
He trashes the portrait. Two months later, we see him destitute in
the park, sitting on a bench. The swell passes, accompanied by a
wife and five kids. Back in the bar, the tramp is prompted to draw
his ex-girlfriend's face on the floor with a piece of chalk. He manages a circle with two eyes and a mouth before going crazy, kicking his fellow drinkers out the door, scrawling incomprehensible
circles on the floor then falling flat drunk.

(In the restored version, some scenes are transposed: The
painter is first seen with a model and the Girl, and the rival's painting comes later, in line with the course of the poem: 'I was work-

ing on a portrait, one afternoon in May / Of a fair-haired boy, a friend of mine, who lived across the way . . .' In the bar, the 'sot' is thrown out, and draws another face on the sidewalk, but since the scenes of him kicking the other drinkers out are included this might be an out-take. Keystone films were recycled often, recut, resold and renamed. In the restoration, it is clear that the wife the 'sot' sees with the rival and five kids in the park after 'a year of misery' is the Girl, and in general Chaplin's intention to satirically mock the sentimentality of the ballad at every level is clearer.)

Charles Chaplin Senior, the 'dramatic and descriptive singer', may have been reluctant to support his estranged wife and pay enough maintenance to keep his sons out of the workhouse, but he still kept a thin thread of communication with the younger, Charlie, as the older, Syd, seemed set on his sea-going plans. During some of the frolics of the Eight Lancashire Lads, A. J. Marriot has found, Charles Senior was on the same bill, notably at the Clapham Grand in mid-August 1900. Charles Senior continued to play the halls, but Marriot has clocked his last appearance at the Portsmouth Empire on New Year's Eve. On 9 May 1901, Charles Chaplin Senior died, at the age of thirty-seven, of cirrhosis of the liver, the disease of the long-time alcoholic. Both Charles and Hannah were registered at the same address at that point, 16 Golden's Place, Lambeth, so she might have even been tending him when he died. His was a common fate, in a tradition stretching back to Hogarth's *Gin Lane*. One does not know whose face he might have scrawled upon the bar-room floor, but it was probably not Hannah's, who, in another common tradition, was left with the consequences of ephemeral pleasures.

The Eight Lancashire Lads continued to cavort, however, well into 1902, though at some point Charles Junior left the troupe, searching for a new stage berth. The group was still in good shape at the Canterbury in June 1902, as reported by *The Era*: 'The Eight Lancashire Lads are responsible for a very fine exhibition of clog-walloping.'

Chaplin's training in pantomime, his maternal model apart, still lay in the future, though its avatars, Fred Karno and his Speechless Comedians, were already a fixture in the halls. At the Manchester Palace, in October 1900, the bill reveals the Eight Lancashire Lads performing after Fred Karno's 'Jail Birds', one of the maestro's most popular skits, involving mayhem in a prison. As Karno had several companies touring at different venues, the two troupes would have shared the programme often. But Chaplin's immediate future lay in speaking parts. A short stint of two weeks in *Jim – A Romance of Cockayne*, a play by H. A. Saintsbury, in July 1903, as 'Sam, a newspaper boy' was followed by the boy's breakthrough role, that of Billy, the pageboy of Arthur Conan Doyle's Sherlock Holmes stories.

His role as Sam the newsboy gave Chaplin his first proper named notice and reviews: the *Era* singled out 'Master Charles Chaplin . . . a broth of a boy as Sam the newspaper boy, giving a most realistic picture of the cheeky, honest, loyal, self-reliant, philosophical street Arab . . .' while the *Topical Times*, slating the play itself, found Charlie its 'one redeeming feature', praising him as 'a bright and vigorous child actor. I have never heard of the boy before, but I hope to hear great things of him in the near future.'

In the event, greatness took a little more time to emerge. Chaplin's trajectory as a child actor from this point has been followed in close detail by both David Robinson and A. J. Marriot, from his successful two-year run as Billy, through his performances in the juvenile troupe of 'Casey's Circus', which ran from 1906 to 1907, via a joint appearance with Sydney, who had abandoned a sea-going career for the stage in Wal Pink's 'Repairs', a slapstick sketch about builders, dubbed by the critics 'a clever example of the low comedy school of humour', and 'a capital knockabout, pantomimic sketch'. This would have been Chaplin's first foray into mime, rather than spoken parts. Marriot has unearthed another 1906 show, 'The Ten Loonies in "Dotty"', but cannot take an oath that Chaplin actually played a part in it. Other curiosities were an appearance in December 1907 at the Foresters' Music Hall in Bethnal Green as 'Sam Cohen – The Jewish Comedian', and his first written effort, a sketch called 'Twelve Just Men', 'a slapstick affair about a jury arguing a case of breach of promise', staged at the Manchester Grand in June 1909. This jury included 'a deaf-mute, a drunk, and other unlikely personages'. By this latter date, however, Charles had already followed Sydney into Fred Karno's company. In between, in 1908, lay his first job with a Karno troupe, as a supporting player in *The Football Match*, which starred Harry Weldon as 'Stiffy the Goalkeeper'. In June, 1908, Karno assigned Charles in a small role to his most successful and verifiably the longest-running sketch in English music-hall history, 'Mumming Birds'.

During this crucial period, Charles Chaplin's teens, there were also some other work experiences, especially during 1902–3, when the schedules are vague, and Chaplin was aged thirteen to fourteen. Hannah's health fluctuated, as whatever meagre support had come from Charles Senior stopped on his death. Sydney was at sea, travelling to New York and Cape Town, and the Chaplins lived at 3 Pownall Terrace, which Chaplin often listed in later interviews as his birthplace. Their flat lay up 'three flights of narrow stairs' that he remembered later climbing up and down 'to empty those troublesome slops'. He recalled, in a broadcast to blitz-struck Britain in 1943, 'the Lambeth streets, the New Cut and Lambeth Walk . . . They were hard streets, and one couldn't say they were paved with gold; nevertheless the people who lived there are made of pretty good metal.'

David Robinson found that Chaplin 'worked as a barber's boy . . . a chandler's boy . . . as a doctor's boy for a partnership called Hool and Kinsey-Taylor . . . He lost the job because he was too small to cope with cleaning the windows . . . He lost a job with W.H. Smith when they discovered he was under age, and lasted only one day in a glass factory.' This one day seemed to have left a strong memory, as he recounted it at length in his interview with the *San Francisco Chronicle* in 1915:

The foreman put me to work. The duties I was called upon to perform bewildered me. But more terrifying was the heat in the glass blowing room. It was hotter than the depths of a fiery furnace. My clothing was soon dripping. My breath came short. I fled to the open air. Out in the yard some workmen were loafing and smoking. They began to make fun of me, and as my theatrical life had sharpened the gift of repartee I answered back in kind.

My retorts to their 'kidding' won loud appreciation. Anxious to win their friendship, I began doing 'stunts,' acrobatic feats and jig steps. Soon I had a large audience of labourers and loafers . . .

Too frail to stand the heat in the glass factory, however, he lost his job, or, following the known chronology, he probably gave it up as far too strenuous. Working a printing press – 'an augury of his battles with machinery in *Modern Times*,' suggests David Robinson – selling old clothes in the street, and other odd jobs followed. In May 1903, aged fourteen, Charles was the man of the family, as he had to bring his mother in to the infirmary, reporting her confused and delusionary behaviour. An 'Order for the Reception of a Pauper Lunatic' was made by a Dr Quarry. Hannah remained in the Cane Hill asylum, where her boys paid her regular visits.

These years of coping on his own, while his elder brother was absent, clearly steeled young Charles to his life and work. Many fourteen-year-olds in those days, as in many harsh cultures today, became adults, taking responsibility for their own fate, as best they could. Chaplin was no pauper, and no illiterate, whatever the judgement of society. Meanwhile Sydney, on board ship, had developed his own skills as a comedian, entertaining the passengers with impersonations and songs. On his return, early in 1906, he joined the Charles Manon sketch company and then found the show he could perform in with his brother, the aforementioned Wal Pink's 'Repairs'. An enthusiastic London reporter wrote of the act at the Hammersmith Palace on 5 May: 'In Mr. Pink's sketch there are superadded strange orations from a boozy painter, terrible pugilistic displays by a huge plumber, a combined worship of Bacchus chorus around a beer barrel, and an extraordinary sand dance for Omnes . . . The acrobatic actors are as smart a crowd as can be found around Variety Land . . .'

By July 1906 Sydney had signed a contract with the Fred Karno company to appear in their pantomime sketches, while Charles danced and jigged his way through 'Casey's Circus'. It was during this act, which Charles remained with for over a year, that he tried on his impersonations of Bransby Williams, Herbert Beerbohm Tree and 'Doctor' Walford Bodie, of which several photographs survive. Chaplin's mentor in this show was the veteran performer Will Murray, who, A. J. Marriot claims, taught him the trick of turning a corner with a special skid on one foot. Aged seventeen, however, Charles was getting a little old for juvenile acts, and it was only fitting that Sydney, already established with Karno, should find his no-longer-kid brother a job with his boss, the famous 'Guv'nor' of English music hall.

At this point, Fred Karno had been established as a variety act entrepreneur for over a decade. Born Frederick Westcott in Exeter in 1866, he was no theatre brat himself, but the eldest of seven children of a cabinet maker who taught his sons a ferocious work ethic. The usual odd jobs followed an early escape from an apprenticeship at a lace factory, including a spell as a plumber. Sent to do a job at a gymnasium, he discovered his skill at athletics, which led to his entrance into show business as an 'equilibrist' and circus acrobat. The legend takes him on tours of the mining towns of south Wales and a short backsliding as a glazier, with a companion called 'Mike'. Tramping to London to look for work, they hit a bad patch when, relates his biographer, J. P. Gallagher:

Nobody seemed to have any broken windows. Fred told the story to his older son, Fred Junior, years afterwards . . . 'We come to this village, see, and we 'adn't a bean, not even t' price of a cup o' tea. I sent Mike off to knock up a few doors and 'e come back with a face all glum, and no jobs.

'Well,' I said, pointing at a small shop winder across the road, 'that there winder could break ternight – a with a little 'elp – and in the morning they'll be bloody keen ter 'ave it fixed . . . That night we bust two winders, at least I did while Mike watched . . . when I started to walk down that village street, a-yelling "Winder-a-mend," the shop-keeper and t' old fellow come running. I did it a few more times in other places and it always worked. At least I ate.'

There are clear echoes of Chaplin's window-breaking in *The Kid* in this account, which may reflect the fanciful invention of Fred Junior for Gallagher's 1971 book, or the possibility that Chaplin got that particular bit of business from the Guv'nor himself. A 1939 biography of Fred Karno omits the window-breaking tale . . . But Westcott's brushes with Victorian poverty were more than mythical. Imbued with great determination, he moved from the circus to variety pantomime, to an act named The Three Karnos. There followed his first entrepreneurial flourish, the adoption of the early phonograph, as the 'Karnograph', for which he recorded some early stars. Playing these recordings at the halls, Karno amazed his audience with this novelty in 1889, the year of Charles Chaplin's birth.

Pantomime was a natural development for Karno, whose skills were physical and who could neither sing nor excel at the comedy patter. In partnership with a mimic named Rick Klaei, he devised a silent sketch, entitled 'Hilarity', which first toured in 1894. Featuring 'a humorous donkey . . . an actively funny footman . . . a couple of lovers, a grumpy guardian and a domestic', it also involved Karno himself gyrating on the high bars, but after nearly falling to the bare stage at a performance in April 1897, he abandoned the dangerous domain of the performer and became a manager behind the scenes. A whole raft of pantomime acts followed, from the hit sketch 'Jail Birds' through 'Early Birds' and the ubiquitous 'Mumming Birds', 'His Majesty's Guests', 'The New Woman's Club' and a host of others which grew Karno's company into a theatrical force, with its own headquarters, prop and costume factory, transport wagons and actors' studios, set in two large houses in Camberwell.

'Fred Karno's Army' became a catch-phrase, a slogan for the First World War, a by-word for mad frolics and an atmosphere of chaos and

mayhem. It attracted the best and most ambitious of already established British comics, like Fred Kitchen and Harry Weldon, and built
up others, like Billy Reeves, Charley Bell, Billie Ritchie, Syd and
Charlie Chaplin and a little later, a gawky Lancashire lad called
Stanley Jefferson, who was to become Stan Laurel.

Pantomime was not, as I have detailed elsewhere (in *Stan and Ollie:
The Roots of Comedy*), originally a major staple of the English music
hall, nor was it necessitated by legal strictures on certain theatres,
as has been mistakenly said in the past. Plays had been censored by
the Lord Chamberlain's Office since John Gay's eighteenth-century
The Beggar's Opera prompted a government clamp-down on subversive plays. Only 'legitimate' theatres were allowed to present
full-length plays, but shorter sketches were tolerated in the non-
licensed theatres and music halls until 1912, when legislation
extended licensing to all theatres. Every written play or sketch, however, had to be passed by the Lord Chamberlain. The only way to
evade censorship was to dispense with a script. Pantomime thus freed
Karno's Speechless Comedians to poke fun at anything they wished –
within the obvious boundaries, such as lese-majesty, public decency,
et cetera.

These Karno spoofs were in the spirit of Joseph Grimaldi's early
nineteenth-century harlequinades. 'Jail Birds' spoofed Her Majesty's
prisons, with convicts larking about and playing practical jokes on
the warders and authority figures. 'Early Birds' presented 'an original
pantomime burlesque' of London's Whitechapel slum, showing 'the
life mostly of the loafer, the thief and the dosser'. Karno himself
played a hook-nosed Jewish travelling glazier, in a sketch that 'caught
the very essence of the hopeless gaiety, the gruesome jollity of English
poverty, wretchedness and crime . . . how it reeks with life and
reality!' enthused *The Era*. At night, 'we are transported to the horrible lair where the human animals fling themselves down in their rags
and tatters at the close of the day.' Fourteen years later, Chaplin was
to recall this world in *Easy Street*, and this was not the only Fred
Karno sketch that would re-emerge as American movie comedy, as
we shall see.

The principle of ECFK – Everything Comes From Karno – remains
an arguable truth about the nature of much of silent film comedy,
although the mayhem of Mack Sennett was already in place when
Chaplin, Karno's main transmission vehicle, began his Keystone

clowning in 1914. Of all the clowns, Fatty Arbuckle, in particular, pre-ceded Chaplin as the master gagsmith, an authentically American madman. But the nature of Karno comedy was markedly English, as a local American reviewer noted when the Karno troupe, with Chaplin aboard, hit Minneapolis in March of 1911:

Broad English humor is very broad indeed. It smacks even more of the slap-stick than our old friend, the burlesque comedian. Yet there are always moments of unexpectedness. Where the American would do the obvious thing, the Englishman does the unusual. Fred Karno's 'Night in an English Music Hall,' now headlining at the Unique, is one of the funniest of all the skits. It is elaborately staged, showing several boxes and a miniature stage, with all the habitues of that place of entertainment . . . There is the inebriated swell, the fresh young chap from Eton . . . and then the typical turns . . . the magician, the village choir singers, the saucy soubrette, and, finally, the 'Terrible Turk,' the whole ending with a wild rough-and-tumble burlesque wrestling match . . .

Karno's 'Mumming Birds' indeed travelled far. But it had already been known in America five years before, in 1905, when Karno had first presented it under its US title for one month, returning the following year in September for a longer engagement.

'I have discovered', Karno told the *New York Telegraph* then, 'that, contrary to the prevalent idea in Europe, Americans are not in the least slow to understand pantomime, but heretofore they have never had pantomime offered to them as a vehicle for real comedy; and I find that comedy is what they want . . . I had no idea New York was such an immense place, and what impresses me the most is the constant hurry that everyone seems to be in. I have been kept on the rush ever since I have been here. But, take it all in all, I rather like it. America is a great country.'

An extended article in the New York *Morning Telegraph* of 7 October 1906 described the Karno pantomime and its main act in detail, as well as the establishment it came from in London:

FRED KARNO, ONE OF LONDON'S FAMOUS PRODUCERS

Versatile Young Man Spends His Time Organising Pantomime Companies, Building Theatres, Putting on Spectacles of 250 Persons, and Between Whiles Fits Up an Establishment Where He Makes Everything the Stage Calls For.

After all, when we want the real thing in pantomime, we have to fall back on our cousins across the water. If we don't go to England for our successful pantomimes, we have England bring her successful pantomimes here . . .

Europe has long known Mr. Karno for a genius of the most unusual order, but it has only been a comparatively short time that America has had an acquaintance with him . . . The first offering of the company was 'A Night in a Music Hall, or the Mumming Birds.' Fifteen people are required for this act, which . . . was received with the greatest favor by New York audiences, and later, on a tour of the country as far west as San Francisco, the metropolitan success was repeated, until to-day Fred Karno's comedians are almost as well known in America as they are in their own land.

'A Night in the Slums of London' is by far the most pretentious pantomime act that has been presented in this city since Thompson and Dundee produced 'The Duel in the Snow' at their then Colonial Theatre. Wherever it has been shown, it has been a headliner, as they say in vaudeville – and you don't get to be a headliner in these days of shrewd managerial weighing and measuring unless you have the requisites . . .

If the pantomimes Mr. Karno has created are interesting in themselves, Fred Karno, the man, is infinitely more interesting . . . His genius was mechanical, as well as artistic, a happy blend of both, and the utilitarian quality found its most notable expression in the establishment of a manufactory which is now famous throughout the United Kingdom. The building is situated at No. 26 Vaughan Road, Cold Harbour Lane, Camberwell, London, which . . . is known as a veritable house of a thousand wonders.

In 'The House That Karno Built' can be made anything in the stage world, from a theatre itself down to a shoestring . . . One of the largest and lightest of the rooms is given over to the painters, and here are produced the scenes for many an important production. Another apartment enchants with its beautiful lacy, filmy effects, its dainty garments and its general air of gladsomeness. This is the costume room, where all the dresses are designed and made.

Another room is given over to 'Props,' and every facility for modelling and fashioning is at hand. White-aproned carpenters hold sway in another room and busy themselves with saw and hammer on the lumber which later appears as the scenery in the public performances. There is a spendid rehearsal room, where the companies are drilled by the most competent of stage managers, and the almost countless other apartments, the uses of which are strange to the layman.

When the companies set out from 'The House That Karno Built,' it is very much in the nature of a pageant. First comes a succession of motor cars, followed by a four-horse coach, with the Karno driver and the Karno footman gaily uniformed and lending a holiday air to the streets through which they pass. Then come the Karno buses, more four-horse teams, and the drays holding the scenery and properties . . .

The rowdiness of the past informs the future.

This was the world the brothers Chaplin were to inhabit together from the beginning of 1908, and through the next four years. But in 1906, it was Sydney, not Charlie, who was touring the United States with the company, and blazing the trail that his younger brother would follow, when he boarded the SS *Cairnrona* in Southampton, in September 1910.

4

A Night in the Show

Synopsis (*A Night in the Show*, Keystone, 1914):

A drunken swell makes trouble in the line for tickets to a show, and continues his disruption inside, moving seats, pushing aside other punters, sneering at an ugly lady, striking a match off the bald head of the tuba player, fighting with the orchestra conductor. Meanwhile, in the upper balcony, among the lower classes, an equally drunk pleb (both drunks played by Chaplin) is also rowdy, yanked back before he can fall down into the stalls. When the acts begin – La Belle Wienerwurst, Tutty-Frutti the Snake-Charmer, male duo Dot and Dash (names added perhaps in later film versions?) and the Fire Eater, the swell intervenes on the stage, fighting with the manager, throwing pies at the singers and dunking loose snakes in the tuba. Finally, the Fire Eater, Professor Nix, is hosed down by the rowdy in the balcony, and general chaos ensues.

In 1915, when Chaplin recalled Karno's 'Mumming Birds' for his San Francisco interviewer, he said (or was presented as saying):

At last came an opportunity to play an 'all-pantomime' role in the most famous of comedy organizations in England. It was Fred Karno's London Comedians, and they presented a repertory of comedies which were very much on the order of the later motion picture productions.

'A Night in an English Music Hall' was the star offering on their list. It was produced with a stage within a stage. That is, when the curtain arose the proscenium of a miniature stage was seen, with boxes on each side and a 'pit.' The 'audience' was composed of typical characters found in any of the 'alls, the lower and upper levels of humanity being seen in the boxes and on the benches beneath the stage . . .

I was cast for the esthetic role of the drunk. This was a part which might have been repugnant to one's finer sensibilities. But after I had studied its possibilities I saw the vast amount of genuine, uproarious fun that could be extracted from it. But what interested me most was that I could play it from beginning to end without uttering a syllable . . .

Chaplin's spin is as ever evident as he presents a portrait of his own innovations in a part already honed for years by others, notably by its progenitor, Billy Reeves, from 1904, and, in the 1908 run, Jimmy Russell. Sydney, not Charles, was the first Chaplin to play the swell. Charlie's first leading role with Karno was not in 'Mumming Birds', but in *The Football Match*, where he replaced Harry Weldon as Stiffy the Goalkeeper in April 1909.

'Mumming Birds' itself had grown out of a sketch called 'Entertaining the Shah', derived from a visit by the fun-loving Persian ruler to the halls in 1902. Comic jugglers, Burton's Leaping Dogs and the Fratellini Brothers made the monarch 'laugh heartily', the whole wrapped up with the Persian national anthem. The drunk interloper was a later invention. The original acts dived further downmarket till they became the Swiss Nightingale, the Prestidigitateur, the Saucy Serio, the Rustic Glee Party and the Terrible Turk, aka wrestler Marconi Ali. The act itself was no longer Speechless, though the first script available from the Lord Chamberlain's archives is dated 1915, with an appended note by the censor, one G. S. Street: 'In spite of Mr. Karno's name on this piece, I can discover no opening in it for anything offensive . . . The only line which is dubious is in the first song . . . "she did look a flirt in a little short skirt," but it seems hardly worth noticing. Otherwise the piece, as it stands, seems quite harmless.'

Charlie's performance in the Keystone film of 1914 shows, as is clear from other Keystones, that he was not yet fully convinced that the Tramp should be his primary, let alone only, face to the world. Another character had already been seen in his early shorts as the Slicker, in *Making a Living* and *The Star Boarder*, or as Lord Helpus in *Cruel, Cruel Love*. This was an unusually demonic alter ego, whom we shall look at in due course. The Swell in 'A Night in the Show' was characterised by a kind of teeth-baring sneer, much like a modern British TV character, Harry Enfield's 'Tory Boy', with his snorted expletive: 'Fnuh!' This typical upper-class idiot and lush originated as Archibald, 'a broken-down swell', as he appeared in Fred Karno's 1909 sketch 'Skating', later to return as Archibald Binks in 'The Wow Wows' in 1910. Both Sydney and Charles appeared in 'Skating' from its inception, in January 1910, and Chaplin would later use its purely pantomime bits in his fifty-eighth short film, *The Rink*, made for Mutual in 1916. In the original sketch, the banter between Archibald and the skating-rink attendant goes as follows:

ARCHIE: Can you put me up for the night?

ATTENDANT: Certainly not, I don't know you.

ARCHIE: Don't you remember Archibald? . . .

ATTENDANT: Why, it's the Captain, my dear old Captain. Why, I haven't seen you since we were in the army together.

ARCHIE: The dear old Salvation Army . . .

ATTENDANT: Do you remember when we were in the Soudan surrounded by the enemy on every side? . . . There we stood with our retreat cut off.

ARCHIE: Our what cut off?

ATTENDANT: Retreat cut off . . . Do you remember those three days and nights without food or water, think of it, not a drain of water, but what did we do?

ARCHIE: Drink it neat.

ATTENDANT: Well, how's the world been using you?

ARCHIE: Now and then.

ATTENDANT: Where are you working?

ARCHIE: Here and there.

ATTENDANT: What do you work at?

ARCHIE: This and that.

ATTENDANT: Do you have to work hard?

ARCHIE: On and off . . .

ATTENDANT: Are you looking for a job?

ARCHIE: Yes and no.

ATTENDANT: Well, you don't look half as smart as you used to.

The old Empire echoes in the background of the young swell and Imperial soldier fallen on hard times, a rare hint of a past life that would of course have been irrelevant to the American audience. In *The Star Boarder* this character simply lurks about, enjoying the attentions of the landlady (played by Minta Durfee, Fatty Arbuckle's wife), who serves him her best grub. Their flirtation, under the baleful eye of her husband (played by Edgar Kennedy), is recorded by a small boy with a box camera, who presents these amorous exploits to the boarders as a naughty slide show. General embarrassment and spanking of the miscreant follow. Marital high-jinks were a staple of Keystone, though not of Karno, whose bumps and grinds eschewed sex for aggression.

In the movie version of 'A Night in the Show', Chaplin split himself in two: the Swell and the 'Rowdy', with the hall split between the middle-class poseurs in the stalls and the riff-raff in the balcony above, which include a blacked-up character among the whites, a rare example of the racial mixing common mainly in the cities, at the working-class level.

Unwelcome flirtation is a staple of the Keystone swell, as he moves seats to press up against swanky Edna Purviance until he realizes he is clutching her husband's hand by mistake, and leans towards the Snake Charmer at the edge of the stage until her snake tickles his nose. This kind of vulgarity would certainly not have been countenanced by Mr Street of the Lord Chamberlain's Office.

In his work for Karno, Chaplin appeared in a wide variety of roles in many sketches, supporting his brother Sydney, Fred Kitchen, Albert Bruno, Gilbert Childs and many others. A. J. Marriot has compiled as complete a list as can be envisaged of the Karno companies' performances from May 1909 through April 1910, when Chaplin began to star in a new playlet called *Jimmy the Fearless*. In that show he appeared as a miner's son who lives out his reading of pulp 'penny dreadfuls' by dreaming himself into the Dog's Nose Drinking Saloon at Deadman's Gulch, where he rescues his beloved from 'Alkali Ike' and moves on to a sword fight with pirates, from whom he wrests a hoard of gold doubloons. Chastisement by his dad provides a rude awakening. (This character would be reborn two generations later as Walter Mitty, the hero of James Thurber's 1939 short story.)

Karno's companies were Charlie Chaplin's training ground, and one can imagine the profound impact of one of music hall's most successful enterprises on a youth who was no longer a boy. Having taken the Karno shilling aged seventeen, he progressed through the ranks till the age of twenty-one, at which point he was one of Karno's star attractions.

As youth dictates, it was also the period of his first love, with Hetty Kelly, a dancer in Bert Coutt's 'Yankee Doodle Girls'. The affair lasted for only a few days, and in the impetuousness of youth, Chaplin later recalled in *My Autobiography*, he first asked her to marry him and then, when she hesitated: 'I think we'd better part and never see each other again.' Such regrets are long lasting, and Charles would recall elsewhere: 'It may have been a childish infatuation for her, but to me it was the beginning of a spiritual development, a reaching out for beauty.' Hetty Kelly remained 'the face on the bar-room floor' for Charlie for many years to come.

In 1909, Charlie encountered a more adult temptation, in the shape of the habitués of the *promenoir* of the Paris Folies-Bergère, where the Karno troupe played 'Mumming Birds' in November. These were the ladies who hung about the great back circle of the stalls, beyond the sumptuous foyer with its magnificent staircases that swung up to the dress circle. Here, Chaplin could see 'bejewelled Indian princes with pink turbans and French and Turkish officers with plumed helmets'. It was the acme of glamour, but when the young lad tried to pick up one of these ladies, he discovered that she expected a small fortune for a short business-like session, rather than the night of desire he had dreamed of: "'*Vingt franc pour le moment?*" "*C'est ca,*" she replied emphatically. "I'm sorry," I said, "I think I'd better stop the cab.'"

Paris would remain a rose-tinted vision to look back at. But Karno's foreign sights were set elsewhere, west, rather than east, across the Atlantic.

In America, at the parallel period to England's music hall, vaudeville was at its peak, experiencing its second golden age after the 'gilded' 1890s. Acts like W. C. Fields, Houdini, Weber and Fields, Nat Wills – the 'Happy Tramp' – Joe Cook, Bert Williams, Eddie Cantor, and grandes dames such as Lillian Russell, Eva Tanguay and Nora Bayes, among the lesser mortals, played the great palaces controlled by America's vaudeville tycoons, Keith and Albee, Klaw and Erlanger and the Shubert brothers. Newcomers of this period who would become famous via the movies included, as well as Fields, the Marx Brothers, whose 'Fun in Hi Skool' began in 1911, and buxom Mae West, belting out 'rap' lyrics and swinging her hips from 1910 on.

Many of the standard acts of American vaudeville were international stars as well: they toured Europe, from London to Paris to Berlin to Madrid, Milan, Vienna and Copenhagen, and further along the great steamship itineraries, mainly throughout the stations of the British Empire – Cape Town, Johannesburg, Sydney, Melbourne, Hong Kong, Calcutta, Bombay and Mysore. Of the long-lasting stars of British music hall, the singer and raconteur R. G. Knowles had been to most places, almost everywhere, in fact, collecting stories that he would transform into a major act called 'Trifles that Trouble the Traveller'. In an age before mechanical means could amplify the human voice, he would stand on his own and transfix an audience, in halls that held over two thousand people, for up to two and a half hours with his tales alone.

Of the American tourers, W. C. Fields's annual peregrinations in the British Isles have been noted – around the halls from Portsmouth to Edinburgh, from Dublin to Hull. In July 1909, Karno's 'Mumming Birds' and Fields's juggling act shared the bill at the New Olympia, Liverpool, though no record of any meeting between the two future

Hollywood comedy stars has been logged. Chaplin would have been at least fitfully familiar with American vaudevilleans during his three Karno years, since the transatlantic route was a two-way street for both British and American acts.

Hindsight is a plague of biography – we see famous people with glittering careers where there is, at the early stage, merely a struggling lad or girl trying to learn the ropes or get a foot at the bottom rung of the ladder. Even as a headliner in the swirling world of variety, life could be precarious. Booze or a sudden collapse of popularity could claim more prominent souls than Charles Chaplin Senior, and his father's fate, as well as his mother's decline, would stand as harsh warnings of the deep pitfalls strewn in the road ahead. You could be lauded as the next best thing by a friendly critic in March and be back in the poorhouse come November. In the Edwardian Britain of the twentieth century's teens, there was no welfare to cushion the fall. The 'Cry of Outcast London' could still be heard in Lambeth, and many other boroughs, even if some alleviation had been achieved by, for example, the Education Act of 1902, which had widened the provision of schooling. An even more crucial National Insurance Act, providing some protection to workers from sickness and unemployment, would not be passed till the end of 1911.

For those performers who dreamed of the American tour, there was a particular dilemma to face. The British and the Americans were very much two peoples divided by a common language, and this gap was not necessarily closed by speechless mime. There was a conceptual difference. American vaudeville was overwhelmingly ethnic, with almost all acts defined as Irish acts, Italian acts, German acts, Dutch acts, Jewish acts, and the separate and unequal black acts, not to speak of the long tradition of blackface minstrel. In contrast, most British music-hall humour was class-based, albeit mixed with the universal seasoning of the sex wars, boy and girl, husband and mother-in-law and the eternal stewpot of family squabbles. George Robey could combine the two themes in a ditty describing his doomed approaches to a rich heiress's father:

> He told me my society was superfluous,
> That my presence I might well eradicate.
> From his baronial mansion he bade me exit,
> And said I might expeditiously migrate.
>   In other words, 'Buzz off!'

Although British class-war humour was not unfamiliar to Americans, who had after all been watching Gilbert and Sullivan operettas since the 1870s, at the lower end of its scale the vast array of regional-accented jokes and rituals were pretty opaque for the American crowds. In the other direction, the Marx Brothers found that their own street-slang repartee was incomprehensible to British audiences as late as 1922, when their presentation of their American hit *On the Balcony* at the London Coliseum was met by a shower of heavy copper pennies. Groucho told the angry audience that the least they could do was throw the lighter shillings, but even the professional critics could not understand what Groucho and Chico were saying in their Yankee and mock-Italian patter.

Charlie Chaplin was an out-and-out cockney, a Londoner bred in the bone. School may have taught him to speak a little more 'proper', and by the time he reached the United States in 1910 he was just another 'Englishman', with all the foreignness that entailed. We, of course, can gauge his speech only from the later sound films, beginning as late as *The Great Dictator* in 1940, with little trace of the London argot remaining. By *Limelight*, in 1952, it has been eradicated completely. The roots, however, were strongly present, and visible, in the character that Chaplin came to adopt in the course of his Keystone apprenticeship.

His Other Self, the Drunken Swell, was transported in the SS *Cairnrona* from Southampton in that September of 1910, when Charlie finally crossed the ocean with the Karno troupe, reaching New York to commence rehearsals for their first appearance at the Colonial Theatre on 3 October. Karno had chosen the sketch his New York troupe, led by manager-director Alf Reeves, would open with. Setting aside the staple fare of 'Mumming Birds', aka 'A Night in an English Music Hall', the cast presented 'The Wow Wows', a new sketch that had opened in England in August 1910. 'A Farcical Sketch in 3 scenes', this once again featured the Hon. Archibald Binks, of 'Skating', and his silly upper-class friends, who are initiating him to the eponymous secret society of the Wow Wows, at their Lodge in Brown's Club House. The dialogue was practically devoid of real jokes, though some must have passed muster at the East Ham Palace or Nottingham Empire, where it opened, apparently with Sydney Chaplin in the lead. Archie's lines were a farrago of puns and *nuls entendres*:

LYDIA: Did you sleep well last night dear?
ARCHIE: No, I had a beastly dream, oh, a fearful dream.
LYDIA: Indeed, dear, and what was it?
ARCHIE: I dreamt I was being chased by a caterpillar.
LYDIA: Oh, how dreadful. I say dear, have you been in for your morning dip?
ARCHIE: Yes, I've had my usual river plunge.
LYDIA: And was the water up to your expectations?
ARCHIE: No, only up to my knees.

And, in the initiation scene:

BRUNTON: Come along Archie, this way, don't be afraid.
ARCHIE: All right old boy, I say, look at that old chap up there with his legs crossed (pointing to skull and bones over door).
BRUNTON: That's the arms of the Wow Wows, now stand there and don't say a word (knocks on door).
BLAZER (in mysterious voice): Who seeks admittance to our secret chamber?
ARCHIE: Here endeth the first lesson.
BRUNTON: Hush! We are your loyal brothers numbers one and six.
ARCHIE: Go on, make it half a crown.
BLAZER: What are your names, brothers?
BRUNTON: I am good brother Nightmare.
ARCHIE: And I am good night Nurse.
BLAZER: Impart to me in secret the sign and password (during this Archie does ballet step).
BRUNTON (gives sign and says): Kiss me!
BLAZER: 'Tis well, brother Nightmare, enter.

In the darkness of the lodge, the 'brothers' make Archie kiss a casket with a haddock in it and dance on an 'electric carpet', then place fly paper on him, and all unmask. Archie uses the ' electric carpet' to give them all shocks. Curtain.

The whole thing did not go well at the Colonial, critics calling it a 'collection of blithering, blathering Englishmen', though *Variety* singled out Chaplin for special notice: 'Chaplin will do all right for America, but it is too bad that he doesn't appear in New York with something more than this piece . . . The Colonial audience laughed at the show Monday night, but not enough. An act of this sort, erected solely for comedy, should register a bigger percentage of laughs. . .'

The troupe soon reverted to the tried and true repertory of 'A Night in an English Music Hall', as well as 'A Night in the Slums', the US title for 'Early Birds', and another variant on the Swell character, 'A Night

Keystone antics, as drawn in 1915.

in an English Club'. *Variety* on 10 December noted that this starred S. Jefferson as 'the dude', and that he 'was really very funny'. For once, Chaplin played second fiddle to Stan Laurel-to-be, but Stanley was soon relegated to his proper junior place, and Chaplin took back the star role. A. J. Marriot has sleuthed another minor addition, a sketch called 'A Harlequin in Black and White', described as a 'Shadowgraph Pantomime', that the Karno group performed in New York in January 1911. Chaplin kept a review of this eleven-minute piece in his archive – a rare outing at Karno for the classical *commedia dell'arte* characters of Harlequin, Clown, Pantaloon and Columbine. It would echo in his memory until its resurrection in *Limelight*, forty years later.

Charlie's Archibald role would have taken care of the transformation of his cockney accent into a more genteel English sound. The drunken Swell of 'A Night in an English Music Hall' stumbled on across the United States, from New York to Pennsylvania, Massachusetts, Chicago, Wisconsin, on into Manitoba, Canada, and down the west coast, to Washington, Oregon, into California – to San Francisco, Sacramento, Los Angeles and back around the western and northern states through 1911 and the summer of 1912. A brief hiatus back home in Britain ensued, and then a return to New York and westwards again in October 1912, continuing through 1913.

The character of the drunk interloper was thus imbued so deeply into the warp and weft of Chaplin's performances that he became difficult to shake when the movies finally beckoned, and lingered on through the Keystone period and beyond. He became an endemic part of the Tramp, always lurking in the wings, ever ready to spring out and disrupt the playing of both stage and reality, the postures of the rich and self-righteous, the parties of the complacent, the innocent flirtation of park-bench couples, the simple pleasures of lunch or just the workings of ordinary folk going about their business. He was the imp on Charlie's shoulder, representing, with a quick sneer and a kick in the arse, his contempt for any social structure or standing, for marriage, for family, for any kind of achievement, and, most of all, for art itself. It was no wonder the surrealists, and before them the Dadaists, proclaimed him the patron saint of their cause.

But of course, it was just a gag, was it not, repeated every night for a fee, just another job, to keep eating, and to survive life's turmoil and graft?

5

The Tramp

Or: Strolling over the country without lawful occupation

Synopsis (*The Tramp*, Essanay, 1915)

Charlie, the Tramp, is walking down the open gravel road in the woods when a motor car zooms by and upends him. He recovers and brushes himself down. Meanwhile, at a farmhouse, the owner is giving his daughter a wad of cash. An unshaven wandering tramp sees the cash; he tries to steal it but Charlie chases him off. Reluctantly he returns the cash to the daughter. She takes him to her home, while the other tramp, with two hungry companions, plots revenge. At the farmhouse, Charlie is offered work and comedy bizness follows with a farmhand, pitchforks, and heavy sacks falling on father's head. Charlie waters trees, tries to milk a cow by its tail and otherwise proves himself useless. When the tramps attack the farmhouse, father chases them off with a shotgun. Charlie is injured in the leg and is put to bed and pampered by the girl. But when her slick fiancé arrives he knows he has no chance with her. Wiping his nose on the curtain, he writes her a note and leaves, the first instance of the iconic shot of Charlie departing sadly down the open trail, then giving a little kick of self-encouragement and proceeding jauntily, iris out.

From Mark Twain's *Huckleberry Finn*

Chapter 5: Pap Starts In on a New Life

I had shut the door to. Then I turned round, and there he was. I used to be scared of him all the time, he tanned me so much. I reckoned I was scared now, too; but in a minute I see I was mistaken . . . I warn't scared of him worth bothering about.

He was most fifty, and he looked it. His hair was long and tangled and greasy, and hung down, and you could see his eyes shining through like he was behind vines. It was all black, no grey; so was his long, mixed-up whiskers. There warn't no color in his face, where his face showed; it was white; not like another man's white, but a white to make a body sick, a white to make a body's flesh crawl – a tree-toad white, a fish-belly white. As for his clothes – just rags, that was all. He had one ankle resting on t'other knee; the boot on that foot was busted, and two of his toes stuck through, and he worked them now and then. His hat was laying on the floor – an old black slouch with the top caved in, like a lid . . .

The American tramp was a familiar figure before Chaplin came on the scene, but his history encompassed barely half a century. Drifters of course had always existed in every country and era, but the word 'tramp' appears to have become widely used during the American depression years of 1873–4. According to an essay by Sidney L. Harring in *Law & Society Review*, 1977, the term was first used by the *New York Times* in 1874, 'to describe the traveling unemployed'. It was often interlinked with the more romanticized 'hobo', to whose lifestyle so many ballads alluded. Initially, and for most respectable folk, he was a figure of fear, like Huck Finn's almost demonic Pap, a drunken vagrant who pours scorn on Huck's schooling, his 'putting on frills' and his 'airs'. 'First you know you'll get religion, too,' the ultimate degradation. The forces of law and order always saw him as a menace, and many states passed Tramp Acts, defining a tramp as – in the words of the New York statutes of 1885 – 'All persons who rove about from place to place begging, and all vagrants living without labor or visible means of support, who stroll over the country without lawful occupation.' Any resident of a town where an offence under this act was committed could 'apprehend the offender and take him before a justice of the peace or the competent authority'.

Fiction writers often saw the tramp, and in particular the hobo, as a kind of inverse image of the journeying of the pioneers of the American frontier. They were the sojourners of Walt Whitman's 'Song of the Open Road', which exemplified

. . . the profound lesson of reception, nor preference nor denial,
The black with his woolly head, the felon, the diseas'd, the illiterate person,
are not denied . . .

But another image was provided by Jack London, in his 1907 record of *The Road*, describing Reno, Nevada, in the summer of 1892:

It was fair-time, and the town was filled with petty crooks and tin-horns, to say nothing of a vast and hungry horde of hoboes. It was the hungry hoboes that made the town a 'hungry' town. They 'battered' the back doors of the homes of the citizens until the back doors became unresponsive.

A hard town for 'scoffings,' was what the hoboes called it at that time . . . Why, I was so hard put in that town, one day, that I gave the porter the slip and invaded the private car of some itinerant millionaire. The train started as I made the platform, and I headed for the aforesaid millionaire with the porter one jump behind and reaching for me. It was a dead heat, for I reached the millionaire at the same instant that the porter reached me. I had no time for formalities. 'Gimme a quarter to eat on,' I blurted out. And as I live, that millionaire dipped into his pocket and gave me . . . just . . . precisely . . . a quarter. It is my conviction that he was so flabbergasted that he obeyed me automatically, and it has been a matter of keen regret ever since, on my part, that I didn't ask him for a dollar. I know that I'd have got it. I swung off the platform of that private car with the porter manoeuvring to kick me in the face. He missed me. One is at a terrible disadvantage when trying to swing off the lowest step of a car and not break his neck on the right of way, with, at the same time, an irate Ethiopian on the platform above trying to land him in the face with a number eleven. But I got the quarter! I got it!

One can almost hear the voice of Charlie himself, with its mock-genteel timbre, in one of the many escapades that were finally encapsulated in the mature sagas of *City Lights* and *Modern Times*.

Tramps and hoboes were often mixed, in public perception and in the suspicions of law and order, with the subversive threat of working-class agitation, and Sidney Harring's aforementioned article is mainly concerned with the 'Suppression of Tramps in Buffalo, 1892–1894', as 'in those depression years as many as several hundred thousand of the three to four million unemployed workers in the United States "took to the rails" in search of work, thereby exposing themselves to the danger of arrest and six months in prison under the Tramp Acts'. According to the New York statutes, interestingly: 'This act shall not apply to any person under the age of sixteen years, nor to any blind person nor to any person roving within the limits of the county in which he resides.' Which may explain, to the literal-minded, why Chaplin's Tramp character could roam about in his own restricted area, and was never portrayed as a full-blown 'rail-riding' hobo, though this, in his first movie year of 1914, was most probably because the natural budgetary constraints of the early Keystones required most action to take place within a couple of miles of the studio at Edendale and Echo Park.

Another researcher, John D. Seelye, of the University of California at Berkeley, examined, in his 1963 article 'The American Tramp: A

Vision of the Picaresque', the dichotomy between 'our distaste for the real tramp and our love for the comic version', the latter being a kind of exorcism of the demonic shadow of the real thing – 'the lazy, incorrigible, cowardly, utterly depraved savage', in the parlance of the time. Even being a free-born white American could not absolve one from this dread condition, brought about by the sudden scourge of poverty. As the balladeer of *The Face on the Bar-Room Floor* announces:

> You laugh as if you thought this pocket never held a sou,
> I once was fixed as well, my boys, as any one of you.

This circumstance, brought about after the chaos of the Civil War, was in fact new to Americans, who might have recalled, in the words of Herman Melville in 1849, that in America 'such as being a beggar is almost unknown; and to be a born American citizen seems a guarantee against pauperism; and this, perhaps, springs from the virtue of a vote.' But Charlie Chaplin, as we know, never voted, and his creator never became an American citizen, a decision which would have its consequences, in time.

The 'tramp problem' lingered in American social discourse through the turn of the twentieth century. O. F. Lewis, General Secretary of the Prison Association of New York, penned an article in 1912 stating:

There is much unclear thinking about tramps. The bulk of people probably do not know what they mean when they talk about tramps. Some of them have learned about tramps from funny papers; some from the stranger in the street, some from having their summer cottages robbed or burned . . . Charitable societies, missions, city lodging houses, courts and prisons have all dealt with, and do deal with, the 'hobo.' When the solution of a problem is hard and costly, and perhaps useless in the end, it is apt to be side-tracked. Thus it is with the related problems of inebriety and vagrancy.

Like many before and after him, Lewis advocated a 'national committee' to reduce the twin evils of vagrancy and drunkenness. Clearly the issue persisted, as strongly as it had been evident over thirty years before, in the year when Charles Chaplin was carrying his own drunk impersonation across America with Karno's troupe.

For the tramp clown, there were already pre-existing models before the iconic moment when Chaplin, according to his own self-made legend, wandered through the Mack Sennett studio's costume room looking for something to put on. As a relative stranger to the

US – although he had travelled its length and breadth for almost three years – he might not have been completely familiar with the resident fauna, but he must have been aware of the swirl of tramp comedians that inhabited the vaudeville halls. 'In the first decade of the 1900's,' wrote vaudeville's chronicler, Douglas Gilbert, 'tramp comics swarmed through vaudeville almost as a national symbol; legit musical stages were heavy with them; and joke magazines and newspaper strips . . . detailed their haphazard lives with jesting abandon.'

There was one of the originals, Ned Harrigan of Harrigan and Hart, the duo who had defined post-Civil War variety with their Irish sketches and plays – Harrigan was said to have wandered through the streets of New York and cadged his latest costume off the worst-dressed bums he could find. There was Nat Wills, the 'Happy Tramp'. There was Paul Barnes, who used a 'red nose, ragged beard, broken derby and disreputable clothes'. There was Lew Bloom's 'philosophical bum', and Charles R. Sweet's tramp burglar, who 'made his entrance with a dark lantern through a window that gave onto a living room and explained that he was examining the property by night because his business affairs were so engrossing in the daytime'. And of course, there were the tramp jugglers, most lasting of them W. C. Fields, who honed his act with Irwin's Burlesquers from 1898 before becoming an international headliner. Appearing in London in 1901, his look was described in the *Black and White Budget* magazine: 'Clothes – old, torn, loose and unclean; boots, big and bulging; hat – an artistic wreck. And the face! Hirsute and blotchy, with a ludicrous expression of countenance that was most diverting.' Unlike most tramp characters, Fields eschewed the usual patter, and – probably in order to make his act popular to audiences speaking many foreign tongues – he eventually became not just 'the comedy juggler' but 'the silent humorist', developing his own form of pantomime. It is possible to believe that Chaplin was so tied up in his own Karno performances that he failed to notice all of these predecessors – but he certainly could not have failed to notice some of them.

Chaplin's account of his own adoption of the tramp costume was sealed in *My Autobiography*, as he described the moment at Keystone studios when he was waiting to shoot his very first film, in January 1914:

I stood where Sennett could see me. He was standing with Mabel [Normand], looking into a hotel lobby set, biting the end of a cigar. 'We need some gags here,' he said, then turned to me. 'Put on a comedy make-up. Anything will do.'

I had no idea what make-up to put on . . . On the way to the wardrobe I thought I would dress in baggy pants, big shoes, a cane and a derby hat. I wanted everything a contradiction: the pants baggy, the coat tight, the hat small and the shoes large. I was undecided whether to look old or young, but remembering Sennett had expected me to be a much older man, I added a small moustache . . . I had no idea of the character. But the moment I was dressed, the clothes and the make-up made me feel the person that he was. I began to know him, and by the time I walked on to the stage he was fully born.

Not quite so, as the young man was still unsure whether he should stick to this new image, or revert to the Cad, or try out the Drunken Swell, or the gesticulating maniac Lord Helpus, throughout his Keystone year. But the tale may be no less true for being an encapsulation of so many influences: from George Robey, the small bowler and cane; from Fred Kitchen and even Little Tich, the oversized boots and the strange swagger that could turn in an instant into a mincing gait, with signature little kick of the heels; from Will Murray, the grinding-on-one-foot turn. In *Photoplay*'s 1915 rendition of 'Charlie Chaplin's Story', the writer, Harry Carr, had a completely different version of the story:

His first costume didn't suit him at all. The Keystone people say he was always poking around the property room trying to hit upon some sort of clothes that would 'register.' One day he came out grinning, with a funny old pair of shoes in his hands. They were long and curled up at the toes. They reached right out and shook hands with Chaplin as soon as he saw them. They had been Ford Sterling's and had been left behind when Sterling quit the company. Chaplin has worn those identical shoes ever since.

Chaplin's transfer to Keystone, from his stage life with Karno, has also been argued by researchers, trying to determine who exactly spotted him in the Karno ensemble at which date. David Robinson quotes a letter from Charlie to Sydney back home in London, in August 1913:

Oh' Sid I can see you!! beaming now as you read this, those sparkling eyes of yours scanning this scribble and wondering what coming next . . . I have had an offer from a moving picture company for quite a long time but I did not want to tell you untill the whole thing was confirmed . . . It is for the New York Motion Picture Co., a most reliable firm in the States – they have about four companies, the 'Kay Bee' and Broncho [and] Keystone which I am to joyne . . . It appears they saw me in Los Angeles, Cal. playing the Wow Wows when they wrote to me in Philadelphia which was a long time after . . .

Chaplin was signing for an opening salary of $150 a week climbing after three months to $175, about the standard for a new Keystone clown. The Motion Picture Company was indeed a power in the business, set up by New Yorkers Adam Kessel and Charles Bauman in 1908 and then removed to California in the wake of the conflicts that became known as the 'Edison Patent Wars': the attempts by Thomas Alva Edison to corral all film companies into a combination that would be bound to use his equipment. 'Independents' scurried to farther pastures to escape the pressure, and Kessel and Bauman set up their studio at Alessandro Street, Edendale, California, in 1909. By 1910, movies were already a major American industry and, like today's 'dot com' companies, these short films proliferated as audiences demanded more and more. As Mack Sennett himself wrote: 'Anything on film made money. The only requirement was that it be reasonably new.' Sennett, having worked with D. W. Griffith at the New York Biograph company since 1908, had become Griffith's comedy director, and then joined with Kessel and Bauman to create Keystone, their comedy arm, with his first comic recruits – Fred Mace, Ford Sterling and Mabel Normand – in 1912. Chaplin claimed, in his letter to Sydney, that he was being hired to replace Fred Mace, who was leaving the company, but in the event it was the big-shoed Ford Sterling whose role as Mabel's foil he was to assume.

The date of transfer is more or less fixed by a legendary telegram – which has never been archived – sent on 12 May 1913 to the Karno troupe's manager, Alf Reeves:

IS THERE A MAN NAMED CHAFFIN IN YOUR COMPANY OR SOMETHING LIKE THAT IF SO WILL HE COMMUNICATE WITH KESSEL AND BAUMANN 24 LONGACRE BUILDING BROADWAY NEW YORK.

And that is as good a story as any. The contract was finally signed on 25 September in Portland, Oregon, where Chaplin was performing in 'A Night in a London Club' at the Empress Theatre, before repairing south to San Francisco. His last week with Karno is logged as 23 to 29 November, at the Empress, Kansas City, Missouri. Chaplin left the troupe with which he had spent his days and nights since 1908, five years at the apex of English music hall's classic traditions. On his first night in Los Angeles, having checked in at the Great Northern Hotel, he went to the Empress Theatre, where he had appeared in October, and by chance met Mack Sennett and Mabel Normand there. Sennett, so the legend goes, was taken aback at how young the mature-looking Drunken Swell appeared without make-up. But the next day, he was off to the studio in Edendale, the ramshackle madhouse that was to transform him into the twentieth century's most recognized man.

6

The Fatal Mallet

Or: Who painted the 'IWW' on the shed door?

Synopsis (*The Fatal Mallet*, Keystone, 1914)

Charlie wanders along a park glade and sees Mack Sennett (also dressed as a tramp) wooing Mabel. He interrupts them. Mabel throws a brick at Charlie, and Mack faces him down. Another suitor, dapper and large-bodied Mack Swain, arrives to claim Mabel. Sennett and Charlie gang up on him, trying to bean him from behind with a brick. Swain chases them off. Charlie and Sennett hide in a shed, where Charlie finds a huge mallet. While Swain continues to woo Mabel in the glade, Charlie creeps up behind him and brains him with the mallet. Sennett and Charlie carry Swain into the shed but Charlie gets the drop on Sennett and locks them both in. Swain awakes and threatens Sennett, but then they decide to gang up on Charlie. Meanwhile, a small boy has cuddled up to Mabel in the glade. Charlie arrives and kicks him away. Swain and Sennett escape from the shed and find Mabel cooing with Charlie. Charlie kicks Mack Swain in the groin and chest, knocking him into the lake. Mack Sennett kicks Charlie into the lake, and walks off arm in arm with Mabel.

A raw piece of aggressive Keystone violence, *The Fatal Mallet* was the fifteenth Chaplin film, released at the beginning of June 1914 and allegedly directed by Mack Sennett himself. In its format, it was a regression to the earliest type of Keystone film, made right at the start of the studio's foundation in the fall of 1912. It is pure essence of slapstick, with no possible hint of a redeeming subtlety or refinement of plot or character. Even Mabel gets hit by a brick in the face at one point. Kicks in the groin and chest, poking in the behind, macho posturing and Extreme Mallet Action prevail. Mabel is the object of desire, in an obvious sense, but in another, the violence itself is the reward and the object of the three suitors' primal savagery. In the end, of course, as is the case in the movies, the director walks off with the girlfriend.

In the first two years of Mack Sennett's Keystone studios, Sennett often appeared in his own movies, sometimes for the hell of it, sometimes to fill in for an unavailable actor. Subtle characterisation, or any characterisation at all, was not his forte. We can scan his on-screen progress from his first appearances in the early Griffith shorts of 1908: a gawky, country rube figure with orangutan arms, he later tried on a French character, Monsieur Dupont (a shameless steal from Max Linder), in 1909's *The Curtain Pole*, chronologically the very first 'Mack Sennett' comedy. A middling actor – though he cut his teeth singing small parts in Broadway musical shows – once Keystone was set up, Sennett proved himself a master producer, parlaying his ramshackle troupe into America's first and foremost comedy company, dominating his field till the 1920s. By 1913, he was recruiting comedians like crazy, sweeping up Roscoe 'Fatty' Arbuckle, Al St John, Edgar Kennedy, Hank Mann and all the staples of the famous Keystone Kops, who first puttered on to the screen in *The Bangville Police*, patently failing to rescue Mabel in peril.

To Mack Sennett, the quintessential 'Father Goose', all his flock of goslings were equal, and he had no reason to think that Charles Chaplin was anything special. Chaplin had consistently good notices as the Karno tour's lead player, though stories about his peculiar 'Englishness' were also making the rounds. The *Philadelphia Record*, in April 1913, quoted manager Alf Reeves about Charlie's strange behaviour in entering an American bar for the first time:

He had only arrived here the day before and the dust of the London streets still clung to his boots . . . we went to a small saloon near the theatre for a 'nightcap.' I ordered a Scotch and soda and asked Charlie what he would like to drink. The bartender leaned over the bar to get the order. 'Well, old Top,' drawled Chaplin, 'I fawncy that I would like a mug of mulled ale and a toasted biscuit.' The bartender thought he was being 'spoofed,' . . . and, reaching for a huge oaken bungstarter, he said in a quiet, but menacing manner, 'You're in Jersey City, young feller, not on Piccadilly; how would you like a glass of beer?' Chaplin took a good look at the bartender and then quietly said, 'I should like it jolly well.'

A toasted biscuit? What were those Philly journalists thinking of? Once ensconced in Mack Sennett's manic barnyard, however, neither Charlie nor Mack had any clear idea what was to happen next, apart from the general Sennett admonition to 'go out there and be funny!' In later years, Sennett would be famous for the big central tower in which he held court, often naked in his large bathtub, cigar clamped between his teeth. But Sennett alternated accounts of the early studio as pure spontaneous chaos with more tempered tales of the extreme care he claimed to take on every movie. In May 1913 Gertrude Price of the *Toledo News Bee* reported,

He builds his plots around current happenings and works them out in the street car or as he walks down the street. He never writes a line, for when the picture is once in his head he has it . . . 'There's just a hair's breadth between melodrama and comedy,' he told me. 'You can make the latter out of the former by exaggerating it a bit . . . It's much more difficult to make people laugh than to make them cry, I find . . . I work my actors as a man moves his checkers on a board. I know the plot . . . it's up to me to keep all the strings untangled and to pull them, each at the right time.'

The star of the Sennett lot, then, was always Mack Sennett – he later described himself as master of the cinematic trades, supervising if not personally writing all the plots, editing the finished films, taking over the direction when he thought fit and, in later years, choosing the inter-titles which were inserted after the movie was shot. In hindsight, after he had made the error of losing Chaplin to the Essanay company, he told the *Saturday Evening Post* (September 1916):

Chaplin's methods of getting laughs at once engaged my attention. There are many comedians who work mechanically, with too apparent force, assuming the attitude: 'Now I'm going to make them laugh!' They are contracted, tense. You can almost hear them grinding their teeth with determination . . .

But Chaplin was wholly unconscious of his audience; just as relaxed in front of twenty-five hundred people as if he'd been sitting at ease in his own bedroom. His were humorous methods.

Chaplin was getting something like seventy-five or one hundred dollars a week [in vaudeville]. I engaged him for a hundred and twenty-five dollars, I think, and took him to the coast. He'd never been in a motion picture studio before. I thought I had the makings of a star in him – a big star – and I could afford to go slow and observe him . . .

Some of Chaplin's early accounts of the studio were somewhat far-fetched, as his serialized account in the *Chicago Herald* informed the bemused readers:

I left New York for California under the flattering and delightful impression that in the movies I was to play romantic and serious roles . . . On arriving at Los Angeles I reported for duty at the producing studios . . . the out-of-door surroundings, the sight of 'interior' scenes open to the sky, the view of distant mountains and the breezy flashes of western life were all amazing to eyes accustomed only to the world behind the footlights and the confining brick walls of the New York and London stage.

I shall never forget my first day as a moving picture actor. I reported for work at an intolerably early hour – it was at least 9 a.m. As I stood in the awesome presence of the stage director my heart beat high and I was thrilled with curiosity as to the type of romantic youth I was to play in the forthcoming film. Somehow I had an idea that it would be a drama of the Elizabethan period, and that I would be called upon to wear doublet and hose and wield a rapier in behalf of my lady love.

The stage director's first words stunned me.

'Good morning,' he said. 'Can you fall off a stepladder?'

I fell back a few steps, open-mouthed.

Unbelieving, I asked him to repeat the question.

'I mean, can you do a funny sprawl off a stepladder without breaking your bones?' he demanded.

An hour later I was falling off the ladder – with frills and variations . . .

This was a tale Chaplin told quite often, probably to present himself as more refined than the average Keystone contract player. Harry Carr of *Photoplay* got a version that seemed closer to the truth:

His first days at Keystone were anything but happy ones. They didn't understand him and he didn't understand them. Chaplin had been carefully trained along the lines of English pantomime. He found the silent drama a la American to be utterly different in every particular . . . a whirlpool of action without any particular technique . . . From all accounts he and the lovely Mabel Normand, now the best of friends and the warmest admirers of one another, got along about as well as a dog and cat with one soup bone to arbitrate. He told Mabel what he thought of her methods and Mabel told him a lot of things. In those days Charlie used to come wandering back of the scenes at the theatres as lonesome as a lost soul. He was ready to chuck the whole business.

'They won't let me do what I want; they won't let me work in the way I am used to,' he complained. His first pictures for the Keystone were not much of a success. In one of them he appeared in the part of a woman. Chaplin was a mis-fit in the organization . . .

The Fatal Mallet was a typical sample of the kind of movie that restricted Charlie to the basic range of comic business. I hit him, he hits me, she gets hit by mistake, big laughs. It was the lowest denominator of comedy, but it ingrained in Chaplin the principle that the building blocks of slapstick always had to be there. As late as *A King in New York*, with its cabaret scene of the painter and client, he knows that the clown is a clown, first and foremost.

The character, however, was another matter, and the grand epiphany of the Tramp remains a myth. Chaplin's first film at Keystone, *Making a Living*, features him as a dissolute and unemployed city slicker, with a drooping moustache, top hat, frock coat and cane. His foil in this case is Henry 'Pathé' Lehrman, another of Sennett's early recruits. Lehrman was a key player in the early Keystones, directing roughly half of their movies. Nicknamed 'Pathé' because of his claim to be French, he was in fact an Austrian national (allegedly from Przemyszl) who had immigrated to the US in 1907. He had met Sennett at Biograph, and they shared an apartment in New York, on West 5th Street, though Sennett later claimed he had recruited Lehrman to the flicks from his job as a movie usher at the Unique Theatre.

Lehrman later proved to be a shrewd operator – setting up his own L-KO (Lehrman Knock-Out Comedies) company – and a controversial figure, hated by many for his ruthless business practices. But at Keystone he was a mercurial presence both behind and in front of the camera. In *Making a Living*, as well as directing, he played a newspaper photographer, from whom Charlie the slicker cadges money and whose girl (Virginia Kirtley, not Mabel) Charlie proceeds to flirt with and steal. Applying for a job as a reporter, Charlie tangles once more with Lehrman, and is chased out. When Lehrman, witnessing a car accident, gets a scoop photograph, Charlie steals his camera and plate and presents it to the newspaper editor as his own. Much mayhem ensues with chases through the city and into a woman's house and bed, with Charlie and 'Pathé' slugging it out in front of an oncoming streetcar, continuing, dragged on its fender, into the fade-out.

A standard Keystone knock-'em-down one-reeler, *Making a Living* nevertheless featured several different locations and some elaborate street settings on a major thoroughfare (Glendale Avenue) buzzing with traffic, marking an effort by Sennett to give Chaplin some space to show his tricks. The Tramp is nowhere in evidence, and though there is some business with familiar knee-slapping and cane, the physical action is more an imitation of the arm-waving antics of Ford Sterling than anything else. In his legend, Charlie disliked the picture, but in the flush of its novelty for him, he had few critical tools with which to judge whether it suited him or not – it was just his first job in pictures.

Nothing stood still at Keystone, and within days Charlie was in the prop department rummaging for that costume that would become his signature, and shooting two more films directed by Lehrman, *Kid Auto Races at Venice* and *Mabel's Strange Predicament*. *Kid Auto Races* was a split-reeler, i.e. half of a reel which also contained an informational film entitled *Olives and Their Oil*. It was based round another Sennett staple, picking out some public event and muscling in on it with the cameras. In this case it was, of course, kid automobile races at Venice Beach. There is no plot, just a series of gags as Charlie, as the Tramp, gets in the way of Lehrman who is trying to film the races. David Robinson wrote about it: 'He is a mischievous child, grimacing at a car that almost runs him down and sticking out his tongue at Lehrman. There is a long shot of him running, leaping and skipping down the track in crazed abandon.'

In short, for the standard already set by even the most mundane Keystone pictures, it was rubbish, despite the seeds of greatness supposedly found in it by scholars. In the minutiae of forensic research into early Charlie, the historians have also examined Los Angeles weather records of January 1914 to determine the true order of production of the first two Tramp pictures, given that Chaplin himself recalled that *Mabel's Strange Predicament* was shot first. *Kid Auto Races* at Venice retains its primogeniture, on 10 January, while the extant one-page synopsis of *Mabel's Strange Predicament* is dated the same day. The outline was most probably written before, rather than after the film was shot, as it features Charlie's character, 'the drunk', quite a way down the story, as a subsidiary foil to Mabel's confused relationship with her sweetheart and another woman's husband who comes on to her in a hotel. When a dog chasing a ball accidentally locks Mabel out in the hotel corridor in her pyjamas, the script goes: 'At this point drunk comes along and tries to flirt with Mabel. In a panic she tries the next room's door and enters husband's room. Latter is standing at mirror and does not observe her. She hides under bed.'

Mabel's sweetheart comes to her room, finds it locked, sees the dog, calls on the husband. Standard Keystone stuff ensues with confusion of the wrong people in the wrong rooms, not to speak of the dog, the wife eventually finding Mabel under her bed in her pyjamas. As the script winds up, most laconically: 'Consternation, etc.'

The shot film, however, has been altered to make the drunk the star part. Charlie is in the frame from the start, staggering into the hotel lobby, twirling his cane, trying the armchair, ogling the women, chiefly Mabel, tumbling over and sampling his flask. The scene in the corridor, where he chases Mabel, leers and declares his love, is pursued by outraged lover Harry McCoy and tangles with beefy wife Alice Davenport and weedy husband Chester Conklin, gives ample room for multiple pratfalls. The 'scenario' by Lehrman was directed in tandem by Lehrman and Sennett over, allegedly, one single day. It would not seem that more was needed. The Tramp, reeking of liquor and beset by an uncontrollable satyriasis, kicks his way into screen history. All tics and spasms, he flutters his hands, wobbles on his feet and presents a whole catalogue of 'English' gestures, from the half-sneer at bourgeois convention to the ear-twist that turns out his tongue. Mabel is all preening and fluttering herself, clearly more tied up with her dog than any of her human admirers, her hiding place under the bed a suitable place to shelter before Charlie's assault.

The onslaught continued in *Between Showers*, another Keystone exploitation of a found event, in this case a rare Los Angeles downpour. Ford Sterling, still on the payroll, co-starred with Charlie as rival 'mashers' pestering Mabel in the street. Ford, frustrated by a broken umbrella, steals a better one from Chester Conklin as the cop cuddling up to Mabel, leaving his bent specimen in its stead. He spies Mabel trying to get across a puddle and rushes to her aid. Getting a plank to help her, he finds it snatched by Charlie, who has sidled up, spying his prey. Pushing and shoving ensues, with Chester eventually feeling Ford's collar for brolly theft.

The rain apart, it is a good moment to compare Ford and Charlie's comic techniques. Sterling, an actor trained on the speaking stage, was one of the men and women swept up by Sennett who had to exchange their vocal skills for pantomime. All swagger and mugging, Sterling broadcasts every move and intention with a swing of the arms, bending knees and wagging eyebrows. Charlie's balletic movements appear to belie his clumsy appearance. This contradiction between the Tramp's circumstances and responses obviously tickled the public's funny-bone. Keystone characters are often mere puppets of the grand Irish giant who pulled all the strings and led their merry dance. Sennett understood comedy in its North American form as 'exaggerated drama'. In the midst of mayhem there was nevertheless a story that the paying public could appreciate: Boy gets girl, girl dumps boy, girl gets another boy, boys beat each other to pulp.

But Charlie's comedy was still of the 'pre-surreal' Karno-type. Behind the rudimentary narrative lies the great absurdity of Life, the harshness of society, the dumb failure of law and authority, the fragility of social structures. Karno and Sennett shared the suspicion of authority, and their contempt for policemen, but Sennett, as an American (or the ex-Canadian he was), looked at the externals, the physical action in the real world. Charlie was already dredging up, from his childhood, the intense, internalized rebellion against the constrictions of reality itself. You saw it in the gestures, twiddles and quirks of his body, the expressions that flitted across the deceptively flat make-up of his face, the eyes that gazed out with a strange compassion that belied the aggression with which he took on all comers – friends or foes.

Something was being born, behind the greasepaint, behind the shabby, dirty jacket, the frayed shirt and pants, the battered shoes. Behind the poverty and the pathetic gait of the drunk – defiance. Not so much the cheerful cockney endurance of Charles Chaplin Senior, with its fatalistic abandonment of all personal obligations, even love – but a more steely determination to survive against all odds.

In *The Fatal Mallet*, as Charlie and the two Macks, Swain and Sennett, dart in and out of their sheltering shed, one can see on the shed door the chalked tell-tale letters 'IWW' – initials of the International Workers of the World. A clear provocation in Big Mack's un-unionized outfit, it may well have been there before any camera team turned up, scrawled by some passing hobo. But might we just imagine that it was chalked there by one of the staff or crew – rebelling already against petty salaries, penny-pinching and the normal course of movie exploitation? Or was it put there by the emerging demon of Charlie Chaplin himself?

Charlie's box-office prowess – as seen in 1915.

7

A Film Johnny
Or: 'I Don't Want Any Bums around Here!'

Charlie's next film, *A Film Johnny*, reprises another old staple, the mayhem of the film studio itself. Why bother to build sets and script characters if you can simply turn the camera indoors? As Chaplin 'described' the scene in Mrs Rose Wilder Lane's version of his 'Own Story':

A glare of light and heat . . . The stage, a yellow board floor covering at least two blocks, lay in a blaze of sunlight, intensified by dozens of white canvas reflectors stretched overhead. On it was a wilderness of 'sets' – drawing rooms, prison interiors, laundries, balconies, staircases, caves, fire-escapes, kitchens, cellars. Hundreds of actors were strolling about in costume; carpenters were hammering away at new sets; five companies were playing before five clicking cameras. There was a roar of confused sound – screams, laughs, an explosion, shouted commands, pounding, whistling, the bark of a dog. The air was thick with the smell of new lumber in the sun, flash-light powder, cigarette smoke . . .

The exigencies of sound, fourteen years later, reduced the studio floor to that terrible hush once the director cries 'Silence!' But the silent film shoot, at Sennett's conveyor-belt film factory, was by all accounts a major cacophony. The director bellowing at the actors through his megaphone, the noise of other film projects in the next lot and the continued building of sets for new pictures at the same time became part of the legend, and in themselves the comedy stuff of the many in-studio films. Doubtless much of this was flimflam, too, since as movies settled down to a more measured schedule even comedians would require some space, and some peace to perform. But Keystone and the other studios producing one- and two-reelers were contracted to churn 'em out hard and fast.

And so the Tramp hangs about the studio entrance, as the employees stream in, and his efforts to get through are barred by the manager who calls out: 'I don't want any bums around here!' Eventually Charlie squeezes through, stumbling on to the sets, tangling with props, flats and carpets, disrupting scenes. The stereotyped over-excited director is chomping his cigar, screaming at the actors to put more pep into their fights. Charlie flirts with the leading lady, gets hold of a pistol and begins firing in all directions. A fire breaks out, and the director cries: 'Just what we need to finish the picture!' Chaotic firemen arrive, dousing all and sundry with hosed water. Charlie, delegated to get a bucket, causes more chaos, fighting with the director, toppling the camera and ending up doused himself. All is reduced to Keystone 'normality'. As Sennett himself once declared, tongue firmly in cheek, to a 'Seeker of Information' from the *Toledo Daily Blade*, in 1917:

Seeker of Information – How do you get the effect of a man flying through space propelled by his own momentum? Everybody knows that can't be done.

Mack Sennett – If it can't be done, why ask me how I do it? You saw him fly, didn't you?

S of I – Apparently your men are thrown or projected through brick walls. How do you do that?

MS – Have you heard of the Fourth Dimension? Maybe we have found the secret.

S of I – In your automobile and taxicab smashups – how do you manage them? Every one is apparently killed, but we know you cannot do that.

MS – That is a simple trick – the machines just run together – you read of it in the papers every day . . .

S of I – Do you really burn buildings?

MS – Oh, yes. No Keystone day is complete without a fire . . .

S of I – How do you manage those explosions where the fellows are blown to smithereens and a whole house is wrecked?

MS – Well, every now and then somebody gets careless with dynamite and accidents will happen. We regret wrecking the homes of prominent citizens – but if the homes get in the way we can't help it. Our fellows are used to being blown up; it's part of the game. They expect it.

There seemed little scope for Charlie Chaplin or Roscoe Arbuckle or even Mabel Normand to develop a coherent character here, rather than a Punch and Judy figure. Mabel was closest to success, as she had already formed her act by the time Mack began directing Griffith's comedies in 1911. At the age of sixteen, she had posed for illustrator Charles Dana Gibson as a 'Gibson Girl', advertising anything from hats, hairbrushes and cold cream to veils, necklaces, frocks, evening wraps and furs. Making films for both Biograph and its rival, Vitagraph, before she was twenty, she fascinated Mack Sennett with her child-woman routines, and thus the myth of Mack and Mabel was born. Playing both waifs and tomboys, she impressed her audience with her boundless energy, playing a girl detective, an aviatrix, a diving girl, a country rascal, often initiating action in her own right. By the time Chaplin had arrived she was a veteran, twenty-two years of age, and directing her own films.

'Fatty' Arbuckle had been tumbling since about 1906, when vaudeville attracted him from a life of drudgery as a waiter to become a man of all showbiz trades: burlesque singing, jumping, pratfalling, even blackface. In 1908 he married showgirl Minta Durfee, who was about one third his size. In 1909 he made his first films for the Selig company in Los Angeles. In 1913, legend relates, he leapt up the stairs to Sennett's office and did a perfect back-flip. 'Name's Arbuckle . . . I bet I could do well in pictures.' As indeed he did. The amiable fat man who moved like greased lightning and could hold his own in any situation, some of his earliest shorts were as a Keystone Kop, before he was teamed with Mabel in what seemed a serendipitous double act. Minta Durfee also became a Keystone player, along with regular dames Alice Davenport, Virginia Kirtley and Alice Howell. The male stalwarts – Kops and others – included Al St John, Harry McCoy, Hank Mann, Edgar Kennedy, Henry Lehrman and Chester Conklin.

Another ex-vaudevillean, who had begun his career as a 'monologuist' – what we would today call a stand-up comedian – in Oakland, Chester Conklin escaped his fate as a carpenter's apprentice in Iowa and soon discovered he could be funnier by donning an immense false moustache. He too had his own legend of his start at Keystone, hanging around for three weeks like the 'Film Johnny' outside the door until at last one day Sennett said to him: 'Say, are you funny?' Chester sighed deeply: 'There is some difference of opinion as to that.' Which tickled Sennett so much that he told him to go to make-up. Sennett was quite easily amused.

Chester's teaming with Charlie would leave a famous echo, as he re-appears in the great factory start-up scene in *Modern Times* in 1936. After Chaplin left Keystone, Sennett teamed Chester with Mack Swain in a series featuring them as 'Ambrose' and 'Walrus.' He was also a capable and distinctive character actor, as his cameo role in Von Stroheim's *Greed* as a stiff German father revealed in 1922.

The stock company swept Chaplin up and whirled him about in thirty short films in quick succession. But still he was not convinced about the Tramp. After *A Film Johnny, Tango Tangles* featured Chaplin without tramp costume or make-up, in suave evening attire as a drunk who disrupts the action in a dance hall. Chester Conklin is in cop costume (dancing with a man in prisoner gear), Fatty Arbuckle is one of the musicians, Ford Sterling the band leader, Minta Durfee one of the girls. The whole piece revolves round a grudge fight between Ford and Charlie over Ford's girl. Charlie rehearses the kind of dancing gait he will use as far ahead as *City Lights*' boxing scene. His own Karnoesque tricks aside, it is a fair example of the Sennett ensemble meshed in a kind of drunken weaving around the floor, with Charlie and Ford getting entangled in their own clothes and coats to no great avail. The next one-reeler, *His Favorite Pastime*, begins with Charlie and Fatty Arbuckle as two drunks in a bar. Fatty mimes to Charlie his brood of children, marking their differing heights with his hand, a gesture we will see Charlie taking up in later films. Charlie staggers out, flirts with a toff's wife in a drawn-up car, then returns for another bout of drinking, picking fights both with other barflies and the swing doors. One begins to see the Tramp's repertoire of gestures and tics building up, the sneer, the regurgitation of beer in the face (a favorite piece of Sennett vulgarity), and later, when he follows the woman home, the epic wrestling match between Charlie and a recalcitrant flight of stairs.

In the next film, *Cruel, Cruel Love*, however, Chaplin reverted to the spiv, as in *Making a Living*, but with his drooping moustache duly cropped. 'Lord Helpus' is courting Minta Durfee but also flirts with her maid, so she turns him out of her house. Going back to his own home, he drinks a glass left by his own flatmate and becomes convinced he is poisoned. There follows an extended and unusual scene of Charlie mugging his anguish to the camera – his face contorted, his hair congealing, clutching his throat, grimacing and panicking. A short insert of hell shows the spiv being grabbed by two devils with pitchforks. Meanwhile the gardener runs over with a message of forgiveness from Minta. But the spiv has called the doctors, who race over in an ambulance, the whole concoction a kind of spoof of the cross-cutting action movies already made famous by Griffith. Interesting scenes of halcyon Silver Lake of 1914 grace the background. But it turns out that what the spiv has quaffed is only water, and he celebrates his survival and reunion with Minta by kicking everybody into a heap. The joke, one gathers, is in Lord Helpus's total lack of acquaintance with water as a tipple, anticipating W. C. Fields's famous radio monologue – 'The Day I Drank a Glass of Water' – by thirty years.

In *The Star Boarder*, once again Chaplin plays the spiv, the favourite lodger of his landlady, Minta, to the fury of her jealous husband, Edgar Kennedy. Edgar's own flirtations, as well as Charlie's, however, are caught by Minta's naughty small boy with his camera. Revelation of the kid's pictures at a slide show causes the expected mayhem, with the husband chasing Chaplin and the boy getting his bottom smacked. No notable advances in the grand art of comedy are logged here.

The three last named pictures were directed by George Nichols, another ex-Biograph veteran. For the next, *Mabel at the Wheel*, Mabel was assigned the direction, also playing a racing driver's girlfriend. Chaplin is again the spiv, in his top hat and frock coat, this time a full-blown Victorian-type villain, mugging and gesticulating, and not averse to punching Mabel in the face when she berates him for allowing her to fall off into a puddle while he was racing her about on his motorcycle. Many bricks are thrown at each other by Charlie, Mabel, her boyfriend Harry McCoy and her dad, Chester Conklin. The second reel of the film, a kind of adult *Kid Races*, exploits another found event, the auto race, at which Mack Sennett plays a rube in the audience, spitting into Chester's hat. (Sennett's stalwarts loved to spit, a soon-to-die-out part of comedy's repertoire.) Charlie and his two thuggish minions seize Harry and tie him in a barn, but Mabel takes the wheel in his stead. The villains try to disrupt her run with bombs and flood the course with a hosepipe to spin the car about, but of course she wins out in the end.

At this point, legend tells us, Chaplin was especially miffed to be taking direction from a mere girl, but he was more likely to be fed up with the villainous subsidiary role, which gave him little scope for any serious laughs. Furious at having his suggestions for some livelier business with the hose rejected, he downed tools, and shooting was stopped for the day. As David Robinson recounts, however, orders were coming through at the Keystone distribution office for more copies of Charlie's previous films, and Sennett and Mabel decided to conciliate and calm him down. The upshot was that Chaplin would get to direct his next picture at the studio.

The first film Charlie is recorded as having directed at Keystone, *Twenty Minutes of Love*, is a quick reel of tit-for-tat action around a park bench: Charlie the Tramp jeers at two lovers (Minta Durfee and Edgar Kennedy) and tries to muscle in on their wooing. Meanwhile a thief steals a watch from a sleeping man. Charlie walks off after another girl, but then sees the thief with the watch and steals it in turn, while a Keystone Kop fails to notice. Much confusion ensues between Charlie, the girl, the thief and the lovers, the Kop intervenes, and everyone gets shoved in the pond.

It is in fact difficult to figure out what directing might mean in this context. It takes a special skill for an actor to direct himself, if he is in practically every shot, and the choice of camera angles would most probably be made by the cameraman. It probably meant that no one mediated or interfered with Charlie's shtick in the film, and indeed here the Tramp is reduced to his basic archetype – a shambling wanderer who arrives from who knows where and tries to assault innocent women. In almost all the Keystone films, the Tramp, and his alter ego the drunken Spiv, are essentially aggressive and predatory. I'll do anything for a bit of aggro and a fuck, seems to be their very English, indeed very London attitude. It is a somewhat un-American trait, even for Mack Sennett's manic-aggressives, who tend to go in more for male-on-male violence, replete with kicks, punches and nose-biting. (Ford Sterling leaps on Charlie in *Tango Tangles* and tries to bite his nose off, as is his wont.) Charlie's assaults on Mabel, as in *Mabel at the Wheel*, may have included some backstage wish-fulfilment.

Be that as it may, Charlie's next film, *Caught in a Cabaret*, can lay claim to being the first in which themes emerge that are recognizable as 'Charlie Chaplin' concepts and situations, despite the fact that it is recorded as being a Mabel Normand-directed picture – or a collaboration, depending on from whom you think the scenario, such as it was, originated. Charlie is a waiter in a tough downtown joint, with singing waiter Chester Conklin, rough-house boss Edgar Kennedy and flirty dancer Minta Durfee. Discarded steaks get picked up off the floor and served. Elsewhere, in a posh house, Mabel is a society girl whose boyfriend is the jealous Harry McCoy. Charlie takes time off work, walking his reluctant dachsund in the park. The toffs are also there, but Mabel is attacked by a lout. Charlie chases him off, and introduces himself with his card as 'O. T. AXLE – AMBASSADOR OF GREECE.' Mabel's folks invite him to their daughter's party, to the boyfriend's outrage. Back at the cafe, Charlie is upbraided for turning up late, but wins kudos for dealing with a tough customer who refuses to leave by braining him (and Chester for good measure) with a mallet. At the garden party, arriving in top hat and proper coat, Charlie flirts with Mabel and gets soused, drinking directly from the bottle. After he leaves, the toffs decide to go off on a 'slumming party' downtown, and arrive at Charlie's cafe, where he is bullied again by the owner. Mabel sees he is just a waiter, and he drops a stack of plates by her side. Pretending he is only disguised as a waiter doesn't wash with Mabel, and a brawl between Charlie and Edgar Kennedy escalates to all-out coal-brick-throwing. Kennedy goes berserk with a pistol, Mabel is mussed up and pushes Charlie over. As a previous script put it so succinctly – 'consternation, etc.'

The rough cafe scene, where singing and dancing can be replaced at any moment with violence and chaos, the waiters bashing each other and the flighty girls waiting for action, was very much a Keystone staple, which was to lay the basis for many similar set-ups in later films. Fatty Arbuckle and Buster Keaton would cut their teeth on this kind of mad environment. Mack Sennett clearly had a close acquaintance in his pre-film acting days with bars in which enjoyment was never complete without a good old Irish punch-up. In 1916's *The Waiter's Ball* he would appear himself as a spaghetti-scoffing diner in an Arbuckle–St John saga set in a dreadful eatery in which pork and beans are referred to as 'one grunt with a thousand on a plate'. This is the kind of place where one wipes one's hands on a barfly's beard and hawks into the spittoon at twenty paces.

Charlie never made a clean break from the original Drunk of Karno's 'Mumming Birds', but he would subsume him into the Tramp, which provided a broader canvas on which to paint his pain, his desperation and his defiance of the cruel world. Subterfuge, dissimulation and attempted infiltration across the class divide to the bourgeois world of plenty – and plenty of free liquor – were to remain abiding themes too.

Between May and the end of the year 1914 Chaplin would appear in twenty-two more Keystone shorts – as well as the comedy feature *Tillie's Punctured Romance*. That was an average of about three films per month. Eighteen of these were directed (probably) by himself, as he learned by leaps and bounds how to master the camera, set the scenes, construct the story and control his own development of comic business and gags. The films came thick and fast: *Caught in the Rain, A Busy Day, The Fatal Mallet, Her Friend the Bandit, Mabel's Busy Day, Mabel's Married Life, Laughing Gas, The Property Man, The*

Face on the Bar-room Floor, etc., etc. In the midst of these, a three-reeler, *The Knockout*, explored the seedy world of boxing, starring Fatty Arbuckle and featuring almost the entire Sennett crew, with Charlie in a small role as a referee in another fight that prefigures another later Chaplin film, *The Champion* (made at Essanay).

As Chaplin continued to direct, he continued to develop more and more of the small gestures that illuminated his character, rather than the broad strokes of Keystone knockabout. In acting terms, he was clearly learning both from Mabel and from Arbuckle, who excelled in the comic dichotomy between his bulky body and incongruously graceful moves. Mabel was very aware of her presence as a comedienne in a world of manic males, for whom she was often no more than a trophy to be fought over in fearsome park pond combat. In *Mabel's Married Life* she is cast as Charlie's dissolute wife, who is caught flirting with the tennis-racket-wielding Mack Swain. Charlie goes off in a huff to the bar; Mabel buys a large punching dummy that vaguely resembles Mack and installs it in her apartment. A long scene ensues in which Charlie comes back plastered and confronts the dummy, which continually rocks on its base, knocking him down after his first attempts to invite it for a friendly drink bear no result. It may be a classic Keystone stand-off, but Chaplin has opted for minimal action, swaying as dumbly as the dummy itself, helpless before his own drunken delusion. All action in this scene appears to be initiated by the dummy, rather than the man. It is a brilliantly conceived presentation of the drunkard's inner state, which will be perfected, two years on, in the Mutual short *One A.M.*

The Property Man returns to the world of vaudeville as Charlie wields the props in a savage show peopled with manic spectators and acts. I have elsewhere (in *Keystone: the Life and Clowns of Mack Sennett*) written about the strange non-stop energy of so many early comedy shorts of this period, that seem to fit the title of a Pathé one-reeler, *Contagious Nervous Twitching*, that showed the whole street being infected by a man (probably Max Linder) who is seized by uncontrollable sneezing. The cinema was still young (though approaching its twenty-first birthday), and the idea of movement itself continued to entrance the audience. The idea of anything standing still seemed anathema in a Mack Sennett movie, and Charlie remaining in place, if wobbling on his feet, could only be a proper use of screen time if it was a prelude to him either being knocked over or breaking into a fit of meaningless violence. In a real sense, Sennett did not understand

Chaplin, or what he was striving for, but he could not ignore the fact that the order book showed that his films were getting more and more popular.

Chaplin continued to experiment, still not convinced that the Tramp was his vehicle. In *A Busy Day* he takes on full-blown drag as an enraged wife or girlfriend whose companion, Mack Swain, goes off to flirt during a big parade, another typical Keystone 'found event'. Kicking, pratfalling and beating up with umbrellas are the order of the day, until the harridan falls off the pier. Chaplin is terribly convincing as an enraged harpy, and if one didn't know it was him, one might wonder which of Sennett's crazies hid in that get-up. Cross-dressing seemed to be on Chaplin's mind at that moment, as in *The Masquerader* he turns up as his unmade-up self at the Keystone studio, larking around at the dressing table with Arbuckle. After cutting another typically manic swathe through the film set, he is sacked by the director, only to return as 'Senorita Chapelino'. The director and crew all dote on 'her' until Charlie reveals himself to the suckers and continues to rip the studio apart. Cross-dressing of this kind was a staple of vaudeville, and practically everyone in the early comedies indulged, including Fatty Arbuckle, who once doubled up as both female and blackface in *That Minstrel Man*, a sadly missing example. Perhaps significantly, blackface was one staple that Chaplin avoided, though whether one can read any particular sensitivity into this, in a period when 'minstrel' comedy was still common, remains an open question.

Other comedy perennials include a dentist picture, *Laughing Gas*, with Charlie causing mayhem in and out of the surgery as the dental assistant. The dentist sketch was another common vaudeville routine, reprised most famously by W. C. Fields. Charlie's pursuit of a pretty girl in the chair, and his straddling with giant forceps upon a terrified patient, prefigures Fields's own toothsome antics in one of the last ever Mack Sennett shorts, the talkie baldly titled *The Dentist* in 1932.

Another prefiguring Chaplin Keystone would be *His Musical Career*, in which he teamed up with Mack Swain as delivery and repossession men, carrying a piano by donkey cart. Their mishaps with the piano falling on top of big Mack, and wrestling it up a flight of steps, before dropping it in the pond, clearly inspired Laurel and Hardy's 1932 film *The Music Box*.

The Drunk remained, however, Chaplin's reliable second string at Keystone. In *The Rounders* he appears with Fatty Arbuckle, two totally blotto men-about-town who arrive back home to be berated by their wives, Phyllis Allen and Fatty's real-life wife, Minta Durfee. Escaping the assault of this tiny but fearsome spouse, Fatty and Charlie, having discovered by a flurry of Masonic signs that they are in the same Lodge, hie back to 'Smith's Cafe', where they outrage their fellow revellers by drawing up the tablecloths so they can sleep on the premises. Chased on by the wives, they steal a boat on the shores of the ubiquitous Silver Lake reservoir and, lying down in the leaking vessel, float off, as the intertitle sombrely tells us, 'Rocked in the Cradle of the Deep'.

While all this was going on, Sennett was preparing *Tillie's Punctured Romance*, his grand experiment as the first feature-length comedy. Lacking confidence in his own comic flock to carry the project, he procured a stage hit, *Tillie's Nightmare*, the tale of a poor working girl who dreams of a sumptuous society wedding to her boyfriend, written for and starring Marie Dressler. Dressler was a big star, who had helped her fellow Canadian Mack Sennett get his first introduction in show business, to David Belasco, about a dozen years before. Chaplin and Mabel Normand would co-star, but he would not play the Tramp. Instead he would return half-way to the spiv, as 'The Stranger', a city slicker who flirts with country girl Tillie and entices her to the city in the hope of getting his hands on her precious jar of cash. In the course of events, her millionaire uncle falls down a cliff while mountain-climbing and she inherits his swanky mansion. Charlie seems to be in clover as Marie's fiancé, but his girlfriend Mabel turns up to spoil his day, which is turned to chaos when the uncle turns out not to be dead and arrives to chase all the usurpers and social climbers off. At the end, Mabel and Tillie both agree that Charlie 'ain't good for neither of us'.

The six-reel movie was not released till November 1914, by which time Charlie had increased his box-office appeal, having added *His New Profession*, *The New Janitor*, *Recreation*, *Those Love Pangs*, *Dough and Dynamite*, *Gentlemen of Nerve* and *His Trysting Place* to his curriculum vitae. *His New Profession* and *Recreation* were two more park movies, with Charlie getting a job wheeling an invalid about with painful results in the former, and more shoving and pushing into the pond with a sailor in the latter. *Those Love Pangs* was another tangle with Chester Conklin and other love rivals, who beat him up for stealing their girls. *Dough and Dynamite* was a standard workplace gag-fest in a bakery involving fun with bread and dough.

Gentlemen of Nerve was another found auto-race picture with Mabel, Chester Conklin and Mack Swain. *His Trysting Place* cast Chaplin, unusually, as a henpecked husband to Mabel, with Mack Swain another unlikely victim of his own wife, played by Phyllis Allen, with much confusion arising when the husbands' coats get switched. A review by the cultural pundit Lewis Reeves Harrington in the *Montgomery Journal* shrewdly picked up on Charlie's innovations:

The comic spirit is entirely too deep and subtle for me to define . . . The human aspect is certainly dominant. It is funniest when it is rich in defects of character. The incongruity of Chaplin's portrayals, his extreme seriousness, his sober attention to trivialities, his constant errors and as constant resentment of what happens to him, all this has to be seen to be enjoyed . . .

Two more films, *Getting Acquainted*, another park episode with Mack and Mabel, and *His Prehistoric Past*, would wrap up Charlie's Keystone oeuvre.

In the meantime, however, events back home in England would have a crucial effect on the fortunes of all the British comedians who had been sampling an American career. In the first week of August the guns opened up in Europe in the first salvoes of what was to be called the Great War. On 9 August, Charlie wrote a letter to his brother Sydney from his berth at the Los Angeles Athletic Club, an elegant refuge for many film colonists, including Mack Sennett, announcing:

Well, Sid, I have made good. All the theatres feature my name in big letters, i.e. 'Chas Chaplin hear today.' I tell you in this country I am a big box office attraction. All the managers tell me that I have 50 letters a week from men and women from all parts of the world . . . I hope to make a bunch of dough. I have all kinds of offers at 500 a week . . . I have my own valet, some class to me, eh what? . . . Since I have been hear I have 4000 dollars in one bank, 1200 in another, 1500 in London not so bad for 25 and still going strong thank God. Sid, we will be millionaires before long . . .

Chaplin was worried whether he could send money to support their mother now the war had started. 'Tell me in your next letter what to do,' he added. 'I hope they don't make you fight over there. This war is terrible.' Mercifully he was sheltered in Los Angeles from the slew of jingoism that was spreading like a toxic cloud on the other side of the Atlantic, taking over the stage and the stage press as well. All the old trumpet calls of the 1900 Boer War were braying, and much louder. By mid-August patriotic plays with titles such as *A Call to Arms* were opening in London and 'patriotic song hits' included 'It's a Glorious Thing to Be a Soldier', 'We Didn't Want to Fight – But by Jingo Now We Do' and 'Don't Waste Your Time in Piccadilly – You'll Find Recruiting Offices near the Fountains in Tra-fal-gar Square!'

Sydney, luckily, managed to get away. With Charlie's recommendation, he joined the Keystone crew in November, playing a character called Gussle in his first film: *Gussle, the Golfer*. Charlie, however, was already weighing up several new offers, and preparing to increase the figures in his bank accounts to even more satisfactory heights. In his letter to Syd, he wrote enthusiastically about a proposal from theatre owner Marcus Loewe to form his own comedy company. But in the event the veteran Essanay company ('S & A', being George K. Spoor and G. M. alias 'Broncho Billy' Anderson), based in Chicago, took him on at his own salary demand – $1,250 per week plus a $10,000 bonus, a king's ransom for the kid who had once scrabbled for pennies and then eked out his pounds in the English music hall.

In his last film for Mack Sennett, *His Prehistoric Past*, Charlie and Mack Swain, swathed in cavemen's furs, compete with clubs for a posse of Mack Sennett lovelies in suitably minimal animal skins. In the end, back as the Tramp, Charlie awakes on a park bench with a policeman's truncheon rapping on his head. Without a second glance back, Charlie picks himself up and wanders out of the frame, the Tramp now ready to be fully hatched out of the Keystone farm's ferocious dawn chorus.

During the waits Chaplin fools around and pulls some of his funniest comedy. While producing "His Prehistoric Past" he broke up business at the nearby Ince Ranch with an imitation of a circus snake charmer.

Prehistoric Charlie with onlookers from the Ince studios.

8

His New Job
Or: Have You the Chaplinoia?

Within six months of his arrival at the Essanay studios, Charlie Chaplin was world famous. At Keystone, his name had spread by word of mouth, without much press attention. There were reviews, such as in the *New York Dramatic Mirror*, commenting on *Caught in a Cabaret*:

It is unwise to call this the funniest picture that has ever been produced, but it comes mighty close to it. It is the usual Keystone type, not overly refined humor, but certainly successful . . . As the Premier, Charles Chaplin is inimitable. Mabel Normand, besides acting and looking very pretty, directed the play. The minor parts are well handled.

But there was little else besides. In Britain, where Chaplin was already known from the Karno acts, Keystone advertisements highlighted his name, and local journals noted that 'he does things we have never seen done on the screen before'. In America, the entire ensemble was the star. At Essanay, however, there must have been some unsung publicist who was quick off the mark. By 10 January 1915, pictures and a feature article on Chaplin had already appeared in the *Chicago Herald*, which proclaimed: 'In one year as a motion picture comedian, Charles Chaplin has achieved greater popularity than any other funmaker of the films,' and related his droll adventures trying to find big enough shoes for his character: 'With a guide from the Essanay studio I started on a tour of the junk shops on State Street. These dens of cast-off fashions had the usual display of old shoes fluttering outside the windows. But somehow I couldn't find any boots that were large enough. . .'

From the outset at Essanay the Tramp would take centre stage, and would subsume, in almost all Chaplin's subsequent movies, the 'Mumming Birds' Drunk and the city-slicker cheat. A review of his first Essanay outing, *His New Job*, noted:

. . . he has emerged from the energetic seethings attendant upon his important comic divertissements for the first time under the Indian-head banner, and he is just as funny a Charlie Chaplin as he has ever been . . . In this display he is a little nicer than he has been in some Keystone confections, but not too nice to spoil his humorous appeal . . .

The manic style, which was the be-all and end-all at Keystone, is still evident, but Charlie, directing himself, now makes sure he has enough scope to develop his repertoire of gestures and gags. From the outset, the gags derive from the character, and then flow into the plot-line. The punch-drunk aggressive part was farmed out to Ben Turpin, as a rival applicant for a job at the movie studios who tries to stop Charlie going through the door for his interview by dragging him back and biting his leg.

Ben Turpin, whose famous crossed eyes were later insured for a million dollars in a publicity stunt by Mack Sennett, was the New Orleans-born son of a candy seller whose family moved to New York when he was seven. He wanted to be a fireman, but settled for vaudeville after four years as an authentic tramp, riding the rails. 'Mulligan stew was my daily bread,' he wrote later; 'it taught me human nature.' In about 1891 (aged twenty-two), so he told the tale, he went on the road with a medicine show as a comedian on seven dollars a week. His trade-mark crossed eyes were the result, he said, of playing the ocularly challenged Happy Hooligan on stage, in a version of the Hearst news-strip cartoon. Knockabout pratfalls were his stock in trade, and he could flip himself head over heels faster and harder than anyone else on stage or in movies. After three years of playing Chicago theatres, sweeping the stage as well as pratfalling on it, he was swept up by 'Broncho Billy' Anderson in 1907 for the new movie company Anderson was forming with film-renter George Spoor. His first ever picture, *An Awful Skate*, featured him 'careening down street in skates, bumping into outraged pedestrians who were later paid two dollars each for their inconvenience'.

Turpin was paid fifteen dollars a week. By the time he was introduced to the new boy on the lot, Charlie Chaplin, in January 1915, he was a veteran. He had been famous enough in 1909 for his story to be told in *Moving Picture World*, under the title 'Life of a Moving Picture Comedian': 'This is a great life . . . I must say I had many a good fall, and many a good bump, and I think I have broken about twenty barrels of dishes, upset stoves, and also broken up many sets of beautiful furniture, had my eyes blackened, both ankles sprained and many bruises, and I am still on the go . . .'

Ben was only one of several dozen working comedians who had a following long before Chaplin came on the scene. And yet, when Charlie signed with Essanay for $1,250 a week, Ben Turpin was receiving only $50 a week! When he found out, Ben was none too pleased. Chaplin wrote later that, when he was looking for partners to cast at the studio, 'there was a chap with cross eyes named Ben Turpin, who seemed to know the ropes and was not doing much with Essanay at the time. Immediately I took a liking to him, so he was chosen.' Ben presented his own view of their meeting, in an interview of 1924:

'Ben,' somebody said to me, 'meet Charlie Chaplin!'

I didn't know who Charlie Chaplin was, but they put me on to work with him.

'Ben,' he said – he had a broad English accent – 'put on your – aw – make-up and let a fellow see – aw – how you look.'

So I went in and got the piece of an old wig that was the only moustache I had. I stuck it on, changed my clothes and came out. Charlie took a look and began to laugh. 'Haw!' he yelled. 'What sort of funny looking egg is this I've got to play against?'

He laughed some more and kept on laughing. Every time he looked at me he started again.

As well he might. Ben Turpin was one of those characters who could raise a laugh simply by shuffling into sight. Their double act marked Chaplin's first two Essanay films – *His New Job* and *A Night Out*. Turpin had a smaller role in the next film, *The Champion*, and a last hurrah as a gypsy smuggler in the later *Burlesque on Carmen*. For their first acts together, Chaplin took Turpin with him from Chicago to Niles, California, outside San Francisco. After his fourth Essanay film, however, Chaplin relocated his own unit to Los Angeles, and Turpin returned to Chicago. Some said Charlie was miffed that Ben was receiving as much attention as himself in their two first movies, but that is not borne out by the press coverage.

His New Job was formally released at the beginning of February 1915, and *A Night Out* – in which Charlie and Ben played two anarchic drinking buddies – on the 15th. The third Chaplin film, *The Champion*, was out in March. By then, the Charlie Chaplin publicity bandwagon was running wild all over America. *Motion Picture*, in March, headlined him as 'The Funniest Man on the Screen', as he enthused to the writer, Victor Eubank:

'I know now why my comedy is good, if you will pardon me for saying that' (and I found he did when he began to talk on comedy), 'but I didn't know when

I first started. I was on a train from San Francisco to Los Angeles. I picked up a train acquaintance. He said, when we got off, "I want to take you to a Motion Picture show and show you a nut." When I saw the screen, there was I. He said, "The man is clear crazy, but he certainly can put across the comedy stuff . . ."'

When I asked Mr. Chaplin about comedy, he pulled a long, long face. 'It really is a serious study,' he said . . . 'it is a serious study to learn characters; it is a hard study. But to make comedy a success there must be an ease, a spontaneity in the acting that cannot be associated with seriousness.

'I lay out my plot and study my character thoroly [sic]. I even follow the character I am to represent for miles or sit to watch him at his work before I begin to portray him. For instance, I recently took the part of a barber. I even went and got my hair cut, which is my pet aversion . . . But I picked out a particularly busy barber shop, so that I could sit there a long time . . . I watched all the barber's ways. I studied out exactly what he did, and what he might be expected to do, in my photoplay. Then I followed him home that night. He was some walker, and it was three miles to his home, but I wanted to know all his little idiosyncrasies . . .'

A curious story, since Chaplin was not to play a barber until a deleted scene in *Sunnyside* of 1918 (to be reprised in *The Great Dictator* in 1940!) but perhaps this was another abortive project. Since Charlie was telling the press any tale that came into his head at this point, including his fake birth in France and the sad lie of his mother's death, he seemed to be labouring hard to avoid repeating himself in this slew of shaggy-clown tales. To reporter Mary E. Porter, for *Picture-Play Weekly*, he enlarged on the topic of his study of comic potential:

I endeavor to put nothing in my farces which is not a burlesque on something in real life. No matter how senseless a thing may seem on the screen, I think that if it is studied carefully it can be traced back to life, and is probably an everyday occurrence, which the would-be critic of the farce had never thought to be a bit funny . . .

Mary Porter wrote that, however: 'He seldom rehearses his own part, preferring to do things on the spur of the moment, thereby getting the "what-will-happen-next" effect which is so enjoyable in his acting.' This seems somewhat in contradiction to his account to Mr Eubank, but perhaps both approaches were integral parts of the technique that Chaplin was presenting by now, barely a year and a half into his screen career, as what we might today call a 'holistic' approach.

The publicity machine continued to rumble. In April, *Picture-Play Weekly* published this strange report:

For some time past rumors have been in circulation to the effect that Charlie Chaplin, the famous Essanay comedian, who is, at the present time, the best drawing card of all motion-picture actors, had been killed while playing in one of his comedies. This report was emphatically discredited by the General Film Company, which includes the Essanay. Charlie is very much alive at the present time, producing side-splitting, multiple-reel films, and had the rumor of his death been true, not only the Essanay Company, but the ten million or more people who daily spend several hours in picture-play theatres throughout the country, would have sorely felt the loss.

This kind of non-story story, so familiar in our present age, was grist to the mill of Charlie's rolling reputation. Along with the stories, there began to appear endless cartoons of Charlie, all over the United States – and abroad – marking the iconic figure of the Tramp with his signature moustache, bowler, cane, baggy pants and huge shoes. One telling cartoon in the *Cleveland Leader* of 9 May 1915, under the heading 'WHO'S WHO NOWADAYS', has two newspaper boys talking in front of a group of kids clustered round a Charlie poster:

'I'd ruther be Charlie Chaplin.'

'Children promised to be good all week if they could see Chaplin on Saturday afternoon,' added the *Leader*. 'Their parents enjoyed seeing him at night.' There were even 'Charlie Chaplin girls', who wrote passionate letters and wanted to know if he was married. The strip cartoons, which enjoyed great popularity throughout the American teens of the twentieth century, began featuring him as a fictional character. Essanay handed out franchises, as to the *Chicago Herald*, which published 'Charley Chaplin's Comic Capers' from May 1915. *Motion Picture* portrayed the stations of his life, 'from a penniless immigrant stranded in New York . . . to the highest paid movie actor', showing the globe of 'the whole world' shaking his hand.

'Man Who Has Made Millions Laugh Can't be Avoided; In New York He Can't', headlined the *New Jersey Evening News* –

'Get Charley Chaplin on a balloon!' . . . Thus bellows the vendor on the curbstone, throwing into the faces of passers-by an inflated yellow bladder on

'The whole world enjoys Chaplin Comedy.'

which is crudely sketched the figure of a ludicrous little man with a tiny moustache, baggy trousers, limber cane and a mop of curly hair surmounted by an absurd derby hat of a vintage now sold only to helpless heathen.

A little further on another curbstone hawker is is offering postcards of Charley Chaplin at the enticing rate of two for a nickel. The man from out of town, having successfully dodged the balloon salesman, gazes curiously at the postcards and then turns into a drug store with the foolish idea that he can get a prescription filled there. Feeling his way through the counters piled with celluloid picture frames, aluminum ashtrays, plumbers' supplies and assorted candy, he suddenly finds himself confronted with a table devoted to plaster of paris statuettes . . . all of Charley Chaplin . . .

The desperate hick tries to take refuge in a theatre, in vain: 'Charley Chaplin is in the lobby on a three-sheet; he is in a frame by the

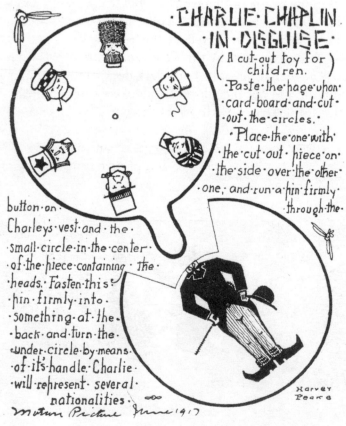

'Charlie Chaplin in disguise' – a cut-out toy for children.

box-office; a scroll-sawed sillhouette of him stands on the sidewalk; a Chaplin figure run by clockwork rolls its eyes, cocks its head, shakes its feet and smokes a cigarette. . .'

Chaplin merchandising was to set the tone for a new Hollywood industry, soon to be followed by Felix the Cat, a succession of comic stars and, most of all, Walt Disney's Mickey Mouse and co. From the start, as early as May 1915, copycat manufacturers muscled into the act and lawsuits flew across the District Court benches. The original Chaplin miniatures, we learn from the *New York Telegraph* of 25 May, were designed by G. Grandelis, the sculptor who had made five hundred figures for the College of the City of New York and 'also decorated the New York Public Library . . . and the Metropolitan Museum of Art.' Fifty thousand dollars had been invested in the Chaplin figures by the Mark Hampton Company, plaintiffs in their suit against the Art Novelty Company of 32 Union Square. But this was only a modest start.

By June, mimicking Charlie Chaplin became a pastime and an art form in its own right. In Cleveland, the local park got so crowded with Chaplin imitators that, as the *Cleveland Plain Dealer* reported on 9 June: 'The management of Luna Park decided to offer a prize to the best imitator and out they flocked. It looked as if Charlie had a score of twin brothers running loose at the park, each with a tiny little moustache and a cute little cane. Remember how it rained Monday? Well, that didn't stop 'em.' The local press named the winner as Elmer Reichard, former circus acrobat, and printed a neat drawing of him with all the runners-up:

Parade of Charlie Chaplin impersonators, 1915.

The Chaplin craze was well on its way! 'HAVE YOU THE CHAPLINOIA?' enquired the *Kansas City Star*, announcing, in September, that 'Kansas City, along with the rest of the country, is in the throes of a movie epidemic, which has been diagnosed as Chaplinoia. The germ has been isolated and found to have been cultured by a certain young Englishman, whose present habitat is Long Beach, Cal. . . .' Sightings of the man himself, in the flesh, seemed to be legion, and the Essanay publicists were making the most of the mass affection that had sprung up. As the *Star* wrote:

If he appears on the beach in his celebrated make-up, a crowd is there to follow him. If he strolls forth as a handsome young man of 24, with serious, almost melancholy eyes, the following is as great . . . In either case Charlie entertains with the droll antics and mannerisms that have become second nature by this time. A large Los Angeles café has a standing invitation for him to come and bring as many of his legion of friends as he wants to. The bill is on the house.

Clearly Chaplin had a voracious appetite for all this public adoration. The consequent perils of fame were not as yet familiar aspects of this early 'celebrity culture'. All seemed spontaneous and natural, give or take some ruthless promotion. In the summer Charlie had given interviews to dozens of newspapers and magazines, and extended accounts to *Photoplay*'s Harry Carr and others. For his multi-instalment piece in the *Chicago Herald* he enlarged on his way of life and philosophy, if perhaps seasoned with some creative ghost-writing:

Next to reading – and I am a bookworm of no slight avidity – walking is my particular hobby. Long walks, endless rambles . . . Human nature in all its gay and gloomy phases, character in its thousand and one types, I seek to study and do study instinctively on every one of the walks I take. There are new stories of life on every hand, in every street, past the residences of the wealthy and through the tenements. I never cease learning about my fellow men and women. Unconsciously they are funny most of the time . . .

The park benches afford superb opportunities for study. There is repose and a sense of amiability which makes people throw away their cold social guards. The 'crabbiest' old miser is sometimes thawed out by the warming sunlight and the singing of birds . . . There are endless things people will talk about on a park bench – baseball, weather, war, socialism and not infrequently Charley Chaplin. My best and sincerest critics are the plain folks who ask me:

'Have you seen this Chaplin feller in the movies? Ain't he a holy show?'

In another passage Chaplin talked about how hard he worked to make his acting seem easy, explaining how 'I am sore in body and in mind after a day's work of many hours, in which I have exerted the combined nervous and muscular force of an astronomy mathematician, a French digger and a parachute jumper. I am fagged to the point of complete exhaustion, and I am credited with earning my salary by means of a few hop-skips and a comic fall downstairs . . .'

Nevertheless, he credited his effects largely to inspiration:

It is the general impression that most of my acting is impromptu . . . without rehearsal or forethought. This idea is largely true. But I do not often think of a humorous action at the moment the picture is being taken on the film. I have invented it perhaps ten or fifteen minutes before, and have gone through one or two rehearsals with the members of my company. I am generally 'one scene ahead' in my comedy inspirations.

The main ingredient, Chaplin said, was 'Enthusiasm . . . my tonic, the elixir for worn muscles, frazzled and outworn patience'. This, clearly, Chaplin had in spades, and he inspired it both in his cast and crew and among his fans, their numbers increasing with each new film that tumbled out of the Essanay studio.

Motion Picture writer Charles McGurk observed him at work for the August 1915 issue:

'Ah!' he said, *sotto voce*. 'Got to limber up. A little pep, everybody; a little pep. Come on, boys. Shoot your set. I'm ready.' The last sentence was shouted. Charlie went thru a few other steps, and then sized up the situation . . . He looked down on those $50,000 feet of his, picked up one of them and stood like a stork as he examined the shoe, put it down again, straightened up and started to shoot a rapid-fire of directions, musings and comments on the world of today. When any actor went thru a piece of business that appealed to Charlie, he was quick to step out, pat him on the back and tell him: 'You're a bear. Good stuff. You're going along all right, old top. Keep it up – keep it up.'

It took a little while, but Chaplin finally injected enough enthusiasm into his people to make them work without thought of time . . . Every one who had worked with Chaplin that morning had the warm spot in his heart that comes with the praise of work well done . . . Chaplin is a paradox, a character, an 'original.' The methods he uses are hoary with the age of centuries, yet his effects are spectacular and brand new. He is an Englishman . . . [but] his type is more the Latin type . . . There is Celtic subtlety in the Chaplin comedies that reminds one of the wit of Lever or Swift; sometimes there is even a hint of Boccaccio or De Maupassant. The subtleties you do not notice. But they are the things that tickle you and make your mirth uproarious . . .

After shooting, McGurk writes,

Charlie was informed that another story was being written about him. Then someone showed him his likeness on the cover of a famous magazine devoted to Moving Pictures, and a third informed him that a Chaplin chorus of show-girls, each one costumed a la Chaplin, was the latest hit on Broadway. Charlie shrugged his shoulders and looked into space. 'Say,' he said. 'Did you see *The Tramp*? I know I took an awful chance. But did it get across?' Finally he unbosomed himself to the interviewer. 'Oh, go as far as you like. You'll write what you please anyway. I'm trying to figure whether or not plucking three feathers from a lady-chicken will get by the censors . . .'

9

The Champion

Synopsis, *The Champion* (Essanay, 1915)

Charlie, with his dog, arrives at Dugan's Training Quarters – 'Partners Wanted Who Can Take a Punch'. Eager for a job, he goes in and joins the bench of punch-drunk hopefuls. Within, various aspiring fighters are tested against the gym's tough guy. Charlie puts his lucky horseshoe in his glove, so he manages to knock out the tough guy, even chasing him down the street, till he hops a freight train to get out of town.

Charlie makes ready to fight the contender for the championship, exercising with weights, on the hoops, fortifying himself with a jug of beer. A spiv offers him 'five big ones' to throw the fight. He ogles the trainer's daughter (played by Edna Purviance). He limbers up for the big fight, shaking his dog's paw before entering the ring. The fight is on. Charlies dances around his burly opponent, who struggles to land a blow. Charlie knocks down the umpire. The bell keeps saving him from disaster. But then he too manages to land some blows. The fighters clinch. Charlie's dog joins the audience, then leaps into the ring to sink its teeth into the opponent's shorts while Charlie lands the crucial blows, to win and become the champ.

The Essanay studio was a different environment for Chaplin from the Sennett madhouse – a somewhat gloomy film factory set in windy Chicago, whose managers initially expected him just to be another hired hand. George Spoor, according to Chaplin's autobiography, was so deep in shock at the sum his partner 'Broncho Billy' Anderson had agreed to pay the new employee that he failed to turn up for days to ratify any payment. After Chaplin decamped to the Niles studio outside San Francisco, however, Anderson smoothed things over and left him alone to organize his own movie unit. Now Charlie could cast the fellow actors who would be his foils: Ben Turpin, Bud Jamison,

Boozing buddies – Ben Turpin and Charlie.

Charles Insley, Lloyd Bacon, Leo White and Edna Purviance. The last three were to follow him into his next Mutual productions.

Ben Turpin, as we have noted, lasted through the first two films, plus his cameo role in *The Champion*, and a return bout in the *Burlesque on Carmen* in the spring of 1916. Their jagged ballet, in *A Night Out*, as two drunk friends who drift from bar to street to nightclub to hotel rooms and corridors, like two live rag dolls, echoed Charlie's double act with Fatty Arbuckle in *The Rounders*, if with a greater rapport. If Charlie was a man-about-town who couldn't resist his tipple, Turpin was a man whom the booze had so deeply inundated that he was merely its stunted vicar on earth. That he could walk or stand at all was a veritable miracle of human endurance. He and Charlie together formed a seedy wave of force that could sweep all that was respectable before it into a well-deserved oblivion. Charlie was still not quite ready to allow the Drunk to depart.

But it was in *The Champion* that he found the themes and the settings that would define the Tramp's world. The Essanay films, now fully restored after decades of being known only in rough and mutilated versions, are the workshop in which the Tramp, like Geppetto's Pinocchio, is hammered out and then let loose from his strings. Drawing on all his memories of his harsh Lambeth life, and fortified by his three years of observing American urban reality, Charlie begins his odyssey through the lower depths of the Land of Promise and elusive prosperity. From the first shot, Charlie and his dog, whom he would return to forcefully in the later *A Dog's Life*, shuffle down the desperate alleyways in pursuit of an honest, or sometimes not so honest, buck. If Keystone's Tramp was a force of destruction, an imp of the perverse off the English music hall, Essanay's Tramp is rapidly changing into a more rounded, complex character, whom Chaplin would eventually call 'The Little Fellow'.

The Keystone period's lustful, aggressive figure has morphed into an eternal optimist, ever ready to take on life's challenges and capable of actual sentiment, even love, a continual round of hope against hope played out with Edna Purviance. She was not at that time an actress at all, but a secretary, whom one of Anderson's scouts had spotted at a San Francisco cafe. She had the qualities that attracted Chaplin, a statuesque blonde look with captivating eyes and figure, immediately striking on the screen. Charlie continued falling in love with Edna for the next eight years, in film after film, and off screen too, though Chaplin never married her. That delight was reserved for Mildred Harris, whom Chaplin was to meet in 1918 when she was only sixteen years old, a pattern that was to be repeated throughout his life. Charlie, on the other hand, preferred the more mature woman, someone who often, like himself, bore the scars of survival. In *The Champion* she has only a couple of scenes, with not much to do, while Charlie's attention is engaged by his male protagonist in the ring.

The desperate tussle, in a seedy, run-down boxing hall, with slavering, goggling patrons and a pipe-smoking old-timer who wreathes the whole frame with his smoke, makes the scene look like some Dantesque suggestion of one of the lower rings of hell, an endless bout alternating hopeless flailing about in the ring with a mad clinch of seconds rubbing

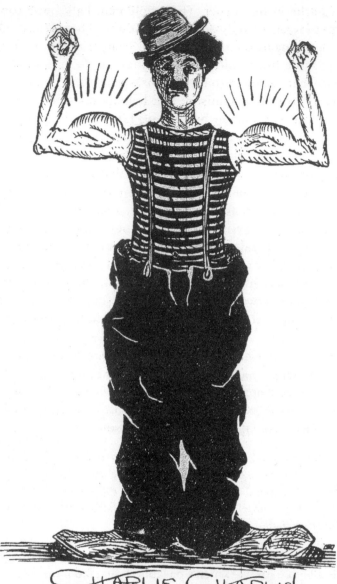

CHARLIE CHAPLIN

Terre Haute Tribune May 9, 1915

Chaplin – the Champion.

down Charlie in his corner. The whole mad ballet was too good a sequence to waste on only one film and it would be repeated, alas without the dog hanging on to the opponent's pants, in 1931's *City Lights*.

Eleven more films followed at Essanay. *In the Park* was a quickie one-reeler that regressed to the old park-bench Charlie, trying to prise Edna away from Bud Jamison, and helping disappointed lover Leo White to commit suicide by kicking him into the pond. *A Jitney Elopement* gave Charlie his first chance to romance Edna fully, revamping and developing themes he had used in *Caught in a Cabaret* – a comedy of love across class lines with Charlie impersonating Count Chloride de Lime. The circular car chase that closes the movie still remains standard Keystone. *The Tramp*, analysed earlier, defined the character as a drifter in the classic hobo mode, appearing as an unlikely suitor to Edna's farm girl and mucking up the barnyard labours. *By the Sea* returned to another old Keystone staple, the pier comedy, with semi-romantic knockabout at the seaside, traditional slapstick frolics between Charlie, Bud Jamison, Edna and other stock characters, the refreshment stall vendor, the holiday couple, and the cop.

In his next film, Charlie strode forth into new vistas, albeit in variations on a theme which was as old as comedy, and a straight reprise, in its central sections, of his 1906 English music-hall stint with Wal Pink's company in 'Repairs'. This sketch featured, to recall a contemporary notice of the show at the Hammersmith Palace:

. . . The Plumber, the Paperhanger, the Whitewasher, the Carpenter, and their various assistants all engaged in their respective fell tasks, breaking windows faster than they mend them, whitewashing the tenants rather than their house, painting themselves rather than the wainscots, or sleeping at their work, but very wide-awake at meal-times . . .

In *Work*, Charlie first appears in a scrum of traffic, striving to pull a cart piled high with workmen's paraphernalia, ladders, buckets, planks and what-not, spurred on by his boss, Charles Insley, who is seated on the cart. In subsequent shots, he strains up a forty-five-degree slope, slipping down as he encounters a discarded banana skin, and then striding up again. The Tramp has fallen into the true hobo's nightmare, a kind of indentured labour, almost slavery, as he doubles up as beast of burden and assistant of all menial tasks. The camera is obviously set at an angle as Charlie heaves and hauls up his impossible trajectory, lifted in the air as the cart lurches backward, and wringing bucketfuls of sweat from his clothes. Another, burlier companion joins the boss on the cart, and both egg Charlie on shamelessly. A traditional gag as the cart is stalled on a tramline provides another perilous image.

The house they are heading to for their decoration job provides a grotesque riff on the 'rich idiots' theme beloved of all early comedy, aimed as it ever was towards its working-class and immigrant audience. The wife is obsessed with hiding her silver from the ill-clad workmen, prompting the workmen to take all their valuables, coins and watches out and secure them with a safety pin in Charlie's own capacious pocket. The husband, played by Essanay regular Billy Armstrong, has to deal with all the intruding annoyances and exploding kitchen appliances, as well as a love rival for his wife, a bearded 'French' dandy who bursts in with flowers – a constant role for Leo White, who played angular weirdos in almost all Chaplin's Essanay films, and followed him to the Mutuals.

Once set to work, the old Karno style dominates. Paint is slapped all over walls and persons haphazardly, while Charlie flirts with Edna the flighty maid. A bucket of paint is upended over the boss, removed to reveal two soulful eyes gazing out of a mound of white gunge. This kind of action remained so basic to comedy that Chaplin reprised it, as noted before, forty-two years later in *A King in New York*. In 1925, Oliver Hardy, before Laurel, was to perform this act too with Bobby Rae in *Stick Around*, aka *The Paperhanger's Helper*, not to speak of Stan and Ollie's classic return to the 'hapless workers' routine in *The Finishing Touch* and *Busy Bodies*. In one scene, however, Charlie sits down with Edna in a close shot, as he relates to her some unspecified tale of woe while picking his fingernails with a spade and leaving his dirty fingermarks on her arm. She is repelled, and he gives a little shrug, and goes back to work and mayhem. Just a small moment of melancholy that prefigures much more to come.

In his next film but one, *The Bank*, Charlie returns to sweated labour, as the janitor who falls asleep and dreams that he has rescued the pretty secretary, Edna, from bank robbers. The dream is set up by another early instance of the clown's pathos, as he sends some flowers to Edna, which she tears up. Charlie's anticipation and woe at his rejection are played in close-up, as those great eyes tell the whole story. The Tramp, we know, is not just a ragged puppet of circumstances and his own primary desires and hunger. There is a lost soul hidden in there. Writer Robert Payne, in his 1952 book, *The Great Charlie*, segued from Charlie's 'deadpan' face to an analogy with 'the Great God Pan', 'the divine prince of knaves and liars . . . the high and presiding genius of sensuality who is also the mocker of sensuality . . . the eternal wanderer on the high cliffs of the mind . . . the spirit of licence in a trammelled world'. Chaplin would often attract this high-flown language from his admirers, trying to answer the literally million-dollar question of Why Chaplin? Why no one else?

By using the straightforward close-up to convey his inner thoughts Chaplin was not inventing the wheel, but utilizing a dramatic trope that was unusual in comedy. In February 1915 Griffith's groundbreaking film *The Birth of a Nation* was released, marking the highest point in cinematic technique, as well as its lowest point in the deployment of racial bigotry by a serious director. Griffith had made advances not only in the structural grammar of film-making – its editing, the cross-cutting that drove the action so powerfully – but also in the direction of the actors: the use of close-ups to depict small gestures and to suggest motivation. Everyone was learning from Griffith, but no one more than Chaplin understood the potential power of the apparently unmoving close-up.

One dramatic actor, the Japanese heart-throb Sessue Hayakawa, expressed this idea in analysing his own performance in Cecil B. DeMille's lurid melodrama *The Cheat*: 'I tried to show nothing in my face. But in my heart I thought, "God, how I hate you." And of course it got over to the audience with far greater force than any facial expression could.' *The Cheat*, however, was not released until the end of 1915, so Chaplin's grasp of this principle of expressing thought takes precedence, and he was to continue to deploy it to its greatest effect, culminating in the soul-searing close-up of the last, fade-out shot of *City Lights*.

'In a sense,' Robert Payne wrote, 'all the films are an attempt to solve the single problem: Who is he?' In his mythical, as well as his practical elements, though, it is not a difficult question to answer, if with a cliché: he is Everyman, the representative of mankind's sorrowful journey upon earth, in his most basic aspect. The genius of Chaplin was to realize that, whatever he wished to do with the character, he should keep him simple, but that, with this simple figure, he could construct a great symphony. It may well be no coincidence that, as he advanced towards his creative independence, he attended to the composition of the musical accompaniment to his pictures, for the set of themes he was to engage in had a symphonic range. Later clowns learned from Chaplin to compress their characters so that complexity hid behind simplicity: Buster Keaton and Harold Lloyd were the prime beneficiaries of this idea; Laurel and Hardy carried it forward; Harry Langdon found a mysterious way to dispense with the complexity. But as Charlie marched on, into sunset after sunset, he began to be more ambitious about what could be contained within the primal figure.

Early hyperbolic comparisons, as those of *Motion Picture*'s Charles McGurk likening Chaplin to Boccaccio and Maupassant, come into play in *A Woman*, the romp which preceded *The Bank*. This curious piece commences as a Keystonesque park-bench assignation mix-up and escalates to a full-blown adulterous farce, with Charlie cross-dressing for his third and last time. Papa, Mama and daughter are slumped in the park, awakened only by the possibilities of billing and cooing among the trees. Pa, Ma, Edna, Pa's flirtatious friend, and the interloper, Charlie, all flirt mercilessly, and Charlie is invited to the women's home. He flirts unabashed with both over doughnuts. Then Pa and the friend arrive and Pa and Charlie fight. Charlie goes upstairs and finds the women's wardrobe, coming down in full female regalia, with one caution, as Edna tells him:

'Get out of that moustache and into a pair of my shoes and you'll make a perfect lady!'

The moustache goes, and Charlie is transmuted into a coquette, flirting with Pa as mother and daughter look on from the next room. Both Pa and his friend proclaim their passion for the 'lady', and are even tricked into a brief mutual male kiss as they close in on Charlie as he steps aside. But Pa soon discovers the subterfuge and more mayhem beckons. The wife, daughter and Charlie beg Pa to make up, so that Charlie can plight his troth to Edna. Pa refuses, till told by Charlie: 'Come on, shake, and your wife will never know what I know.' Still enraged, he throws both Charlie and the friend out into the street.

Chaplin was still not convinced that the Tramp was his complete destiny. This may be apparent by the next but one Essanay short, *A Night in the Show* (synopsised previously) in which he reprised the Karno 'Mumming Birds' drunk. The film before and the next but one after it, however, returned Charlie to his new element: the world of work and how to shirk it. October 1915's offering, *Shanghaied*, is a compendium of on-board-ship gags. Charlie is a drifter whose rather perfunctory early flirting with Edna is baulked by her side-whiskered father. Ambling off, he is offered a few dollars by the first mate of a vicious ship-master (played by Wesley Ruggles, later a comedy director) to bop a couple of other drifters on the head and 'shanghai' them aboard as forced crew. In the event he gets shanghaied as well. Meanwhile, Edna, disguised as a boy, has stowed away, making her Pa frantic because he has plotted with the master to sink the ship for the insurance. The main virtue of the film is a series of ludicrous scenes of cooking, eating and getting along in high winds, as the ship yaws madly from side to side. It appears as a kind of rehearsal of the similar and more well-known sequence of the yawing ship in *The Immigrant*. Here, too, plates careen madly from side to side on a table and slide off to be smashed to smithereens. The camera was swung strongly about on a counterweight to produce the effect, and a special cabin was built on rollers to match the onboard shots in the studio. The crew keep falling overboard, and Charlie's attempts to hide with Edna in the hold may have inspired the Marx Brothers' stowaway antics in barrels of kippered herring in their later *Monkey Business*. In the end, Edna and Charlie are rescued by her distraught father, who rushes up in a launch, but demands that Charlie jump overboard. He does, but climbs aboard on the other side of the boat, and kicks Pa into the sea as he roars off with Edna in his arms.

Also in October of 1915, Cecil B. DeMille's swashbuckling romance *Carmen* was shown in cinemas, starring the New York opera star Geraldine Farrar. At about the same time, a second *Carmen* (this one now a lost movie) was released, directed by Raoul Walsh and starring Theda Bara. Not to be outdone, Chaplin felt he had to make his own version, and *Charlie Chaplin's Burlesque on Carmen* was produced, with Edna Purviance as the feisty tobacco-worker and Charlie as 'Darn Hosiery'. The settings, if not the plot of the DeMille version were followed quite closely as the gypsy brigands pour through a breach in the city wall while Darn Hosiery is romancing. Since Chaplin was negotiating for a new deal with Mutual, completed in March 1916, Essanay took the two reels of *Carmen* and expanded them to four, adding new scenes with their contract player Ben Turpin, brought in as Don Remendado. Chaplin had no power, in the months that followed, to prevent the re-editing of his picture. In the event, it remains fitfully amusing, but Chaplin did manage to achieve, in the

In "Carmen" (Essanay) Charlie Chaplin discards his famous derby and cane, but he still retains his celebrated feet.

Chaplin in *Carmen*.

wreckage, a scene of proper dramatic pathos at the end when he stabs Carmen, and contemplates his deed in a close-up of abiding melancholy.

Charlie's last appearance for Essanay, in *Police*, however, returned the Tramp to his proper place as a representative of battered humanity. 'Once again in the cruel, cruel world,' declares the title, as Charlie is released from prison, only to be accosted within a few steps of the gate by a preacher who beseeches him: 'Let me help you go straight!' Charlie wipes his welling tears on the preacher's beard and is affected enough to withstand the temptation to lift the watch of a swaying drunk in his way. Instead he samples the fruit at a fruit-stand, discarding each piece after a bite. Sliding away from the fruiterer, he spots the preacher this time in a near-clinch with the drunk. When the preacher moves away Charlie discovers the man of God has stolen the drunk's watch. Turning another corner he is accosted by another preacher, this time smooth-chinned but with the same shtick: 'Let me help you go straight!' Annoyed, he knocks the preacher over and rushes off, knocking over a cop for good measure.

'That night,' Charlie, destitute, gets in line for a seedy flophouse, run by a ragged Jew in large skullcap and beard, who is soft-hearted enough to allow a coughing man in for shelter without the requisite coin, but who chases Charlie off when he tries the same sob story. (The flophouse scene was said to be the first to be shot, as part of a larger project, possibly a feature, called *Life*, that was not made, and subsumed into the subsequent short.) Once again, Charlie wipes his tears with his protagonist's beard. Outside, Charlie has to shake off the cop again, hooking him off his feet with his cane and running away. Stopped at a house by a man with a gun, he and the gunman recognize each other as old cell mates.

Charlie reluctantly agrees to rob a house with his old mate, even though the suspicious cop has followed them. Trying to jemmy open the window, then finding the door open, they go in, knocking furniture over and alerting Edna, who phones the police. Here, Charlie can't resist a dig at the old Keystone Kops, as the policemen hang around their office, in no hurry, daintily drinking tea and buffing their nails. Continuing to make a racket, the burglars set to work, only to be interrupted by Edna in her nightgown, telling them, 'Please be quiet as my mother is very ill!' She invites them into the kitchen and sets the table, as the cops leisurely approach in their car, smoking cigars.

Charlie's mate spots a ring on her finger, but Charlie is again being given the treatment, this time by Edna, with the old line of 'Let me help you to go straight.' She points to God above. Charlie is not moved, and proceeds to stock up more loot. He shakes her hand and tips his hat, picking up some furniture on the way out. He is ready to go but his mate stops him, suggesting that there must be more to get hold of upstairs. Edna repeats the tale of her ill mother – 'the shock will kill her!' – but the uncouth ruffian insists. Charlie stops him and they fight, getting tangled with the cop from outside who has finally staggered in. When the other police arrive, they still stand around lazily. Charlie gets shot in the bum by his mate. The police finally dawdle in, catching Charlie, but Edna defends him, saying, 'He is my husband!' In a typical bit of business, as the cops file out, their captain holding his hand out for a handshake, Charlie feels in his pocket as if for a tip but then flicks his ash into the outstretched hand. The original cop who had seen the break-in is, however, still at the door, and Charlie parts with Edna, as she reaches down into her combinations to bring forth a few dollars for him. She sends him on his way, without his swag, and he exits towards a suburban street leading up the hill, stretching his arms out, in an uncharacteristically Christ-like pose, in the sunlight of a new day, before the cop chases him off again.

The big money chases Charlie Chaplin.

One feels, here, that Charlie Chaplin has found an alternative medium between the old slapstick mayhem and the new pathos of his evolving character, as that final stretch in the sun seems to say: At last, I know who I am! But that may be an early delusion, a recognition still filtered through the artist's desire to keep experimenting, to keep trying new angles. He has found a creative space, and a financial freedom, to explore these without let or hindrance. Now he can finally proceed to exploit this unexpected gift to the full.

10

Easy Street

Or: 'I Will Now Play You the Hungarian Goulash'

SIGNING CONTRACT FOR HIGHEST SALARY EVER PAID TO ANYONE
EXCEPT KING OR EMPEROR!

March 1916 was the time of the accession. John R. Freuler, of the
Mutual Film Corporation, was photographed looking rather sombre
beside twenty-seven-year-old Charles Chaplin, with his elder brother
Sydney looking on rather more cheerfully. The newspapers calculated
that Charlie was going to earn $4.46 per minute, $268 per hour,
$2,147 a day, $22,884 a week, or $670,000 dollars for the year.

The *Kansas City Star* had a nice story about Charlie Chaplin paying
a visit to the Internal Revenue office in New York, at Wall Street, to
enquire what his tax might be –

. . . standing hat in hand while fifty employees of the internal revenue department and thirty citizens carrying income tax papers but forgetting to file them
scrimmaged for the honor of shaking the hand that made lemon meringue pie
famous . . . 'This is Chaplin,' said the even, melodious voice that few of the
Chaplin millions have ever heard. 'Yes, I'm living at the Plaza, you know, and
have been advised that I should report my income to this office. It's a bit puzzling, for I have never kept any accounts. The officer in charge here has kindly
granted me an extension of thirty days . . .'

Nonsense about celebrities is not confined to our own time . . . The
Deputy Collector picked up the tale for the *Star*:

Mr. Chaplin is very amiable . . . He wasn't at all flashily dressed, but fastidious, you might say, in the English way. He was wearing a brown derby, a
fairly short coat and patent leather shoes with light kid tops. Of course, he
wasn't wearing his moustache, but I recognised him from his eyes and nose.
All the young women wanted to be introduced to him, and as he didn't mind
they all met him, and the men too.

From now on it would be difficult for Charlie to meet all his fans in person, as he discovered on his train journey east. Crowds in Kansas City
and Chicago, when he stopped off, were massive and in New York he

had to avoid Grand Central station because the crowds had gathered all day. On his return west, the *Los Angeles Enquirer* noted that 'Next to the war in Europe, Charlie Chaplin now is the most expensive item of contemporary history . . . for a man of his age he is doing reasonably well,' purred the paper, under the heading 'Film Comedian and His Moustache Return to Los Angeles Exuding Gold'.

Chaplin was literally on the money, as a *New York Times* item of January had noted in a report about Charlie Chaplin coins that 'have been tumbling by thousands' into vending machines and telephone slots. The coin was apparently 'sold in cigar stores and such places for a cent. On one side is the familiar face cast in lead and surrounded by stars, and on the obverse a laurel wreath.' An elastic cord passed through a hole in the rim, so that the 'Disk of Jest' could be retracted at will into one's cuff. Unfortunately, it was the same weight as a nickel, and the offending souvenir was recalled.

Chaplin the man would become less and less accessible, the more Charlie the Tramp became familiar as a daily fact of life, both in America and abroad. Boys in the most remote parts of the world imitated Charlie Chaplin's walk, and played games based around his character, doing the hop skip and jump chanting his name. Nearer home, in Brooklyn, the Chaplin walk even led to a murder, when an old man, Pasquale Caruso, domiciled near Borough Park, was goaded by kids who kept shouting: 'Charlie Chaplin! Charlie Chaplin!' at him because of his rheumatic walk. The old man asked the kids' father, Joseph Certona, to stop them, and when he refused, a fight broke out, in which Pasquale was stabbed and, in revenge, shot his assailant with a blunderbuss.

The more mundane downside of fame was manifest in continual imitations. All sorts of fairground acts blossomed as 'Original Charlie Chaplins', playing the violin or offering 'Come in and see Charlie Chaplin fight the bull!' According to *Motion Picture* in April, he had been unmasked in various places in his real name: Charles Fitzgerald, Otto Barger, Patrick O'Flaherty or Nicolai Lapidovitch. Other Chaplins accused him of borrowing their own original ideas: the hat, the cane, the pants, the shabby shoes and the toothbrush moustache. Reporters desperate for an angle made up tales – 'that he spent time in an asylum; that he is a dope fiend; that he is married . . .' His death was reported more than once. Ordinary folks sent in verses to the papers:

Charlie Chaplin's the funniest freak;
Makes you laugh till you can't even speak;
  I think he's a daisy,
    Some think he's plumb crazy;
But who wouldn't be for a thousand a week?
              (Frank O'Hearn, of 209 E.64th Street, Los Angeles)

Or, in a mockery of his failure to rush off to join his countrymen in the French trenches:

Poor little Charlie Chaplin,
He's breaking his heart in Los Angeles,
His salary's grown so big, poor chap,
They won't let him wear a khaki cap.
Though he's terribly anxious to do it,
He's written to say so – pass the cruet.

It was no wonder that Mrs Rose Wilder Lane and the Bobbs-Merrill company weighed in with *Charlie Chaplin's Own Story*, which Chaplin laboured so successfully to suppress. He clearly realized that his old habit of telling tall tales to the press undermined his efforts to control his own narrative, now he had an image that had to withstand the closest possible scrutiny.

It was unlikely, too, that he could continue his quiet walks through the streets of Los Angeles watching ordinary people's behaviour. He continued to stay at the Los Angeles Athletic Club, that all-purpose film community residence-cum-training-centre-cum-watering-hole, where his ex-boss, Mack Sennett, also lived until 1920. It would be six years before Chaplin would move into his own long-term residence in Summit Drive up in the Hollywood hills, after a series of rented homes. From the LAAC he could commute to the studio at which his new Mutual films would be shot, a lot on Lillian Way and Eleanor Avenue, just south of Santa Monica Boulevard and west of Vine Street, which was revamped and renamed the Lone Star Studio. By the end of the year he had a Japanese chauffeur, Toraichi Kono, who remained with him for eighteen years, and a personal valet/secretary, Tom Harrington, a 'lean, solemn, ascetic-looking man' who became an indispensable amanuensis, friend, messenger and even intellectual mentor, guiding Chaplin, as David Robinson reports, in his discovery of such authors as Lafcadio Hearn, Frank Harris and James Boswell.

Money, mounds and mounds of it, was separating Chaplin from the everyday life of his fellow citizens, not to speak of the reality of the Tramp himself and the host of characters that made up his streetwise world. It did, however, give him a closer insight into the upper crust, whose strange and pretentious antics he was to lampoon with greater insight and force.

Above all, Chaplin had no intention of resting on his laurels, and was determined to use his financial muscle to deepen his art, and make better films. He was brimming with ideas, but they still lacked structure, and the piled sediment of his years in music hall and Keystonery was sloshing about in his mind, a seething inchoate mass of ambition, of potential gags, character tweaks and endless shards of possible stories.

It was with the twelve Mutual shorts that Chaplin honed his method of picture-making. This was in complete contrast to the method of any other major film-maker, apart from Griffith in his earlier days. Chaplin's use of the shooting process itself as his later almost endless rehearsals was an impossible procedure for any other director, particularly of dramas, to adopt. Even comedy films, as the Mack Sennett archives reveal, required a script, often lengthy and detailed, even if it was altered in shooting. Griffith had shot *The Birth of a Nation* without a script, but there still had to be an enormous amount of planning and preparation for his spectacular scenes. Most directors could not afford to burn money, to change tack and reshoot at will. But Chaplin's great advantage was that he was not shooting epics. He was shooting chamber pieces, small comic melodramas, which might feature at their most extravagant a ballroom, an ornate drawing room or the seedy front porch of *The Cure*. Later, in his features, larger-scale scenes would become necessary, the most spectacular being the long line of Alaskan prospectors winding up the Chilcoot Pass in *The Gold Rush*, in 1925.

Chaplin's films were becoming spectacularly profitable, but the outlay was not onerous, once he had control of his own lot. To the repertory crew that he brought over from Essanay (having lost Bud Jamison and Billy Armstrong to their own headlining series), he added two key actors who would define the Chaplin Mutuals: Albert Austin, an old Karno hand, became a kind of irascible foil, as often a bent as a straight man. Born in 1881 (or 1885) in Birmingham, he had arrived in the US in 1912, and was eking out a living in stock theatre in Denver before Chaplin picked him out for the Mutuals. Chaplin's

Charlie with Eric Campbell.

trawl though old Karno hands also brought him to Eric Campbell, an amiable Scottish giant who would become Charlie's most fearsome adversary, whether as the fuming fork-bearded gouty monster of *The Cure*, the demonic eyebrow-twitching waiter of *The Immigrant*, or other representatives of anarchic nemesis and doom.

Born in Dunoon, Scotland, in 1879, Campbell remains the most recognizable of Chaplin's on-screen foils for almost everyone who has seen a Chaplin picture, well beyond the field of movie buffs. The gentle giant – six foot four and twenty stone – morphed under Charlie's direction into a kind of human mountain, a cartoon-like character of indestructible ferocity and comic malice. He had been a Karno player before Chaplin, toughened before that by years of stock acting around Scotland in any role that fitted his girth, and then arrived in America in 1914 with one of Karno's post-Chaplin troupes. Taking bit parts in Broadway stage productions, he was spotted by Charles and Sydney in George M. Cohan's play *Pom Pom*, while the brothers were closing the Mutual contract. He was an inspired choice for Charlie, matched only by Chaplin's reunion with Mack Swain, in *The Idle Class* of 1921, and most famously in *The Gold Rush*. Charlie might have retained Campbell on the team for ever, were it not for his tragic death in a car accident in 1917. (His tale is told in a fine 1996 documentary by Kevin Macdonald, *Chaplin's Goliath: In Search of Scotland's Forgotten Star*.)

Chaplin's unique shooting method at Mutual was comprehensively revealed on film by Kevin Brownlow and David Gill in *Unknown Chaplin*, featuring footage of out-takes and private frolics kept by Chaplin's estate and collector Raymond Rohauer but unseen till 1983. This shows how Chaplin tirelessly reshot scene after scene of his pictures to find the right combination of story and gags, arranging and re-arranging his actors, props and bits of business, discarding entire sequences, holding back major gags that would be used later, constructing his films by intuitive leaps. With no written script or plan, apart from a general theme, the films evolved out of a process of trial and error.

Another new member of the crew was Roland Totheroh, who had been a cameraman at Essanay concentrating on Broncho Billy's own films before being brought by Chaplin to the Lone Star studio. Describing his early work many decades later, in 1972, Totheroh told the magazine *Film Culture*:

He didn't have a script at the time, didn't have a script girl or anything like that, and he never checked if the scene was in its right place or that continuity was followed. The script would develop as it went along . . . He'd have an idea and he'd build up. He had a sort of synopsis laid out in his mind but nothing on paper. He'd talk it over and come in and do a sequence. In a lot of his old pictures, he'd make that separation by using titles about the time: 'next day' or 'the following day' or 'that night' – that would cover the script gaps in between.

Chaplin would alter and rebuild entire sets, as in *The Cure*, where the out-takes reveal numerous attempts at staging an establishing scene of the drying-out hospice where even the staff are terminal alcoholic wrecks and the patients are rushed about in wheelchairs, with Chaplin directing the traffic. Eventually the entire structure of the front porch was remade, to include the pure water well that would be a source of multiple gags, and a dunking place for Eric Campbell with his great gouty foot.

The Immigrant, which we have looked at as a narrative of the Tramp's world revealed in its chronological origin, in actuality emerged from its second half, the searing scene in the cafe, with

Charlie and Edna in thrall to Campbell's menacing waiter, and the panic of the lost coin. Originally, the lost footage reveals, it was an idea about the uncouth Tramp in a cafe, with Charlie making up to Edna at the next table, and another Chaplin regular, Henry Bergman, as the fussy but not very frightening waiter. Short of another reel of action, Chaplin came up with the immigrant ship as a prelude to the cafe, and reshot the whole film to fit, as well as replacing Bergman with Campbell's monstrous figure of towering terror.

Chaplin's method shows his perfectionism, but it also reflected a continuing tension between his creative ambition and the character that had so powerfully captured public affection – he was still not sure about the Tramp. Later comedians, like Keaton, Lloyd, Langdon and most effectively Laurel and Hardy, would learn from Chaplin that fixing a popular character ensured their pay packet and their very survival as film-makers, though only Harold Lloyd was able to match Chaplin's precious independence. The movie historian and biographer can chart the convoluted and complex path the artist took to achieve a successful result – but the audience can be satisfied simply by that result: the appreciation that the imagined creation has come to life in its own right.

In a simpler sense, Chaplin was also approaching his film-making as an old-fashioned vaudeville artist. Bits and pieces of business emerge out of the mulch of ideas fretted over before the player reaches the stage, the kind of stuff W. C. Fields used to rehearse in front of the bathroom mirror. For Chaplin, the mirror was the camera lens itself, and the bathroom his entire personal lot.

Chaplin's Mutual films shot at the Lone Star studio continued the experiments in style and theme that began at Essanay, but with more time and better resources. With meticulous attention to the details of gags, background and character, the dozen two-reelers Chaplin turned out between May 1916 and October 1917 include his first proper masterpieces. Of the first seven films – *The Floorwalker*, *The Fireman*, *The Vagabond*, *One A.M.*, *The Count*, *The Pawnshop* and *Behind the Screen* – at least two, *One A.M.* and *The Pawnbroker*, arguably fall into this category, and the next five – *The Rink*, *Easy Street*, *The Cure*, *The Immigrant* and *The Adventurer*, set the tone and the quality for the shorts and features that were to follow.

The first two films in the series were gag-rich pieces which did not advance the Chaplin character much beyond the frantic imp that he was eager to outgrow. *The Floorwalker* brings him into 'The Big Store', a cornucopia of props with which the Tramp can play with wild abandon. A shelf of toilet requisites gives him the opportunity to have a quick shave and brush-up. Stacks of boxes just waiting to be knocked over enable him to drive shop assistant Albert Austin crazy. At the back of the set a marvellous new contraption, automatic escalating steps, rolls up, waiting for the moments when Charlie will milk the last ounce of use from it in a series of chases, as Eric Campbell flails after him in the climactic moments.

In Campbell's first outing in a Chaplin film, he is attired in his cartoonish jagged eyebrows and beard as the shop manager whose embezzlements have been found out and who is about to skip the joint with a bagful of cash. Lloyd Bacon, as the assistant manager and fellow crook, is a sombre-faced Charlie lookalike, and their encounter in the manager's office is a precursor of sorts of the mirror routine used by Max Linder in 1921's *Seven Years' Bad Luck* and then to great effect by the Marx Brothers in *Duck Soup*. (Looking closely, one can see many moments of Chaplin shtick that Groucho, wittingly or unwittingly – though Groucho is seldom if ever unwitting – picked up for future use, including his funny walk, prefigured by Charlie in *The Count*.) Charlie and Lloyd Bacon look at each other, startled, reach out as to a mirror, double-take and then rush perturbed for the door. When Charlie finds himself alone at last with the money, he cries out, in a title: 'Spondulicks forever!' and dives headfirst into the bag.

While *The Floorwalker* explores Charlie's gags and movements within a space filled with artefacts that are as much his foils as the people, *The Fireman* returns to a Keystone-type world of Men at Work, or rather Men Shirking. Eric Campbell is the fire-chief, less villain than bumbling oaf, his love for Edna leading him to accept a deal from her top-hatted spiv father: 'Let my house burn. I'll get the insurance and you can wed my daughter.' Of course the daughter is in the house and Charlie, after a tangle of fire-cart and hoses, has to climb up the front of the burning house to save her. Charlie – or his stuntman – clambering up floor by floor looks ahead to Harold Lloyd's more spectacular climb in *Safety Last* of 1923.

But it is the third Mutual film, *The Vagabond*, in which Charlie begins to break new ground and explores further the pathetic vein examined in *Police*. *The Vagabond* opens with a shot of Charlie's signature boots arriving from behind swing saloon doors. Two badges of beer, Extra Pale and Falstaff, adorn the doors. Charlie emerges from behind the doors with hat, cane and violin, an instance noted by one reviewer who wrote, 'For the first time . . . Chaplin, who assays the role of an itinerant musician, brings into play his famous violin of which so much has been written . . .' The press in May 1916 had already posted the news that Chaplin's 'chief hobby is found in his violin. Every spare moment away from the studio is devoted to this instrument. He does not play from notes excepting in a very few instances. He can run through selections of popular operas by ear and, if in the humor, he can rattle off the famous Irish jig or some negro selection with the ease of a vaudeville entertainer.'

Charlie takes up position in a corner by a side door and begins to saw his strings. As he begins, a four-man brass band complete with drummer arrives at the front saloon doors and opens up, Albert Austin conducting the blast. Charlie shuffles into the bar, holding out his hat. The bar set has been stripped to its necessary minimum: a few bottles and glasses, a couple of posters on the wall, a few plates of ham. As one of the bandsmen comes in to collect, the barflies cry out, 'What? Again!' and a fight breaks out between the player and Charlie which segues into a Keystonesque chase, in and out the swing doors and round and round the set, with a proper measure of smacks and pratfalls. As everyone chases his own tail, Charlie finds himself alone for a moment in the bar, pours himself a drink, shrugs and departs through one door as everyone else trudges back in by the other.

The opening scene done, we are in a rich house, with two women sewing. The mother of our tale draws out from her sewing basket a portrait of a young girl. Iris-in the next shot, to 'The Gypsy Drudge', Edna Purviance in rags by the steps of a caravan, elbow deep in suds at the wash-tub. She is the girl obviously snatched in childhood by gypsies, a rare instance of Chaplin pandering to a racial or ethnic stereotype. The image of her oppression is harsh and cartoonish – a harridan crone who chivvies her on, a brutish clan of men led by Eric Campbell, unsparing with the whip – one can imagine the torments Edna faced with Chaplin's usual multiple takes.

Charlie saunters down the path, observes her weeping and climbs over a fence, in apparent compassion, but the intertitle states his thoughts: 'I ought to do good here!' He plays, his passionate crescendo driving Edna to a paroxysm of vigorous clothes-scrubbing, just as the strains of Brahms' 'Hungarian Dance' over the radio would dictate the movements of the Jewish barber at his job in *The Great Dictator* twenty-four years later. Chaplin falls into the tub but continues playing – as he will do in the orchestra drum even later, in *Limelight*: no good move was ever wasted by Chaplin. As Edna has no money he nevertheless tells her: 'I will now play you the Hungarian Goulash.'

Gypsy Eric enters, making free with his whip. Charlie grabs a plank, following the gypsies to their own caravan, and, shinning up a tree, brains them one by one. The scene ends with Charlie driving Edna's cart off down the road, as she herself beans Eric from the back, and his fall pulls all the other pursuers down like skittles.

The next morning ushers in the first of several scenes in Chaplin movies of Charlie 'awakening in Paradise': he has rescued the bedraggled girl, and after offering her a rake to comb her tangled hair, he bathes her face in a bucket, 'civilizing' the ingathered waif. The caravan is parked by an idyllic path leading off into a hilly distance. The vagabond's Eden is, however, soon interrupted by a handsome snake: a bourgeois artist, set up with his easel, but bereft of inspiration, until Edna appears with her little bucket in search of water, and he decides to paint her as 'The Living Shamrock'.

As the Artist joins them to 'dine', Charlie, having set a check shirt over the bucket, breaks some eggs into a skillet with a hammer, and, looking at Edna as she prattles on and gazes adoringly into the interloper's eyes, he realizes, as the title redundantly informs us, 'His romance fading'. For the first time in a close-up, those Chaplin eyes, shining out of the white sheet of his facial make-up, find that expression of the deeper melancholy of the clown that marked Charlie's existence on the screen. The moment of pathos is mitigated, as Chaplin always makes sure, by some little piece of comic business, in this case, Charlie catching imaginary flies off the meal set before them, and flicking one vainly into his rival's face – again, a set of movements that will be reused several times in Chaplin's continually postponed performing flea act, that would eventually be seen on the screen over thirty years later, in *Limelight*.

The Artist leaves, with a handshake, and Edna is left pining, unconsoled by Charlie's drawing of her on the caravan canvas and his promise that 'I'll learn to paint, kiddie!' But the Artist's painting of *The Living Shamrock*, exhibited in a city gallery, catches the eye of the pining mother, who exclaims: 'That birthmark – my child!' Chaplin's perfectionism required, according to the press, that he borrow some genuinely famous paintings from Los Angeles friends, among them 'a genuine Rembrandt, loaned to Chaplin by a Coast connoisseur'. For *The Living Shamrock*, Chaplin used 'a splendid oil painting of Miss Purviance completed and forwarded to her by a leading New York painter'. But probably only Chaplin and his patrons might have noticed all this in the brief gallery scene.

As Edna continues to pine, a posh car drives up to the caravan and the top-hatted Artist and the distressed mother pile out to a tearful reunion. Mother and child embrace, as Charlie returns from a walk to the nearby farm to purchase some eggs. Mother's limp hand and her offer of a wad of cash to Charlie is spurned, as he bids her 'Goodbye, little girl.' The car door slams, the car drives off down the once idyllic path, while Charlie is left, gutted, alone by the caravan, attempting to lift his spirits with a little kick and brushing of the hands but subsiding to a limp hunch. In the car, however, as the girl is driven off, 'The awakening of the real love' prompts her to call for the car to turn around, and she surprises Charlie with the call: 'You come too!' He grabs his violin, hat and cane, and climbs into the car, which turns yet again down the open road.

The ending of the film, and indeed its entire tone, is completely Griffithian, echoing the grand moments of separation and redemptive love that ever formed one of the building blocks of cinema narrative. In *The Vagabond*, for the first time, Chaplin stretched his wings as a director of drama, not just of strings of brilliantly achieved gags. The Tramp's soul, if one might chance a concept of those bygone days of simpler contrasts and direct appeals to conventional ideas and emotions, now emerged from behind the ragged costume, the awkward walk that could ever break into the most exquisite ballet, the sneer of the Drunk, and the imp of park-bench subversion.

Chaplin had finally found Charlie in the dressing-room mirror. He was no closer, perhaps, to the artist's question of 'Who am I?' But he was considerably closer to the craftsman's query to his creation: 'Who art thou?'

A PICTUREVIEW WITH CHARLES CHAPLIN;

11

The Adventurer
Or: More faces on the bar-room floor

Synopsis: *The Adventurer*
(Mutual, Lone Star studio, 1917)

On a beach under a cliff, prison guards are rushing about with guns in search of an escaped convict. Charlie's head emerges from the sand just behind a resting guard. He pulls himself out, attired in striped convict uniform, and a chase ensues up and down the cliff, through guards' legs and a cave that leads to the sea. Finally Charlie grabs hold of a guard's gun and, backing off, swims out to sea, the guards in pursuit capsized by a wave.

At a seaside pier, a distraught girl – Edna Purviance – calls out for help as her mother is foundering in the water. Her companion, fork-bearded Eric Campbell, is too cowardly to jump in, so she leaps into the water. Charlie, swimming by, rescues her and her mother. Meanwhile Eric, joined by another over-weight onlooker, falls in from the pier too. Charlie rescues him, pulling him by his beard, but is pushed back in the water when Eric climbs out up a ladder. Edna, in her car with her mother, gets the chauffeur to pull Charlie out. Pretending to have been on his yacht when he saw the women in distress, Charlie gets an invitation to Edna's palatial home.

Much butt-kicking ensues between Charlie and Eric as he ventures downstairs the next morning to meet Edna's house guests. To his dismay it turns out that her father is a judge. Eric spots Charlie's picture as the escaped convict in the morning paper, and alerts the judge, but Charlie has altered the picture to add Eric's beard. Eric is frustrated again, and further embar-rassed when he tries to dig out some ice cream that has been tipped from Charlie's hand down the back of a stout lady's dress.

Meanwhile, in the kitchen, the maid has been dallying with one of the prison guards, and Charlie is threatened again with exposure. A grand chase ensues up and down the stairs, Charlie disguising himself at one point as a lampstand. Edna is appalled

at the revelation that he is a convict, but he can only console her
with a quick embrace and a kiss before fleeing again, pursued
by the guard.

Despite the epiphany of *The Vagabond*, Charlie continued oscillating
between the Tramp and the Drunk. And in his proliferating legend,
writers sprang in to fill the gaps between the public imagination and
the enigma on the screen. Movie magazines had for some time published 'novelizations' of feature films (such as Cecil B. DeMille's *The
Squaw Man* and others), and for *Motion Picture*, Alexander Lowell
fleshed out Chaplin's *One A.M.* in the style of free verse 'made popular by poet Edgar Lee Masters in his *Spoon River Anthology*':

It is one a.m.
A taxi speeds up Broadway, mocking the stillness with dissolute horn,
Wakening the honest burgher from the nightmare of a married man
Who dreams of stubbed-out shoes and butcher bills.
'Scandalous!' sniffs his wife; 'I hope he is arrested.'
But, in the darkness, her husband smiles a reminiscent smile.
And turns upon his sober pillow to dream anew a dream of long ago, and
highballs, and pretty chorus ladies.
And one a.m . . .

Charlie's *One A.M.* declined to flesh out his character with any such tan-
gible back-story, reducing the narrative to its basic component of the
cosmic battle between one sozzled late-night boozer and the orneriness
of household ornaments: the keyless door, the rug that aspires to slip
from under him, the stuffed big cats that close their teeth on his shoe, the
round revolving table with its whisky decanter that is pulled out of
reach, the symmetrical stairway either end of the entrance hall, which
cannot be scaled without the proper rig-out of Alpine climbing rope and
pick, and, at the upper landing, the great pendulum of the grandfather
clock that swings throughout the first reel, ready to deliver the *coup de
grâce* to the miscreant when he finally manages to ascend.

The film is an early sample of Chaplin's sense of the frame (what the
auteur theorists called *mise-en-scene*). Griffith and other early masters
deployed the power of editing to flow action, building the now-
conventional panoply of camera positions to show long shots, medium
shots, close-ups. Chaplin would more often than not have Rollie
Totheroh, his cameraman, hold back to show the entirety of a set, with
Charlie given space to interact with the other actors, the props and the

decor. The camera shifted position when Charlie's actions so required, but with the confidence that it was not necessary to show off the camera's multiple capacities to make the scene work as it should. We might note the obvious, that all movies shot before the advent of television assumed the presence of an audience in a theatre, gazing at a large screen. Like many comic screen acts, Chaplin's films still work mainly in such a theatrical setting, rather than as an individual experience on the home screen, however large it grows in our own day.

In *One A.M.* – apart from the opening scene in which a taxi draws up driven by Albert Austin, with Charlie in the back, struggling to find a way to open the cab door while the driver sits in front, frozen as an icicle, waiting for his fare to alight – Charlie is alone in the film and set against the material objects that are nevertheless alive with malevolent intent. *Motion Picture*'s writer Lowell re-imagined him as 'the new caretaker – Charlie' to one 'Arthur Arkwright, the naturalist, now in Peru'. Even at the instant, people were misunderstanding Charlie, for it is surely the master of the house himself, drunk as a lord, in his top hat and cape, entering the house stacked full of the souvenirs of a life once spent in action. He is, to stretch an analogy a little, a precursor of Groucho Marx's irrepressible Captain Geoffrey T. Spaulding, the African Explorer ('did someone call me shnorrer?') of 1930's *Animal Crackers*. The animal skins, artefacts and spoils of fortune are, to the Drunk, natural obstacles to be overcome with the proper sangfroid of a man of the world, who will not be defeated by a dead cougar or the ubiquitous folding bed. On the way we are treated to two pure Chaplin moments – his ascent of the staircase in full Alpine regalia, only to tumble down head over foot at the end, and his mad run on top of the revolving table, his feet frantically turning the great wooden top with its unattainable whisky jug. It is as much a metaphorical image of 'modern' man as Harold Lloyd's famous hanging on to the hand of the clock far up above the Hollywood traffic.

Chaplin told the *New York Telegraph*, in one of his numerous – and often repetitive – 1916 interviews, about the 'Psychology of Comedy':

Making fun is a serious business. It calls for the deepest study – the most concentrated observation. Business that causes some people to laugh makes others frown. That can't be helped. What matters is how to make most of the people laugh all the time. How to do this is the problem.

Did you ever see what happens when a policeman in uniform slips on a greasy street and takes a tumble? The policeman's uniform and his club are symbols of his authority. He is a power in the land. When he slips and gets mussed up the crowd shrieks with laughter. Why? Well, even good people have a sneaking dislike for a 'cop.' They like to see him get a tumble.

Visualize a bloated capitalist with Dundreary whiskers, light trousers, spats, frock coat, silk hat – all the insignia of a million dollars . . . Even the most inoffensive among us has some time or other considered the idea of pulling those whiskers . . .

There is fun in striking contrast. One minute there is a picture of pride and dignity, stalking solemnly through the labyrinths of human life, austere, exclusive, apart. If I hook that chap with the crook of my cane, drag him almost off his feet, pull his Dundrearys and step casually on his silk hat, the audiences shriek with laughter . . . It is because they never in all their lives believed that anybody would have the effrontery to pull a millionaire's whiskers or step on his hat.

Today, we live in a world which may be no less divided between rich and not rich, but we are inured to the spectacle of 'the great and the good' having their whiskers pulled. Chaplin's world, of course, was far more segregated on many levels. The masters of the universe might be glimpsed now and then passing by in their glistening motor cars. To ordinary people they were imaginary rather than real. Chaplin packed these remote beings into Eric Campbell, with his forked beard and painted devil's haircut, and proceeded to torture him in exquisite ways, pulling the beard, kicking him in the stomach, crushing his gouty foot and dunking him off a Los Angeles pier. Though Eric, often, was no more a millionaire than Charlie, merely an obese arriviste who pretended to a class and honour he wholly did not deserve.

Eric's ability to present himself as a cartoon character, but at the same time to express an almost bottomless well of an excruciating and palpably ridiculous desire to be loved and accepted in society, is played out in several of the Mutual shorts. This is first explored in *The Count*, in which Eric plays the tailor to Charlie's assistant, both deciding to turn up as the fake 'Count Broko' to a dinner held by Edna Purviance – 'Miss Moneybags'. Charlie gets there first and Eric has to fume throughout as his secretary, eyebrows and beard twitching in rage. Both indulge in a great deal of bottom-kicking and punching before the real Count turns up, exposing them as fakers. In this instance, both Charlie and Eric are impostors, each treating us to a demonstration of his prowess upon the slippery ballroom floor, with many inevitable pratfalls and Charlie waddling off in his pre-Groucho walk. Eric's beard comes in very useful when Charlie has to haul him off Miss Moneybags – although Charlie himself is the greater upstart, as he is also indulging in a flirtation with the maid. The apparent order of society is of course a mask beneath which all the destructive desires of Men and the dashed hopes of Women are played out, and Charlie responds to a wine-glass sprinkled in the face by an outraged dandy (Albert Austin) by drenching him with the entire punch-bowl.

The slippery ballroom of *The Count* later becomes the skating arena of *The Rink*, in which Eric appears as Mr Stout, another would-be bourgeois, oddly married to Henry Bergman in drag as Mrs Stout, and caught up in a love triangle with Edna and Charlie, while Mrs Stout is being wooed by Edna's dad, played by James T. Kelley. Henry Bergman had joined the Lone Star company earlier in 1916, a musical-comedy singer whose first appearances on screen included the serial *The Perils of Pauline*. Roles with various comedy companies led him to Chaplin's troupe, in which he gave stalwart service in all Charlie's subsequent films up to *Modern Times* in 1936. An amiable presence, stout in loyalty as well as body, his dedication to Chaplin became, in David Robinson's words, 'his ruling passion. He assumed the role of assistant, confidant and indulgent aunt.' His characterisation as a 'bachelor', and his evident delight in cross-dressing, suggest he was another of Hollywood's many unsung early gay actors.

Mr Stout becomes terribly embarrassed, along with Mrs Stout, when both are caught out in their dalliance at the skating rink. There ensues one of Eric's great duels with Charlie, as they face off in the centre of the arena, Charlie holding Eric back with his cane as the big man swipes helplessly at him. At the end the entire body of skaters swoops in a daisy chain out of the rink into the public thoroughfare.

The rich in Charlie's films are a direct extension of the class chasms of English Karno life. A load of posturing oafs, the posh idiots of comedy-land are high on etiquette but extremely low on any element of genuine grace – one suspects that they, too, have only come off the boat the week before. Eating spaghetti or chewing on watermelon is fraught with peril, let alone galumphing over the dance floor. They are, of course, the working-class audience's image of what the rich are like, fodder for the tumbrils and the guillotine of humour. Chaplin's imitator and later equal in the comic stakes, Stan Laurel, had it perfectly when, as a waiter, he misunderstood the lady of the house's instruction to serve the salad undressed. But Chaplin knew his audience too, in the widest possible sense, as he explained to the readers of the *New York Telegraph*:

I'll tell you one important reason why the Mutual pays me $670,000 a year. It isn't because I can amuse the American public alone, but because the same stuff that makes an American laugh, also makes the Chinaman on the Yang Tse rock himself out of his seat, or cause the Japanese audience in Tokio or Kioto to laugh vociferously, splits the visage of the Turk in Constantinople and gets the money that the Russian Moujik used to spend on vodka. In short what we have discovered is the one touch of nature that makes the whole world kin . . . Once or twice I've tried to entertain audiences in a polite, restrained manner – the high-class, subtle sort of thing, you know. I can't say it was a huge success.

Chaplin was probably referring to the first outing the Karno company had in New York with 'The Wow Wows', which was already long in the past. The same essay gave Chaplin an opportunity to indulge in another piece of instant myth-making, stating that his signature walk originated with 'an old character they called "Rummy" Binks' who hung out at the cab-stand outside the Queen's Head pub in London:

He had a bulbous nose, a crippled up rheumatic body, a swollen and distorted pair of feet and the most extraordinary pair of trousers I ever saw. He must have got the trousers from a giant and he was a little man. When I saw 'Rummy' shuffle his way across the pavement to hold a cabman's horse for a penny tip, which was his daily occupation, I was fascinated. The walk was so funny that I imitated it. When I showed my mother how 'Rummy' walked she begged me to stop, because it was cruel to imitate a misfortune like that, but while she pleaded she had her apron stuffed in her mouth. Then she went in the pantry and giggled for ten minutes. Day after day I cultivated that walk . . .

'The principle [*sic*] thing you've got to do', Chaplin wrapped up his piece on the Psychology of Comedy, 'is to make the audience think it is superior to you in intelligence and analytical sense. You've got to be the clown. I make people laugh with me, but it is a sort of patronizing sympathy. They think I'm an awful ass, but then I'm a funny one and that covers a multitude of sins.'

In short, the comedian's act, like the actor's in general, is a deception, in which the audience colludes, more often than not without thinking about it. Which can make the relationship between the person behind the mask and the audience awkward, even at times dangerous, as the adoration-cum-resentment of celebrities in our own day demonstrates sharply. The clown dances, as ever he danced in the days of the *commedia dell'arte*, on the edge of an abyss. Turning without end on his revolving table, or, in another gag Chaplin reprised more than once, round the revolving doors of a hotel.

Who art thou? The question returns in Charlie's next but one film after *The Rink*: *The Cure*. This can be seen as a sort of sequel to *One A.M.*: The Drunk, perhaps still 'Mr. Arthur Arkwright, the naturalist', late of Peru, presents himself at the sanatorium where he is to be dried out, alongside a cast of male and female inebriates and social sliders led of course by Eric Campbell with his great bandaged foot. Brownlow and Gill's meticulous film *Unknown Chaplin* reveals all the twists and turns of trial and error by which Chaplin emerged, after several hundred abortive shots, at the final version of this Rake's Progress. The central well, around which Chaplin designed his front porch, contains the curative brew that the Drunk manages to avoid imbibing by spilling it in his hat, but which finally sends him heaving with disgust back to his trunkful of liquor, albeit depleted by the bottles quaffed by the geriatric bellboy (played by James T. Kelley). Even the temptations of fellow inmate Edna fail in this instance to console him, until the revelation that his whisky has been dunked into the well by male nurse Albert Austin leads to general delight.

The Cure is a torture chamber of society's solutions for the demon rum's malign authority – the chief torturer, apart from the water well, being Henry Bergman's fearsome masseur, who pummels and bends his victims into pretzel shapes before tossing them peremptorily into the gym's pool. The revolving door exemplifies this failed attempt at moral resurrection, as Charlie's cane traps Eric and the nurse in its stalled panels. There is no cure for society's ills, as it is incurably insane.

Charlie had returned to the Drunk after his descent into the lower depths again in *Easy Street*, perhaps his most iconic short. This, as noted before, was a fairly faithful reprise of Fred Karno's 1903 sketch 'Early Birds', with its portrayal of the 'gruesome jollity of English poverty, wretchedness and crime'. That pantomime of London's Dickensian Whitechapel came complete with its central conflict between a young heroic defender of the poor and the 'brutal, remorseless "rough"', whom the hero finally beats down with a table.

Charlie's *Easy Street* is his most merciless depiction of the poor, devoid of any morsel of sentimentality or even ordinary pity. Here is the clown-director at his most cruel. Destitute, the Tramp arrives at the Hope Mission to take his place among the down-and-outs waiting for their soup while harangued by Albert Austin's priggish preacher. A contretemps with a baby's bottle, however, softens Charlie up for the squeeze between Albert and Edna, the good-hearted missionary, so that he pulls out the poor-box he has stuffed in his pants and returns it to them before leaving the mission. Still penniless, Charlie answers the 'Policeman Wanted' sign at the cop shop, unaware that the cops have been depleted and hospitalized by Eric Campbell's giant bully, the 'rough' who has all of Easy Street in his thrall.

The set of the street is one of Chaplin's best, a spare, theatrical stage of a symmetrical T-junction, with the tenement houses at each end of the street a bare refuge for the denizens who dare to sneak out, from either side of the frame, only to be chased back en masse by Eric, strutting alone among his spoils – the shredded pants and jackets of the beaten policemen, with the few coins that have been shaken free of their folds.

Reality as Fable: The balletic dance of terror reaches its peak when the new cop, all of Keystone rolled into one uniform, dares to walk his beat as Eric swaggers up and down the pavement. A vital prop, the gas lamp-post, with the police telephone box, looms between them. Charlie had managed to drop Eric with a mere tap of his club in *The Vagabond*, but Eric has grown in power, and bends his bare head engagingly to the useless hammering of the new cop's truncheon. Like a great beast of the jungle, Eric flexes his muscles and bends the lamp-post, enabling Charlie to pull the gas-filled lamp down over the ruffian's head, and choke him into unconsciousness. The timid policemen arrive, carting off the giant, and Charlie is the new king of the street. The inhabitants creep up and then dart back into their tenements just as they did with Eric before.

Catching a hungry woman stealing from a grocer, Charlie takes pity on her and accompanies her up the stairs to a home teeming with small children and a weedy father upon whom Charlie bestows his badge of puissance. Meanwhile, in the police station, the giant awakes, tearing open his handcuffs and wrecking the station.

Biographer Kenneth Lynn has suggested that Chaplin's Easy Street cop, and his fairy-tale ending of Law and Order restored, with even the bully and his wife become respectable citizens, reflected a dream of Chaplin's in his Lambeth childhood, of order triumphing over primordial chaos. But Charlie, the Tramp, had no more belief in order than his alter ego, the disruptive Drunk. Charlie the cop scattering food to the kiddies in the tenement room reflects the harsh reality that was a matter of record for the reformers of Victorian England. But if Chaplin had benefited from the reforms that had provided his basic schooling, he retained the necessary anarchist roots that had kept him going against the odds. Chaplin's order was not the social handcuffs of the police station and the Dundreary-whiskered fat cats he so often lampooned, but the make-believe structure of the stage and the studio lot. Like Karno, he was an instinctive ironist, who saw the Empire and its social lions as a zoo containing wild and savage animals. He would have agreed with George Bernard Shaw, who famously proclaimed that he hated the poor and looked forward eagerly to their extermination. When their monstrous leader returns to Easy Street to wreak his revenge, Charlie and Edna are seized by the mob and deposited in a cellar, where Lloyd Bacon's addict lurks with his needle under two portraits that appear to be the Russian Tsar and Tsarina. Charlie's fortune, in falling on to the needle and being injected with its magical energy, enables him to rise up and beat the entire mob into the ground. (Taboos on drugs and censoring of the unpleasant facts of addiction were not yet as strict as they would later become . . .) The final title, 'Love backed by force; forgiveness sweet; Brings hope and peace; to Easy Street,' is not Chaplin's dream. It is the audience's delusion, to which the clown panders. Both the audience and the clown wink to each other and know that this is not the way the world is.

12

Shoulder Arms!

Faking it among the rich apart, Charlie the Tramp made two more forays into the world of work during Chaplin's Mutual period. In *The Pawnshop*, Charlie 'assists' the Jewish pawnbroker (Henry Bergman in his first major supporting role for Chaplin) by feuding with his other assistant (John Rand), committing all possible mayhem with a ladder and the pawnshop's signal three balls. The classic moment is Charlie's demolition of an alarm clock brought in by a customer (Albert Austin). Having laid it open, unpicked its coils and emptied every little cam and spring on to the counter, he finds the scattered innards refuse to die, squirming like snakes and stricken beetles even when squirted with black oil. Finally the remains are swept back into the empty casing by Charlie and handed back to Albert – not working.

To watch the scene is to become aware not only of the skill of the performance, creating a maximum effect through a minimal expenditure of bodily movement, but also of the technical ingenuity that enabled the inanimate objects to come alive. Another ingenious technical effect was tried by Chaplin in his next movie, *Behind the Screen*, a third remake of Keystone's *A Film Johnny* and Essanay's *His New Job*. Streamlining the old mayhem-in-the-film-studio act, Chaplin worked on a sequence in which he walks through a rehearsal of a French period scene featuring an axeman, whose razor-sharp blade just misses Charlie as he sashays by. The out-takes, examined closely by Brownlow and Gill in *Unknown Chaplin*, show that the apparently death-defying shot was achieved by Charlie walking skilfully backwards as the film was reversed in the camera, so that the axeman could lift the axe at precisely the right moment, rather than smack it down. After multiple takes to ensure the scene would work properly, it was eventually left out of the movie. Chaplin's perfectionism was such that even perfectly achieved results could be sacrificed to the overall pace and thrust of the film.

The last two Mutuals were *The Immigrant* and *The Adventurer*. Whatever the convoluted and exhaustive process used to achieve his results, those results were now seamless, as if they had been meticulously planned and structured in advance. The process was quite unique among film-makers, and revealing of the odd and singular nature of Chaplin's intuition. He seemed to have no clear image in his mind, beforehand, of the shot he wanted, and, being both director and actor, had to view the result in the 'dailies' before he could make up his mind. But once the right shot had emerged, he recognized it unerringly.

The second reel of *The Immigrant* provided, like *Easy Street*, a potent fable of the real pain of poverty. The setting was simplicity itself, the seedy cafe presided over by Eric Campbell and his crew of thuggish waiters, ready to beat the living daylights out of a diner who had enjoyed the baked beans of solitude and then come up ten cents short. At this point, of course, Charlie discovers that the coin with which he was expecting to feed himself and Edna, the immigrant waif, is counterfeit, and bends in Eric's steely teeth, leaving him broke, with a brutal doom looming before him.

Another coin, appearing miraculously on the floor, becomes the target of a cosmic battle between Charlie's need and waiter Eric's big foot stamping on it, until Charlie and Edna are finally rescued by the *deus ex machina* of Henry Bergman – 'I am an artist!' – who wants to paint Edna, and whose tip is enough to pay their meal. Exiting into the street, Charlie drags her round the corner to a door with the sign 'Marriage Licenses'. And thus a happy ending is wrung from the tale.

Three and a half years into his career in movies, Chaplin's legend continued to grow, manifested in articles, interviews, photographic spreads and cartoons, as well as popular doggerel, not all of it adulatory. One C. T. Barr of Martin's Ferry, Ohio, wrote on Charlie's accession to his $670,000 salary, and apropos *One* A.M.:

> As an actor who only gets drunk,
> Chaplin gets quite a large chunk of junk,
>   But my Unk thinks he's punk,
>   And his thunk ain't all bunk,
> As my Unk can get drunk on a plunk!

Murmurings about the downside of Chaplinoia increased through 1917, as the *Minneapolis Tribune* reported on 13 March about the categories of films 'to which Minneapolis teachers and ministers object'. These included 'Thrillers. Vice exposes. Uncensored Wild West films. Annette Kellerman sans clothing. Charlie Chaplin "when he's drunk." Theda Bara, on general principles, all the time.'

Already in 1916, Pastor H. Lester Smith, 'preacher at the noonday services in the Detroit Opera House', had announced, according to the *Detroit News*, that 'the fact that Charlie Chaplin now receives the largest salary paid to any man in the United States . . . is a clear evidence of the enormous numbers of low-grade, unintelligent, shallow-minded men and women in the United States.' The pastor was delivering a sermon entitled 'The Deepening of Life' to a 'big crowd of business men and women'. He also denounced 'the simpering sweetness of Mary Pickford, which appeals to the callow sentiment of the crude and undeveloped intellect, or the coarse, vulgar slapstick of Chaplin, which passes for humor with the witless and coarse-grained person of a low order of intellect'. This could of course be laughed off, but it was one thread of a whole embroidery stitched by mainly religious worthies, whose interventions would lead in three years to the laws prohibiting alcohol, and then lead on to further denunciations of Godless Hollywood that would merge with the moral panic sparked by the Fatty Arbuckle trials of 1921 to the appointment of an overall screen censor – the long-lasting Will Hays. Debate over the censorship of the 'vulgar' movies was in fact rife from a much earlier period, and raged in the pages of the trade movie magazines throughout the 1910s. Early objections focused not so much on the content of films, but on their places of exhibition – theatres with dimmed lighting in which women and small children could fall prey to the kind of seedy low-lifes whom the objectors imagined to be the main audience of the flickers.

Box office, then as now, could override this, but not completely, and one can see how even the comedy movies bent, after the first rush of hyper-anarchist Keystonery, towards a less savage tone. When, in *The Count*, Eric Campbell, defeated by Charlie on the dance floor, pulled a gun and shot Charlie several times in the bottom, he was merely following a general comic convention that a bullet in the bum is just a minor annoyance to the working comedian.

The scribbling classes, however, and certainly those in the movie business, were in little doubt on the issue of 'Is He Worth It, and Does He Get It?' as John Tillman Melvin wrote after the release of *The Rink*:

'Say, you don't mean to tell me that you think that fellow Chaplin is funny, do you?'

Despite the fact that Charlie Chaplin has one of the largest followings of any living man, you will find any number of people who will ask you the above question, and just as many others who will tell you confidentially that 'he doesn't get all that money.'

Well, if you can't laugh when your favorite horse-play funster requests the second comedian to put the soft-pedal on the soup-spoon sonata . . . when he cavorts on a moving staircase while the villain still pursues him; when – but what's the use of naming other equally laughable maneuvers – if you can't laugh at the ones already mentioned, you're hopeless! Possibly you belong to the dry-humor gang who are afraid to laugh from the diaphragm because some of their associates might accuse them of low-browness . . .

'In filling the house at each performance,' Melvin wrote, 'these pictures will draw at least two hundred more dimes – in many places quarters – than will the general run of comedies, or "features" for that matter. Why, a hundred dollars a day should be a low estimate of the average box-office increase when Charlie flickers across the screen. And . . . these comedies are sent broadcast over the face of the globe.' Chaplin was certainly earning his money.

From vulgarity to art, he was already established. As the press reported his meeting with the world-famous opera star Caruso, in 'one of the large New York hotels' in April 1916:

'Ah, ze Caruso of ze cinema, I greet you!' exclaimed Caruso with his characteristic modesty.

Chaplin hesitated only a second, advancing smiling and with outstretched hand.

'Delighted – the Chaplin of the opera, I congratulate you.'

Comparisons of Charlie and his movie contemporaries were also noted. During the release of *The Cure*, the *Cleveland Leader* reported Max Linder and Chaplin would 'lock horns in Cleveland this week in new pictures at neighbouring theatres . . . The new Chaplin dido, christened "The Cure," unscreens itself one of Charley's most pretentious efforts. For Linder, it is fair to say, his two other made-in-Chicago features failed to score. But in his latest offering, called "Max in a Taxi," the dapper Frenchman has found himself and he soundly whacks the bell.' The reviewer, John De Koven, praised the 'Rabelaisian capacity for burlesque' which characterised both comedians.

Chaplin's debt to Linder was not in doubt, as the Frenchman's films had been popular in both England and the US while Charlie was still a Karno novice. Little encyclopedias of comic gags and business, Linder's films, from 1905 on, provided all putative film comedians with a mass of moves and gestures, though one of his own early pictures, 1907's *At the Music Hall*, was itself a pinch of Karno's 'Mumming Birds' sketch. Linder had in fact been invited to America by George Spoor to replace Chaplin at Essanay, even though he had suffered a nervous breakdown in France in 1916, following injuries sustained while a despatch driver at the front in the first months of the 'Great' War. Linder visited Chaplin at the Lone Star studio in May 1917, and Chaplin gave him his photo inscribed 'to the one and only Max, "The Professor" from his Disciple, Charlie Chaplin'.

In April 1917, America had entered the war in Europe, increasing mutterings about Chaplin's lukewarm enthusiasm for the cause of fighting for freedom against the villainous Hun. The *Toledo Blade*, in mid-1916, during the release of *The Vagabond*, reported, under the heading 'Chaplin's Patriotism', that:

They say that poor little Charlie Chaplin is no longer popular abroad, because he did not go to the front, and has not devoted some of his alleged colossal earnings to the conflict. Can such piffle be true? asks Alan Dale. Surely there must be two sides to patriotism. If a man's country is unable to take care of him in his time of need, and he has to look for support elsewhere, can that country logically claim him when he has found that support – elsewhere? If so, why?

Chaplin made his name famous without the intervention of his native country, and now that native country is aggrieved . . . However, Chaplin should worry! Nationality is the least of his anxieties. Chaplin made his reputation and his cash in U.S.A. and that is where the former should be enjoyed and the latter spent.

Questions of Chaplin's national loyalties would rumble on for a long time, as his fate in the 1940s will demonstrate, but the sniping was set to increase when the US abandoned its former policy of non-involvement, and American troops shipped off to France. Men were drafted, women lined up to knit Sox for the Boys, old men joined keep-fit classes, kid doughboys drilled with wooden rifles and Red Cross ladies packed peach pits to make gas-mask filters. Army posters declared: 'ENLIST – ON WHICH SIDE OF THE WINDOW ARE YOU?' over a young man in tuxedo and bow tie looking out over a parade of khaki and the ubiquitous stars and stripes. In Los Angeles, Cecil B. DeMille became the captain of his Lasky studio Home Guard unit, and studio workers marched up and down Vine Street with a brass band in tow.

Charlie contributes to the war.

In February, the press had reported that Chaplin had sent a sum of $150,000 to the British war effort, for a 'Win-the-War' bond issue, and a cartoon showed him back-kicking a bag of swag marked $150,000 to a figure of John Bull. At the time of America's enlistment drive, however, he was otherwise engaged in efforts to renegotiate his contract with Mutual, or sign a better deal elsewhere. Mutual's president John R. Freuler offered him a cool million dollars for twelve further pictures. Chaplin counter-proposed the same sum for eight films. The top movie stars' vast earnings were coming under scrutiny by tax authorities who were considering a war tax to cut into some of these vast sacks of loot. At the end of June, Chaplin announced that he had signed a deal with the First National Exhibitors' Circuit, headed by Samuel L. Rothapfel, brother Syd having beavered away successfully to clinch the deal. He would, as he had wanted, get his million dollars for eight two- or three-reel films.

While American troops filled the trenches in northern France, Chaplin laid the foundations, in November 1917, for his own purpose-built studio at the confluence of De Longpre, La Brea and Sunset Boulevard, by a Colonial-style mansion that would serve as his house. As this was a residential district there would be no factory appearance, but a façade of old English architectural houses 'adding a quaint and welcome touch to this exclusive section'. Charlie and Sydney were photographed wielding pick and shovel to break new ground for this half-million-dollar construction.

A while earlier, *Motion Picture* writer James E. Hilbert described his day at the location shoot of Charlie's last Mutual film, *The Adventurer*, in July, at a 'summer camp . . . situated between the rugged mountains and the great Pacific ocean':

There was some excitement in the camp the morning he arrived; tents were deserted, and the little store at the camp did more business in ten minutes than it usually does in a week. We all gathered around, and Charlie treated the bunch to ice-cream and soda-water; and then he promptly offered $5 for a cup of English breakfast tea, which the storekeeper could not provide. One of the campers came across with tea and hot water, and Charlie made the tea himself . . . He had on a convict suit used thruout the picture, and while drinking his tea he posed gracefully for our cameras, poising his cup and saucer in an I-don't-care-if-you-do-fall fashion.

Having paid for the tea and posed for several more private cameras, Charlie and his company started for the 'location' where the first scene was to be taken, with the campers bringing up the rear. It was quite a procession. Charlie, in his jail suit, took the lead; then came the jail guards carrying their rifles, and the camera-men with their cameras over their shoulders, and an actress in a fancy bathing-suit was next in line . . .

After a suitable location had been found and Charlie had viewed it from every angle, with his hands over his eyes, sailor fashion, he breathed a sigh of relief and smiled blandly at the crowd below. He ordered the cameras up and proceeded to take the picture. A dummy dressed as a prison guard was to be rolled down the mountainside . . . It did not reach the much desired bottom; instead it dangled from its coat-tail in midair from a shrub on the mountainside . . . With much difficulty the dummy was recovered, and once more started on its way down, with better results . . .

Action was soon on again. As if lightning had struck him, Charlie bit the dust, for the special purpose of tripping a guard . . . I am sorry to say that Charlie got real mad. A flivver [the ubiquitous Ford car] was in the picture, and it had to be done all over again . . . The scene was started again, but just as Charlie made his getaway and the guards were starting down, a lovely big rattlesnake loomed up on the trail . . . A long pole was procured, and Mr. Snake was promptly executed. Charlie tried again, and to make sure everything was right, he went thru his dialog:

'No more flivvers coming? No. No more snakes in sight? No. Are you ready up there, you bum guards? Yes. Are the caps off the cameras?

Remember, Joe, I will trip you right here; fall heavy and get up quick. Then you know the rest. All ready? Camera!'

At this point some one mentioned that it was 'Friday, July 13th,' and, with an exclamation of annoyance, Charlie said with the air and tones of finality:

'We shall all go home at once. This is my Jonah day, and I *absolutely* refuse to work any more today.'

'Absolutely?'

'Absolutely!'

But there were few bad-luck days for Charlie in this year that was a bad-luck year for so many poor souls caught up in the twentieth century's first great global conflagration. After all, it was what he was for, as another poetic fan, Dora April, of 823 Hunt's Point Avenue, the Bronx, NY, aptly put it:

> When a thing don't go your way
> And you're out of sorts all day,
>   See Chaplin!
> He will rid you of your pout,
> Turn your dark clouds inside out,
> Keep you laughin' till you shout,
>   Say, you see Chaplin!
> And when hubby comes home sad,
> Business rotten awful – bad,
>   Take him to see Chaplin!
> Billy soon will lose the blues,
> Stick his troubles in his shoes,
> He's forgotten all bad news,
>   When he sees Chaplin!

A Los Angeles cartoonist, in August, imagined 'If They Do Draft Charlie' – a uniformed Charlie with his wide shoes and cane, over an image of the Tramp 'Somewhere in France', waddling through no man's land, the Bosch soldiery collapsing in giggles as they cry out: 'Ho-Ho, make him stop it!' 'Mass formation charges will lose all terror with Charlie on the job,' imagined the artist; 'why not put on an act and tickle 'em to death?'

Chaplin would not respond to this, in his own inimitable fashion, until *Shoulder Arms*, released in October 1918, about three weeks before the armistice that was finally to end the war on 11 November. But he was present at the front in the form in which he was at his most

"If They Do Draft Charlie"

effective, as correspondent Junius B. Wood described in the *Chicago News* one year before, in November 1917:

Field Headquarters, American Expeditionary Forces, France, Oct. 10 – All around this little French village French troops were camping for the night . . . All day the click of marchers' feet on the cobblestone, the hum of motor trucks, the rattle of wagon trains, ambulances, loaded and empty, and the rumble of freight cars loaded with cannon had echoed through the town. On every road through the country we had passed marching troops, trains of hundreds of trucks, each camouflaged and marked with a frog, rhinoceros, mule or some other distinguishing insignia of the unit. Wet, tired and glum we came back through the mud and rain to our hotel.

'Let's take a chance in the movies before the rush for dinner . . .' Soldiers in blue uniforms filled the little theatre back of the café. One had his wife. Two others had their arms around new found acquaintances. That comprised the feminine portion of the audience. Two feeble lights battled in the darkness in the unpainted walls and wooden seats. An Italian reel of a faithless wife and lover, ending in a shooting did not evoke a ripple among the spectators. A string of scenes of ruined portions of France brought sighs and muttered curses.

Then came American films. A philanthropic woman was leaning over the side of her automobile shaking hands with her fiance on 5th Avenue, New York. Next she was in the south among the cotton pickers. Then came a picture of a real American railroad train, and an office with telephones, and one could almost think of taking the elevated home for dinner.

Finally appeared Charley Chaplin. Even the soldier's wife forgot that her husband was leaving at daylight and laughed until her cheeks were tear streaked. Charley sat on the stove, carried the baby by the middle of the back . . . wiped his nose on the door and slammed a custard pie in the face of a man wearing a silk hat.

Outside it was still raining. The café was crowded with more soldiers. Others were sloshing through the streets, bent under the weight of their soggy packs. Dinner was late. At one table a dozen French officers, little more than boys, going to the front, were drinking champagne at what they called their last party.

'The war will be over in September,' one, wearing an aviator's leather jacket, kept repeating in English . . . The middle aged waitress was distracted in the rush. The soup was all gone. One was lucky to eat at all.

'It is wartime in our dear France,' she said. It seemed a favorite expression. Charley Chaplin was back home, thousands of miles away, and we were in the midst of battle racked France again . . .

13

His Trysting Place

Heywood Broun, one of New York's cultural heavyweights, in reviewing *The Rink*, had written, tongue in cheek, in a review headed 'NIETZSCHE HAS GRIP ON CHAPLIN', that Chaplin's comedy had become, rather than 'the old comedy of submission', the work of a kind of comic superman, following the German philosopher's dictum that 'it was comic to kick, but never to be kicked'. But, as the Tramp character became more rounded, deepened, the melancholy of both vagabond and drunk sunk into the reflecting well of his eyes, he was becoming a much more fragile being than the destructive imp who rampaged through the Keystones and the Essanays. His first film for his new independent studio, *A Dog's Life*, honed this image to its sharpest, clearest point.

As if starting literally from scratch, the Tramp enters the frame as one of the many iconic American vagrants of lore, penniless, hungry and ever on the lookout to steal a sausage and evade the cops. His alter ego, Scraps the dog, is an equally hungry mongrel whom he rescues from a dog fight. The slum street through which Tramp and Dog careen is Easy Street revisited, another retread of the Karno vision of poverty row, London-cum-Everytown. Lining up at the labour exchange, Charlie has his hopes of employment dashed by all the other desperate applicants one by one shoving him out of the way, until the exchange's window is shut.

A cutting-continuity script (typed during rather than before the shoot, the earliest instance of a script in Chaplin's films) describes the opening of the film – depicting the early morning sunrise 'over the gas tank and roof tops of tenement district'. Scene Two is described as 'shooting from elevation in direction of Hester and Essex street corner then panning down into vacant lot in foreground. On right foreground Charlie is asleep with head resting on a small barrel.' Clearly Chaplin envisaged Lower East Side New York as the setting for the film, though on-screen the slum is generic.

'A tender spot in the Tenderloin' ushers in the seedy cafe of *The Immigrant* combined with the rough-house dance hall of *Caught in a*

Cabaret. Edna Purviance is the down-and-out shy girl who is hired to flirt and clip the customers. 'If you smile and wink, they'll buy a drink,' says the surly owner. As an added bonus, there is an appearance by brother Syd Chaplin as the walrus-moustached owner of a street lunch-wagon, whose pies Charlie proceeds to snaffle.

Charlie's duel with Syd is the first on-screen opportunity for the brothers to spark off each other, a masterclass in the old 'speechless comedy'. As Charlie leans against the wagon, snatching pie after pie, with Scraps licking his own chops below him, Syd twists and turns around to try to catch Charlie in the act. Syd's demeanour, as he sets his eye on the depleting pan of pies, might be seen to mask a deeper level. After all, Syd knows Charlie is snaffling the pies, but the rules of the game require him to catch him pie-handed, with Charlie freezing in wide-eyed innocence every time Syd whips around to face him, then scoffing another pie when Syd turns back to his knives. Finally, Syd turns to administer the *coup de grâce* with a massive sausage, only to connect to the cop who has sidled up behind Charlie in a vain flanking manoeuvre.

The scene gives us a taste of Syd's own comic genius, so nobly sacrificed to his younger brother. At the same time that Charlie released his Karno remake, *A Night in the Show*, for Essanay, Syd Chaplin had been lauded for his role in *A Submarine Pirate*, still in the employ of Mack Sennett's Keystone. One reviewer called it 'one of the funniest films that has yet been put forth by any motion-picture manufacturer'. Syd was lauded as 'a daring and intrepid comedian, with a keen sense of the ludicrous'. Among other stunts,

. . . he goes leaping gayly across a 5 or 6-foot gap between buildings 'way up there' over New York's head. Then he goes down in his real sure enough submarine, and last night he had a big audience . . . laughing at everything he did. Officially, he may not have removed his brother's laurels from that derby-hatted brow, and it is certain there is room enough in the field for both . . .

After 1916, Syd's movie appearances dwindled, as he took on the full-time job of managing Charlie's resources, but he turned up as an army sergeant and as the Kaiser in *Shoulder Arms* and again in minor parts in *Pay Day* and *The Pilgrim*. He then returned to the screen in his own right in a dozen more films until 1928. Once talkies came, he bowed out, but remained at Charlie's side.

Charlie's partnership with Scraps the dog (played by Mutt) was a perfect one. At one point they appear to merge bodily, as Charlie stuffs

Scraps down his baggy pants to bring him into the dog-free cafe, and Scraps' wagging tail emerging from Charlie's butt keeps banging the orchestra's drum, confounding the drummer until Charlie reveals the subterfuge. A drunk at the table is knocked cold by the sight of this white-tailed biped, but it does not seem too out of place in the crew of grotesques scuffing the dance floor.

The sleazy cafe is all of Charlie's showbiz past rolled into one, the essential reduction of small-time vaudeville. 'A new singer sings an old song' – as Edna's awkward sentimental tune prompts floods of tears from the accompanying players and guests alike. Grown men and hard-boiled women weep and the barman stuffs the wad of cash he has stolen from his employer back in the till. Henry Bergman, in another cross-dressing role as a gross matron, soaks Charlie at his table below with two massive streams of tears, drenching the drummer with the soda spritzer for good measure. Then, as the hooch dancer replaces the singer, all is frenzied shaking and desperate gaiety once again. One is reminded of Groucho Marx's memory of the way an old-timer would judge a vaudeville act: Is it sad or high-kicking? Everything else is just grist to the mill.

Edna is sacked by the owner for failing to flirt, and Charlie vows to save her from this den of iniquity, succeeding by managing to filch the ill-gotten gains of a pair of robbers who have rolled a drunk for his wallet and stashed it in a hastily dug hole. Scraps digs the wallet up, Charlie takes it and rushes to the cafe to collect Edna, only to be waylaid in turn by the crooks. The crooks celebrate their gains inside the cafe while Charlie creeps up on them behind a curtain. Another tour-de-force double act ensues, with Albert Austin as the crook, as Charlie brains him with a bottle and then sticks his hands from behind the curtain through Albert's coat, miming to his partner to get him to hand over the money. The old cheesy parlour trick is transformed by Chaplin into a strange, mute dialogue that results inevitably in discovery and a frantic chase.

In the end, Charlie rescues Edna, Scraps rescues Charlie, and the lunch-vendor's wagon is trashed, a forlorn and undeserved fate for poor Syd. The tramp-clown, concerned only for his own immediate needs and his new-found love, has no care for the uncaring world at large. But a fabulous epilogue ensues, 'When Dreams Come True', in which Charlie is planting seeds in clean furrows in an idyllic field. Edna is his adoring wife, waiting for him in their homely cottage. They gaze into a cradle by the fire, but it contains not their own delightful offspring but Scraps's litter of pups, the mutt having either switched gender during the film or despatched his own spouse to some other, off-screen kennel. The rapture of the poor is, as ever, truly absurd. Perhaps Charlie was not so far from Nietzsche, after all . . .

'Stardom's Height' was the title of another piece of doggerel, from London, England, celebrating Charlie:

> To raise the Jester to a thing sublime,
> To leave where other memories come and fleet,
> A stardust imprint on the sands of Time,
> For 'bootless' emulation – Chaplin's 'feat',
> Oh, sacred misfits, great twin 'soles' of mirth,
> In painful pacings o'er the silversheet,
> The giddy height to stardom from this earth,
> Ye scaled and found it measured – just two feet!
>
> *E. Codd*

The strangest and perhaps finest encomium to *A Dog's Life* came two years later, when Chaplin met the deaf and blind savant Helen Keller. He described the entire film to her 'by means of "vibrations" – tapping with the feet and hands, the golden buffoon succeeded in making her understand the gist of the story and the spirit of the humor.'

At the height of his fame, Chaplin was becoming a major social lion in the city that had grown into the great hive of show-business industry. America's participation in the war slowed it a little, but it was to gather pace when the war ended, to enter its true golden age. A *Los Angeles Times* writer of August 1918, Alma Whitaker, recalled:

The first time I met Charlie Chaplin . . . soon after he had broken into society. The Los Angeles 'four hundred' had 'taken him up,' and were giving him the rush of his life. He wore an air of expectant alarm and had obviously decided that discretion was the better part of valor . . . His conversation was largely a sequence of intelligent smiles and amiable acquiescences. If the stylish grande dame said it was so, far be from it from him to contradict a lady . . .

Clearly no overturning of the punch-bowl or kicking the guests in the bum occurred in real-life Charles's entry into the upper class. As Alma Whitaker continued:

He was a genius at circumventing cross-examination, and was desperately niggardly with opinions. As for ultimatums, he avoided 'em like the plague.

He was still wearing ready-made suits, though just blossoming into silk shirts, and his attire was as modestly unobtrusive as his manners. He was very observant, and could be caught silently watching social nabobs with the sort of studious interest a collector gives to a new species of butterfly.

But Chaplin had soon learned to play the new field, noting all their little foibles while remaining on the right side of his new friends for business. Perceiving the new mood for war, he joined the march of Hollywood's celebrities to raise money for the Liberty Bonds first launched in June 1917. His closest relationships within the movie colony, at his own level, were with Douglas Fairbanks and Mary Pickford, who had written, in her daily column in August 1916, of her own first encounter with Chaplin when she was dining with her mother and a man came and sat at the next table – 'a very good looking, ascetic young man with large, melancholy dark eyes, a shock of wavy black hair and a rather drooping mouth . . . "I think he is a poet," I whispered to my mother, for he wore a dark tie around his collar and had the abstracted, dreamy manner of one who is eternally seeking rhythm in words . . .'

Mary Pickford and Douglas Fairbanks, who were to become Hollywood's most famous couple, were already in love during the first Liberty Bond tour of Hollywood celebrities in April 1918 (both were still married to their first spouses at the time). The party travelled east to Washington, where, David Robinson relates, Chaplin 'was carried away by his own eloquence, and fell off the platform,' taking robust Marie Dressler with him, and landing on top of a young Assistant Secretary of the Navy, Franklin D. Roosevelt. Chaplin met President Wilson and proceeded to New York, where, on 8 April, a crowd of up to thirty thousand people jammed Wall Street. Fairbanks lifted Chaplin on his shoulders on the steps of the Stock Exchange, and Chaplin made his first public speech, calling for financial aid to Uncle Sam in his time of need against 'that old devil, the Kaiser!' The crowd cheered him to the skies.

Chaplin told Alma Whitaker about this event:

We were all trying to appear modest and dignified . . . and genteelly indifferent to our personal ovations . . . We could see the crowds waiting for us, and we were all wondering whether the cheers were for Doug, or Mary, or Charlie, and sternly reminding ourselves that we were on a lofty patriotic mission and must comport ourselves accordingly . . . It was dreadfully thrilling. We at once adored these crowds and suspected them of invidious discrimination on behalf of each of us. And then, after the excitement had died down, we looked sheepishly at each other, and it took all our histrionic abilities to appear calm and unmoved, trying to look a bit blasé, as if we had been used to these wild national acclamations all our lives.

That was, Alma Whitaker recorded, 'one of the charms of Charlie Chaplin. He is under no illusions about himself, revels in his popularity and engagingly styles himself a parvenu celebrity.' The natural narcissism of the actor was inevitable, but one of Chaplin's undoubted gifts was his ability to analyse and utilize this, too, for his material, as he would do to stunning effect years later, in *The Great Dictator*, dissecting his darkest real-life alter ego . . .

Whitaker was able to coax Chaplin into reminiscing about early romances. He told her about a letter he had just received from his first love, Hetty Kelly – though he did not name her for Whitaker:

You know she threw me down. Wasn't in the least interested in me. It was when I was about 18, and she was a struggling little chorus girl. I thought she was the most wonderful girl in all the world, the most beautiful and intellectual. By and by she went away with her sister to Paris and moved in stylish society, because her sister had married well. She certainly looked down on me with pitying contempt in those days. I had a wonderful time nursing my tragic sorrow for six years. Then I heard she had come to America and that's what brought me to this country . . .

Chaplin recalled his first trip back to England, speaking presumably of the summer break in the Karno tour which took the troupe back to play 'Mumming Birds' from July to October 1912:

I have never been so rich as I was when I saved $2,000 nearly six years ago. Oh, but I was the gilded millionaire! I decided to go back to England, to the scenes of my worst poverty, and give all my old friends a treat. Oh, what a homecoming! All my old friends had gone – one drifts a long way in a year or two in the slums. I couldn't find anyone that knew me. I remembered the Trocadero, that had always been to me the arch-palace of luxury, a gaudy London restaurant . . . I was scared to death of the waiter, who patronized me shamefully. I longed to shout at him and tell him I had $2,000 in real American money. I ate gorgeously in lonely dejection . . .

As with Rose Wilder Lane, Chaplin was wont to mix up his movie plots with his memories, or were the fearsome waiters of his movies real avatars of that earlier trauma? Just as in a Chaplin movie, his first love, at that point of dejection, nearly ran him down in an automobile in Regent Street and, exclaiming, 'Why, it's Charlie!' she 'graciously, serenely, offered me a lift. She was so kind, and though I tried to act like $2,000, I couldn't drag it into the conversation, because she seemed so used to $2,000 worth of things. We parted politely. The next thing I heard she had married an Australian captain.'

Nevertheless, Chaplin told his interviewer, he had found consolation with Edna Purviance, though he offered no intimate revelations, merely relating that he had met her during a spirtualistic party, when she had agreed to pretend to be hypnotized by him: 'I decided she was the actress I was looking for, and Edna Purviance has been my leading lady ever since.'

Chaplin's tale of his second meeting with Hetty Kelly shifted over the years, but the letter he received from her was clearly genuine. His letter replying to her was found by David Robinson: 'Your charming personality is evident,' Charlie wrote, 'you ask how I am, etc., etc. Well, physically I am perfect; morally? – well, I am all that could be desired of a young man of twenty-nine years. I am still a bachelor, but that is not my fault.' The letter was dated 18 July 1918, and Chaplin had already met the sixteen-year-old girl who was soon to be his wife, Mildred Harris, a child actress since the age of ten. In June, press reports of their coming marriage were denied, despite rumours that she was pregnant. Mildred and Charlie were married on 23 October 1918, a few days after the release of *Shoulder Arms*.

Hetty Kelly, in the event, did not last out the year. She died, in the great influenza epidemic that swept across the globe, on 4 November 1918. News of her death never reached Chaplin. She had, in fact, married a pukka Englishman, a soldier, Lieutenant Alan Horne, in 1915. The Australian captain was a myth.

Chaplin's liking for not-quite-child brides would be an abiding feature of his marital life, courting controversy and intense press attention again and again, down to his last marriage with Oona O'Neill, whom he first met when she was seventeen years of age. He was fifty-four years old when he married her in 1943.

The relationship between the Tramp and his creator was becoming ever more complex, raising the question of who was the master, the maker or the mask?

Judgements can always be made from our moral hindsight, from the passage of history, from the arguments and analyses of historians, but in the end the Tramp was who he was because of the combination of the elements that made him, consciously and subconsciously, in his own time and place, and the audiences who made him famous, who filled the theatres, who wrote the endless doggerel, who poured their own dreams into those baggy pants and that dusty jacket, who walked the splayed walk with him, twirling their imaginary canes.

Chaplin was, in this reading, just a conduit through which this strange, intangible connection was made. But in the power of the mask he too became an object of intense study; his everyday actions and his foibles, talents, idiosyncrasies, and to some even crimes and eventual treasons, were minutely examined. Who Was He? joined the other queries of Who Am I? and Who Are You? in the clown's own eyes.

During the First World War, however, he was most eager to please. Too new an immigrant, he couldn't afford to fail to fall in line with the patriotic madness of the hour, particularly as he had managed to side-step the question of why he was not donning a British uniform, however much he might have studied the military manual, just in case. The manual, in fact, must have come in useful in preparation for the one great contribution Chaplin was labouring on for the war, his despatch of Charlie to represent him in the trenches.

Shoulder Arms was shot between May and September 1918, a long period for a three-reel film. Charlie had been mulling over it since 1917, and began shooting with a more structured plan than hitherto applied for his movies. In keeping with the tradition derived from vaudeville's time-slots for a single sketch, there would be three episodes, each lasting about one reel: Charlie as a civilian, being drafted; Charlie in the trenches; Charlie defeating the Kaiser single-handed. The third episode would of course be, as in *The Bank*, a dream.

In the event, the first part was deleted, but survives in the out-takes, and is included in current DVDs of the film. Charlie has become a family man, dragging three small children home with him and parking them by the saloon while he takes some fortification before arriving home to a barrage of thrown objects from his wife – who remains off-screen. The draft order is delivered. At the recruiting office Charlie, undressed, has to dodge about, waiting for his examination, while a lady clerk goes about her brisk business. In the examination room a surreal scene ensues, in one shot, taken through the glass window of the surgery of 'Dr Francis Maude', with the doctor and Charlie as shadow puppets. The doctor inserts and loses his spatula inside Charlie's gullet, and has to fish for it with tongs, which are also swallowed and have to be retrieved with a hook on a string. The process concluded, the door is opened and Charlie is declared fit for service.

This was one of three attempts by Chaplin, during his First National period, to evade the Tramp and give Charlie a new persona as an everyday working family man. The second try, with *A Day's Pleasure*, shot in 1919, was a comic take on a day's family outing by flivver (Ford car) and pleasure boat. This featured some nice gags, but Charlie as family man never gelled. (Pay Day (1921), his last two-reeler, at least dispensed with the superfluous kids.) It could work, technically, but the character lacked credibility. However much he might try to escape, Chaplin was stuck with the Tramp.

Shoulder Arms, as we know it, starts with Charlie as a new recruit at the training camp. In 'the awkward squad', Charlie has to learn to straighten out those splayed feet. Arrived at the trench, among the exploding bombs, Charlie bunks down with his fellow soldiers, among them brother Syd, already a veteran. Meanwhile, in the next-door trench, the Germans, a conglomeration of odd-sized freaks, are tyrannized by their midget officer.

Chaplin, who was never in any army, captures perfectly the mixture of wistful boredom and terror that rules the trench, although he could not, would not capture its dire stench and vile sanitary conditions. Daring to make fun of pain, as he after all had been doing for five years with poverty, Charlie nevertheless shows the soldiers trying to get their sleep in a flooded bunker, with a toad leaping off Syd's foot into the sump, and a candle floating by burning his toes. Finally, Charlie manages to escape Syd's snoring by uncoupling the phonograph horn and using it to breathe underwater.

In a poignant double exposure, the makeshift 'Broadway' of the trench is juxtaposed with the authentic avenue, with a nostalgic shot of Henry Bergman mixing drinks at a familiar bar. A letter arrives for another doughboy, and Chaplin's expression as he reads it over the man's shoulder acts out its contents, till the soldier whips it away. Charlie's own parcel from home turns out to be hard tack and Limburger cheese, that staple of old silent comedy, which can only be tackled by gas mask. Tossed over the trench, the cheese plasters the midget Hun officer, interrupting his bragging toast 'To the Day!' In the morning, Charlie wakes in the water-logged trench, massaging his foot, which turns out to be Syd's, a gag that will be reused to great effect by Stan Laurel and Oliver Hardy, years later.

'Over the top in fifteen minutes!' The last minutes of waiting cut between the sombre faces of the soldiers and Charlie's nonchalant attempt to light his cigarette. Up the ladder and over – Chaplin glosses over the battle – cutting to his miraculous capture of the enemy trench and all its soldiers.

Officer: 'How did you capture thirteen?'

Charlie: 'I surrounded them!'

Charlie is perhaps as close here to a Nietzschean Superman as he will ever be: spanking the midget Hun officer when he spurns his cigarette; potting enemy soldiers one by one and marking them off, even picking off one who seems to be flying above, as Charlie and Syd's eyes follow his off-screen fall. A cigarette is lit from a passing shell.

Then Charlie volunteers, pushing Syd aside, rashly, for the officer tells him: 'You may never return!' Within the enemy lines Charlie, disguised as a tree, manages to avoid being chopped down by a passing German patrol and even saves Syd from a firing squad when Syd, out behind enemy lines too, is captured. ('More heroic acts', explains the intertitle.)

Hiding in a ruined house, Charlie is discovered in the bed by French Edna, who tends his wounds and helps him escape when the Germans enter the house. More turning of the tables, and a machine gun, on the enemy ensues, till Edna is taken 'for aiding the allies' to Hun headquarters, which are then visited by the Kaiser. The stage is set for Charlie's Great Heroic Achievement, capturing the Kaiser, with Syd, Edna and he disguised as the German Emperor's drivers. 'Bringing Home the Bacon': the Kaiser – played by Syd in his second role of the film – is paraded before the cheering doughboys, helped on his way by Charlie's kick in the pants. 'Peace on Earth, Goodwill to All Mankind' (except the Kaiser and his minions, of course), pronounces the title, and then Charlie awakes from his dream of glory, still in his tent at boot camp.

Chaplin's longest film to date, at thirty-six minutes, *Shoulder Arms* is full of gags and frenetic action, a propaganda comic strip of the Tramp as – for the first time properly – the iconic 'Little Fellow', Everyman turned heroic saviour. His rendition to Edna of his American identity, by knocking himself on the head and miming the stars and stripes, is just one of many small throwaway moments. Charlie as a tree running through the woods is a scene that anticipates, as so much else of the silent comedies, the surrealists, who had to dredge their imagery from intellectual depths rather than the junkyard of ordinary absurdity that the comedians deployed instinctively – just to get one more laugh.

The irony of the splendid morale-boosting of Chaplin's film is that it arrived in the cinemas at the end of October, just before the armistice of 11 November 1918. It was in fact part of a raft of war movies that had turned up during the last months of the conflict, mostly shrill propaganda efforts with titles like *The Kaiser – the Beast of Berlin*. The scenes of the beastly Hun officer assaulting Edna, however, bear some resemblance to scenes in Cecil B. DeMille's more layered war film with Mary Pickford, *The Little American*, released the year before. The laughs that greeted the movie were a catharsis for the real terrors of the war, and the heart-stopping wait of so many American families to find out whether their boys would come home or not. 'It was altogether too much,' wrote the *Chicago Herald*, 'peace and Mr. Chaplin on the same day! Still, Chicago, with its remarkable capacity for assimilating every situation, assimilated both peace and Mr. Chaplin yesterday with nearly equal enthusiasm.' And the Ohio press wrote that 'there is no doubt that Charlie Chaplin is becoming more of an American institution . . .'

During the last weeks of his shoot among the upper slopes of Hollywood behind Beverly Hills that provided the woods and fields of Normandy, Chaplin also turned out a short promotional film, released as *The Bond* in September 1918. This was a quick series of tableaus in painted sets: 'The bond of friendship' had Charlie and Albert Austin meeting under a lamp-post to chat amiably until Albert touches Charlie for a loan. 'The bond of love' showed Charlie and Edna flirting on a park bench while Cupid shoots his arrow into Charlie's behind and ties them neatly up in silk. 'The bond of marriage' shows Edna and Charlie bashfully idyllic before the altar, until the pastor signals for his pay. Then 'The Liberty Bond' shows Charlie as The People, handing bags of cash to Uncle Sam, who hands it to the American worker, who hands a gun to the army and the navy in turn. This wraps up with Charlie smashing the Kaiser into the ground with his big Liberty Bonds mallet.

Perhaps just in time, before the US government ran out of cash, the allies achieved the real thing, clinching the armistice deal in the French Marshall Foch's railway carriage in the forest of Compiègne. No one checked to see if all the trees outside this historical event were static, or whether one of them shook with a disorderly glee.

Million-Dollar Charlie.

14

Those Love Pangs
Or: Finer, More Cautious Fabrication . . .

After completing *Shoulder Arms*, Charlie was at a loss what to do next. Young Mildred, whom he had rushed to marry because of her apparent pregnancy, turned out not to be pregnant after all, though this was soon remedied and Chaplin awaited his first child. His next film, however, was plagued by an unusually high level of indecision. More days were spent not shooting than shooting, and the studio was idle for long periods well into 1919. The film, titled *Sunnyside*, was finally released in June, a full eight months between one three-reel film and the next. *Photoplay* magazine wrote about the new picture in its September issue:

I have never seen in my life a film of finer, more cautious fabrication than 'Sunnyside,' the latest Chaplin exhibition. Perhaps the extreme caution with which it is developed killed the spontaneity, for the truth is that despite moments of real exalted artistry, and a few big laughs, 'Sunnyside' is not a first-class Chaplin offering, when judged by his recent standards. Charlie as a farm-hand, kicked not from pillar to post, but from bed-post to bed-post, is the subject of the pantomime. The funniest and most original moment is that in which, catapulting off a culvert, he alights on his sphere of reflection, and . . . beholds a bright bevy of half-nude dancing girls prancing for his delectation . . . What we get is a perfectly staged and really exquisite burlesque of the 'classic' craze . . . The Chaplin spirit of jest slumbered for a moment, perhaps, but his artistry, his determination to put forth first-class work, shines forth as strong as ever . . .

Once again, Chaplin made an experiment in stepping sideways away from the Tramp to create a kindred rural spirit, set in a village that is introduced by an iris out from the cross of the church spire. Charlie is a kind of happy idiot in a town of buffoons – his boss the brutish manager of a decrepit hotel, the morning church service featuring a dwarfish father and a giant son, and Edna as a dreamy simpleton who comes to buy something but has forgotten what it is she wants. If Charlie's urban world is a realm of desperation and violence, his rural world is a dreamland of country cousins, where the egg is cracked into the pan fresh from the chicken and milk squeezed into a cup straight from the cow. 'The Unwilling Sinner' is the title that describes Charlie the farmhand as he hies off down the path with the cows: 'His church, the sky, his altar, the landscape.'

Apart from Edna, he seems lumbered with an idiot brother, whom he sends blindfold into the fields, and a rival, a 'City Chap' who is brought into the hotel unconscious and then recovers and steals Edna's heart. But this rivalry too is a dream, and Charlie and Edna can frolic in their bucolic paradise.

A deleted sequence, found by Brownlow and Gill for *Unknown Chaplin*, shows Charlie setting up the hotel's ragged barber's chair to give Albert Austin a terrifying shave, filling his face with lather and burning his scalp at the heating furnace, while doggedly stropping his razor. This would later feed into the barber scene in *The Great Dictator*, but was left this time on the cutting-room floor.

Plagued with an unusual imprecision, Charlie's rural character fails to gel into a set of coherent and consistent gags. Where did this character come from? How did he get to the village? Has he always been there? And if so, what differentiates him from all the other village idiots? The dream of the dancing nymphs comes close to opening a door on Chaplin's own priapic fantasies of girls not far grown from puberty, and their sudden morphing into the bunch of yokels who toss him back into the ditch on his head might signal fears of things yet to come. Unease over the marriage with Mildred, or fears over the coming child?

On 7 July 1919 Mildred gave birth to Chaplin's first son, named Norman Spencer Chaplin, but the baby died after three days. The child was laid to rest in Inglewood cemetery on 11 July. Within ten days, David Robinson writes, Chaplin was already 'auditioning babies' for another production, which was tentatively titled *The Waif*. He had already found a co-star for it, the small son of a vaudeville performer, Jack Coogan. He interrupted the shooting of his next First National contract film and threw himself into this endeavour, which would take a full year to complete. Then, in October, he returned to the half-made film and completed it in a couple of weeks. Named *A Day's Pleasure*, the two-reeler was released at the end of the year.

In *A Day's Pleasure*, Chaplin departed once again from the Tramp. A family man on a day out, he is taking his wife Edna and two kids off for a boat trip, commencing with a lengthy attempt to get his Model T Ford to start up and run. It was a sad irony that Charlie had two children in his new movie at the very moment his creator lost his first child, and, given its interruptions, it is perhaps no surprise that the film appears truncated, barely structured and somewhat lame.

On the boat, Charlie gets into a punch-up with a jealous husband who finds him lurched in his seasickness up against the man's fat wife. There is a black jazz band, whose trombone keeps wiping Charlie's nose until he pulls it out and throws it overboard, the band themselves as seasick and glaze-eyed as anyone else on the coastal cruise. The inevitable deckchair-folding fiasco is played out, until Charlie tosses this too into the sea.

The film presents a kind of snapshot of a weekend's outing, LA-style, at a particular moment of the return to 'normalcy' after the war. The scene with the flivver that rocks and rattles as it is wound up, but coughs to a halt whenever Charlie tries to climb into the driving seat, is reprised in many American silent comedies, notably by W. C. Fields, who first performed the same scene in a sketch called 'Off to the Country' in the Ziegfeld Follies of 1921.

Cultural historian Frederick Lewis Allen wrote about the idiosyncrasies of the 'high, hideous, but efficient Model T Fords of the day' in his book about 'The Fabulous Twenties' – *Only Yesterday*, describing the antics of his fictitious driver, Mr Smith:

He climbs in by the right hand door (for there is no left-hand door by the front seat), reaches over to the wheel, and sets the spark and throttle levers in a position like that of a clock at ten minutes to three. Then, unless he has paid extra for a self-starter, he gets out to crank. Seizing the crank in his right hand (carefully, for a friend of his once broke his arm cranking) he slips his left forefinger through a loop of wire that controls the choke. He pulls the loop of wire, he revolves the crank mightily, and as the engine at last roars, he leaps to the trembling running board, leans in, and moves the spark and throttle to twenty-five minutes of two . . .

Eventually, the whole majestic caboodle can be ridden off.

Chaplin himself would not have had to fiddle with this monstrosity, as he had his Japanese chauffeur, Toraichi Kono (who can be glimpsed in one scene as Edna's driver in *The Adventurer*), to drive the eight-seater Locomobile he had bought in 1916. The gulf between Chaplin and Charlie could only widen further over time. While Charlie struggled with his attire and deckchairs, Chaplin's valet-cum-secretary Tom Harrington saw to his sartorial and other needs: 'When traveling,' the *Ladies' Home Journal* recounted in an article of August 1918, 'his secretary pays all the bills and tips. "Mr. Chaplin," he will say, "I have put twenty dollars in your pocket." '

Writer Rob Wagner, who penned this account, also waxed lyrical about 'Chaplin's passionate love of beauty', and claimed that

. . . the modesty of his material wants are strongly expressed in his personal life. Able to live in any extravagant manner that he chooses, he prefers a modest bachelor apartment, consisting of one large room and a bath. Here he has his piano, talking machine, violin, cello and books, and this is his refuge from the world. He rarely entertains in his own apartment; only a few intimates have ever been inside of it.

Of course, Chaplin had his home from home in his studio, his personal playground which contained not only the shooting stages, editing suites and prop and costume departments but also the laboratories for processing and preparing the films. When he married Mildred, the temporary apartment flat was superseded by a leased house in North Hollywood next door to that of Cecil B. DeMille, at 2000 DeMille Drive. This house was described in its palatial grandeur by the *Detroit Journal* in its January 1920 issue, the awestruck writer Marjorie Daw having been taken round the premises by Mrs Chaplin:

The Chaplin home is gorgeous. Her own room is the most wonderful of all . . . exquisite in every detail. From thick carpets to ceiling lavender was always the tone – two stately four-poster beds prettily wrought in ivory . . . lavender shaded light streaming from a tall standing lamp . . . Mrs. Chaplin showed me through her lovely gardens – apologising for the fact that because they were only a year old she had none of the hardy flowering species that take [more time] . . . [the thing about] Charlie, said Mrs. Chaplin, 'is that he has a whole brood of miscellaneous ancestored dogs around the house and won't let me have a pet dog of my own because he says dogs are meant for the open air – and not even tears would move him from his decision . . .

The two four-poster beds may have said it all. After a few months, the Chaplins moved to another house in South Oxford Drive, where Charles and Mildred lived the remainder of their stilted marriage, nursing their private woes, until their troubles spilled over into public view in March of 1920.

The release of *Sunnyside* had prompted comments that perhaps the Tramp had lost his way. 'IS THE CHAPLIN VOGUE PASSING?' asked one Harcourt Farmer in the June 1919 issue of *Theatre*:

A couple of years ago it would have been deemed treasonable to cast the smallest of critical stones at Chaplin. He was the biggest thing in laughs in the whole of America . . . But today is not a couple of years ago – and a review of Chaplin's last release, 'Sunnyside,' fills the analytical mind with grim foreboding. It wasn't a success, to put it bluntly. And, honestly, when you consider all the Chaplin films in the order of their manufacture, can you truthfully call them great art? Even if you allow that 'A Dog's Life' was funny – which many people deny – and even if you affirm that 'Shoulder Arms' was not an uncouth reflection on army life but a clever satire, you must admit that these two films were, in essence, but a rehash of the earlier 'Carmen,' just as 'Carmen' was a recooking of 'Behind the Screen,' and so on and so on.

In other words, I contend that the extraordinary Chaplin vogue is based upon the simple law of repetition – that each film contains precisely the same elements – that the appeal of every Chaplin picture is to the lowest human instincts – and that, in the natural course of events, the Chaplin vogue in five years will be a thing of remote antiquity . . .

This was of course no new tune, but one that had accompanied Chaplin from the start of his fame. Proof of his thesis, Farmer continued, was in the fact that

. . . every Chaplin picture, without exception, is constructed upon the psychological principle that pain is diverting – that you'll laugh at the concept of someone else suffering injury. And you do. When one of the bewhiskered artistes in a Chaplin exhibition picks up a pitchfork and delicately impales another member of the cast through the seat of his trousers – the packed mass in front of the screen chortles and screams and kicks.

As of course they always did and will always do. Chaplin had noted in his 1916 comments on the 'Psychology of Comedy' that 'world travelers have told us that naked blacks in the Congo would laugh themselves into hysterics if one of their number was caught stealing by the Lead of a safari and whipped. The others thought it made the whipped man look ridiculous to be whipped. So it amused them.'

The 'polite, restrained manner', as Chaplin put it, was not box-office gold. He would give no apology for deploying the ugly and indeed cruel nature of human beings when faced by another's humiliation. And in fact, his attempts to be a little more 'refined', in *Sunnyside*, had palpably failed.

The problem, however, was clearly deeper than mere technical artifice. Put dramatically, when Chaplin tinkered with the cosmic forces that had been unleashed by the Tramp phenomenon, he did so at his artistic peril. Jokes about milking cows into cups and goats bleating a wrong note behind a piano had a limited appeal, and Charlie as a rather slow-witted farmhand, however impish and elvish, was not what the punters had paid to see.

'Chaplin isn't a great artist,' wrote the portentous Farmer:

What's the difference between a John Barrymore and an unknown ham? The answer is *brains*. Barrymore mixes his colors with brains, consequently he's a great comedian. Chaplin, happening by the drift of circumstance, to make a lucky strike in a low comedy characterization, has repeated that particular role in every public appearance . . . The funny walk, the acute gestures . . . the sporadic vulgarities – they've all given us a deal of unaffected pleasure in the past; they were quite all right in the days when people went into a movie to kill time – but can't we look for something better and funnier in the future?

Chaplin may or may not have read this diatribe, though he clearly followed his reviews closely and *Theatre* was a prestigious journal. He had no cause to worry over his box-office figures, even if one or even two movies dipped a little. But he did yearn, in his new-found social milieu, for a better use of his own gifts and his popularity, to do something more. In his heart, he probably agreed with the comments about 'low comedy', which still remained his bread and butter. In 1920, in an interview with the *New York Times*, he would redefine himself, telling writer Benjamin De Casseres:

My clowning, as the world calls it – and I dislike the word clown, for I am not a clown – may have esoteric meanings. I prefer to think of myself as a mimetic satirist, for I have aimed in all my comedies at burlesquing, satirizing the human race – or at least those human beings whose very existence in this world is an unconscious satire on this world. The human race I prefer to think of as the underworld of the gods. When the gods go slumming they visit the earth. You see, my respect for the human race is not 100 percent . . .

And so Chaplin wrestled with his desire, his pretension even, to use the primal elements of pantomime to break out of the cycle of tit-for-tat slapstick and make his mark on a changed world. For 1919 saw not only the rise of leisure, the ubiquity of the flivver, the temptations of 'normalcy' and the supposed 'end of all wars'. It was also the era of labour unrest, strikes and the big Red Scare in the wake of Russia's revolution of October 1917, which had sent rumbles all over the world among both the rulers and the ruled. In the industrial heartland of America there were, by November 1919, at least a million men and

women on strike against their employers for better pay and conditions. In September the United Mine Workers' motion to strike even
demanded the nationalization of the mines. The Industrial Workers of
the World were an openly socialist and revolutionary movement,
fomenting and supporting strikes up and down the land. On the radical
fringes, anarchist militants committed direct acts of violence, including
sending explosive devices in packages to government figures and prominent capitalists. In June 1919 a bomb exploded at the home of Attorney
General A. Mitchell Palmer. A few months later, on New Year's Day of
1920, the Attorney General would send police and agents to seize
Communists or those suspected of Communism. Six thousand persons
would be arrested. Anti-radical rhetoric had been increasing throughout
the year to hysterical heights – foreign Bolsheviks with bombs and
beards were said to be spreading their doctrine of terror and the
overthrow of the State all over America. Amid this, as if to top up the
hysteria, the Volstead Act providing for the complete prohibition of
alcohol was passed in October 1919 and would become the law of the
land within months.

Sympathy for the Bolshevik revolution, however guarded, had
incurred another stigma during the war, when Lenin's government's
withdrew from the fight at the end of 1917, leaving American soldiers
more harshly exposed. But by early 1919 Chaplin was openly meeting
with prominent radical left figures like Max Eastman, introduced to
him by the same Rob Wagner who had written about his passion for
beauty and his modest needs in *Ladies' Home Journal*. On their part,
left-wing activists were as keen then as now to make the acquaintance
of Hollywood stars, the real arbiters of the popular taste of the day.

Whatever his political views – and we still do not know who scrawled
'IWW' on Mack Sennett's shed door during *The Fatal Mallet* – Chaplin
did not air them directly, yet. He continued to give interviews about
movies, the charmed life in Hollywood, and his thoughts about how
comedy worked. But, as one who always observed reality, he was looking intently at the bigger picture beyond the infinitesimal gestures of
daily life. He was wondering whether he could continue to dance in his
small, 'vulgar' post-vaudeville circus, or whether he could find a vehicle
that would allow him to speak with a firmer voice about what he saw,
and what he thought.

As ever, in Chaplin's acts and methods, there was a great blurring of
cause and effect. As is well known, he was considering the idea of a

comedy feature film from his Essanay days of 1915. His Essanay and Mutual contracts, however, precluded this. His contract with First National still committed him to eight films. But he was freer now to try his hand at the longer subject, if he could find a story that would stretch far enough, that had enough to say.

Given the strangely coincidental chronology, it is difficult to say how directly the death of his child influenced the subject of Chaplin's first feature film, but it certainly seems to have galvanized him into action. David Robinson writes that it was some weeks before the death of his son that Chaplin had, 'in the depressed period which followed the completion of *Sunnyside* . . . gone to the Orpheum, and seen there an eccentric dance act, Jack Coogan'. The dancer had his five-year-old son with him, who 'took a bow, gave an impersonation of his father's dancing, and made his exit with an energetic shimmy'.

If a dog, Scraps, could be a canine Charlie to partner him in the rough joints of the tenderloin, why not a child Charlie, reminiscent of his own years as a junior actor? With thoughts of his son almost due, Chaplin bonded with Jackie, and met him again at the Alexandria Hotel in Los Angeles. As both Coogan parents had been vaudevilleans, Chaplin got on well with them, and his 'moment of enchantment' with Jackie, Robinson writes, 'was when he asked Jackie what he did, and Jackie serenely replied: "I am a prestidigitator who works in a world of legerdemain."'

Chaplin gave Jackie his first try-out as one of Charlie's two kids in *A Day's Pleasure*. But within a month he had put aside the partly shot short and begun shooting the feature film that started life as *The Waif* and would be released, in February 1921, as *The Kid*.

PART TWO

The Pilgrim

Synopsis, *The Pilgrim* (First National, 1923)

A warder pins a poster of an escaped convict – Charlie – to the wall. A clergyman dipping in the river finds his clothes are gone. In a small town, Charlie turns up, in pastor's gear. A runaway couple try to enlist his help to marry them, but he runs off, evading the cops, and takes a train down to Texas. At his destination, however, he is greeted by the local sheriff, as the town congregation have been awaiting their new minister, Reverend Pim. The stout deacon (played by Mack Swain), accompanies him to the church, where he is expected to take the collection and give a sermon. He mimes the tale of David and Goliath, to the delight of a small boy but the stony glare of the parishioners. Later, at his lodging house, he meets the landlady and her daughter Edna, and an older guest couple (the father played by Syd Chaplin) and their small aggressive boy. The boy sticks Dad's hat on the plum pudding, which is then served, to great consternation. While wooing Edna, Charlie is recognized by an old cell mate, who gets invited into the home and proceeds to steal the landlady's life savings. Charlie pursues the thief, interrupting a hold-up in the town saloon, grabs the cash and speeds back, only to be arrested by the sheriff, who has discovered that he is a convict on the run. Edna pleads with the sheriff, showing him the money Charlie has returned, the evidence of his redemption from sin. The sheriff takes him down to the borderline with Mexico, egging him across the line to pick some flowers on the other side. Charlie misunderstands, and keeps coming back, till the mounted sheriff takes him by the scruff of the neck and kicks him across to Mexico. Freedom's joy is shattered by the gunfire of desperados in the bushes, and Charlie hightails it through the desert, hopping with one leg in Mexico and the other in the United States.

15

The Bond
Or: *In the World of Legerdemain*

From *Photoplay*, April 1920, Editorial Page

A Letter to a Genius:

CHARLES SPENCER CHAPLIN:

It is a daring thing to call any man a genius, for that word, like fame, is a tremendous description, almost always absurdly applied. But we will venture to call you a genius, for your performances are unique and your renown has girdled the world in an inflammable band embroidered with sprocket-holes.

Yet, we must call you a genius-on-vacation. And we must add that it is time your vacation were over. How many people are wishing that now!

We haven't seen you since 'Shoulder Arms.' 'Sunnyside' was anything but sunny. 'A Day's Pleasure' certainly was not pleasure.

Perhaps your contract is irksome – you may think it unfair. Perhaps your remuneration seems very little as an emolument to your illustrious talents and a recompense for those diamonds, your working hours.

But you didn't think that agreement unfair when you made it, not so long ago. To most of us, who have to grub and grind for what is a pittance to you, it seemed a very wonderful thing. But that is not for us to decide – pardon!

What is plain to anyone is the manly alternative in such a case. Be quit of your self-made fetters by honest, sportsmanlike effort. If your present ties are shackles, break them with your best blows . . .

Charlie! – we have no part in your quarrels; we have no will to meddle in your business. But all of us, from North, East, West and South, from as many sides of the water as there may be, are imploring, because we are doleful and bewildered in a bewildered and doleful world. Give us again those magic hours of philosophic forgetfulness, that you once set out so charitably, like beacons of a kindly neighbor.

We are not commanding nor advising nor even criticizing; we speak because we need you – because you made this turbulent God's marble a better thing to live on – because since you have been out of sorts the world has gone lame and happiness has moved away. Come back, Charlie!

The Kid, when it finally surfaced, was Charlie in his most Dickensian aspect, drawing broadly on *Oliver Twist* – itself filmed as early as

1909, the 1912 version being perhaps the cinema's earliest American feature. Chaplin's year of work was condensed into a mere hour of compact story-telling, blending the echoes of the Victorian novel, pictorial lessons from Griffith, age-old Karno-mania, the intensity garnered from his own childhood and the emotional turmoil of the loss of his son.

Since Chaplin had conceived the idea of co-starring with a child before this tragedy, it was most likely born of his thoughts about fatherhood during Mildred's pregnancy. In place of his wife, however, the story emerged with 'The Woman, whose only Sin was Motherhood', Edna Purviance, released from the Charity Hospital with her little bundle of grief. One wonders what Mildred, who was parting from Chaplin amid allegations of his cruelty, might have thought of this deflection of her own traumatic experience to a tale of the wages of unplanned parenthood. Unlike a later wife, Lita Grey, she has left us no account of her own apart from the breathless reportage of contemporary journalists.

A failed marriage that had been reluctant from the start, a cruelly curtailed paternity, could not fail to have deeply influenced Charlie, even though he recorded, decades later, in *My Autobiography*, that he had not been in love with Mildred, and that in her own almost childish enthusiasm 'she had no sense of reality'. Of the loss of their son he wrote baldly: 'After we had been married a year, a child was born but lived only three days. This began the withering of our marriage. Although we lived in the same house, we seldom saw each other.' Eventually, he wrote, Douglas Fairbanks approached him with 'rumors concerning Mildred'. They consented to a divorce, and 'separated in a friendly way'.

Throughout, Chaplin was at pains to separate the creation of *The Kid* from the creation and doom of his own kid. After over forty years, the pain still lingered, but had been overtaken by so many more ups and downs. Such are the perils of late-blooming reminiscences. But the impact of the immediate events is evident in practically every frame of the movie.

In a scene in *Limelight*, made nearly thirty years later, the clown Calvero insists to Claire Bloom, whom he has taken in after her attempted suicide, that 'in my last years, I must have truth!' But 'truth' is what shines out of the character, Charlie, at every step, and it was that cinematic truth that Chaplin was looking for every time he designated a filmed shot either to the out-takes or into the project at hand.

He could not define it, but he knew it when it appeared in rushes on the screen. Clearly it was a fragile thing that could spring out in a spasm of action, or in a composition, or in a look. Sometimes he might mistake it, as he thought he had in a number of scenes in *The Kid* which he cut out fifty years later, when he recorded a new soundtrack for the film in 1971. The three scenes are indicative – all over-emotive for a later era: a lingering scene by a church, as Edna sees newlyweds come out, a stained-glass window forming a glowing halo behind her head; a scene when she wanders distraught after abandoning the child, standing by a bridge as a toddler breaking free from his nurse totters towards her; a later scene when she confronts 'The Man' who was the cause of her downfall, and he tries to make amends. None seems relevant now, but they appeared essential enough in 1920 for Chaplin the perfectionist to include them in the finished film. He also left, even in 1971, a metaphorical insert still of Christ toiling uphill with the Cross, after Edna has left the hospital.

'The Man', whom Chaplin might have dispensed with too, is seen briefly after the Woman's exit from the hospital, an artist chatting with a friend in his studio while a photograph of Edna, precariously perched on his fireplace, is dislodged into the fire. Picking up the half-charred picture, the Man considers it for an instant before casting it back in the flames. In the event, Chaplin balked at omitting the real father completely, leaving Edna in an even more terrifying limbo, a much too 'modern' conceit for him to contemplate. The short scene was in any case required to emphasize her abandonment.

Considering that Dickens's *Oliver Twist* was published in 1838, in the cauldron of Britain's Industrial Revolution, there is a direct analogy between the harshness of that era of the forced orphanage with its disciplinary horrors and the hard world of Chaplin's contemporary nightmare of 1920, with its busybody reformers dragging the Kid away from Charlie the surrogate father. It was clearly this theme, and the idea of the two Tramps, adult and child, that guided Chaplin, with his nagging thoughts of the rights and wrongs of society seeping in as the project progressed.

Karno remained, nevertheless, also deep in his bones. According to Karno's 1971 biographer, as we have seen, Karno, before he joined the circus, tried his hand as a glazier, working with a friend called Mike at a short-lived career of breaking windows at night and then fixing them by day. Whether this was Chaplin's art following Karno's life, or

Karno's life reinvented in line with Chaplin's art, in the film it was a brilliant character gag illuminating the bond between man and boy.

The early scenes of *The Kid* – once Edna has deposited her baby on the back seat of a rich man's parked car, in the desperate hope that the child might have a good life – proceed with a rigorous, economical logic. The plot-line has been honed to a set of just-plausible-enough circumstances to bring the child into Charlie's life: a pair of thieves steal the rich man's car. They park it in the slum and hear a baby crying. They haul the baby out and chuck it by some garbage cans up against a wall, then drive off. Charlie enters the scene.

The Tramp, reborn after the hiatus of *Sunnyside* and *A Day's Pleasure*, is now no longer the bewildered immigrant at his wits' end. He is clearly an habitué of this rough world, a hobo to the manner born, dodging rubbish thrown out into the street from an upper floor, pausing to select a proper smoke from his battered tin of stubs. Discarding his threadbare mittens in the garbage, he notices the crying child and looks up to see from where on earth this piece of flotsam has come. A woman with a pram passes. Assuming the babe belongs to her – 'Pardon me, you dropped something' – Charlie dumps it on her, only to be beaten off. He tries putting the baby back by the wall, but a cop strolls up, and he rushes off, babe in arms again. A doddering old man passing by is the next to be handed the kid. He, in turn, rushes after Charlie, spies the pram, and Charlie, avoiding the cop again, strolls by the pram and is chased by the mother, who bops him on the head with her umbrella and hauls him back to the pram by the scruff of his neck, just as the cop has come into shot again. Charlie picks the child up and walks off, pausing to sit down by a grate to think things out. He lifts up the grate, and glances at the child and the sewer below, a terrible solution looming for a quick moment. Then, looking into the folds of the child's swaddling clothes, he finds Edna's scrawled note: 'Please love and care for this orphan child.'

Scene by scene, the story is told in a succession of long shots, the camera unmoving except to slightly adjust composition, from the moment Charlie spies the child to the moment he sits by the grate. Once the camera is closer, and the note implores him directly, the bond to the child is made. Back to long shot, as Charlie walks out of shot, the grate still looming in the foreground. As he approaches his own tenement room, one of the women lounging in the street outside asks him: 'Is that yours?' He nods. 'What's its name?' He pauses, goes into

Chaplin presents *The Kid*.

the room and comes back to tell her: 'John.' The entire sequence, from the moment the Tramp has noticed the child, lasts just over three minutes.

After Charlie has entered his room with the babe, we are back with Edna, running in agonized fear back to the rich man's house in search of the baby she has abandoned. She rings the bell and a rich lady comes out, but her chauffeur has discovered that the car is stolen. Edna faints on the steps. A brief scene of Charlie rigging up a hammock and an ingenious way for the child to be fed and to wee into its pot follows, then fade to the title: 'Five years later', which will bring us to Jackie Coogan.

Finding Jackie was a phenomenal stroke of good fortune, as his performance is both luminous and comical, free from false sentimentality and mirroring Charlie in more than just gesture and mimicry. From the moment the small urchin, watched by a baffled cop, buffs his nails on the pavement, then rises and yawns as the Tramp has done from time immemorial, one knows Chaplin's choice is sound. There follow a series of iconic episodes: Jackie breaking windows and Charlie sauntering up with his new glass to fix the damage. Charlie and Jackie at home, sharing a stack of pancakes, or a mess of porridge from a bucket. Jackie challenged by a boy in the slum alley, and Charlie being promised a beating by the aggressor's bulky Big Brother if his kid dares to win.

The year's shoot with its evident mountain of footage has been stripped down to its essential content, as if Chaplin is impatient to get to the meat of his story – the uncaring authorities' attempt to 'steal' Jackie from his 'father' after a report by a brusque 'country doctor'. The plot-line requires, however, that Edna be brought back into play. Having been taken up by the rich family, she is 'now a star of great prominence', showered with gifts and wooed by such luminaries as the impresario 'Professor Guido' (Henry Bergman in one of his two roles here, the other being the night-shelter keeper). She has also become a charitable worker ('Charity, to some a duty – to others a joy', says the intertitle), bringing toys to kids in the slum. As she cradles a baby and remembers her child, Jackie appears in the doorway beside her, ravishing her with his smile. But she will walk away, not knowing his identity, at this point.

Later, when Edna has stepped in to stop the fight between Jackie and his rival, and between Big Brother and Charlie ('Remember, if he smites you on one cheek, offer him the other'), she unwittingly sets the train of her reunion with her child in motion, telling Charlie that 'this child is ill – get a doctor at once'. When the doctor asks Charlie: 'Are you the father of this child?' Charlie answers, 'Well, practically,' and shows him the old crumpled note, stuck within the dusty pages of the *Police Gazette*.

The doctor huffs, 'This child needs proper care and attention,' and the 'proper care and attention' is summoned, the brutal enforcer and his van from the County Orphan Asylum. No one forgets the tearing away of the child, Jackie pleading from the back of the van, Charlie's desperate fight and his rush over the rooftops to leap into the van, knock the enforcer off and clutch Jackie, chasing off the dumb-founded driver at the gates of the asylum. There then follows a reprise of the flophouse scene from Essanay's *Police*, this time extended and deepened. The flophouse features a cameo role from Jackie's real-life father, Jack Coogan, as a drunk pickpocket whose roving hands turn up a coin Charlie didn't even know he had, so that he dips the thief's other hand into his other pocket, hopefully. The two Tramps sleep in one bed, each kicking fitfully in his sleep, in perfect syncopation. But the bearded keeper, having stuck Charlie for payment even for the child, spots an item in his newspaper which promises: '$1,000 reward – lost child wanted. No questions asked. H. Grafton – Chief of Police.'

The film then moves to its final apotheosis. The keeper snatches Jackie. Charlie awakens suddenly to find the Kid gone. He pulls the blankets from all the sleepers and rushes out into the street, calling his name. Finally, slumped by a doorway, he dreams. Chaplin developed the fey scene in *Sunnyside* into a kind of slum epiphany. It is a 'dream-land' out of the epilogue of *Easy Street*: All the people in Charlie's courtyard are decked with wings, even the cop, and Charlie is kitted out with his own, Jackie beside him with his miniature pair. The 'angels' cavort with their brass instruments. Charlie flies off 'for a spin'. A bunch of devils, however, get through a hole in the gate of heaven, and begin seducing the happy folk. Chaplin cast a twelve-year-old girl, Lillita McMurray (later to be Lita Grey), as a flighty and flirtatious angel – 'Innocence' – whose boyfriend is the familiar bully, played by his regular tough guy, Charles 'Chuck' Reisner. Made up to be much older, she winks at Charlie, who then gets embroiled with the jealous rough. Feathers fly, paradise is disrupted, the cop chases Charlie through the air, the cop fires his gun and Charlie falls dead.

Lying by the doorway, he is shaken by the scruff of the neck to wake with his collar seized by the policeman, who hauls him off, shoves him in the back of an expensive car and deposits him at the steps of the rich folks' mansion – where Edna and Jackie, reunited, await him.

THE END.

The abrupt end of the picture is puzzling, until one realizes that Chaplin has distilled the essence of his story and it cannot end any other way and still fulfil the brief of comedy rather than tragedy. 'A Picture with A Smile, and Perhaps a Tear', as it was prefaced, could not end with the Tramp's defeat. But it is full of defeats, and spikes of triumph, as the parted are brought together only for fragile moments among the hammer-blows of reality. Paradise is shut down by a cop's bullet, and the final cathartic moment of Mother and Son jubilant is momentary and rapidly faded out.

Where is the movie set? By now, the audiences were quite used to the idea that Charlie Chaplin movies were set in Charlie-Chaplin-Land, an Easy Street reductively familiar from previous episodes in the life of the Tramp. He is still not quite the 'Little Fellow' that he will become in Chaplin's hindsight mind. Chaplin required in the frame of his movies precisely what he required, and no more. The doorway, the bare grate, the entire courtyard, or the whole street that Charlie and Jackie Coogan work, with enough scope for a chase. Even the rooftops do not open out to a wider view of the city within which these dramas unfold.

Historians have hied to Pownall Terrace, one of the Chaplins' childhood addresses, to which he himself would make a pilgrimage in his coming trip abroad, looking for similarities, or models. But between London and Los Angeles, with a whiff of Lower East Side New York, Charlie lived among the generic tenements. The closest he came to a direct London reference was in the courtyard scene, with its lumbering bowler-hatted bully and the neighbours clustering round the brawling kids. What is missing of course is the pubs, the saloons so ubiquitous in the early Keystones, Essanays and Mutuals. *The Kid*, therefore, signals the departure of the Drunk, the rending of Charlie from the stage Archibald – though he would have one more come-back, a year later, in *The Idle Class*. From now on, Charlie would live completely in fable, *sui generis*, a creature wholly of the screen. Perhaps it was Chaplin's great irony that, in the post-war world of America's new consumer culture, Charlie is no longer a social reminder at the very time when Chaplin begins, in earnest, to develop his own social creed.

Chaplin's cutting of the film proceeded, through 1920, in a flurry of anxiety over his divorce from Mildred, and an extended wrangle with First National over his eight-film contract, of which *The Kid* was only the fifth of eight films promised, two years after the initial deal. Should *The Kid* be cut into separate shorter films or be the seven-reeler that Chaplin wanted? Fearful that First National and Mildred's lawyers might band together to attach his picture, Chaplin decamped from Los Angeles to Salt Lake City, to cut his film in secret in another state. Having done this, he decided to preview the picture unannounced in a local Salt Lake theatre. The audience loved it, but a subsequent screening to First National executives was less exciting, and its fate was not yet assured. Chaplin and his staff had gone east, to New Jersey, where the film was completed in a studio disguised as the 'Blue Moon Film Company'. Chaplin then took residence at the Ritz Hotel in New York, where he met the writer Frank Harris and a host of New York luminaries. Harris was then still editor of the US edition of the literary journal *Pearson's Magazine*, but he had not yet published his five-volume saga, *My Life and Loves*, celebrated, denounced and banned for its sexually explicit tales. Chaplin did not relate if he had a preview, but Harris later wrote his own account of their meeting amid Mildred's continued recriminations and legal demands. As Harris wrapped up his description of Chaplin cutting short one of her hectoring calls: 'Charlie Chaplin strolls away from the 'phone with a smile on his lips and a little sub-acid contempt for human, and especially for feminine nature.'

Evidently a meeting of like minds . . . But Chaplin did not stint in his enjoyment of the upper stratum of New York's intellectual elites, hob-nobbing with such as the magazine mogul Condé Nast, Frank Crowninshield, editor of *Vanity Fair* and *Vogue*, and 'the pick of the Ziegfeld Follies girls'. As he recounted much later, he met the poet Hart Crane, the novelist and essayist Waldo Frank, the suffragette Margaret Foster and the radical Max Eastman – already an old acquaintance.

This was the point at which American intellectuals finally embraced Chaplin and began to see him as part of the revival of the American arts that they were seeking after the epoch-changing war. Eugene O'Neill's first major play, *Beyond the Horizon* – which would win the

1920 Pulitzer Prize for drama – opened in February 1920 at the Morosco Theatre, and Chaplin recalled meeting the Provincetown Players who were rehearsing O'Neill's second play, *The Emperor Jones* (which opened in November). It may have been too early in the decade for him to have met the future diners of the Algonquin 'Round Table' who would lionize and 'discover' vaudevilleans like the Marx Brothers and W. C. Fields, but he was in a very real sense his fellow-artists' trail-blazer. Journalist, author and poet Benjamin De Casseres recounted Chaplin's whimsical reflections about his art and life, and his unusual desire to play more serious roles, in his article headed 'The Hamlet-Like Nature of Charlie Chaplin' in the *New York Times* of 12 December 1920:

Midmost in this his mortal life 'Charlie' Chaplin, the most famous man in the world, has declared that he is tired of a dog's life. He intends to shoulder arms against a sea of laughter and by opposing end it – by playing Hamlet – maybe . . .

But hold your smile for a while, as I held mine. One may smile and smile and be a villain – and one may smile and smile and be a Hamlet.

'Charlie' Chaplin smiles and is a Hamlet. He has clowned, cavorted and somersaulted in every city, town and mining camp in the civilized and uncivilized world; but there is no man I have ever met who, intellectually and emotionally, comes nearer to the Hamlet-type of being than Charles Spencer Chaplin, whose stage personality is better known than any other human being . . . and who has more completely hidden his real personality than any other world-figure.

In many hours easy conversational talk with Chaplin I discovered a spirit of very rare vintage – a poet, an esthete; a dynamic and ultra-advanced thinker; a man with a thousand surprising facets; a man of many accomplishments; a man infinitely sad and melancholy; a man as delicate as violin strings that register the world-wail and the world-melody; a Puck, a Hamlet, an Ariel – and a Voltaire . . .

Having redefined himself to De Casseres as a 'mimetic satirist', Chaplin charmed his way around his interlocutor, as he always did, by offering some nugget of his innermost thoughts, contrived or spontaneous as they might have been:

'Nothing fails like success,' he replied when asked how it felt to be a millionaire when one had known the most desperate poverty, as he had. 'I mean by that that money never satisfied a spiritual or intellectual need . . . I doubt if a rich man ever has a real friend – for how when one is fixed for life in this world's goods can one tell friend, enemy or fawner? I always understand poor artists; rich ones always seem to me a contradiction in terms.

'A part of my childhood was passed in a London orphanage. When Christmas time came around a big table was spread, and on it were laid little presents – tin watches, bags of candy, picture books and other trivial things – for the inmates.

'On this particular Christmas I was seven years old. We all formed in line, and long before it was my turn to reach the table and select what I wanted I had picked out with my eye a big, fat red apple for my present. It was the biggest apple I had ever seen outside of a picture book. My eye and stomach got bigger and bigger as I approached that apple.

'When the line had moved up so that I was fifth from the table a house-keeper, or somebody in authority, pounced on me, pushed me out of line and took me back to my room with the brutal words:

'"No Christmas present for you this year, Charlie – you keep the other boys awake by telling pirate stories."

'I have always found that red apple of happiness just within reach when some invisible presence or force drags me away just as I am about to grab it.'

De Casseres returned to their original topic in one of the nocturnal walks he reported Chaplin took along 'the streets at night for hours with some friend discussing art, religion, books, theories of beauty and his own ambition to be a tragedian' –

'And Hamlet?' I asked him on one of these nocturnal excursions. 'Would you like to play Hamlet?'

'I am too tragic by nature to play Hamlet,' he replied. 'Only a great com-edian can play the Dane.'

With which enigmatic answer he switched into a long dissertation on Freud and the tremendous light the latter had thrown on his own Hamletic nature.

I have never met an unhappier or a shyer human being than this Charles Spencer Chaplin.

16

The Idle Class
Or: My Trip Abroad and What I Found There

Synopsis, *The Idle Class* (First National, 1921)

'The summer season' at a swanky resort. Chauffeurs wait to collect the city slickers at the railway station. Among a posse of silly duffers, well-dressed Edna awaits her husband, whom she has asked to meet her. An uninvited guest, our Charlie, has arrived, riding the rails under the carriages.

'An Absent Minded Husband' – Edna's husband is Charlie the Drunk, stuck in his hotel room with his liquor, and venturing in to the lobby without his pants. Edna, arriving at the hotel, sends him a message: 'I will occupy other rooms until you stop drinking.' He appears desolate, his shoulders shaking with apparent grief from behind, until he turns, and we see he is handling the cocktail shaker.

'The Lonely Tramp' – evidently a social climber, trips his way on to the golf course, mixing with and enraging the upper-crust players. Having no ball of his own, he uses theirs, until an encounter with a sleeping tramp enables him to pop up all the golf balls that have fallen in the tramp's open mouth by pressing on his ample stomach. Charlie sees Edna taking a canter on a horse, and dreams of rescuing her from a fall, riding his donkey. A fantasy wedding, and a fantasy baby, beckon for a brief instant, but it is not to be.

'That Evening' – at a masquerade ball, Edna has given her drunk husband his last chance to turn up. He is present, but unfortunately dressed in a full suit of armour, whose visor snaps over his face. Meanwhile, outside, Charlie, mistaken for a thief on a bench, is chased by a cop and runs into the ballroom, where he is mistaken by Edna's father (Mack Swain, one of the golfers) for her man. Edna takes him by the hand: 'You look so strange, won't you sit down?' The drunk sees her through his visor: 'My wife! And flirting!' But Charlie, introduced to the guests as Edna's husband, says coyly: 'Oh, no, we're not married!' This insult leads him to be chased round the dance floor by Mack Swain, while the visored drunk also tries to intervene. All in a heap – Charlie tries to open the drunk's visor with a hammer, then a tin-opener, which cuts off the metal, revealing his alter ego. Charlie, understanding the misunderstanding, takes off, but Edna asks her father to go and apologize to the strange man for all his troubles. Mack, attired in a kilt, does so, but is kicked in the butt for his pains, and Charlie runs off, iris in, down the road.

Jokes about golf? What has the Tramp come to? Following his conflicts with First National and his stint on the east coast, Chaplin returned to his studio at the end of January 1921 to attend to his ongoing eight-movie contract. The result was *The Idle Class*, an unfunny comedy with some fine interspersed gags. The problem was not any waning of the craft, as Chaplin's mastery of the frame, and the timing of action, was as good as ever, but Charlie himself was out of character, hob-nobbing with the nobs on the golf course. It may well be that Chaplin still felt the need to give the Drunk of *One A.M.* and *The Cure* his last hurrah, but locking him in a suit of armour, which solved the problem of having both Tramp and Drunk in the same shots, with a Chaplin-face-alike for the tin-opening sequence, was not the best send-off. Two great images were added to the Hall of Fame, however: the cocktail-shaking gag, with its cheat of emotions, and the Drunk, discovering he has no pants on when he ventures with tux and topper into the hotel lobby, emerging from his hide-out telephone booth crouched in a midget's gait.

The film marked, as well, a welcome return to Chaplin's crew of Mack Swain, old Keystone partner, after Eric Campbell had died so suddenly, in an alcohol-fuelled car crash. The jagged gap left in Chaplin's repertoire for a full-blooded mock-Victorian villain was never filled, but Mack provided a different kind of foil: heavy in girth but more nuanced in his subsequent portrayals, whether as the amiable deacon of *The Pilgrim* or the starving, 'chicken'-chasing Alaskan prospector of *The Gold Rush*. In *The Idle Class* he still wore the moustache and face mask of his Keystone character, Ambrose.

Edna Purviance's hurt portrayal of the neglected wife seemed to mirror her status in the Chaplin ménage, as she had seen herself supplanted by Mildred, and left behind while Chaplin dallied with the swankier damosels of New York. Nevertheless, she was still his leading lady, and would remain so through *A Woman of Paris* of 1923.

The scandal that would curtail her career, involving Mabel Normand and a shot oil tycoon, would not occur till New Year's Eve of that year, a further blow to the carefree image of Hollywood that began to be shaken in September 1921 – the moment of Fatty Arbuckle's doom. Coincidentally, and almost as if he were sniffing some intangible trouble to come, Charles Chaplin decided to depart on his trip to Europe just one month before, in August.

Earlier in the year, two important events mitigated Chaplin's ongoing jitters about his First National contract and the divorce from Mildred. In March, a long-hoped-for reunion could be set in motion when his mother Hannah was granted a visa to come to live with him in the United States. Throughout his film career till then, Hannah had remained in the Peckham House asylum, looked after first by Charles and Sydney's aunt Kate, then by her son, Charles's cousin Aubrey. Sydney was arranging the necessary permits as early as April 1919, but Charles, already beset by his troubles with Mildred, and anticipating the birth of his son, cabled him to postpone the project. His son's death, and the year's work on *The Kid*, delayed the immigration of Hannah Chaplin still further. Finally, Chaplin sent his factotum, Tom Harrington, to bring her from England. Her entrance into the US was slightly marred when, as David Robinson writes, 'on her arrival in New York . . . she mistook an immigration official for Jesus Christ.' Chaplin clearly had to use his clout to get around the immigration rules that barred a person in her condition from entering the United States. The ruse, it appears, was to grant her a limited stay to undergo medical treatment. The London *Times* wrote (on 30 March) that she was detained on arrival at Ellis Island for 'medical observation', and then released when 'the necessary formal assurances for her support and care were furnished by her son'. Mrs Chaplin, as *The Times* reported that officials were informed, 'has been suffering for two years past from a severe nervous affectation which had its origin in a shock occasioned by the repeated air raids in London during the war. Only recently has her health improved sufficiently to enable her to make the journey to the United States.'

Whether this fiction was provided solely for the press or was the tale prepared for Ellis Island is unclear. Four years later, in March 1925, according to the *New York Times*, immigration officials refused an extension of Mrs Chaplin's permit and ruled that she had to leave the US. In the event, Chaplin's attorneys must have managed to get this ruling quashed. Hannah remained, until her death, in California, with a personal carer, 'in a bungalow with a pleasant garden near the sea'.

The second positive event for Chaplin, in April 1921, was the formal incorporation of United Artists, the company that had been announced in January 1919 by Chaplin, Douglas Fairbanks, Mary Pickford, D. W. Griffith and W. S. Hart, as a declaration of independence by the film-makers against the combinations and trusts. Chaplin, however, still had two films to make for First National. He began work on another two-reeler, which would eventually emerge as *Pay Day*, in early August, but stopped after a few days, shut the studio and took the train to Chicago and New York, en route to Cherbourg and Southampton. His Trip Abroad was about to begin.

In New York he met up again with his intellectual friends – with Max Eastman, with the rising young turks of the press, Heywood Broun and Alexander Woollcott – and attended the premiere of Fairbanks's new drama, *The Three Musketeers*. Already in Chicago crowds had gathered, and hordes of pressmen fired their questions at him:

'Mr Chaplin, why are you going to Europe?'

'Are you going to make any pictures while you are there?'

'What do you do with your old mustaches?'

'Are you going to get married while you are in Europe?'

'Mr Chaplin, are you a Bolshevik?'

Chaplin's subsequent book, *My Trip Abroad* – co-written with a newsman who was to become his assistant director, Monta Bell – chronicled his first return to England and Europe since his second embarkation with the Karno troupe to New York in October 1912. The question 'Are you a Bolshevik?' recurred in New York, when Chaplin replied: 'I am an artist. I am interested in life. Bolshevism is a new phase of life. I must be interested in it.' Charlie was not averse, however, to enlarging on his cultural and political views to the newsmen who gathered round him at the Ritz Carlton Hotel, as the *New York Times* reported on 30 August:

Charlie Chaplin thinks short skirts are terrible. Also he thinks that women should all wear tailored suits, that they should bob their hair and that if it contributes to their comfort they should wear rolled stockings . . . [but] he would much rather discuss problems which, if they are no more difficult of solution, are of greater social moment, problems such as Government ownership of railroads, socialism, unemployment, and the relations of capital and labor. In such questions of the moment does he take an interest . . .

'Labor is not to be fooled with grand epigrams,' said he. 'The working class is becoming better educated all the time and is learning to face facts. Particularly now that he has not had his drink to dull his senses, the laboring man is thinking and capital must realize that this thinking must be met with thought and not pretty words. Of course, there must be working people, and there should be, for work is noble. It is good for prosperity. There must be an adjustment in this country before there can be any degree of contentment, and capital must realize that a little more of the profit must go to the workers. If capital wants to control the situation, it must be on the level.'

This was not quite red-blooded Bolshevism, and perhaps we might revise our speculation on who scrawled the 'IWW' on Mack Sennett's shed door. Chaplin's conservative view of Prohibition might be seen in light of the fact that, at this early stage, the criminal bootleg empire the law gave birth to was as yet a squalling infant. His own view of the demon rum, however much he mimed its dubious delights as the Drunk, was clearly coloured by his own father's fate.

Other reports showed him equally cautious in these interviews, stating that 'my radical views have been much misunderstood. I am not a Socialist, nor am I looking for a new order of things. But I do believe that conditions can be much improved.' He praised Henry Ford, who 'gives value received for his merchandise, and on the other hand he considers his workers, pays them a fair wage, and has made profit-sharing absolutely practicable.' He was in favour of a bonus for returning soldiers, income tax and peace for everybody. 'War is bad for progress and I hope to see all the nations disarm.' He was, surprisingly, supportive of 'intelligent censorship', and to the question 'Will German films cause great competition in this country?' he replied: 'A work of art does not compete – it stimulates.'

In his book, however, Chaplin was at pains to portray himself as an entertainer, not a politician abroad. 'I felt proud that I was in the movies,' he wrote, though there was a downside to fame, as he later described the moment the crowd of fans closed in: 'I felt a draught. I heard machinery. I looked down. A woman with a pair of scissors was snipping a piece from the seat of my trousers. Another grabbed my tie and almost put an end to my suffering through strangulation. My collar was next. But they only got half of that . . .'

In his brief stopover in France, the deluge began in earnest. Once again the marauding pressmen:

'Why did you come over?'

'Did you bring your make-up?'

'Am I going to Russia?'

'What do you think of the Irish question?'

'Are you a Bolshevik?'

In Southampton, he was greeted by the mayor and a host of dignitaries and their relatives. 'I am in England. There is freshness. There is glow. There is nature in its most benevolent mood . . . I am in another world . . .'

Entraining to London, the familiarity of the buildings overwhelmed him, as the train clattered through south London towards Waterloo. Here the crowds were waiting in earnest:

Thousands are outside. This also thrills me. Everything is beyond my expectations . . . There is real warm affection. Do I deserve even a part of it?

A young girl rushes out, breaks the line, makes one leap, and smothers me with a kiss. Thank God, she is pretty . . . They are coming on all sides. Policemen are elbowing and pushing. Girls are shrieking.

'Charlie! Charlie! There he is! Good luck to you, Charlie. God bless you . . .' Bells are ringing. Handkerchieves are waving . . . I am bewildered, at a loss, wondering where it is all leading to, but I don't care. I love to stay in it.

This adulation of the crowd was new, and its overpowering waves washing over from his own native Londoners were intoxicating – and addictive. Everyone, it seemed, wanted a piece of Charlie Chaplin. Even before he arrived, his published plans to visit his old school 'somewhere in Kennington' stirred up instant recollection from such claimants as a Mr T. A. Murch, headmaster of St Agnes Church School, Kennington Park, who told *The Times* that though he had never seen a Chaplin film, he had vivid memories of 'Charlie' as a certain 'curious boy he knew between the years 1904 and 1909'. The school register showed one Chaplin, Charles, son of Chaplin, Charles, at the school till June 1909. 'I last saw him when he was perhaps 16 years old, in Brixton road, a somewhat ludicrous little figure, I thought, with his hands covered with cotton gloves much too long in the fingers,' who spoke of his desire to go on the stage. Chaplin was obliged from New York to deny this story, and name the school he had attended as 'Hanwell, or Handwell Schools, Kennington'. The other 'Charlie' Chaplin remained a mystery.

On 12 September, the London *Times* reported on Chaplin's eagerly awaited visit to his old haunts:

Soon after Chaplin had arrived in London he carried out his intention of slipping away and revisiting the scenes of his childhood. He went to Kennington, to Brixton, where he watched with great delight the efforts of a hawker to dispose of his tin baths; to Vauxhall, and to the New Cut. For the most part he went unrecognized, but it was always the children who 'spotted' him first. At one point a little girl recognized him and was about to spread the news when Chaplin begged her to keep the news to herself: money changed hands and he was able to escape. But occasionally he was detected, and then a hasty flight by taxicab was the best way out of the situation. In the New Cut, he says, he felt like the Pied Piper of Hamelin because though he was recognized the crowd followed him at a distance of a few feet and never attempted to worry him.

Later, at the London Ritz, the journalists besieged him again with questions about unemployment and Bolshevism, 'but he denied the rumour that his next picture was to be *Charlie the Bolshie*'.

Throughout the morning a large crowd awaited his appearance, including two little girls who refused all suggestions from the police that they should 'move on'. They sent up a message to the comedian that they had often been 'spanked' for staying at the pictures to see the Chaplin film twice. Now they were willing to go to prison, but they had no intention of leaving the Ritz until they had seen their hero in the flesh – a request which was eventually granted.

A few days later Charlie did bond with his 'old school', attending a 'special performance at the Globe Picture Theatre at Acton', with an audience of five hundred boys and fifty officials of the Central London District Schools at Hanwell, the proceeds of the performance to be 'handed to the managers of the schools for disposal as they think best'. Chaplin wrote later, in *My Trip Abroad*, about his mixed feelings at revisiting the poverty of his cockney London, observing, even as he crossed Westminster Bridge,

. . . the same old blind man I used to see as a child of five, with the same old earmuffs . . . the same old clothes, a bit greener with age . . . a bit more grey in his matted beard. He has that same stark look in his eyes that used to make me sick as a child. Everything exactly the same, only a bit more dilapidated . . .

London, unchanging London, after the shattering changes and transformations of America . . . But by the time he reached Lambeth, he was ready with his rose-tinted eyes: 'I just walk down Chester Street. Children are playing, lovely children. I see myself among them back there in the past . . . Somehow they seem different from those children with whom I used to play. Sweeter, more dainty were those little, begrimed kids with their arms entwined around one another's waists . . .'

Things do seem different when you revisit them at the distance not only of time but of your own transformed social circumstances, the distance of class transcended, and with the armour of adoration. Charlie is aware, indeed, that 'I am the wrong note in this picture that nature has concentrated here. My clothes are a bit conspicuous in this setting, no matter how unobtrusive my thoughts and actions. Dressed as I am, one never strolls along Lambeth Walk . . .'

He drives past Kennington Cross, 'where music first entered my soul', when, he recalls, he heard a harmonica and a clarinet playing 'The Honeysuckle and the Bee'. But soon he is back across Westminster Bridge, in Haymarket, 'back to the Ritz to dress for dinner'.

There is another England waiting for Chaplin: his friends, his travelling companion the actor Edward Knobloch, driving past Adelphia Terrace, 'where Bernard Shaw and Sir James Barrie live'. Chaplin postpones his meeting with Shaw, but soon he is meeting the 'Immortals': J. M. Barrie, author of *Peter Pan*, meets the author of *The Kid*; Thomas Burke; H. G. Wells, who seems 'very much like an American . . . very young and full of "pep".' They talk of Russia, but appear to come to no conclusions. Chaplin wrote that he thought he came across as flippant, and we might conclude that he was intimidated by these confident gentlemen who had carved out their places with apparent ease. Perhaps he ached for a ballroom which he could skate around, knocking them down with his cane. It may have been this social unease that Thomas Burke picked up when he later wrote of Chaplin that he seemed 'not much interested in people, either individually, or as humanity. The spectacle of life amuses or disturbs him.' Or perhaps it was the English intellectuals who made him twitchy and tense.

From England Chaplin hurried on to France, was greeted as 'Charlot' at Calais and rushed off to Paris, where the language problem stymied his attempts at communication. Crowds mobbed him at Pigalle, but he escaped to enjoy the gay life of the Latin Quarter and drift among its cafes. Then it's off to Berlin, the capital of the terrible enemy of the Great War. But Chaplin finds Germany beautiful: 'Germany belies the war. There are people crowding the fields, tilling the soil, working feverishly all the time as our train rushes through.'

The streets of Berlin, however, are dark and gloomy, still wearing the cloak of war and defeat. The expressionistic Scala Cafe impresses him with its sea-green mottled walls, 'leaning outward at an angle, thereby producing an effect of collapse and forward motion . . . the lights are hidden, the whole system of illumination being based on reflection . . . the whole effect is weird, almost ominous.' (*The Cabinet of Doctor Caligari* had premiered in the US in April 1921.) At the Palais Heinroth, however, there is an American jazz band, and a movie colleague, Al Kaufman of Famous Players-Lasky, who introduces him to Pola Negri. They hit it off: 'Offered a drink, she clinks my glass and offers her only English words, "Jazz boy Charlie."'

Back and forth to Paris and London, Chaplin walks the Lambeth Walk no more, but bonds with poet Sir Philip Sassoon, H. G. Wells again, boxer Georges Carpentier, and a gaggle of princes and princesses, et cetera, at the Paris charity premiere of *The Kid*. His cup runneth over. On the ship back from Southampton, he meets an eight-year-old girl who says to him, 'Oh, Mr. Chaplin . . . I've been looking for you all over the boat. Please adopt me like you did Jackie Coogan. We could smash windows together and have lots of fun.'

'You like smashing windows? You must be Spanish,' says Charlie.

'Oh no,' she says, 'not Spanish; I'm Jewish.'

'That accounts for your genius,' he tells her, 'all great geniuses had Jewish blood in them. No, I am not Jewish,' he hurries to add, 'but I'm sure there must be some somewhere in me. I hope so.' On this throwaway exchange much future speculation ensued.

He returns to New York, meeting Frank Harris and leaving with him on a strange trip to Sing Sing. There, in this 'outcry against civilization', he sees the chastened relatives and loved ones visiting their incarcerated husbands, brothers, the resigned men, their spirit crushed. The cells, 'built by a monster or a maniac . . . built of hate, ignorance and stupidity'. The hideous death house – 'the chair – a plain wooden armchair and a single wire coming down over it . . . cold blooded and matter of fact'.

It would be a quarter of a century before this grim vision would find its way into a Chaplin picture, in *Monsieur Verdoux* . . .

Chaplin has had his holiday. He saw his old haunts, and satisfied himself that they lay in the past. He met new friends, invariably of the rich and famous, and supped with them as 'Jazz boy Charlie'. He did not kick them in the arse, throw punch-bowls in their faces, trip them on the dance floor, stomp on their stomachs, upend them into wells, or propel them in their wheelchairs off the Santa Monica pier. He behaved impeccably, noted down their addresses, collected his hat and coat from the butler, and stepped into his chauffeur-driven limousine.

Iris in, and fade.

17

Pay Day

Back in Los Angeles, Chaplin completed *Pay Day,* the film interrupted when he had rushed off to Europe, and then shot *The Pilgrim*, which fulfilled the eight-picture contract signed with First National in June 1917. *Pay Day*, a workmanlike two-reeler about the perils of a labouring life, reprised a standard comedy formula that preceded Keystone and would remain a staple up to the present day. Reel One: At a building site, comedy biz with bricks, mortar, the foreman and the foreman's daughter unfolds, with a break for lunch-hour gags involving brick-like sandwiches and eggs. Reel Two: the fatigued working man retires to the 'Bachelors Club' en route for home and the harridan wife (played by Phyllis Allen) who leaves him a pittance for his pleasures. 'Solving the peace problem' outside the club, Charlie and fellow clubbers – including brother Syd and Henry Bergman – warble 'Sweet Adeline', do some gags with canes, grates and umbrellas, and then scrum for the last streetcars home – a set of gags akin to Harold Lloyd's many streetcar adventures that were being aired as early as 1919's *Off the Trolley*. Trying to get on board, Charlie is invariably squeezed off the packed carriage, and ends up so boozed he is left hanging on to a sausage in a very static lunch wagon.

Stan Laurel would soon embark on his own solo-starring series of work films with titles such as *The Noon Whistle*, *White Wings*, *Pick and Shovel*, *Collars and Cuffs*, *Gas and Air* and *Oranges and Lemons*, all made in 1923. The situation that closes Chaplin's *Pay Day* is most similar to the later Laurel-and-Hardys: the fearsome wife waiting for him in bed with a rolling pin while he tries to crawl into their room late and drunk. The 5.30 alarm clock foils his drowsy plan and he ends up sleeping fully dressed in the bathtub – close-up on the scolding wife and THE END.

As in *A Day's Pleasure*, and the unused prologue of *Shoulder Arms*, Charlie is miscast as a long-suffering husband, a bona fide working Joe, although still bearing the costume of his peripatetic alter ego, the derby hat, cane and shoes. The building-site gags would be better developed by Stan and Ollie in 1928's *The Finishing Touch* and 1933's *Busy Bodies*, but a piece of business of Charlie building an instant wall with bricks tossed from below up and between his legs must have given him a chance to use the trick he had discarded in *Behind the Screen* of filming a shot in reverse motion. *Pay Day* is better shot than previous Chaplins and the night scenes look forward in their contrasty light and shadow to the atmospheric sequences of *A Woman of Paris*. The warbling drunks in the night and the monstrous streetcars sliding off with people hung like bunches of grapes are vintage Americana, evoking, with some of the tenement scenes of *The Kid*, the same world of melancholy urban observation that later defined artists like Edward Hopper.

Chaplin's First National films tend to inhabit a more specifically American world than many of his previous films, with their continual return to London's Lambeth memories. Even *A Dog's Life*, with its strong autobiographical echoes, was defined in planning, as we have seen from its continuity script, as taking place on New York's Lower East Side. In its harsh depiction, it could have been spliced on to the first reel of *The Immigrant*, as an alternative trajectory of the pathetic waif fresh off the boat. *The Kid* straddled both the Old World and the New, while *The Idle Class* could be set anywhere where the rich cavorted among their own. *The Pilgrim*, however, was wholly an American tale, and was titled 'Western' in its working draft.

This is the first Chaplin for which preliminary script notes survive, depicting Charlie as one of a group of escaped convicts who dresses as a clergyman and fetches up in the town of 'Hell's Hinges', a den of iniquity, as the notes state: 'Men rough with women . . . Card game that ends in a fight . . . gun play . . . Show a Chinaman or two shot down by the rough element in casual fashion . . .' Charlie was supposed to be mistaken for a new reforming minister come to replace the failed previous incumbent. In the film the plot is simplified to change the location to a typical small-town hick congregation, with a saloon robbery coming in to chivvy the plot along close to the end. The gags mostly derive from Charlie dissimulating in the embrace of 'proper' society. The harsh mockery of rural churchy America that was so awkward in *Sunnyside* has segued to a more gentle satire, with Syd Chaplin again playing a foil, this time a buttoned-up father whose little boy torments Charlie, much as Baby LeRoy would torment W. C. Fields a few years down the line. Just as Fields would do, however, Charlie boots the offending child in the rear. The final image of the film, when the sheriff has unceremoniously thrown him over the border into a gun-torn Mexican desert, with Charlie rushing along the border, one foot in and one foot outside America, was a perfect metaphor for his divided allegiance, his reluctance to become a US citizen. In his later feature scripts, the title page would always read:

A DRAMATIC COMPOSITION
by
CHARLES SPENCER CHAPLIN
of
GREAT BRITAIN
Domiciled in the United States
At Los Angeles, California.

The Pilgrim was a bona fide, if slightly askew, adventure for the Tramp, on the run from one of his clearly regular episodes doing penal time – an aspect of his life that would have to await *Modern Times* of 1936. His creator, however, was still not convinced that he could not escape the constrictions of the tramp mask. Documents show that Chaplin was offering an alternative to First National in case they turned down *The Pilgrim*, in the shape of a two-reel picture called *The Professor*. This appears to have been a fragment of a film begun but not completed in 1919, during the period when Chaplin was shooting *The Kid* and in the midst of the interruption of *Pay Day*. Kevin Brownlow and David Gill found a five-minute (450-foot) sequence of this film which is included in their *Unknown Chaplin*.

The Professor, if completed, would have been the most radical departure Chaplin took from both the Tramp and his alter ego, the Drunk. The surviving scene takes place in a dosshouse similar to the one first seen in *Police* and then reprised in *The Kid*. The tramp costume has been replaced by a long coat and top hat, more akin to the spiv in *Making a Living*, and the moustache has grown to a fairly hefty black brush. An introductory shot shows the Professor staggering down a dingy street, carrying a box. As he enters, weary, into the dosshouse, picking out a coin for the proprietor, we can make out the label on his box: BOSCO'S FLEA CIRCUS.

There follows the most elaborate sketch of the flea act that Chaplin would try several times to include and then drop from his films until it fluttered on to the screen in *Limelight*. Itching and scratching, the

Professor extracts one of his fleas from inside his jacket and rehearses its leap from fist to fist. Spying a sleeping man scratching his beard he pounces to extract a flea, which turns out to be a freelance and is carefully put back in the beard. As Bosco lies down to sleep, his foot knocks over the box. Massed scratching erupts among the dingy beds. Bosco leaps up, taking out his circus-master's whip and ordering the fleas, one by one, to return to their box. The final missing miscreant located, all go back to sleep. But a mangy dog, nuzzling in the box, lets the fleas loose again and begins biting itself in a frenzy. Bosco wakes, sees the dog and pursues it desperately out of the dosshouse and into the street from whence he came.

This brief and tantalizing glimpse of Bosco is a rare window into so many Chaplin might-have-beens. Bosco is neither Tramp nor Drunk but a wholly realized other character, an exhausted foot-soldier of the army of vaudevilleans that trudged the boards of small-time variety or the ubiquitous freak shows, fairground and medicine shows that traversed turn-of-the-twentieth-century America, keeping one step ahead of destitution, or, in Bosco's case, already fallen. Chaplin's great skill is evident in the way in which slight variations in body language and facial tension turn the familiar into a completely new mask. The hair is thick but slicked down with some kind of lubricant, as if the man still has some vanity of his appearance; the corncob pipe clutched in the teeth denotes a determination to control. Some part of the itching and scratching is still of Charlie, but the walk is different, less jaunty, strongly evoking, even in a few steps, the long march of an unemployed but self-imagined master of his minuscule universe. For the beauty of the sequence, of course, as of the brief moment in *The Vagabond* when Charlie catches flies for Edna, is that there are no fleas in reality – there is only Charlie Chaplin's peerless mime.

By July 1922, Chaplin had finished *The Pilgrim*, and with it his conflict-ridden contract with First National, and was free to start work on his first production for the creative hub of United Artists. His book on his European tour, *My Trip Abroad*, had already been published in April. The *New York Times* wrote of it that readers would find revealed in it 'another Charlie, and a very different one from the humorous star of the movies. They will find a young man eager to see things of consequence and to meet people who count in the world, who has his own ideas about the world's problems and who wants, above all things, to get at the heart of life and see and touch its inmost springs.'

In the mulch of these experiences of a homecoming to a different social world of intellectuals like Barrie and Wells who treated him as their equal, and the limpid memories of Berlin and Paris, grew very quickly the kernel of a different kind of movie from those he had made so far. Already in *The Kid* there were ambitions to make a statement, to speak out about matters other than the fate of flea-circus masters or the happy hooligans of Keystone-born mayhem. But there is no doubt that Chaplin, becoming more and more omnivorous and conscious of art, his own included, would have been aware of a different kind of cinema emerging, both foreign and home-grown. The Scandinavian films of directors such as Mauritz Stiller were known in America since the early 1910s, with adult-themed social satires such as *Thomas Graal's Saga*, also known as *Marriage à la Mode*, of 1918. Chaplin never acknowledged a debt to Stiller, nor to the US satirizer of 'modern' marriage, Cecil B. DeMille, though he could hardly have been ignorant of his hit adultery and divorce movies such as *Old Wives For New, Don't Change Your Husband* or 1921's *The Affairs of Anatol*. In all these movies DeMille made use not only of flighty heroines like Gloria Swanson, but of sets and props deriving from the French-inspired movement of Art Nouveau, and the seeds of the later Art Deco. These were part of a trend, in post-war America, of examining the entrails of male and female relationships, mixed with sharp observation of new cultural trends of material consumption and the temptations of the 'Jazz' age.

From another direction, Chaplin was aware that his Art, with a capital 'A', was being discussed by the self-appointed high priests of new intellectual movements, particularly in France, where as early as 1915 Guillaume Apollinaire, poet and enthusiast for all artistic innovations, took his friend, the artist Fernand Léger, to a movie theatre while Léger was on leave from the army. Léger, already a major force among innovators and rebels such as Picasso and Braque, a cubist turned 'tubist' in his own startling paintings, recalled being utterly taken by this 'funny little guy, a kind of living object, dry, jerky, black and white, with nothing of the theatre about him . . . For me he was the first image man . . . He depersonalizes himself and reaches the depths of life, the drama of human destiny, by means of the plastic rhythm of gesture and the most total silence.' Léger drew and painted Charlie several times, including a series of panels (in 1923) for an unmade animated film, *Charlot Cubiste*, representing 'Charlie as a mechanism'.

Another major player to be, the proto-surrealist Luis Buñuel, recorded how he and his fellow students in Madrid adored the silent American comics, though they appeared to prefer the grotesque antics of Ben Turpin and the Keystone madcaps to the more urbane – and more popular – Charlie. But in France, by 1922, 'Charlot' was an idol, exemplified by this encomium published by Elie Faure – already well into his multi-volume *Histoire de l'art* – a pioneer of the idea that the cinema, the perfect child of the machine age, was the primary art form of the twentieth century:

Poor Charlot! People love him, and pity him, and yet he makes them sick with laughter. It is because he bears within him, like a burden which he cannot lay aside even for an instant – except when he calls forth from us a joy which helps him to endure it – the genius that belongs to the great comic spirits. Like them he has that exquisite imagination which enables him to discover in every incident and in every act of daily life, a reason for suffering a little or much . . . and for seeing the vanity that lies beneath the charm and splendor of appearances. Before Chaplin came we knew that beneath all drama there is farce, and beneath all farce there is drama, but what do we not know now! This man appears, and by his revelation he has taught us to recognize all that we dimly knew before . . .

By his spirit, Chaplin conquers fate and removes the sting from death, therefore the Gods flee from him:

. . . because Chaplin judges impersonally the passions which devastate him; and even if he accepts their domination, he refuses to yield them his respect. Thus he wins the right to judge our passions and to make us face without shame our own infirmity, our own wretchedness and our own despair . . . Chaplin can make us laugh at hunger itself. His meal at the coffee-stall, his tricks to hide his pilferings and to appear absent-minded and indifferent, even at the moment when his hunger is sharpest . . . and the policeman is approaching: these things draw their comic force from sufferings that seem least suitable for laughter. Why then, do we laugh, when we ourselves have been hungry, when our children have been hungry? Mainly, I think, especially where the contrast is all the more terrible, because of the victory of the spirit over his own torment. Than this there is nothing that so stamps a man as a man, whether he be a clown or a poet.

Faure's words may have resonated strangely to Chaplin, when they were translated in the *New York Times* in March 1922. But his own trip to

Europe would have helped him realize that, while Americans mainly took to Charlie's antics for sheer entertainment, in war-ravaged Europe, in the wake of four years of disaster and misery, audiences read a Message in the pure rebelliousness of his attitude to life's ordeals. Millions of soldiers returned from the front in complete despair at a world churned into mud and blood by overwhelming folly. While America rushed into the brassy cadences of jazz and ballyhoo, goggling at Gloria Swanson's gowns, Paris and Berlin danced in cabarets that celebrated smoky ruins, while art found new anarchic, 'Dadaist' and later 'surrealist' shapes, dreamlike landscapes of a twisted continent, the provocative protests of George Grosz's dark urban nightmares or Otto Dix's *Cardplaying War Cripples* and Goya-like drawings of the war's trenches. We might be brought up short today, reading a well-fed intellectual like Faure assuming that 'we ourselves have been hungry', but for that generation, this was no mere fancy.

And so Chaplin was aware that, at least in some circles, he was being taken seriously, and that in his own art there were new trends and departures, even if, much later, in his *Autobiography*, he was to claim about his next film that 'it was the first of the silent pictures to articulate irony and psychology'. As ever, Chaplin wished to represent himself and his ideas as *sui generis*, arising from his own insights and intuitions, rather than a recognition that the movies had moved on. DeMille apart, the maverick Erich von Stroheim had just released, in January 1922, his third directed feature, *Foolish Wives*, denounced by *Photoplay* magazine as 'an insult to every American . . . a gruesome, morbid, unhealthy tale . . . that sickens you before you have seen it half told'. Since his first film as director, *Blind Husbands*, of 1919, Stroheim had been innovative in the use of psychology to drive the plot-lines of his tales of seduction and betrayal in European settings. From *Blind Husbands*, he set new benchmarks in the 'realistic' portrayal of emotions, with his characters reacting to each other as they would in real life, rather than in the accepted convention of the movies. 'Realism' was long a target for film-makers, to capture, even in the speechless gestures of the silent picture, truths of life, relationships and the inner thoughts of people. Chaplin had brought this principle very effectively into comedy. There was no reason why he should not try it, as the '*nouveau Charlot*', in drama.

Naturally, however, he could not expect audiences to accept him on the screen in a serious part. Changing costume and mask would not be enough. Chaplin would have to stay behind the camera, resolutely off screen. And so his next feature would be heralded by an announcement:

TO THE PUBLIC – IN ORDER TO AVOID ANY MISUNDERSTANDING. I WISH TO ANNOUNCE THAT I DO NOT APPEAR IN THIS PICTURE. IT IS THE FIRST SERIOUS DRAMA WRITTEN AND DIRECTED BY MYSELF.

18

A Woman of Paris – A Man of Los Angeles

Time and Destiny
are relentless and they plunge humans in strange byways–
some rise by sin while many fall by virtue–
fate has blazed no stranger trail than that path
taken by Marie Arnette–

For the first time, Chaplin had no option but to have a proper script, or at least copious notes for a script, well in advance of shooting. He made a decision which would have been considered extravagant for any normal producer working to budgetary constraints and studio schedules: to shoot his movie drama in consecutive order – in the chronological time of the story. This was a great boon to the actors, who could follow the plot-line as if in stage time, but wasteful for set builders who would have to hold their sets idle while the story proceeded elsewhere before returning to a locale already used. But Chaplin was swimming in money. Testimony at the long-running trust suit against Famous Players-Lasky (who were accused of controlling the film industry) in May 1923 showed, in an intriguing sidebar, that Chaplin had made $1,400,000 from *The Kid*, of which his own company pocketed one million. This was in addition to whatever sums Chaplin had trousered from the original million-dollar First National contract plus additional sums of $100,000 per picture for the later two- and three-reelers.

The rich man proceeded, for the first time, to examine the milieu of social climbers and arrivistes that he had been able to observe in the course of his own leap to the top. The story, legend and Chaplin himself recount, derived from a combination of factors: Chaplin was looking for a non-comedy idea to star Edna Purviance, who was still his leading lady despite being replaced in his personal life with younger and more ambitious women, like the German star Pola Negri and the vivacious social climber of the century, barber's daughter Peggy Hopkins Joyce, who had segued a job in the Ziegfeld chorus into a marry-go-round with a series of millionaires. She had run away with a vaudeville bicyclist at the age of sixteen and zoomed to celebrity status with only her natural charms and unlimited confidence, unburdened by any great artistic talent. She may be viewed with W. C. Fields in the portmanteau movie *International House* of 1932, the butt of a blue joke that got by the censors, when he loses his cat while both are in his 'gyrocopter' and she exclaims: 'I'm sitting on something!' to which Fields ripostes: 'It's a pussy!' Four years before, she teased Harpo Marx by inviting him to dinner at her villa in Monte Carlo, only to lay upon him a stack of comic books, from which he had to read out all the 'Bang! Sock! Pow!' dialogue. In 1922, she already had a stack of her own stories, tales of her adventures in Paris with 'a well-known French publisher', a Monsieur Henri Letellier, one of the many glittering guests at the French premiere of *The Kid* that Chaplin had attended the year before.

Peggy's tales of Parisian high life and gaiety chimed with Chaplin's memories of Montmartre and its restaurants, in one of which he recorded, in *My Trip Abroad*, an encounter with a dazzling Russian singer-dancer: 'There is something refined and distinguished about the little girl. She is different. Doesn't belong here. I am watching her very closely, though she has never once looked my way. I like this touch of the unusual in Montmartre . . .' The girl dazzles him and some unlikely dialogue ensues about her origins as the daughter of a Tsarist general and a Bolshevik mother. Though Chaplin fantasizes about introducing her to a life of stardom in America or in the French Follies, nothing comes of this.

Between bouncy Peggy and Montmartre's Russian 'Skaya', and the need to fit something around Edna's melancholy and declining beauty, the new project, first named *Time and Destiny*, began resolving itself into central characters: Marie Arnette, later to become Marie St Clair, the woman 'for whom Fate has blazed no stranger trail'. Pierre Revel, a rich philanderer, 'the modern paradox' who 'makes a supreme ceremony of living and a mere gesture of the conquest of big business'. Marie's flighty friends – 'Fifi, a joyous little lady from the Follies and a friend of Marie' and Paulette – 'another daughter of pleasure and companion to Marie and Fifi'. The story that would link them swirled in a flurry of aphoristic notes and exploratory intertitles:

The consciousness of our misery is all the more bitter when we learn that others know our plight . . .

King 'Jazz' promises that brand of joy and laughter that will banish worry if only for a moment . . .

Innocent intentions often give birth to dangerous results – a woman may love her lover but mostly she loves, love.

The force is yet to be found that will successfully combat the call of youth and the repression of nature makes its conquest all the more inevitable . . .

One of her greatest charms, inconsistency, has always been with woman whose brain will seldom sit in agreement with her heart . . .

That interference which brings forth the perpetual clash between love and duty leads often to sorrow because of the moral cowardice that is a part of all of us . . .

The quarrels of lovers are often but the renewal of love . . .

Revenge is a weird sort of Justice but human beings often have weird thirsts . . .

Those who would inflict must also be prepared to suffer . . .

Women: past, present and future – Victims when wrong and martyrs when right.

Youth fades, love laughs, friends vanish but a mother remains – a mother . . .

The story that emerged was of Edna as Marie, 'a woman of Paris . . . woman of fate, a victim of the environment of an unhappy home'. She is introduced in the film in a velvet small-town night, preparing to meet her lover, with whom she plans to elope under the gimlet eye of her father, who bolts the door against her return after their tryst. When she tries to get in, he refers her sternly to her boyfriend: 'Perhaps he will provide you a bed for the night.'

Meanwhile the 'boy', Jean, played by Carl Miller, is also a victim of the prejudice of his father, against whose hard moral tone – 'Get that woman out of this house!' – his tender mother is helpless. The lovers decide to elope to Paris, and go to the town railway station to check out the trains. These early scenes already reveal Rollie Totheroh's ability to rise from the journeyman role of just photographing Chaplin, as it might have seemed to many. A restored print enables us to gauge the fine tones of the high-contrast shafts of light in shadow. A simple trick of passing a plank with holes in it before a strong light provides the illusion of a train's lighted windows reflected as Edna stands waiting on the platform. Jean has gone home to pack his bags before rejoining her, but after a last confrontation with his parents, the father has fallen dead. Edna calls Jean from the station, and he tells her their elopement must be postponed, but she turns from the phone before he can explain to her why. In despair, she takes the train to Paris alone. Chaplin makes a pre-Hitchcock-type appearance in the scene as a porter who just dumps a trunk and hurries out of the frame, as unrecognized as he entered.

'A year later in the magic city of Paris, where fortune is fickle and a woman gambles with life . . .' Marie's life has been transformed, from country runaway to the mistress of Pierre Revel, 'a gentleman of leisure, whose whims have made and ruined many a woman's career'. The casting of this role was the grand success of the film, as Adolphe Menjou inhabits the part to the manner born.

Before *A Woman of Paris* Menjou had already appeared in over thirty films, mostly in small parts. He had a supporting role beside Valentino in *The Sheik*, and had played Louis XIII in *The Three Musketeers*, both in 1921. There was nothing in his background to suggest the sophisticated seducer he would become in movies from the moment Chaplin placed the star upon his brow. Born to a French-American father and Irish mother in Pittsburgh in 1890, he had eluded the career of a restaurateur like his father to enter vaudeville and later the films. Some said he was sighted on screen as early as 1912. Legend has him pointed out to Chaplin by Peggy Hopkins Joyce in a restaurant as a good bet for Revel. In his own account, he shadowed Chaplin to his favourite Hollywood Boulevard eateries, arriving 'coincidentally' at the same time in suitably elegant attire, asking for 'fresh escargots in white wine sauce'. More likely it was Edward Sutherland, Chaplin's assistant on the film, who suggested the dapper man for the role. Within a year, he was launched on his career as the suave man of the world in Ernst Lubitsch's *The Marriage Circle*, itself directly inspired by Chaplin's movie. Lubitsch's movie inaugurated a new type of sophisticated comedy both in his own work and for those who came after him, including, along the daisy chain, the early Frank Capra, Rouben Mamoulian, Preston Sturges, and, across the ocean, Michael Powell.

A Woman of Paris remains unique for its demonstration of Chaplin as director. Chaplin always favoured a 'theatrical' style of filming, in which the camera most often films the action head on, as if each composition were a stage. Great argument has raged back and forth over this concept, between those who see this as a fundamentally 'uncinematic' flaw in Chaplin's movies and those who argue that this kind of filming is a no less valid way of shooting films than any other. It was functional, and served the main purpose, when Charlie was on screen, of presenting the character to the best advantage, of his actions, his body language, movements and gestures. As in the traditional way cinema covered dance – before recent assumptions that no audience can watch a shot for more than a few seconds – there was a necessity to see the moves in their context, often in standard long shots, then in close-ups if emphasis was needed. The last thing one wanted in comedy was some gimmick – an unconventional angle, an unnecessary montage, anything that distracted from the performance. Exceptions were the grand trickery of some of Buster Keaton's riffs on modern life's thrall to machinery, or his surreal changes of locale and scenery behind a static motor car in *Sherlock Junior*. Chaplin did not favour this kind of thing: the Tramp was anchored firmly to reality.

Chaplin's primary approach to his projects was nevertheless overtly theatrical. In later scripts, such as *The Gold Rush* and even into *The Great Dictator*, an early draft would be an actual stage play, with instructions such as 'Curtain up' and prop setting to 'right' or 'left' of stage. In the case of *Limelight*, it was practically a novel, a narrative text which explained the detailed background of his characters to a level not presented on the screen.

Chaplin remained forever a vaudevillean, imbued with the sense of the stage event and its audience. Like all other stage comedians turned film actors, he fretted endlessly about the fact that one could not gauge the effect on the audience until the film was finally cut and shown. This obvious obstacle lay at the root of his almost pathological reshooting and experimenting with every possible permutation of a comic idea, until something clicked in his mind and the 'Eureka' moment dawned – THIS shot, THIS situation, not the others. It was in this sense that a script was of minimal use to him in comedy. Of course, once scenes were shot, their content was recorded, and this emerged in the cutting continuities which followed, not preceded, the filming.

In drama, Chaplin still followed the stage idea, shooting directly head-on to his actors. In *A Woman of Paris*, this resulted in great attention being paid to the content of each frame, the light, the decor, the architecture of the village houses, the glittering nature of the Paris restaurants, cafes, boudoirs and living rooms. Since Chaplin was shooting in his studio, his ersatz Paris had to come to life in its carefully planned details, furnishings and props. This much is obvious, but Chaplin pushed it further, into the details of the movement, responses and psychology of the characters. If the early scenes, with their unyielding fathers, expressed a kind of harsh Protestant America underlying the paternalistic French Catholicism, the Paris scenes expressed the combination of freedom, luxury, indolence and decadence that Chaplin had observed on his visit.

'From the drabness of the village to the gayety of Paris,' Edna as Marie arrives at a lush cafe with Pierre, all haute couture with feathered hat. As they take their table, they are compared with another couple, a louche and bored young man accompanying 'one of the richest old maids in Paris'. Revel, 'the richest bachelor in Paris', is waited on hand and foot by the maître d', played by Henry Bergman, who serves them the speciality, champagne truffles. The title explains to us that these are 'Truffles rooted out of the soil by hogs – a delicacy for pigs and gentlemen,' a dig Chaplin clearly couldn't pass up. Before the serving, Pierre has taken a visit to the kitchen, where the chef is enthusing over some odorous fowl delicacy – probably woodcock – which all the other kitchen-crew are holding their noses at, but complains after Pierre has gone that, 'These perfumed handkerchieves stink my kitchen out.'

At table there is the highest level of service and hierarchy – the maître d' even bawls out the assistant waiter who has the effrontery to pour the champagne himself. All is perfect, apart from the many worms in the apple that have already been signalled.

Marie's apartment too is of the highest luxury money can buy. The maid dutifully dusts and friend Fifi turns up to try to budge Marie from her bed. Back in his own pad, lying by his unwinding ticker-tape, Pierre enjoys reading the society magazine which features his coming wedding to a suitable lady of his class: 'Event will link large fortunes.' Marie's friends discuss the magazine but she pretends not to be put out by it. Pierre arrives to find her mildly distressed: 'You're not worried about that, are you?' he asks, adding, 'it makes no difference to us, we can go on just the same.'

This is certainly a very non-American story, and it is the reaction of the characters to each other that sets the film in Paris, more than its decor, thoroughly researched as it was by Chaplin's two assistants, Comte Jean de Limur and Henri d'Abbadie d'Arrast, a future Hollywood director himself. Chaplin coaxed from his actors a difficult mixture of light banter underlaid with Edna/Marie's anxiety and the fragility of her existence. One scene often picked out by critics has her undergoing a massage while her girlfriends prattle about their affairs. Chaplin cast his studio secretary, Nellie Bly Baker, as a workmanlike masseuse. As her hands ply professionally over Marie's back, the masseuse's face subtly reveals her disapproving thoughts about these hedonistic girls, the scene becoming a small masterclass in expressing class-division succinctly and with elegant style. The other class division of the film is more overt – Jean, Marie's village lover, has also found his way to Paris, with his widowed mother, and plies his trade as an artist in the Latin Quarter.

Chaplin took great pains to make coincidences work organically and logically in the film. Marie is on her way to a wild party in the Latin Quarter but goes to the wrong house, where she finds Jean. 'Time makes strangers of old friends and formality covers their real emotions,' says the title. In this scene, she finally discovers the reason Jean had not come to the station to join her, his father's death that night. She commissions him to paint her portrait, so that they can meet again. But when he paints her, it is as she was in the village, not as she models herself in her Parisian gown and hat. 'Why bring up the past?' she asks. 'Because I knew you better then,' he replies. Still in love, he offers her marriage, to begin a new life.

Marie's subsequent scene with Pierre Revel plays out her anguish against his lassitude. Chaplin places him on a chair tooting on a horn while she tries to express her true feelings. 'I want a real home, babies and a man's respect.' Pierre shows her, out the window, real marriage, an exhausted man and a woman, their kids in tow, staggering across the street. He points out her advantages, luxury, pearls. She tears her pearls off and throws them out of the window, only for them to be picked up quickly by a passing tramp. In a touch that Ernst Lubitsch – among many – would learn from Chaplin, she rushes out of the house, down the road and snatches her pearls back from the tramp, while Revel can't contain his amusement. Coming back, she merely comments, 'Idiot!', while he continues to laugh.

Within the standards of melodrama, Chaplin was learning to make the silent film reflect human beings in the really convincing details of a relationship. Throughout there are small touches and revelatory bits of business: Revel casually entering Marie's apartment and finding his handkerchief in her chest of drawers, showing that they share the room and bed. Later, when Jean comes to see her, Revel enters again and one of his collars drops out of the drawer, revealing the facts of their life to Jean. More than in his travails as the Tramp, Chaplin demonstrates in *A Woman of Paris* the acuteness of his observation of the minutiae of people's foibles. It gives the lie to Thomas Burke's statement that Chaplin was not deeply 'interested in people, either individually, or as humanity. The spectacle of life amuses or disturbs him.' But that amusement or disturbance was at a high level of perception.

The film wraps up in a conventional manner. Jean proposes to Marie but his mother objects – 'it's the type of woman she is.' Marie reaches their door just in time to hear him agree in a weak moment to renege on his proposal. Pierre consoles himself with Marie's friend Paulette, but she returns to him and they dine at the restaurant, where the girls are literally swinging above the ballroom floor. Jean takes a gun and follows them to the restaurant. He tussles with Pierre and then goes off into the lobby, by a large ornamental fountain. The shot of his suicide off screen reverberates in Marie's sudden shock. Marie faints by Jean's body. The police take the body home to his mother, asking policemen's questions: 'What was your son's age? Was he a resident of Paris?' In a somewhat implausible touch, the mother picks up Jean's pistol and goes looking for Marie, but comes back after a fruitless search to find her weeping over Jean's corpse. The two women recognize that 'Time heals, and experience teaches that the secret of happiness is in service to others.' In early script notes for this scene (when Revel was called by another name, Poiret) Chaplin put it thus:

News broken to boy's mother – She reads the real truth in the evasions of those who tell her – Knows it is the woman – resolves to kill – takes gun as she bundles herself in her clothes and goes to her boy with revenge in her heart for girl – there is no chance – Doctors can do nothing – Boy dies on sumptuous bed in home of man who took woman from him – Mother arrives goes to room and there sobbing at bedside is notorious woman – mother falls on other side of bed and thus these two women so far removes [sic] that they live in different worlds, meet on common ground in their grief – Gone are her thoughts of revenge – They clasp each other in their arms and weep for the boy.

Then reaction – in her boudoir with Poiret holding her hands nervous – reporters – headlines in papers – very ill and getting a sentimental emotional knot from this grief – Show vanity even as she is in tears fixing her hair before mirror – Poiret very tender and kind – most considerate of her grief – She wants to go away – is sick of her erotic life – wants to go back to clean living and right thinking – Poiret pleads common sense though he does not become violent – But she resolves to leave – he offers money – she takes it – he shrugs shoulders – Figures and predicts she'll be back – She says 'Never' – Poiret moved at their parting. Poiret will get another woman – If Hope looks good when she returns he will let her come back – It is his scheme of life – Things of the sort do not worry him.

She goes away to Central America [crossed out] Canada. . .

None of the stuff with 'Poiret' is in the movie. We fade from the corpse of Jean Millet to see Edna surrounded by children in a village house, with mother. Then 'father' comes in – the priest – and we gather the facts of Marie's new vocation. The priest says to her: 'Young lady, when are you going to get married and have some of your own?' But she goes off in a cart with a group of yokels and an accordion. Meanwhile, as Pierre's car, en route to Paris, whizzes through the countryside, his companion in the back seat asks: 'Whatever became of Marie St Clair?' Pierre shrugs, as his car passes the cart at great speed.

In another alternative end – in notes written intriguingly on blank Western Union telegrams – Pierre sends her a cheque for her orphans. He comes down to her village in his car and Edna meets him. He tells her: 'You know where you can find me. I shall always love you. Goodbye.' This idea was developed further, along the lines of a reconciliation. But Chaplin eventually decided that there was no point in granting Pierre Revel this redemption.

Agonizing about his ending, Chaplin even toyed with the idea of Marie going off to redeem herself in a leper colony. But this was clearly a passage too far. David Robinson describes this process as the standard way that Chaplin refined his scenes down to the essential kernel of the idea. But it is, arguably, a weak coda, which bolsters rather than challenges received ideas.

The weak ending may reflect Chaplin's uncertainty about his own powers as a director of drama, as well as the contradictions of his own upbringing and origins. Man of the world as he was beginning to see himself, he was still a poor kid from Victorian London who had made good, still an onlooker in many ways upon the feast of the fortunate and the wise. He was thirty-four years old. His father had been a drunk and his mother was still mentally ill. In the moral world from whence he came, there were wages of sin that could not be withheld. The innocent suffered while the guilty made hay. Nevertheless, he had created, in the character of Pierre Revel, quite literally a reveller who made his own fate, cushioned by his wealth from the perils of poverty, and by his supreme self-confidence from the consequences of his exploitation of others. In conventional terms, he had sinned egregiously against Marie St Clair, and she had sinned in her acceptance of his poisoned chalice. Jean Millet, on the other hand, was unlucky – tragedies befell him by bad timing and chance, but he was also crippled by the pride of the humble, the inability to rise above his misfortunes. The pride of the poor was punished by death. The weakness of the woman was redeemed by pious kindness. The cheerful sins of the seducer, on the other hand, were unpunished.

Should one read more than the mere creative flourish of the narrative artist into this? In a sense, Chaplin had redeemed his own relationship with Edna Purviance with the film. He had given her, at the moment of her decline, a starring role which she would not have had otherwise. He could not have known that within three months of the film's premiere she would fall from grace, in the latest of the series of scandals that had begun with the Fatty Arbuckle case of 1921 and continued with the unsolved murder of director William Desmond Taylor in February 1922, bringing the full wrath of the reformers down upon Hollywood. On New Year's Eve 1923, Edna and her friend, Mabel Normand, were caught in the house of one Courtland S. Dines, '35-year-old oil operative and clubman of Denver', when Dines was shot by Mabel's chauffeur, Horace A. Greer (alias Joe Kelly), who turned out to be a fugitive from a chain gang. The chauffeur's tale was that Dines had got Mabel drunk and was about to assault her, so he acted in self-defence. Mabel's alibi was that she was with Edna Purviance at the time, and that neither was involved. The press said the chauffeur was 'full of hop'.

Rather than the temptations of Paris and the champagne truffles, it was good old Hollywood sex and drugs and booze that brought down both the Hollywood stars. Mabel's own new film, *The Extra Girl*, had premiered some weeks after *A Woman of Paris*, but the two films suffered from the outrage of moralists and the decision of various state censors to withdraw them both. The press also reported that Edna might be dropped from the new film that her mentor, Charlie Chaplin, was casting at the beginning of 1924. Chaplin was quoted as denying 'that the publicity arising from the Dines shooting would influence his choice'. But, in the event, she did not star in his next film, *The Gold Rush*.

Chaplin, on the other hand, continuing his charmed life, had already moved on from the 'bizarre but brief' wooing of Peggy Hopkins Joyce to the embrace of Pola Negri, which lasted through the shooting of *A Woman in Paris*, with an engagement announced by the press and then cancelled in July 1923. 'Recently', said the *New York Times* on 29 July,

... it was whispered in motion picture circles that all was not well with their romance, but there was nothing definite until Friday night, when both were seen at a public place of amusement, but not together. Chaplin was escorting Leonore Ulrich, the actress. With Miss Negri were William T. Tilden 2nd, national tennis champion and Manuel Alonso, Spanish tennis star, now playing in the Southern California championship tournament.

Said Miss Negri:

Mr. Chaplin is a charming fellow ... We are still friends. I say 'Hello' to him, but I realize now I never could have married him. He is too temperamental, as changing as the wind. He dramatizes everything. He experiments in love. He has no quality for matrimony. I am glad it is over, for it was interfering with my life, my work. I have great ambitions, and I am sure I could not be a great actress as Mrs. Chaplin. Yes, I am glad it is over, and I have profited by the experience.

Other reporters described her spitting all this out through a mouthful of peaches, which 'she disposed of ... as completely as she had disposed of Charlie Chaplin'. He seemed to have been relieved to see her go. He could then concentrate on his own publicity, rather than hers, and prepare the grand premiere of *A Woman of Paris* at the Criterion Theatre on 26 September, a sumptuous event that attracted Hollywood's cream: Irving Thalberg, Mack Sennett, Fairbanks and Pickford, DeMille et al. For the New York premiere a few days later Chaplin added a note to the programme which suggested his somewhat uncertain mood:

In my first serious drama ... I've striven for realism, true to life ... However, it is not for me to say that I am right. My first thoughts have been to entertain you. The story is intimate, simple and human, presenting a problem as old as the ages – showing it with as much truth as I am allowed to put into it . . . I do not wish that *A Woman of Paris* should appear as a preachment, nor am I expounding a sort of philosophy, unless it be an appeal for a better understanding of human frailties . . .

I was over seven months making *A Woman of Paris* and I enjoyed every moment of the time. However, if I have failed in my effort to entertain you, I feel it will be my loss. Nevertheless I enjoyed making it, and sincerely hope you will enjoy seeing it.

Critics raved, Robert Sherwood claiming in the *New York Herald* that 'there is more real genius in Charles Chaplin's *A Woman of Paris* than in any other picture I have ever seen'. *Variety* commented that 'Chaplin . . . straying far from his haunts of yore, comes forth as a new genius both as producer and director.' *The New York Times* chimed in with 'this film lives, and the more directors emulate Mr. Chaplin the better will it be for the producing of pictures.'

If critics ever could make a picture, Chaplin's future as a dramatic director would have been assured. But the audiences did not warm to the idea of a Chaplin behind the camera rather than on the screen. The seven-week run at the LA Criterion netted Chaplin about $40,000, but at the New York Lyric a meagre four weeks resulted in a net loss of nearly the same sum ($39,405.41). Costing $350,000 to make, Chaplin's first drama was measuring up to be a flop. As a rich producer, he could afford to absorb the losses. But the message that audiences were conveying could not be mistaken: We want Charlie Chaplin, but not the famous artist – the Tramp.

19

The Gold Rush

*Or: 'A Stowaway? Heck, that's Big Jim's
partner – the Multimillionaire!'*

A Script in 3 acts–

Act 1

Scene: The interior of a miner's cabin in Alaska. Many miles from any habitation; out in the open spaces.

Description of setting: A rough boarded cabin . . . Door at right and left stage . . . Door in upstage rear . . . Window left and right upper wall . . . Bunk in upstage against rear wall under window. Bunk upstage against side wall (right). Stove on left side (center). Table center; chair and box under table. Shelves on side walls; dishes, pots and pans etc. Blankets, etc. on beds.

At curtain – The lone prospector is seen peering through window (rear); sees cabin empty; slowly enters; sits on bed (rear); his dog sits by him. He looks round cabin; sees large bone in box (right); comes forward; ravenously starts gnawing bone; breaks off piece and gives it to dog as–

Black Larsen enters (Larsen owns cabin, and is a fugitive from justice and has been hiding in this out of the way place)

LARSEN: WHAT ARE YOU DOING HERE?
LONELY: I'M LOST AND HUNGRY – I SAW THE CABIN AND CAME IN . . .

Tries to get out, but wind blows him back in, OLD TIMER blown in, all stay in cabin . . . draw lots to go look for food, Larsen loses, takes dog . . .

Three days later – steaming platter, Lonely serves up shoe: WILL YOU HAVE THE LIGHT OR DARK MEAT?

LONELY: WE SHOULD BE GRATEFUL FOR THIS. OUR FOREFATHERS, SO
  HISTORY TELLS US, WHEN THE DONNER PARTY CROSSED THE ROCKY
  MOUNTAINS, HOME SEEKING AND BLAZING THE TRAIL FOR CIVILIZA-
  TION, THEY HAD NOTHING TO EAT BUT ROASTED SHOES. HOW MUCH
  BETTER IT IS TO HAVE BOILED SHOE LEATHER.

Picks off nails: WANT TO MAKE A WISH?

Curtain lowered to denote lapse of time.

The Gold Rush can be said to be a film that is so well known that it attains a status not just as a 'classic' but as a vital part of cinema's DNA, the elemental structure of twentieth-century movie-making. It looms so large in the frame of Chaplin's work, has been so endlessly analysed and critiqued, placed on a pedestal of incomparable art, then removed and demoted to the gallery of overrated artefacts, that perhaps one excuses so many critics for sidelining a simple question: Why?

By 1923, Chaplin, despite the commercial disappointment of *A Woman in Paris*, was still in total control of his own output and schedules, able to choose his film subjects as he liked, in comfortable ownership of his means of production. He could well afford to cry out, like the Floorwalker of Mutual films: 'Spondulicks forever!' as he dived into his big bag of swag. His previous film had declared his interest in a new kind of 'realism that will portray emotions intelligently . . . a realistic treatment to a point which is true to the times – a modern treatment'. Why then in his next film did he veer so powerfully over to another tack: a period picture, set in a fabled Alaska of frontier mythology, a studio fantasy of crags and crevasses? And this at the very moment when Jazz-age America was plunging into its golden age of urban syncopation, a dizzying pursuit of material well-being and social climbing that was best defined in comedy by Harold Lloyd's splendiferous 1922 feature *Safety Last*. Harold desperately hung on to a clock high above teeming Hollywood, but Charlie trudged off, hat, cane, battered shoes and all, into the snowbound wastes.

One might note that another rival, Buster Keaton, had just presented *Our Hospitality*, a keen nostalgic look at the Old West with its primeval pioneering railway train and derring-do among forests and waterfalls. But Chaplin had demonstrated, in his first two features, that he did not follow trends.

The legend of how Chaplin conceived of *The Gold Rush* and the convoluted tale of its making has been often told: How he 'strove, thought and brooded' for an idea, saying to himself: '"The next film must be an epic! The greatest!" But nothing would come.' Then one weekend at Fairbanks and Pickford's paradise home, he sat with Douglas, looking at stereoscopic views, as one did apparently on Sunday mornings in Hollywood, and chanced across a series of views of the old Alaska Gold Rush of the 1890s, 'with a long line of prospectors climbing over its frozen mountain'. As he later described in *My Autobiography*:

This was a wonderful theme, I thought . . . In the creation of comedy, it is paradoxical that tragedy stimulates the spirit of ridicule, because ridicule, I suppose, is an attitude of defiance: we must laugh in the face of our helplessness against the forces of nature – or go insane. I read a book about the Donner Party who, on the way to California, missed the route and were snowbound in the Sierra Nevada mountains. Out of one hundred and sixty pioneers only eighteen survived, most of them dying of hunger and cold. Some resorted to cannibalism, eating their dead, others roasted their moccasins to relieve their hunger. Out of this harrowing tragedy I conceived one of our funniest scenes . . .

Indeed. But why this story, not another? If Chaplin was going to return to the Tramp, having yet again tried vainly to escape him, and if he felt a vocation for a 'modern treatment' of human characters and relationships, why did he not choose a story that set the Tramp in his contemporary world? After all, the project he would settle on was going to engage all his energies, and all his resources, and crew, and actors, for many months, if not years. He could not afford to choose on a whim.

Perhaps, on the other hand, it is true that Chaplin did exactly that, just as he chose various ideas out of the creative void during his Mutual period, trying, failing, retrying, waiting for the moment when his intuition told him the right shot had wound through the camera. Perhaps in his disappointment with the 'modern treatment' of *A Woman of Paris* he chose the opposite. The vaudeville comedian's instinctive fear of failing to amuse the audience would have been a major factor. A dedicated dramatic director might have shrugged, or cursed, and tried again, in Samuel Beckett's phrase of a future age: fail again, fail better. But failure was too bitter a pill for Chaplin, by now a full-fledged addict of adulation.

One might speculate about *A Woman of Paris* with Charlie starring, rather than Adolphe Menjou. The old priapic imp, a version of the Drunk and the Spiv combined, might have carried through a very different dalliance with Edna, in a very different form, but that had not been Chaplin's intention. In any case, these Charlie alter egos had long outlived their use. It would have had to be the Tramp, or nothing.

And so the Tramp returned. Again, the labours of the film have been oft told, allowing a brief summary of the main points: how Chaplin took his crew out to Truckee in the Sierra Nevada, having found, in lieu of Edna, a new leading lady in Lita Grey (Lillita McMurray), the angelic figure from *The Kid*. She was almost sixteen, but Chaplin cast her not only in his film but in his love life. During the course of filming she got pregnant, and Chaplin found he had to replace her and reshoot a major part of the film. The scenes that survive from the early shoot are the magnificent opening sequence shot on location: the long line of weary prospectors trudging through the snow and up the pass on Mount Lincoln. Two and a half thousand extras, many of them vagrants, who 'trudged through the heavy snows of the narrow pass as if gold were actually to be their reward, and not just a day's pay . . . They were to be seen in a picture with Chaplin, the mightiest vagrant of them all. It would be a red-letter day in their lives, the day they went over the Chilkoot Pass with Charlie Chaplin . . .' Then the crew hied back to Los Angeles, to construct the iconic cabin scenes with Charlie, the Old Prospector (alias Big Jim McKay, played by Mack Swain), and the villain on the run, Black Larsen, played by Tom Murray. The fake mountains and models of the cabin that was to be tossed and whirled in the snowstorms consumed 239,577 feet of timber, 22,750 feet of chicken wire, two hundred tons of plaster and 285 tons of salt, a hundred barrels of flour and four cartloads of confetti, according to David Robinson.

The crew shot till September – until Lita's pregnancy precipitated the crisis. Once again, Chaplin was forced into marriage by his own recklessness and his penchant for very young women. The couple rushed off to Mexico to be married in the small town of Empalme. This was only a few days after Chaplin's near-embroilment in yet another of Hollywood's iconic scandals, the death of producer Thomas Ince aboard William Randolph Hearst's yacht, the *Oneida*, off the Californian shore, on 19 November 1924. Legend has constructed an entire conspiracy theory involving the principals: Ince, Hearst, Hearst's mistress Marion Davies, Charles Chaplin – who was dallying with Marion, DeMille actor and dancer Theodor Kosloff, actress Seena Owen and journalist Louella Parsons, whose silence on the events of that night was said to have been purchased by Hearst with the gift of her career as Hollywood's hottest gossip columnist. Did Hearst shoot Ince when he caught him in flagrante with Marion? Or was it Chaplin who was caught and the bullet hit Ince by mistake? Recent research suggests that the original finding of death by heart failure was correct, but the alternative rumours began immediately and did not die down.

Lita's replacement as the star of *The Gold Rush* was Georgia Hale, an eighteen-year-old beauty, previously Miss Chicago, who had been cast by Josef von Sternberg in his first film, *The Salvation Hunters*. Douglas Fairbanks had seen the footage and apparently wanted her for his forthcoming *Don Q, Son of Zorro*, but Chaplin hastened to snap her up.

And then the reshoots: all the dance hall scenes, set, according to the early scripts, in Sitka, Alaska, but announced in the film only as 'One of the many cities in the north, built overnight during the great gold rush'; the scenes in the cabin with Georgia and the girls of the 'Monte Carlo' dancing troupe. The four thousand-plus slates of the film were finally done in May, while Chaplin was already cutting the film. On 5 May 1925 Lita gave birth to Chaplin's first surviving son, Charles Junior, six months after the Mexico marriage. Finally, the film was premiered on 26 June 1925 in a great splash of an event at Grauman's Egyptian Theatre in Los Angeles. This time there were no excuses and no appeals to the indulgence of the audience. Chaplin knew well what he had wrought, even in the crucible of so many doubts and confusions.

The plot of the film is easily summarized: Charlie, a lone prospector in the Alaskan gold rush, braves the snowy wastes and a lumbering bear to take refuge in a cabin which is a shelter for two other men, Black Larsen, on the run from the law, and Big Jim McKay, who has just made a claim on his 'mountain of gold' but is torn from it by a storm. Larsen goes out to forage for food and leaves them stranded when he takes a sled full of provisions from two lawmen whom he kills. Charlie and Big Jim face starvation. Charlie cooks one of his shoes. Big Jim mistakes him for a chicken, and chases him around with gun and axe, before a bear lumbering in to be shot provides them with enough food to survive. Big Jim goes to his claim but Larsen has found it and they tussle. Big Jim is knocked out and loses his memory, while Larsen dies when the ledge he is on collapses.

Meanwhile, in the frontier city, the Monte Carlo dancing girls and dazzling Georgia are wooed by the handsome and confident Jack. Annoyed by his advances, Georgia chooses to dance with Charlie, who has just ambled into the dance hall in his shabby clothes. When Jack tries to bully him, Charlie is saved by a clock which falls from the wall, knocking Jack out.

Wandering alone and hungry, Charlie comes across the cabin of Hank Curtis (Henry Bergman), a kindly prospector, who takes him in and leaves him in charge of his cabin when he goes up north. Tending the cabin, Charlie meets Georgia again when the girls fetch up at his doorstep, throwing snowballs. The girls see that Charlie is keeping a photograph of Georgia and decide to tease him, suggesting they all come to dinner in his cabin on New Year's Eve. Naïvely, he prepares for the festivity, falling asleep and dreaming of their presence. For Georgia, he performs a dance of the bread rolls with forks. But the girls are whooping it up in the dance hall and Charlie is left alone. He wanders down to the dance hall, while the girls, remorsefully recalling their pledge, sled up to the cabin and find that 'the joke has gone too far'. Back to the dance hall: Georgia writes an apologetic note to Jack, whom she rejected the previous night, but Charlie gets the note, thinking it is meant for him. Before he can approach Georgia, however, Big Jim, who has suddenly remembered the cabin, recognizes Charlie at the bar and drags him off, shouting at him: 'Take me to the cabin and I'll make you a millionaire in less than a month!'

At the cabin, however, another storm hits the two prospectors, and the cabin is tossed and whirled by the wind to the edge of a chasm, where it is held teetering by a rope caught in a cleft. At the edge of certain death, Big Jim manages to get out to find that his claim lies just outside the cabin. He hauls Charlie free, just as the cabin falls into the abyss.

In an epilogue, the new 'multimillionaires' are aboard ship, and Charlie poses in his old mining clothes for photographers. Georgia, who is travelling by steerage, sees him and thinks he must be the stowaway she has overheard the ship's officers talking of. She 'rescues' him, but the truth is soon uncovered. Charlie and Georgia pose for a kiss for the photographers, who exclaim: 'Gee! This will make a wonderful story.'

One can see that this naïve tale has little truck with realism, or any hint of modernity, but it is, in fact, a perfect Karno spectacle. One can imagine the 'Guv'nor' enthusing over the kind of set which could include a teetering cabin, crazy louts chasing each other with axes and the chicken scene. Karno's 1910 sketch 'Wontdetania' had featured a luxury liner which could be set rolling by pistons under and behind the scenes, just as Chaplin had deployed in *Shanghaied* and *The Immigrant*. The teetering cabin, one might point out, also featured in a Larry Semon film, *Lightning Love*, released in October 1923, in which the now forgotten comic, one of the early 1920s' biggest comedy stars, had a storm throwing a whole house on to a ledge. Semon steps out of the house and falls all the way down a cliff, on his head. Such was the bread and butter of comedy. Who pinched what from whom, or whether great minds think alike, is a perennial game of film history. D. W. Griffith's dramatic ice-floe rescues, in 1920's *Way Down East*, may have provided enough of a model.

The iconic scenes of *The Gold Rush*, however, cannot be taken away from Charlie, derivative as they might be. Eating the cooked shoe, with Charlie munching the sole, twirling the laces like spaghetti, and daintily licking the nails, while Mack Swain looks on, digustedly chewing his bit of hard leather. The dance of the bread rolls, which may have been prefigured by an old Fatty Arbuckle short of 1917, *The Rough House*, in which Fatty sticks forks in two bread rolls to parody a Charlie Chaplin walk – Chaplin paying back the compliment, as it were. The teetering cabin, with Charlie and Mack inside, steadily realizing that its movements are not due to 'the stomach'; the chicken scene – all remain timeless. Legend tells that Chaplin tried out a stand-in for the chicken sequence, but it just looked like a man in a chicken suit; when Chaplin donned the suit himself – he *was* a chicken.

The New Charlie, however, was a departure. The Old Charlie, Keystone's imp of the perverse, the ragged seducer and instigator of mayhem and chaos, has been softened, much further than the raw sentiment of *The Kid*. When Charlie entered the dance hall in *A Dog's Life*, and was refused entry because of the dog, he returned, literally wagging his tail. The hungry tramp then had no hesitation in stealing, kicking a policeman in the rump, fighting it out with crooks for a snatched wallet. When Charlie enters the dance hall in *The Gold Rush*, he is an all but defeated figure, picked up against the backlighting of the revellers, a fully pathetic, lonesome character whose dream of love is a figment of his imagination. One shot, in which the screen is split between the strong light of the New Year's Eve revel seen through a window, with the right side of the screen black, as Charlie's silhouette gazes in the window, is enough to chill the heart.

The Old Charlie survived by dint of his indefatigable spirit. This was the source of his tremendous popularity – he made audiences laugh, of course, but he also made them feel that even the lowest of the low could come out on top. Even if he could not get the girl, he would either shrug and walk back down the path to further adventures, or, more often than not, hightail it down the road, outpacing all enemies, running away only to return in the next film. The New Charlie, however, owes his fortune, and his very survival, to a narrative miracle, a real *deus ex machina*: the storm that blew him on to Big Jim's claim. His love, Georgia, merely teases him: despite her rough treatment by Jack, she really favours the big handsome lout. In the epilogue, we might imagine, she herself has been abandoned, reduced to the Tramp's status, chastened – but Chaplin does not explore this element at all: it is just another twist of chance and fate.

Charlie, bullied by Jack, is saved only by the falling clock. His own efforts merely bring him to the brink of despair, and beyond. Success exists only in dreams. Life in pursuit of these dreams is a savage nightmare, where, as Chaplin defined it much later: 'We must laugh in the face of our helplessness against the forces of nature – or go insane.' Critics have read into this an emotional overreaction to his own marital and love affairs at the time, the entanglement with Lita, which she herself described years later, in her own book (*My Life With Chaplin*), in pretty lurid terms, recalling Chaplin's bitterness at her family's demands surrounding their marriage and his description of them as a 'bunch of money hungry scum'. But the principal elements of *The Gold Rush* were in place long before the marriage, when she was still his darling and star.

Others, like Mordaunt Hall of the *New York Times*, saw behind the bleakness of *The Gold Rush* still 'something of the comedian's early life – the hungry days in London, the times when he was depressed by disappointments, the hopes, his loneliness . . .' And doubtless that theme too was there, although Chaplin had dealt with it pretty comprehensively in *The Kid*. In an interview with Hall in the run-up to the New York premiere, Chaplin told the critic:

'To my mind, the underlying motif of a story should be bright, not depressing. Motion-picture audiences like cheerfulness and don't like to see too much suffering . . . I wanted the audience to cry and to laugh. Whatever may be the public's opinion of this effort, I have at any rate been successful in clinging to my original idea . . .'

He spoke of his friend Thomas Burke; of Burke's latest book, 'The Wind and the Rain,' which the screen star described as 'so full of bitter pathos.'

'Do you know,' said Charlie, 'Burke and I went to school together? It was at Hanwell, in the Parish of Lambeth. Burke writes about himself in this book, and remembers how hard were those beginnings. I haven't forgotten, either, those early squalid surroundings in which I struggled. You will find something of me in "The Gold Rush."

'In one sequence . . . I am a millionaire. But I can't resist stooping down to pick up a cigar butt. I suppose this sort of impulse comes to many persons whose youth has been full of hardship . . .'

Chaplin was by now, however, a sponge of influences, and a voracious reader. His European trip had whetted his appetite for the intellectual life he had had no access to as a boy. We may recall that Heywood Broun had written, tongue in cheek, of Chaplin as 'superman' in *The Rink* in 1916, musing on the influence of Nietzsche's 'will to power' upon the clown. But the philosopher who seems to have a greater grip on Charlie in 1925 might well be Schopenhauer, whose basic idea that the world is not a rational place appears to hold sway over *The Gold Rush*. Schopenhauer's 'principle of sufficient reason' was held to answer the question 'Why is there something, rather than nothing?' though his more arcane thoughts on the relationship of subject and object might be beyond the scope of the Tramp.

The power that Chaplin's films hold over his interpreters derives from the contradiction of the surface simplicity of his narrative and images set against the emotional response that they generate. The familiar caveat operates: comedy is in the eye of the beholder, and those who do not warm to Chaplin's comedy or presence will not be persuaded by the entire panoply of Chaplinalia. Responses to classic comedy also vary over time: Ben Turpin made a career in comedy out of his crossed eyes, but the sight of a poor man with an ocular handicap hardly causes gales of laughter nowadays. Furthermore, one laughs at the familiar, and Charlie's world, that was so familiar in his heyday, is history now – one stays to admire, rather than guffaw.

The 'theatricality' of Chaplin's images is perhaps never stronger than in *The Gold Rush*. Scenes viewed head on: the hallucinations of starvation in the cabin, the dance hall, the girls in the dream feast with Charlie, the heightened drama in the tussles on the ice, the proscenium of fake snowstorms. Even the storm-tossed cabin could be created by some modern Belasco on the stage. And yet, stage settings are, however contrived, still real. But *The Gold Rush* exists in fable – a modern-day fairy tale that only the cinema could create.

In all this, Chaplin found a new range for the most crucial landscape in the picture – the painted mask of his face. He has added black marks under his eyes to accentuate the starkness of the Tramp's hunger: the

The Gold Rush.

eyes gaze at the audience from an intangible depth. The term 'pathos', so often used about Charlie, is a strange one for us to conjure with in a post-Auschwitz, post-Hiroshima, post-September 11, post-Iraq War age. We have become inured to so many images of terror, mass murder, raw anguish and destruction that we can barely respond to that condition described by the dictionary as 'the quality that raises pity'. Pity, of course, is no longer enough; we are supposed to do something about the horrors that afflict our planet – protest, demonstrate, vote out governments, subscribe to rock concerts, rise in rebellion, 'make a difference' in some way. We may have little time any more for 'the Little Fellow', who stood in for humanity's inability to do just that. Charlie's pathos is a paralysis in the face of overwhelming odds – personal failure, society's strictures, economic disaster, and the elements. Through Charlie, audiences cathartically experienced the full extent of his helplessness, that required, as we have seen, a miraculous narrative contrivance to reverse into a stunning success. Charlie in his thousand-dollar fur coat dives for a cigar stub. Big Jim places his massive paw in the hands of a manicurist on the ship and says to her: 'Not the nails – the corns!'

Chaplin, the real millionaire, returned to commune with his young wife and newborn son in their new permanent home on Summit Drive, between Douglas Fairbanks and Mary Pickford's mansion and the demesne of Harold Lloyd. Here his first two surviving children, Charles Junior and Sydney, born in 1926, would grow up, enmeshed in their father's peculiar double life and assuming that it was all normal.

Seventeen years after the release of *The Gold Rush*, Chaplin returned to it, reshaping some scenes, choosing alternative shots with different angles, chopping out the intertitles and replacing them with his own commentary, read in his voice, that had by then become known after the screening of *The Great Dictator*. The 1942 version subtly changed the relationship of Charlie with his audience, mediating it through his narration, softening the cruelty of Georgia's teasing, reducing the overall bleakness. Recent restorations (by Brownlow and Gill) do, however, enable us to revisit the original. Comparing the two, we can now make a judgement: Charlie does not require a mediator, even his own puppet-master, his maker.

There is no need to see the strings.

20

The Masquerader
Or: The Hole into which Everything Falls . . .

On 5 July 1925, the *New York Times* had published the following story:

CHARLIE CAPTURES AFRICA'S GOLD COAST
By Eric Berry.

. . . Not Harvard's, but the original Gold Coast, on Africa's western littoral jungle – ju ju, war drums, black men and all. I was visiting in Accra, homesick . . . I wanted to see the lights of Broadway, and the pretty ladies with their painted lips, and a movie . . . and of all the movies I wanted to see that cosmic clown, Charlie. Charlie on the Gold Coast? Much chance! . . .

'There's a cinema (that's the British term) in Accra,' said my hosts. 'We'll go down and see what they have tonight. It's the only cinema house on the coast, the only movie within thousands of miles . . .

We turned down the wide dark street of Accra. The car whirled up past flourishing little native markets . . . Then the glare of a movie lit up the dark street. The sign read 'Accra Picture Palace' . . . A small building . . . Four ornate and somewhat crooked pillars formed an arcade under which the market women liked to congregate. Wading through a mob of yelling humanity, which sprawled gossiping on the steps . . . We were whisked inside, and on the screen I caught a glimpse of galloping horses, sagebrush covered plains and familiar California mountains. There was a loud burst of shouts and yells and we looked down into a sea of black faces.

Here were Fanti savages from Ashanti land, up-country Kroo boys who work along the docks . . . black mammies, their frizzy traces straightened and stiffened with lard and charcoal . . . Some brought babies peacefully sleeping in a sling . . . Most of the audience were men . . . most of them were naked to the waist, their black bodies shining in the gleam of the electric lamps . . . Then the band started . . . they have a fife and drum arrangement, with a piano to bind the thing together, as it were . . . They played the 'Banana' thing, and 'Marjy' and 'Peggy O'Neill.'

At last the lights went out. No title flashed on the screen, but a funny little man with wide wonderful round eyes appeared – a strange wandering walk, a little cane and a derby hat. It was Charlie! My own recognition was no quicker than that of the wildly transported native audience. There was an immediate chorus of shouts. 'Charlee! Charlee!' Few of them knew any more

English than that, but they did know his funny little hat, his hobbled walk, his amazing shoes . . .

It was a film from the remote antiquity of filmdom . . . so patched and pieced and repieced that all continuity was gone, a piebald hash chosen from the remains of various comedies and stuck together with no plot. Just slapstick. But Charlie had survived even that, and how they did love it!

Charlie kicked the villain in the usual place, and the villain responded by closing the door on Charlie's nose . . . Charlie, creeping softly, came back with a big wooden mallet, and by mistake of course, hit the lady heroine on the head . . . the audience roared and shouted approval . . . No doubt Charlie Chaplin has richly earned the respect of the natives of the Gold Coast, because, in their opinion, he knows how to treat a woman . . .

Indeed, beyond the casual contemporary racism, one gleans the news of an umpteenth re-run of *The Fatal Mallet* in West Africa. Nor was the British colony of the Gold Coast (today's Ghana) exceptional in its reception of Charlie Chaplin movies. 'The Savages Roar and Shout with Delight!' trumpeted *The Times*, but no region of the world that had some ramshackle building, a generator and a projector was too remote for Charlie. In Indonesia, traditional shadow-puppet shows acquired a new figure, with the cane and hat. In Japan, as we will see a little later, his on-screen antics would be attended by a phonograph disc that played music and a translation of the dialogue. In Siam (Thailand) and China 'They Delight in Charlie Chaplin' was a 1920 headline for the *New York Times*, which cited the London *Daily Mail*: 'Charlie Chaplin rules the risible muscles of the West. He is the comic king of the Celestials. His poster outside a Chinese picture palace is as great a draw as his electrically lighted figure in the Strand. The children imitate him in their games just as the western youngsters do, begging for coins to go to see their idol.'

This popularity with audiences was not surprising, but Charlie's co-option into the repertory of experimental art and the latest intellectual fads and movements was less expected and more complex. In Weimar Germany, reeling from the trauma of defeat in the war, this began with the echoes of Charlie's adoption by the burgeoning avant-garde in France. A very early echo was a 'cinema-poem', '*Die Chapliniade*', by Ivan Goll, aka Isaac Lang, a friend of Hans Arp and among the founders of the pre-surrealist Dada movement. Goll's poem appeared in 1920. To him, Charlie was not, as he was to the jolly people of Accra, a figure of eternal recognition, beyond history, but the very embodiment of modernity. Charlie rebelled against bourgeois society, but he was also a perfect example of the marriage between art and technology, high and mass culture. Charlie's social qualities came second in this paean, but Goll also called upon him to bring on 'the communism of the soul'.

What attracted the Dadaists to Chaplin was the vision he presented to them of a cinema freed from the constraints of film realism, that explored the purely aesthetic qualities of the movies. In this, of course, they misunderstood Chaplin, and his continual striving for his own perfect realism, but comprehension has never been a requirement for intellectual adoration. German cinema itself – which had embarked on its own highly adventurous journey into psychology expressed by technology, i.e., lighting – was not strong on comedy, and Charlie came to fill that gap. While the radicals embraced Chaplin as a great twentieth-century artistic innovator, conservative and proto-Nazi critics would later verify that choice by branding Charlie as 'the hero of the sub-human' or 'a little mongrel without race', a perfect sample of the immorality of Anglo-American cultural decline.

Some left-wing German critics, not far off tune with the conservatives, did not share the Dadaists' enthusiasm either, pointing out that 'Chaplin is unable to provide a philosophy of life . . . immediate humanity, for he has no soul, he himself is not a human being but only a very wise, a very artistic puppet that has assumed for us a typical expression.' The ever-perceptive if often prescriptive film-writer Sigfried Kracauer, reviewing *The Gold Rush*, placed Chaplin wholly outside society and wrote that 'other people have an ego consciousness and exist in human relationships; he has lost the ego; thus he is unable to take part in what is usually known as life. He is a hole into which everything falls; what is otherwise connected bursts into fragments as soon as it comes in contact with him.'

The Gold Rush had opened in Berlin in February 1926, in a gala screening that certainly seemed to bind Chaplin to formal, acceptable society, as it was attended by the American ambassador and 'representatives of the German Government', according to the *New York Times*. Preceding the film itself, there was 'a dance in which the statue of Aphrodite comes to life under a rushing gold cascade'. Proceeds of the premiere were donated to German newspaper charities and afterwards 'the Press Association sent a telegram to Chaplin greeting him as the "great master" of the world's cinema'.

Chaplin was certainly bridging the gap, in his own fortunes, between the kitsch of society and its fundamental critics, though not all the zealots of progressive arts could follow Kracauer into his deeper Freudian caverns, as he continued to define Charlie in *The Gold Rush* as 'a human being without surface, without the possibility of contact with the world. In pathological terms, this would be called ego dissociation, schizophrenia . . . However, out of the hole the purely human emanates disconnectedly . . . the human that otherwise suffocates below the surface, that cannot shine through the layers of ego consciousness.' Much discussion went on, when Chaplin presented *The Circus* and then *City Lights*, as German critics sought to define his revolutionary credentials – 'No, no! Chaplin is anything but a convinced revolutionary . . . He is a revolutionary against his will.' But Walter Benjamin, writing in 1929, could only produce the platitude that 'In his films, Chaplin has turned to the most international and revolutionary affect of the masses, laughter.' As if the bourgeoisie were unable to guffaw.

Before the critics, painters and graphic artists integrated Charlie into their own output, as Léger had done in France. The first international Dada fair, the famous Dada-Messe, of 1920, featured a copy, by Otto Schmalhausen, of the well-known 1812 mask of Beethoven with a lock of unruly hair and a small Chaplin moustache. The third issue of the *Dada* journal, in the same year, sent Chaplin, 'world's greatest artist and a good Dadaist', greetings, with a protest against the ban against his films in Germany, still in force because of *Shoulder Arms*.

Artists like Otto Dix, George Grosz and Rudolf Schlichter drew on images from mass media, postcards and posters, to enlighten their art, and the satirist Hans Reimann described Grosz's studio as a place where 'Chaplin smiles on the wall, George Grosz's Mona Lisa'. Ivan Goll, in another riff on Chaplin, wrote, in an essay entitled '*Apologie des Charlot*',

Charlot is the genius of our age. Who is it that pays him millions for a film? The fat, sweaty bourgeoisie? An idea. He rolls himself a cigarette and grins. Then, when he climbs a lamp post like a rose-colored Jacob's ladder and dives headlong into space, so many unhappy shopgirls, soldiers, miserable men on strike, poor, poor people, sob with laughter. Charlot is the best man of our era. He doesn't really grin. He dies of laughing desperation.

The Soviet Union was another place in which comedy was considered a very serious business. As early as 1922, avant-gardists led by Grigori

Kozintsev and Leonid Trauberg issued a manifesto on 'Eccentricism in Action', declaring that 'Protest is inevitable, just like Charlie Chaplin's moustache,' and 'we prefer Charlie's arse to Duse's hands!' The 'Eccentrics' were overtaken by events, but Chaplin remained a potent symbol of freedom. In 1936, when the theatre producer and innovator Vsevolod Meyerhold delivered a lecture entitled 'Chaplin and Chaplinism', he gave an outline of Chaplin's work from Keystone to *Modern Times*, and asked:

Why have we failed time and time again to create Soviet comedy, to create the kind of comic film our people would love and our country needs? I believe our failure lies in not finding anyone who knows how to discover the 'mask' within himself . . . Let me repeat Pushkin's formula: the drama has begun to master the soul and passions of men. Have we made any effort to create a 'mask' from human passions?

In his own production of Ostrovsky's *The Forest*, Meyerhold wrote, he had built on the character Arkashka 'new traits drawn from Chaplinism'. This he defined as High Comedy, which is 'based not on laughter alone, but on character development, and it not infrequently comes close to tragedy . . . Is there comedy in Chaplin's work?' he asked, somewhat ingenuously – 'what do we find when we analyse such a picture as *The Gold Rush*? We find comedy close to cruelty and grief.'

The Gold Rush in particular might well have resonated with the Russian audience's experience of peril and starvation in a snowy wasteland, though in 1936, at the height of Stalin's purges, Meyerhold could not dare to diverge from Pushkin and Art . . . At the time of its release, ten years earlier, Chaplin was as popular in Russia as anywhere, and the *New York Times* reported on 18 January 1926 on a peculiar approach from Leningrad, where 'the Soviet State's motion picture monopoly has invited Charlie Chaplin to take part in a film based on Nikolai Gogol's satire on Russian life, called "The Overcoat." Picture experts are of the opinion that this vehicle would give Chaplin an opportunity to distinguish himself as much by his overcoat as he has done by his trousers and shoes.'

One might point out that Meyerhold could not, in 1936, publically assert the prerequisite for the emergence of Chaplinesque comedy, the condition of artistic freedom, often constrained in movies by commercial limits, but not for Charlie, whose box-office receipts were hugely augmented by *The Gold Rush*. Indeed, he was not subject to the constraints of the 'fat, sweaty bourgeoisie', or even the thin lean types. Neither state policies, nor artistic theories, could match this. Chaplin's was an American success. But it was not just in central and eastern Europe that Charlie was lauded as the working man's best champion, as even in England George Lansbury's *Labour Weekly* published an open letter to him in the wake of the opening of *The Gold Rush* in Britain in September 1925: 'Yours is the kindest sense of comedy: you wear your heart on your trouser leg. We are proud to remember that you are a Socialist, and we do not think it fantastic to say that no one who had not the Socialist's knowledge of and belief in humanity could do the trick as you do it . . .'

Clearly this was Charlie's great strength in his heyday: that he was all things to all men. This was indeed 'the hole into which everything falls'. In Bologna, Italy, researchers dug out an old claim that Chaplin was a bona fide native of the city, his family, the Caplinettis, having set sail for America only a generation before.

Only in Spain had acceptance of Charlie been slow to catch on, as some early critics, expounding the skills of his predecessor, Max Linder, found him vulgar, and his marriage problems and divorces were a matter of some disapproval in the press. In 1918, a surly critic, Joaquin Adan, opposing the Keystone type of slapstick, had written that

. . . the war removed Max Linder from the cinema, and in that absence caused by noble goals, Chaplin the acrobat crept in, somewhat surreptitiously. This clown, who to make people laugh has to don voluminous drawers and dislocate his feet, has presumed to overshadow the refined elegance, the naturalness, the style of Max. The docile submission of the masses to this grotesque actor has annoyed us on many occasions . . .

By *The Gold Rush*, however, Spain's scribes too were at Chaplin's feet, the poet Rafael Alberti penning '*Cita Triste de Charlot*' in 1929:

> My hat, my cuffs,
> my gloves, my shoes.
>
> The butterfly knows nothing of the tailor's deaths,
> of the shop window's defeat of the sea.
> My age, gentlemen, is 900,000.
> Oh!
>
> I was a child when fishes did not swim,
> when geese did not say mass,

and the snail did not attack the cat.
Miss, let us play cat and mouse . . .

It snows, it snows
and my body turns into a log cabin.
Wind, I invite you to rest.
It is already too late to dine on stars.

Another admiring writer, Fernando Vela, was particularly taken with *The Circus*, of 1928, writing of its scene set in a hall of mirrors that 'Chaplin is a tramp who has lost his way in the world. He lived in a different world, but one day, without realizing it, he half-opened a door and fell, making a famous clown's entrance, into a world with fewer dimensions, where the mirrors cannot be stepped through, where every step is a stumble.' This image of Charlie in a particularly Spanish realm of heightened imagination evokes the Spanish sur-realists, Dalí and Buñuel, who were soon to commit their own act of imaginary rebellion in Paris with their short film *Un Chien Andalou*. Yet another writer, Francisco Ayala, who described Chaplin as 'an unmistakable product of the modern city and of modern restlessness', reported on a children's song heard in Madrid, almost certainly deriving from *The Gold Rush*:

> Chaplin eats no meat–
> Chaplin is going to die . . .

In the home of Don Quixote and Sancho Panza, Charlie was an old friend. Later, in 1930, Chaplinitis would come full circle when Hollywood would bring together both Chaplin and Buñuel, and Chaplin and Eisenstein, the former invited by MGM, and the latter by Paramount, which fantasized that the great Soviet film-maker might shoot either Blaise Cendrars' *Sutter's Gold* or Theodore Dreiser's *An American Tragedy* in the United States. In the event, nothing came of this unlikely alliance, and Eisenstein and his assistant Alexandrov departed to Mexico, to attempt another eventually abortive project, *Que Viva Mexico*. Chaplin kept himself and his money out of such shenanigans.

It was in 1937 that Charlie would receive his apotheosis in poetry, from the pen of Russia's great modernist poet, Osip Mandelstam, soon to disappear and die in Stalin's gulags. The first poem celebrated Chaplin's *City Lights*, with its description of Charlie:

In his oceanic bowler, with absent-minded precision,
He swaggers restlessly with his flower girl . . .
There, with a rose on her breast, in two-towered sweat,
Her spiderweb shawl turns to stone . . .
Bend your neck, little atheist
With a goat's golden eyes,
And with crooked, lisping scissors
Tease the heaps of cheapskate roses . . .

The second poem, 'As I'd Ask', is more directly a paean:

Charlie Chaplin
   Left the movie house,
Two soles,
   And a harelip,
Two peepers,
   Full of ink
And marvelous
   Astonished powers . . .
We're all living wrong somehow—
   Strangers, strangers . . .
And very softly
   Charlie says:
Why am I known and loved
   Even famous.
And the big highway takes him off
   To strangers, strangers. . .
Why
   Does Chaplin have a tulip,
Why
   Is the crowd so kind?
Because—
   This is Moscow, after all.
Charlie, Charlie—
   You must keep taking risks,
You went soft
   At exactly the wrong time.
Your bowler hat—
   Is an ocean too,
And Moscow is so close, even if you love
   The road, the road.

Italy salutes *The Circus*.

21

The Circus
Or: 'Bring on the funny man!'

Synopsis, *The Circus* (1928)

Under the big top, the circus is a place of oppression and misery: The ringmaster (played by Allan Garcia) scolds his daughter, the equestrienne (Merna Kennedy), for missing the hoop in her pony jump; the clowns (headed by Henry Bergman) are a dejected lot and the crowds are bored. Around the side shows, 'hungry and broke', the Tramp enters, stealing some bites from a baby's sandwich. A crook steals a wallet, pushes it in the Tramp's pocket, and a comedy of errors follows: crook and Tramp pursued by a cop in and out of the hall of mirrors. The Tramp, chased by a mule, rushes into the big top pursued by the cop, upsetting the acts and delighting the crowd. Wandering by the circus caravans, the Tramp befriends Merna, who has been sent to her berth hungry by her brutal father. The ringmaster offers him a job and commands the clowns to train him, but they fail to teach him how to be deliberately funny. The Tramp is fired, but when the hired hands quit the show, the Tramp is taken on, and proceeds to mess up the magician's act. The ringmaster keeps him on, without revealing to him that his antics have made him the hit of the show: 'He's a sensation but he doesn't know it – keep him on as a property man.'

The Tramp is in love with Merna, who is still treated brutally by her father, as she rehearses her trapeze act. The Tramp is locked in the lion cage by mistake but gets out. Meanwhile, as prophesied by the fortune teller, Merna meets a 'dark, handsome man', but this is not, as the Tramp believes, himself but a new tightrope walker, Rex (played by Harry Crocker). The Tramp tries to teach himself the tightrope walk, and when Rex fails to show up one day he takes his place, having bribed a stagehand to fix a hook in his belt. Climbing high above the crowd without a safety net, disaster strikes when the hook comes off, and a bunch of escaped monkeys clamber up on top of him as he teeters on the wire. He survives the act, but realizes that Merna loves Rex, and sees him only as her 'friend'. Observing Merna's father's continued abuse of her, the Tramp encourages Rex and Merna to marry, so that her father's hold on her can be broken. The circus moves on, but the Tramp remains behind, alone in the great sawdust circle. He shrugs, gives a little kick, and wanders off, alone, in the fade-out.

The Circus was Chaplin's most troubled production, beset not only by the usual Chaplin indecision about the story and individual scenes but by a fire that burned down the set, the theft of the caravans, and most of all, the breakdown of his marriage to Lita Grey. Once again, Chaplin felt he had to remove footage of the film to a safe place in case of its sequestration as part of his wife's suit for divorce. This time the marital battle was fought in the full glare of mass publicity that continued for months in vivid headlines and ghastly allegations about his sex life.

In the beginning, during 1925, the familiar flurry of script ideas, scribblings and notes emerged. In its primal form, the film was titled 'The Traveler', and was set in a specific milieu that would return the Tramp to his roots as a bona fide American vagrant. Once again, Chaplin tried to insert his stubborn 'flea circus' sketch. The draft reads:

Suggestion for opening:

Under the archway of a bridge are a jungle of hoboes. Some asleep – some sitting around – one stirring food in a can over the fire. Charlie comes into camp. He looks around fastidiously – takes out a handkerchief – dusts off a rock and sits down. One bum looks up and inquires – 'What's your line?' Charlie answers: 'I am a circus man.' Bum looks at him incredulously. He notices looks and takes from under his arm a small box labelled 'Flea Circus.' – Business ad lib with fleas.

In putting fleas away for night, Charlie discovers one gone – goes over to bum with long beard – picks up flea from beard, regards it and puts it back. It is evidently not one of circus.

All asleep. In movements in sleep, flea circus is overturned and fleas escape. Scratching commences among bums but fleas concentrate on dog . . . [the dog jumps in the lake and Charlie is in despair as the fleas drown.]

Next morning bums prepare to board train. They will all ride brakebeams. Charlie spies mail-sack in brackets – removes same and stands in brackets. Mail clerk is asleep. Charlie rides at ease, enjoying view, while bums gaze enviously from underneath car. Passenger in car in front of Charlie throws cigarette out of window. Charlie catches same and smokes it – dropping butt with gesture to one of the bums underneath car. Arrives in town to discover circus in progress.

As was his wont, Chaplin discarded this as well as other 'suggestions' about a dog trainer, circus elephants, camels and so forth. Whittling away, he pared down the sequences until he emerged with the essence of the tale he wanted to tell.

In legend, according to a later account by Henry Bergman, the entire movie originated in a nightmare gag that Chaplin had described to him, in which he was 'on a high place troubled by something else, monkeys or things that come to me and I can't get away from them'. Bergman then suggested that he might develop this idea in a circus setting, on a tightrope. Whatever its origin, the scene had Charlie, high above the ground, assaulted by ferocious monkeys, who rip off his pants, leaving him exposed. It was not difficult for subsequent writers to see in this image the real nightmare of his collapsing marriage, with the monkeys standing in for the babies he had fathered. The deep melancholy of the film, the thwarted love, the brutal family life, the sadness of the clowns, Charlie's sacrifice in allowing all possibility of love, companionship, a coherent society, to drift away from him, leaving him with nothing but the paraphernalia of the Tramp and a final kick against the pricks of life, clearly reflect his state of mind at the time. But Chaplin was also the consummate professional, the film an all but inevitable summation of the character he had spent so much time creating and recreating, a salutary return to the roots of show business in its most naked and vulnerable form.

In its opening sequence, the film is set in a generic fairground – filmed at Venice Beach – which could be any seaside pavilion: England's Brighton or the working-class paradise Blackpool might come to mind. A small incident, a crook picking a man's pocket, sets off a frenzied Keystone riff, as the crook, being rumbled, shoves the wallet in Charlie's pocket and protests his innocence. Charlie, meanwhile, has moved off to a hot-dog stand, relieving his hunger by taking bites out of a baby's sandwich as the child is held over its father's shoulder. The crook moves in, trying to retrieve the wallet, and gets caught by the cop, who 'returns' the wallet to an amazed Tramp. As Charlie hurries to order up a dozen hot dogs, the robbed man wanders up, recognizes his wallet and calls another cop. Charlie runs off, still with the wallet, and merges in the subsequent chase with the crook, chased by yet another cop. Charlie darts into the House of Fun, past its mechanical moving dummies, into the Mirror Maze. The crook runs in too, and they both charge around each other and their reflections, till Charlie gets out but, spying the cops, joins the mechanical figures and pretends to be a dummy himself. A perfect simulacrum, he turns and judders with the funfair's beat. The crook, coming out of the maze, tries to blackjack Charlie, but gets caught in the mechanical simulation, as Charlie seizes the cosh and proceeds to bludgeon the crook in a classic Punch and Judy routine. As the crook falls, however, the magic is broken, and Charlie runs back into the Mirror Maze. The cop enters, collars him, but is caught in the maze, asking Charlie: 'How d'you get out of here?'

As well he might, but Chaplin's logic from scene to scene is impeccable. The Tramp eludes the cop, runs out, is pursued again. Cut to the interior of the big top. Two clowns are chasing each other on a revolving podium, to a completely bored audience. Charlie and the cop burst in, toppling the clowns and replacing them on the spinning platform, much as Chaplin the Drunk had spun, in *One A.M.*, upon his own table in pursuit of an elusive drink. The crowd wakes up, electrified by the 'new act'. When Charlie and the cop rush out again, and the clowns troop back in, tumbling lacklustrely, the crowd shouts: 'Rotten!' 'Get off!' and 'Bring on the funny man!' The ringmaster looks on, nonplussed. Outside, Charlie stops the cop, hands back the wallet and rushes away, collapsing in an empty cart. Fade out.

Thirteen minutes of the film have gone by, and Charlie has integrated his wandering Tramp organically into the circus milieu. It could all have gone much faster if he had simply wandered about and been offered a job as a stagehand when a group of them quits because of the ringmaster's stinginess, as occurs a bit later on. But this would have missed out, as well as some of Charlie's best knockabout action gags, the whole idea of fate driving the story.

As was his common procedure in his previous comedies, Chaplin's gags emerged out of the day-to-day process of the filming itself, rather than from script or even notes. This was still in line with the old practice in Keystone when scripts simply noted 'Ad lib comedy biz', though none had the resources and time that Chaplin commanded to work this out week after week, month after month. Mack Sennett, Hal

Roach and other comedy studios were still going strong at the tail end of the silent era, producing prodigious numbers of two-reel comedies. Sennett films starred Billy Bevan, Raymond McKee, Andy Clyde and Charlie's old partner Ben Turpin, who followed a long list of spoof films such as *The Shriek of Araby* and *Three Foolish Weeks* in the early twenties with comeback films like *A Harem Knight* and *Pride of Pikeville* in 1926. While Chaplin was shooting *The Circus*, Stan Laurel and Oliver Hardy were being spliced into legend in the series of dazzling shorts that would carry them into the sound era. Keaton made *Battling Butler* in 1926 and *The General* in 1927 and was shooting the gag-rich *Steamboat Bill Jr*. Harold Lloyd made *The Kid Brother* and prepared *Speedy*. Harry Langdon had teamed with Frank Capra and Arthur Ripley to make *The Strong Man* and *Long Pants*. And there was a host of others still in play, even as the death-knell of the silents was clanged by Al Jolson warbling 'Mammy' in *The Jazz Singer*, opening in October 1927, while *The Circus* was still in production.

Still, Charlie continued to be a world unto himself, as the personal woes of his shotgun marriage to Lita Grey played themselves out, first in private turmoil, and then in the full blare of the press. For the tale behind the scenes we have only one detailed account, that of Lita herself, written four decades after the events, and published in 1966 as *My Life with Chaplin: an Intimate Memoir*. And intimate it certainly is. Lita Grey Chaplin provided a blow-by-blow narrative of her first encounter with Chaplin in the filming of *The Kid*, their reunion as Chaplin prepared *The Gold Rush*, and the uncomfortable tale of his wooing her while she was not yet of the legal age of sixteen. She described 'Charlie's eyes, ceaselessly pursuing me,' his attempts to get her away from her mother, meeting her on street corners in his Locomobile driven by Kono the chauffeur, taking her into his house with its 'hodgepodge of English, French and American contemporary, wedded oddly to Chinese and Japanese décor. The overall aura was Oriental, from the profusion of jade to the faces of the servants.' The bedroom, with its 'masculine bureau', on which stood 'a bottle of cologne marked Guerlain's Misuko [*sic*]'.

'"Is that what I smell all the time?" I asked, "In your dressing room at the studio, in your car, on your clothes, on – you?"

'"You like it, eh?"' One can almost read into this the mischievous stare, the little Charlie simper, the ogle, the twirling of a non-existent moustache. The real seduction, when it finally comes, is in the bath-room, 'all white tile and white marble', with an anteroom 'containing a built-in slab of marble . . . "My private steam room."' There, with the 'foglike mist' billowing, like 'every picture I'd ever seen of queens and princesses bathing in royal tubs', Charlie takes her – 'it's easier this way . . . we can't see each other . . .'

'Lovemaking is a sublime art that needs practice if it's to be true and significant. But I suspect you're going to be an excellent student, Lita.' All this specific dialogue remembered so long after the event may or may not be properly recalled, as may be the case with all the later fury over the blighting of love by unwanted pregnancies and her disdain for Chaplin's encounters with his famous peers and even more famous strangers: 'I'm sure that Dr. Einstein is a great man,' she complains to him, 'but can't you understand that I'm starved for friends of my age?' But when some young kids are finally allowed in the house and play the phonograph, Chaplin bursts in and orders them all out, accusing her of turning his place into a 'whorehouse' and then brandishing a gun when she begins to mention divorce.

Is this how it happened? One might well guess that Chaplin's frus-tration over his child-bride's pregnancy, while denying his own irre-sponsible conduct, would be incandescent. The original Tramp could well have been an imp, a seducer, manic and violence-prone, in his imaginary character, but hoisting that subterranean presence, that id, into the ego of his creator had a costly and damaging effect in real life. Lita wrote:

Charlie's movies reflected him as a man of compassion, as a sworn enemy of anything violent. Then I remembered that no dream had been uglier than real-ity; he did hate me, and he did want to get rid of me. He became so intense about it, in fact, that, as I discovered some months later, he had an electrical eavesdropping system installed and hidden in my bedroom . . .

This would have been to monitor her conversations with her mother, so that he could argue in court that they were conspiring against him. In the event, Lita's family proved to be pretty adept at playing a hard game themselves, her uncle Edwin McMurray coming up, in January 1927, with a divorce complaint that pulled no punches, and was so sensationalist that Lita herself saw fit in her book to disassociate herself from its contents. The document bored into Chaplin's alleged sexual misconduct, to wit:

Plaintiff alleges with regard to the sexual relations heretofore existing between said parties, that the defendant's attitude, conduct and manifestations of interest therein, have been abnormal, unnatural, perverted, degenerate and indecent . . . Throughout the entire married life of said parties and at times too numerous for plaintiff to more particularly specify, defendant has solicited, urged and demanded that plaintiff submit to, perform and commit such acts and things for the gratification of defendant's said abnormal, unnatural, perverted and degenerate sexual desires, as to be too revolting, indecent and immoral to set forth in detail in this complaint . . .

The only specific act mentioned was 'the act of sex perversion defined by section 288a of the Penal Code of California', which covered sex with minors. The whole was a typical sample of the sort of thing hurled about in American courtrooms, where the aim was to blacken the reputation of the 'defendant' so thoroughly that a desired result was assured. In Lita Grey's own account, her uncle told her he was 'going for millions' in her action against Charlie.

All this was sheer manna for the newspapers, from the first rumblings in December:

WIFE QUITS CHARLIE CHAPLIN, TAKING CHILDREN . . .

SPLIT PERMANENT, CHAPLINS DECLARE . . .

PARTY ROW SPLITS CHAPLINS – He Spat at Her She Says . . .

WIFE SAYS SHE 'NEVER, NEVER' WILL GO BACK . . .

MRS CHAPLIN PREFERS $1,000,000 TO DECREE . . .

CHAPLINS MUM AS LAWYERS HIGGLE OVER CHILDREN. . .

LITA WILL SEEK CHURCH SOLACE – Baptism of Two Children by Priest Denied . . .

CHAPLIN'S WIFE HURLS CHARGES – [he brands] Wife 'Gold Digger' . . . 'Blackmailer' . . .

CHAPLIN SUED FOR DIVORCE – HE MARRIED HER TO AVOID PRISON, WIFE DECREES . . .

The petition declares that on their way back from their hasty marriage in Mexico, Chaplin remarked to friends in the party that 'this is better than the penitentiary, but it won't last long . . .'

(*New York Daily News*, 11 January 1927)

WIFE IMPOUNDS CHAPLIN RICHES . . .

LITA CHARGES CHAPLIN BOASTED OF HIS OTHER LOVES . . .

Told of 5 Loves, Says Lita . . .

CHAPLIN ACCUSES LITA OF FRIENDLINESS WITH MEN – Declares
Home a Hell With Wife Accusing Him and Revealing She Didn't
Love Him . . .

SUIT RACKS CHAPLIN – 'IT'S TERRIBLE . . .'

CHAPLIN'S STORY – WOE . . .

Actor Hints Scandal Raised May Mean End of His Screen Career . . .

On 16 January 1927, the *New York Times* reported that 'Charlie Chaplin has had a nervous breakdown and is confined to his bed,' according to Dr Gustav Tieck, New York nerve specialist. Chaplin's attorney, Nathan Burkan, denied that the comedian was under guard and that fears were entertained that he might attempt suicide. 'He is a highly strung man, as most actors are,' he told the press, somewhat unconvincingly. 'We do not regard his condition as alarming.' He was preparing to accompany Chaplin back west to Los Angeles, to prepare his 'cross-complaint against Mrs. Chaplin'. Arthur W. Kelly of United Artists told the press that Chaplin was 'a man of extreme sensitiveness and naturally feels keenly the present situation . . . He is in private life a serious and thoughtful man, who would not be taken for a humorist.'

Be that as it may, production of *The Circus* had already been interrupted in December 1926 and would not resume until September 1927. The bulk of the film had been shot between the Decembers of 1925 and 1926. Its main tenor and themes therefore anticipate, rather than follow, the events of Lita's suit for divorce.

Nevertheless, the messiness of the marriage itself, and her unwanted pregnancy, fed into the tone of the film. It emerges as Chaplin's great meditation on the central contradiction of show business – its economic and social harshness set against the gaiety it is supposed to arouse. In its very first shot – the camera literally tearing the star in the centre of a paper hoop as it reveals the big top – the film announces itself: Not a tale of the big fish of showbiz, but of its innumerable small fry. Its central quadrangle, Tramp, Girl, Father and Lover, mirrors the basic set-up of *The Vagabond* of 1915, when Charlie rescued Edna from gypsy brute Eric Campbell but lost her to the painter who wooed her away. Eric Campbell long gone, the brute is Allan Garcia, a Chaplin regular since *The Idle Class*. Where Eric would have been inevitably funny in his comic-book menace, Garcia is played straight, as nasty and foil.

In fact, nobody is funny in *The Circus*, except Charlie, and possibly the hapless Professor Bosco, magician, whose name has been borrowed from Chaplin's unmade work, and who is played by another silent supporting actor, George Davis, with an Andy Clyde-type moustache. As Charlie charges into the show, pursued by the cop, he gets mixed up with the magician's cabinet and trapdoors, releasing all the pigeons and piglets that should have stayed in his hat.

The basic point is that Charlie the Tramp, in *The Circus*, is only funny when he erupts in his spontaneous business, but cannot be trained to be deliberately funny as a hired act to save his life. The world's most melancholy clowns, led by Henry Bergman in a performance of quiet humanity and an essential dignity that a life of failure had not totally crushed, fail to teach him either the 'William Tell' act or the even simpler barber-shop routine, in which everybody in turn is to get covered in soapy gunge. This is a sketch Chaplin will return to – in total incongruity – in *A King in New York*. The William Tell act, an ancient circus standard, unearthed by movie researchers in a film scene deriving from 1900, has the patsy, whose apple on the head is to be shot with an arrow, spoiling the game by eating the apple. Charlie can't even master this one: the apple has a worm, and his suggestion that they use a banana has the circus people outraged. It is a classic use of one of the oldest chestnuts of comedy to squeeze out one more impossible variant. *The Circus* continually tells us that there are no new jokes, and no new dramas or tragedies, just the drum roll of the old staples, time and again reborn from the essential skill of the clown. Art here is at its most naked, shorn of its myriad trappings and airs.

Chaplin cast as the Girl Merna Kennedy, a childhood friend of Lita's. Her role was clearly to be pretty, and tragic, and then unattainable. As an object of desire, she is strictly ephemeral, lacking Edna's underlying melancholy, or the modern vivacity of the next Mrs Chaplin, Paulette Goddard. Her future career in cinema was in a minor key, roles in twenty-seven standard pictures, including *Come on Tarzan*, of 1932, the best known of her oeuvre being probably *Jimmy the Gent*, 1934, a James Cagney movie directed by Michael Curtiz. It is no wonder that, as *The Circus* pans out, Charlie delivers her to the muscular arms of Rex the tightrope walker, showering them with rice from behind as they march out of their rapid nuptials. This ending, which seems totally out of character for the Tramp – when Merna has after all run away from the circus to join him by his night-time campfire – is nevertheless in character for Chaplin, who could clearly abide no further matrimony at this point. It might be perhaps the only time in one of his features that Chaplin overrides Charlie.

The grand climax of the film remains, however, the great tightrope scene, with Chaplin's (alleged) origin-gag played to its utmost: his quick shinning up the pole, hauled on a concealed rope by the stage-hand, posing on the wire, the rope torn loose, dangling before his hor-rified eyes as he realizes his predicament, and then the monkeys swarm. As is his wont, Chaplin has carefully set up the scene, showing the monkeys escaping from a trunk he upturns searching for the missing Rex's costume. The ringmaster's call: 'You can do the act, can't you?' is followed by the foreman's: 'He'll kill himself!' and the master's snide riposte: 'That's all right, I've got him insured.'

The record shows Chaplin shooting over seven hundred slates for the tightrope scene, which was thoroughly prepared with story-board sketches, the mechanics of the sequence meticulously worked out. Although many of the close shots could be cheated reasonably near to the ground, long shots required Chaplin to be up the wire in harm's way several times. The monkeys were a perfect nightmare, high or low. In the culminating gag, as Charlie gratefully reaches the other end of the rope, he seizes Rex's trick bicycle and whizzes down another rope, out of the big top, into the street outside and into a hardware store. The Tramp staggers out for applause into a busy street.

In Chaplin's output, *The Circus* was downplayed for many years, despite its commercial success at the time. In 1928, movies were already talking, singing and honking in a variety of ghastly squeaks and squawks. In other countries, slower to adapt to talkies, silents could nevertheless be augmented with commentary, as in *The New York Times*'s description of a screening of the film in Tokyo, Japan, during which a phonographic disc emitted music and then some descriptive narration in Japanese (translated back into English by the United Artists Tokyo rep for the *Times*):

A pretty looking girl is appearing. Showing a feat. She is mounting on a white horse, and the girl looks especially charming and beautiful. But the spectators never give her cheers because the feat is of no interest at all. After the feat

finished a man of stern-looking came before the girl. He is the chief of the
circus.

'You stupid! What is the matter of this? Don't you see the spectators are all
getting tired of seeing the feat?' the chief cried.

'Very sorry, boss. Please pardon me . . .'

And so forth. The circus chief says to the circus audience: 'She will
show you a dancing combined of future, present and past. It is called
the dance of devil.' Clearly Charlie's material had to be spiced up
for the foreign market. As the Japanese narrator filled in the basic
character of the universal Tramp:

The beautiful lady returns to the room of the chief . . . she finds there a man
of slightly built. 'Hey! Get up,' the chief cries, 'What are you?'

'. . . I am a man just as you look . . . with an old and high hat on, with the
battered shoes, baggy trousers, a bamboo cane, is Charlie.'

'Well, well. You are Charlie. Don't you join in my circus? I am now in
trouble of finding a proper comedian.'

'All right. Then I shall be employed.'

Indeed. Years later, Chaplin still could not bear to speak of *The
Circus*, according it just one mention in *My Autobiography*, and that
only in passing, when referring to his mother's illness during its shoot.
Of Lita he writes only: 'During the filming of The Gold Rush I married
for the second time. Because we have two grown sons of whom I am
very fond, I will not go into any details. For two years we were
married and tried to make a go of it, but it was hopeless and ended in
a great deal of bitterness.'

In 1971, however, Chaplin returned to *The Circus*, composing a new
score and adding a song for Merna in the opening credits – 'Swing,
Little Girl' – to go with her fatigue on the trapeze. Today, it benefits
from a fine restoration in film and its DVD version, including some
extended footage of a deleted scene and its out-takes: in the aftermath
of the studio fire, Chaplin took his crew down Sunset Boulevard to
shoot a sequence in which he meets Rex, during a walk with Edna, and
they all hie to a nearby cafe. In the cafe, Chaplin devised a bit of business with two twin prizefighters, although Charlie thinks there is just
the one. The first fighter torments him from a nearby table by chucking
sugar cubes at his hat, till Charlie takes him aside and tips him some
money to pretend to be knocked down in a fight, so he can impress
Merna. This works out fine, till the second twin arrives, who doesn't

know the deal. Charlie gets knocked about, and Rex saves the day by KOing the boxer. The out-takes show Chaplin, again and again, shooting the brief scene in which he sits down with Rex and Merna and the taunts of the fighter begin. Version after version, with Charlie, Merna, Rex and a waiter positioned in every possible manner, this small sequence, that was clearly irrelevant to the film and was doomed to be cut, is given the Chaplin treatment of repeated takes, marking slates numbered 3,417 through 3,645, over several days of shooting. Again and again, Charlie turns to his tormentor, turns back to sit and has his chair yanked from under him by the boxer.

Such compulsive behaviour by a director towards his actors might well be ruthless and tyrannical. Such an attitude towards himself put Chaplin in another bracket entirely. No wonder that, when asked how his ideas came to him, Chaplin replied that 'ideas come from an intense desire for them', and that his method of working was 'sheer perseverance to the point of madness'.

This, clearly, was his mode of living as well.

22

City Lights
Or: Dreams Do Not Speak

In *Film Daily,* on 4 March 1927, Thomas Edison, widely regarded as the father of the cinema, made the following proclamation:

I don't think the talking moving picture will ever be successful in the United States. Americans prefer silent drama. They are accustomed to the moving picture as it is and they will never get enthusiastic over any voices being mingled in it. Yes, there will be novelty to it for a little while, but the glitter will soon wear off and the movie fans will cry for silence or a little orchestra music . . . We are wasting our time in going on with the project . . .

No one agreed more heartily with Edison, on this subject, than Charlie Chaplin. American movies were staggering towards speech from 1926, when two sound systems, RCA and Western Electric, started competing to bring this old bogey of the silent cinema to practical theatrical use. Warner Brothers won this race in 1927, in their 'Vitaphone' partnership with Western Electric that produced the caterwauling of *The Jazz Singer*. Al Jolson starred in *The Singing Fool*, in September 1928, by which time other studios were moving to respond to audience demand for the new medium. Two months earlier, *The Lights of New York* had introduced the talking gangster in a minor movie that became an unexpected summer hit. The old moguls of the movies were still sceptical, however. Adolph Zukor, Paramount's little Napoleon, stated: 'It is obvious that the talking picture has its definite place in the films scheme. But this does not mean that the silent picture is doomed. On the contrary, it will remain the backbone of the industry's commercial security.' Joseph Schenck, president of United Artists, agreed: 'Talking pictures will never displace the silent drama.' This seemed a reasonable stance in 1928, as records show that only ten all-talking and twenty-three part-talking feature films were released by the Hollywood studios that year, alongside 220 silents. In 1929, however, only thirty-eight silent movies were released, and 216 part- or all-talking films. By the end of the year, the silent movie was all but dead, and 1930 began the flowering of sound. At the end of January 1931, however, Chaplin released a film with recorded orchestral score and some sound effects, but no speech whatsoever: *City Lights*.

Chaplin had been, from its earliest echoes, an enemy of the talking feature. As late as June 1930 he was said to be allocating five to ten million dollars 'for a new studio in the San Fernando Valley where he would direct two silent dramas annually and produce five silent features a year by other directors'. In November 1930 he stated his case as boldly as King Canute facing the incoming tide:

I shall never speak in a film. I hate the talkies and will not produce talking pictures. The American industry is transformed. So much the better or worse, it leaves me indifferent. I cannot conceive of my films as other than silent. My shadow appears on the screen as in a dream, and dreams do not speak. Artists, like Will Rogers, Bebe Daniels, Gloria Swanson, Bessie Love are interested in interpreting the talking films because they are thus able to present the maximum of their talent. But they are actors; as for me, I am a mime and all the nuances of my art would be destroyed if I were to accompany them with words or with sound effects.

Chaplin was not as fundamentalist as he seems here, as he told his friend, the writer Rob Wagner, in December 1929 that he had ideas about exploiting sound synchronization as far as music was concerned:

By far the finest marriage is that of pantomime and music. It always has been, but heretofore all we could do was to have some one score a picture to well known themes and then hope that the organist would play them . . . Now, however, we can absolutely determine the music . . . as it is part of the mechanical projection . . .

The spoken word, however, was condemned: 'In drama they are trying to marry the conventions of the theatre with the realism of the screen, and the result is an illegitimate child.'

Other comedians had, nevertheless, succumbed. Laurel and Hardy had taken to talkies like ducks to water, 'Unaccustomed as We Are'. Harold Lloyd had adapted, remaking his classic *Safety Last* as a successful – if somewhat tedious – talkie, *Feet First*. Keaton had made *Free and Easy* and *Doughboys*, though these marked a rapid decline. Mack Sennett had taken the leap and rejigged his studio, though he had been left with his 'B-list' stars, and forcing poor Andy Clyde and co to talk slowed down the comedy to a practically laugh-free zone. New types of comedian were about to thrive: the gravelly voice of

W. C. Fields, unveiled in *The Golf Specialist* of 1930; the four Marx Brothers, wise-cracking in *The Cocoanuts* and *Animal Crackers* of 1929 and 1930 respectively; and, of course, Mae West's inimitable 'Beulah, peel me a grape.'

Chaplin's principles, however, were also driven by necessity. The idle reader, noting the long gaps between Chaplin movies since *The Kid*, might conclude that he spent these periods twiddling his fingers or enjoying his wealth, but as we have seen, this was not so. Powered by their multiple takes, the four thousand-plus slates per picture, the painstaking creative process, Chaplin films were in production far longer than almost any other movies, excluding perhaps those of Erich von Stroheim, who had already been creatively assassinated after his last truncated silent saga, *Queen Kelly*, of 1929.

Chaplin had begun work on *City Lights*, therefore, in the New Year of 1928, just before the premiere of *The Circus*, a mere two months after the release of *The Jazz Singer*. Earlier during the production of *The Circus* he had also, as reported by David Robinson, taken on a producer's role in a picture written and directed by Joseph von Sternberg, *A Woman of the Sea*, designed as another comeback for Edna Purviance. Production records of the film exist in Chaplin's archive, but no print of it seems to have survived. Von Sternberg claimed (in his autobiography, *Fun in a Chinese Laundry*) that Chaplin suppressed the film, but this is as yet an unsolved mystery. In any case, Chaplin's attention was soon devoured by his studio troubles and the Lita Grey follies.

The creative engine room, however, did not shut down for long. *City Lights*, despite its reputation as yet another Chaplin picture wholly developed scriptless in the shooting process, nevertheless emerged from a plethora of notes, script ideas, large folders of scribbled and typed sequences. Many versions, false leads and entire plotlines were discarded along the way, before the purified simplicity of the central themes of the film emerged as if they had been crystal clear and obvious from the start.

Shooting did not begin until December 1928, giving Chaplin almost a year to develop his written ideas. On 28 August that year his mother Hannah died at Glendale hospital, ending her long illness in a peaceful setting. She was buried in the Hollywood Cemetery, far from the poverty of Lambeth. Chaplin informed her other two sons, Sydney, then in Europe, and their half-brother Wheeler Dryden, in New York.

Lita Grey and Chaplin's two small children attended the funeral. At the least, her death finally released Hannah from her long suffering, and from her wanderings in her own unknown realm.

By 10 September, having paused only briefly, the work-in-progress was taking shape. The version written in notes contained several elements that are extraneous to the *City Lights* that we know. The 'story sequence' was like this:

Dream – Awakening – Wandering – Clock episodes – Dawn – Statue – Slums – Park – Finding of dime – Meeting with flower girl – Water in face – Seeking shelter – steam shovel – Introduction of millionaire – Café sequence – Millionaire's home – Ejection from millionaire's home – Ignored by millionaire – Meeting with Negro newsboy – Working in theatre – Loss of job – Proposition about fighting – Refusal – Chance meeting with blind girl on street – Business of escorting her home – Discovery of her condition – Search to find negro – The acceptance of the fight – the Meeting at Larry's – The Training – The Fight – Being knocked out – Being with the millionaire – Second café episode – Discovery of blind girl in street in early morning – Giving her the $20 bill – The Tramp being called 'The Duke' by the drunk.

The whole character of the 'Negro' never found its way into the final version of the movie, as was the case with the theme of the theatre, part of the original setting of the movie as a specific London story:

Exterior of Theatre. Night. The crowds coming out, as they part to go in various directions, the lone figure of the Duke is uncovered and behind him is the bill-board, 'The Last of the Dandies'. Following on with his wanderings, the episodes as shown by hours on the clock. Dawn, the Westminster chimes, the striking of 4 a.m.

The story sequence as of 24 January 1929 was:

Opening up with the dream sequence and dissolving into the awakening and it is night, into the city in the vicinity of the theatre. The crowds are starting for home. The Tramp is a lone figure. He tries to sleep but is ordered on by a policeman. He wanders aimlessly until he is spotted by the millionaire drunk and he is taken into the café and after a hilarious venture, he is dropped. It is close on 4 o'clock. He starts his lone walk towards the public square. Fade out and fade in to the statue sequence . . .

On 2 May 1929, the bare list of shots that would open the film was more clearly a variant on the 'rhythm of a city' theme, which would be dropped and then used in the opening of Chaplin's next film, *Modern Times*:

1. City lights out and sunrise on deserted city.
2. Factory whistles, etc.
3. Huge factory wheel starting slowly.
4. Crowds belching from sub-ways, ferries and trains.
5. Cattle train.
6. Crowds entering office buildings.
7. Cattle driven into slaughter house.
8. Wheel still going.
9. Interior of office – typewriters, adding machines, etc.
10. Stock tickers.
11. Riveters.
12. Press working.
13. Wheel still going.
14. Busy corners of city with traffic, etc.
15. Charlie enters and comes to traffic island.

On 13 May 1929 there was another character, a 'girl', whom Charlie takes to a restaurant:

Sequence of Charlie walking with girl. Charlie and girl walking along street. Girl says she is hungry and would like apple. Charlie has no money and has to pretend to buy apple and in reality, steals it. Charlie takes girl into cheap restaurant. He has only enough money for one dinner which he gives girl while he pretends to eat himself – drinks water out of water glass with spoon for soup – gives her middle portion of her own ice-cream . . . business of tip at end of meal. Girl detects bluff on part of Charlie and realises about his sacrificing himself to feed her. She attempts to carry on deception to please him but is unable to do so and breaks down and weeps.

On 21 May, the London setting is still clearly present:

Opening sound is of Big Ben chimes. This continues through main title. Fade in on city aglow with soft lights. Lap dissolve to busy thoroughfare, twinkling with signs, automobile headlights, etc.

Lap dissolve to dressy crowd of ladies and gentlemen emerging from theatres.

Lap dissolve to crowd of drunken men and girls drunkenly getting out of limousine and entering night club. Millionaire drunk will be among them. Descending the social scale, we come to a dark street corner where a man with a gun holds up his victim.

Lap dissolve to darker streets where prostitutes walk.

Lap dissolve to huddled up figure asleep in park. It is Charlie.

From an apartment house window, a dark woman in an extremely cut dress, summons Hindu servant and points out of window. Cut to Charlie still asleep. The servant pulls him to his feet and tells him, 'I want you.' The Hindu takes him to the apartment house where the servants treat him most graciously. He is put in a barber chair and given tonsorial attention which will account for change in his make-up. He is manicured and given a uniform for his meeting with the woman. 'You are a lucky man, monsieur,' says the French barber.

As alternative, woman may drive past Charlie and have Hindu summon him in.

This sequence, which Chaplin continued to work on, would involve Charlie entering to find a woman lying on a settee who coos to him: 'My adorable man, come to me.' They kiss, a butler brings in a feast, leading to, as the notes have it, 'conflict between his desire for love and food . . . As he is again kissing her passionately we lap dissolve into the dog licking his face and the police, who chase him off the bench . . .'

Charlie then goes to a cafe, where the millionaire sees him and takes him in as part of a bet with his friends. This too was reworked, and on 6 June 1929 the 'Continuity of Story' was baldly:

Dream – Awakening – Wandering – Statue – City busy – Albert – Art store – Chips – Girl – Fade out – Fade in – Banana – 6 o'clock – People going home – Helping girl across street – Girl at home – Predicament of girl – Charlie meets drunk – Home of Drunk – Café – meets girl again.

In the event Chaplin decided that London, the theatre, the 'Negro' (aka Albert), and the Hindu woman dream would complicate his central theme needlessly. None of it is in the picture. The structure of the film as we know and view it today is as familiar as any in the movies:

The Tramp wakes up, having found a night's refuge in the arms of a statue of civic virtue ('Peace and Prosperity') that is about to be unveiled. Wandering through the shopping streets of the city, he comes across a blind flower girl who offers him a flower. He gives her his last coin, but when she hears a limousine door slam she assumes the buyer is a rich man who has left without his change. The Tramp tiptoes away. Later, at night, on the embankment, he saves the life of a drunken millionaire who is trying to drown himself in the river. The millionaire takes him home, then to a wild nightclub, and then gives him a stash of money, which the Tramp rushes over to hand the flower girl to buy up her whole basket. He drives her home in the millionaire's car, cementing her belief in her unseeable benefactor. Back at the millionaire's house, the rich man is sober, and kicks the Tramp out. Later, meeting him in the street, drunk, he takes the Tramp in again. Cast out again as the millionaire departs on a European trip, the Tramp finds work, determined to get money to help the blind girl and her mother, to pay their overdue rent and to fund an operation to restore the girl's sight. To get more cash, he takes on a fixed boxing match, but ends up with another opponent, who thrashes him (after a revamped version of Essanay's 1915 *The Champion*). In the continuing twists of fortune, the millionaire, returned from Europe, takes him home again, giving him a thousand dollars, just as crooks, hiding in the house, try to rob him. The Tramp calls the police, but when they arrive, finding the money on him, he is accused. He runs off, gives the money to the blind girl, and is then caught. Coming out of jail after nine months, destitute, he comes across the flower girl again: now she is cured, and set up in a fancy shop with her mother. She has pity on the Tramp, but it is only when she pins a flower on him and feels his hand that she realizes that he is her benefactor. The picture fades on the moment of her realization, and his look of hope against hope.

The scenes of Charlie's first encounter with the flower girl, played by Virginia Cherrill, were the subject of long and repeated try-outs, painstakingly shot, again and again, day after day, week after week. Home-movie shots, unearthed by Kevin Brownlow and David Gill, give us glimpses of Chaplin meandering about on the set in his tramp costume, trying to work out how he could convincingly portray the moment when the blind girl mistakes the Tramp for a toff. Virginia Cherrill was an untried twenty-year-old society girl and coaching her to provide the exact responses he wanted was an arduous and frustrating experience. Apart from this, Chaplin could not find the solution for the basic mechanics of the moment when she mistakes him for a rich man, the central conceit of the movie. A German visitor, one Egon Erwin Kisch, another of Chaplin's radical European acquaintances, was invited to watch Chaplin viewing his rushes at this point, together with novelist Upton Sinclair. Both were consulted on the spot as ordinary viewers about this 'dead centre' in the production. Kisch's tale, published in Germany, was relayed in his own words by the *New York Times* on 18 August 1929.

And now we want to see the film run off. Thus far only a quarter of it is finished . . . 'Great, great,' we whisper after the fragment has been run off and the projection room is light again.

The boss protests and asks, 'Can you tell me what you have seen?'

'Of course. Willingly. A girl is selling flowers on the street corner. And along comes Chaplin.'

'Oh, not yet.'

'First there comes a man and his wife and buys a flower.'

'A man? What kind of a man?'

'A man who looks a little like Adolph[e] Menjou.'

'Yes, an elegant man with a lady. That is important now; and then?'

'Then Chaplin comes round the corner. He sees a fountain in the wall and takes off his glove in order to drink. That is, not the glove as a whole, but finger by finger. One is missing and Charlie tries to find it, in vain.'

'You see, Charlie?' shouts Harry Crocker (his assistant director), triumphantly.

'No, it isn't clear. We will run that over again . . .'

And after further chewing over the matter of the glove–

'Hold on! There's something before that.'

Chaplin looks sharply at Sinclair and myself, almost fearfully, entreatingly. 'Something in between . . . an auto comes along!'

'Yes, an auto comes along. A gentleman gets out and walks past Chaplin . . .'

'And what does the auto do?'

I answer that I don't know.

And Upton Sinclair opines that it goes away.

'The devil, the devil,' murmurs Chaplin. 'It's all spoiled.' And his fellow workers are in despair . . .

Kisch tries to explain what he saw in the rushes: The girl handing Charlie a flower, its fall to the ground, his realization of her blindness, he walks away, then comes back, she dumps water in his face, he comes back again and buys a flower –

'And –'

'She is in love.'

'With whom?'

'With Chaplin.' . . .

Chaplin buries his face in his hands, the picture of gloom . . . And his collaborators are sad. What has happened? Where is the disaster if I, a chance foreigner fail to understand a gag, an idea?

But it is more than a gag. It is the basic idea of the film, which, absolutely unintelligible, has fallen under the table . . . If the public doesn't grasp the tragic quid pro quo in a second – Charlie's powerful emotion, his realization of his poverty and his instant decision to resort to swindling and theft for the sake of this masquerade, for the sake of his love, for the sake of her love – if the public doesn't grasp all this as something elementary all is lost.

'We must do the whole thing over again,' said Chaplin.

And so the work ground on. The solution – Chaplin stepping through a limousine to get around a traffic jam, the slamming of the limousine door confusing the girl into thinking he was its rich owner, who had bought her flower – was not achieved until late in the shoot.

As *City Lights* was Chaplin's fourth full-length feature, and his seventy-fifth film, one might ask, again, why he required this arduous, long, costly process to arrive at a structure that was more or less pre-ordained: the Tramp enters the world, which, with all its familiarities, is a hostile place to him, full of pitfalls and tribulations, in which opportunities present themselves either fleetingly or as miraculous visitations. This was, in fact, the common ground of comedians, although some, like Harold Lloyd, adopted a more congenial persona to the audience, or like Keaton, a more robust innovator in the modern world of machines. W. C. Fields, a self-made original, was often seen as a kind of stranger dropped from another planet, nonplussed by all ordinary matters, be they bathroom mirrors, doors, hats that never quite could be placed on one's head, bank managers, wives, children or society at large. Chaplin, on the other hand, always recognized the world, though he knew it to be a place of infinite peril.

In a real sense, *City Lights* can be seen as a sequel to *The Circus*, a direct continuance of its last shot: relinquishing love, and employment, Charlie walks out of the sawdust ring left by the big top and wanders off, into the twentieth-century city, with its crowds, wheels, clattering offices, shops, cafes and monuments. In the shade of Peace and Prosperity, he gets half-impaled on society's sword, then poses for a moment on the statue with its outstretched hand literally thumbing his nose. The assembled dignitaries, meanwhile, squeak and prattle in a mechanical gibberish, Charlie's contemptuous comment at talkie speech. Film buffs might cross-reference to another 1930 film of fearsome anti-bourgeois sentiment, also featuring gesticulating bearded burghers, Buñuel and Dalí's surrealist outrage, *L'Age d'Or*. Buñuel had in fact met Chaplin in Hollywood in the summer of 1930, though only

City Lights.

his previous film with Dalí, the silent *Un Chien Andalou*, was privately screened there at the time. Buñuel was offered his ticket to Hollywood after an unnamed MGM representative saw *L'Age d'Or* in Paris, just before it was banned. Buñuel recalls, in his autobiography, *My Last Breath*, how he visited Chaplin, having demolished a Christmas tree in his presence at a party attended by several other mad Spaniards. Chaplin invited them to his own New Year revels, obligingly providing another tree, telling Buñuel: 'Since you're so fond of tearing up trees . . . why don't you get it over with now, so we won't be disturbed during dinner?' Buñuel pronounced himself opposed to patriotism, not greenery, a sentiment that would have endeared him to Chaplin. Buñuel states that he screened *Un Chien Andalou* for the Tramp more than once:

I remember the first time. The movie had hardly begun when we heard a loud noise behind us and turned around to see Chaplin's Chinese majordomo, who was running the projector, flat out on the floor in a dead faint. (Much later, Carlos Saura told me that when Geraldine Chaplin was a little girl, her father used to frighten her by describing certain scenes from my movie.)

The 'surrealism' of American movies, however, emerged out of the absurdities of social reality, a thing Salvador Dalí signally failed to grasp when, a few years later, he wrote an unfilmable script for the Marx Brothers – *Giraffes on Horseback Salad* – which Harpo Marx swiftly binned. Buñuel's main actor in *L'Age d'Or*, Gaston Modot, rushes across the street to kick an innocent blind man, but Chaplin's un-Spanish take on blindness is of course far more gentle. The Tramp's compassion for those more unfortunate than himself is an old Victorian virtue, stretching even to the poor millionaire who is determined to kill himself, though he is only an anonymous drunk when he first stumbles into Charlie's view on the riverbank, tying a noose round his neck.

For this role Chaplin cast Harry Myers, a veteran comedian who had worked for almost all the studios – including a leading role in an early Stan Laurel solo short, *Get 'em Young* – and starred in a number of 1920s movies, starting with *A Connecticut Yankee in King Arthur's Court* in 1921. (Myers replaced Chaplin's original choice, Henry Clive, after Clive was allegedly reluctant to get dunked in the water.) Myers's timing as comic partner is flawless. Their initial scene together, as Charlie tries to put him off suicide and the rope entangles both of them, sending them into the river together weighted to a stone, is once again a return to the tried and true of pantomime comedy – Karno to the gills. A manic variant on Chaplin's *One A.M.* drunk, the millionaire is a perfect avatar of the City itself, madly poised between enthusiasm and despair. Charlie's invocation to him: 'Tomorrow the birds will sing! . . . Be brave, face life!' would have been rejected by Keystone Charlie with a familiar kick and sneer.

Despite the repetitious try-outs, Chaplin kept returning to his old well-tested sequences: the nightclub cafe scene of two blotto revellers, as in Keystone's *The Rounders* and Essanay's *A Night Out*. The boxing fight, as aforementioned, a perfect ballet of punch-drunk louts. The drunken party scene, shades of Mutual's *The Count*. Moments of sentiment are punctured with slapstick, as when the Tramp sits down to admire the blind flower girl and she inadvertently flings a bucket of slopwater in his face. As he ogles the girl from outside her window he gets struck by a flowerpot knocked over by a cat and falls over a barrel. The Tramp is still a clown, if only just . . .

At the end of his two-year shoot, Chaplin emerged once again with a compact narrative that fulfilled his definition of the performer appearing on the screen 'as in a dream'. The melancholy air of the Circus seeped into the City, deepening the isolation of the Tramp, now wholly cut off from any imaginary community of hoboes, beggars of the road, whether it leads to Moscow, London, Paris or New York. He drifts like flotsam, alighting on a suicidal madman here, a gambolling crowd, a group of civic posers, until he meets his female counterpart, who, unlike him, remains static, fixed in her own darkness, exuding that inner radiance that Charlie had not found with his wives. The magic of money, that alone can conquer hunger and want, will come to his aid by necromantic coincidences, so that her darkness can be lifted, and when lifted, she will see before her the Tramp in his absolute, destitute essence.

That last look, which critic and fan James Agee set on a pinnacle, describing it as 'enough to shrivel the heart . . . the greatest piece of acting and the highest moment in movies', may well mean different things to different people, a moment of stasis that was typical of Chaplin's refusal of anything that we today call 'closure'. In itself, it left open both options of her acceptance or refusal, leaving the Flower Girl on the threshold of pity. And we might note that, as for Griffith a generation earlier, Chaplin's women were either generically female, or named after the actress of the moment: Edna, Georgia or Merna – only the luckless heroine of *A Woman of Paris* had her own fictional name. But the Tramp himself has been left at the fade-out in an even more uncertain pose. It is as if Chaplin the creator dreads the truth of the moment that would come were it not for that rapid fade to The End. My own conceit is that it could only be inevitably Charlie's Awakening. As in *The Bank*, as in *Shoulder Arms*, as in *Sunnyside*, as in the angel fantasy of *The Kid*, it would have had to be that old chestnut: he woke up and it was all a dream. Back in the arms of the unveiling civic statue, and then, inevitably, carted off to jail.

The Tramp, it appears, cannot abide reality, with all its dangers, its trammels, its looming disappointments. Outwardly indomitable, and able to survive the slings and arrows, there is nevertheless a defeated soul inside. In the world beyond Charles Chaplin's studio, by the time his film was made, the economic slide that was becoming known as the Depression was inexorably shattering the 'Prosperity' part of the monument. The 'Peace' part was destined to receive its bashing only a few years down the line. It might have been better, in fact, for the Tramp to sleep on, in the stone arms of that lofty sentiment, and dream. That part of Chaplin that was Charlie understood this too well, as did his audience, dreaming with him for the eighty-eight minutes of the film.

PART THREE

Modern Times

Synopsis, *Modern Times* (1936)

'A story of industry, of individual enterprise – humanity crusading in the pursuit of happiness.' After a montage of sheep in their pen dissolving into the crowds of a modern city, we are in the offices of the Electro Steel Corp., whose manager (played by Allan Garcia), watching all phases of his enterprise from a giant television screen, urges more speed in the works. On the factory floor, Charlie, a workman, mechanically tightens a stream of bolts rushing past on a conveyor belt. Even in his break, his hands still twitch repetitively. He is chosen from the line to demonstrate a new feeding machine which would enable management to cut out the lunch hour, but it goes haywire, spilling soup, frying the corn on the cob and pushing bolts into his mouth.

Under the pressure of the speeded-up conveyor belt, Charlie goes berserk, and is stuck in the great cogs and wheels of the machine. He pulls levers and switches, sprays his boss with an oil can, and is carted off by men in white coats.

'Cured of a nervous breakdown but without a job, he leaves the hospital to start life anew.' It is the height of the Depression. Men are marching for work. Wandering innocently in the street, Charlie picks up a red flag fallen off a truck and finds himself in the vanguard of a demonstration that is broken up by mounted police. Arrested as a ringleader, he is swept off to jail. Meanwhile, in the streets, a 'gamin', a streetwise girl (played by Paulette Goddard), steals fruit to feed her younger sisters and unemployed father. In jail, Charlie tangles with his criminal cell mates, takes a heavy dose of cocaine which a fellow prisoner has hidden in the salt-shaker, and, in his drugged frenzy, foils a prisoner's escape single-handed.

Outside the safety of jail, where Charlie is a privileged inmate, 'there is trouble with the unemployed'. The Gamin's father is shot dead during a riot and the juvenile authorities snatch her sisters, but Paulette escapes into the street. Charlie, after an episode of tea-gurgling with a visiting minister's wife, is given his pardon and a letter of recommendation to work. His first job on the docks, however, is disastrously ended when he takes a wedge from under a ship in construction, which drifts off and sinks. 'Determined to go back to jail,' he encounters the Gamin when she steals a loaf of bread, and, failing to get arrested for that, goes into a cafeteria and gorges himself before revealing he has no money to pay. Charlie and Paulette meet in the police wagon, but a chance swerve enables them to escape. Destitute together, he dreams of an ideal country life, with a cow outside providing fresh milk. But a policeman's nudge moves them on. Charlie takes work in a department store, and encounters some burglars who include the out-of-work fore-man from the old steelworks. He goes to sleep on the job and spends another ten days in jail. Released, he finds his 'idyllic' shack with Paulette on the waterfront.

The newspapers announce that factories are reopening. Rushing to the steel plant, he is put to work with engineer Chester Conklin to fix the giant machine. Chester gets caught in the gears as the lunch whistle blows, but Charlie manages to get him out. However, the men go out on strike, and in a fracas with the police, Charlie ends up back in jail. Meanwhile, Paulette's street dancing has got her a job in a cafe. She takes in Charlie and the boss (Henry Bergman) gives him a try-out as a singing waiter. A reprise of waiter scenes from old Chaplin shorts ensues, ending in chaos with a mislaid plate of duck. Sent in to sing, Charlie writes down his lines on his cuffs but loses them, and the Tramp gives voice for the first time – but in a gibberish song. He is a hit, but the juvenile authorities have caught up with Paulette. As they try to take her away, Charlie confounds them with a domino pile of chairs, and they escape together.

At dawn, on a country road, she despairs: 'What's the use of trying?' Charlie tells her: 'Buck up – never say die. We'll get along!' For the first time, the Tramp goes off into the sunset, towards a range of hills, together with his chosen loved one.

23

His Regeneration

From 'A Comedian Sees the World', *Woman's Home Companion*,
September 1933, by Charles Chaplin

The disillusion of love, fame and fortune left me somewhat apathetic. There
seemed nothing to turn to outside my work, and that, after twenty years, was
becoming irksome. I needed emotional stimulus.

I am tired of love and people and like all egocentrics I turn to myself. I want
to live in my youth again, to capture the moods and sensations of childhood,
so remote from me now – so unreal – almost like a dream. I need to turn back
time; to venture into the blurred past and bring it into focus . . .

Chaplin's second and longest trip abroad stemmed from a more
modest initial plan to attend the London premiere of *City Lights*, after
its New York opening on 6 February 1931, and then see some sights
in Europe. In New York, Mordaunt Hall, the *New York Times*'s force-
ful film critic, found him in good fettle, exhilarated and more recon-
ciled to sound, emphasizing *City Lights'* specially synchronized score
composed by himself and arranged by Arthur Johnson. It was not, in
fact, Chaplin's first score, as he had, according to Chaplinologist
Jeffrey Vance, composed themes for *The Kid* and *The Idle Class*, and
a special score with conductor Arthur Kay for *The Circus* – which was
replaced decades later, in 1970, with the score that is now played with
the film. Vance found that Chaplin had to his credit three previous
songs: 'There's Always One You Can't Forget', 'Oh, That Cello!' and
'The Peace Patrol' as early as 1916.

Chaplin was so mellow, on his New York trip, that he even
discussed with Mordaunt Hall the kind of accent his character
might have were he to speak which, Chaplin hastened to add, would
be never:

He said that the little tramp might be imagined as speaking punctillious
English, almost in a whisper . . . If he were asked if he had the time, he would
pull out his watch and look at himself and then say 'Yes, I have the time,' and
put the watch back in his pocket without giving the desired information.

Years ago he said that his character symbolized a down and out London toff and in his imagination the little fellow's speech must be in keeping with his bearing . . .

However, all this was strictly theoretical, as 'personally, I prefer to express myself by pantomime.'

The premiere itself, at the George M. Cohan Theatre, Hall observed, was another Chaplin triumph, 'a joyous evening. Mr. Chaplin's shadow has grown no less.' But at this point in the advance of the talkies no one could credibly pretend, not even Chaplin, though he mouthed the words, that silent movies were still 'the substantial medium'.

It was clearly time for a break, to seek a renewal of energy, though Chaplin took a detour before his embarkation to Europe, to present *City Lights* at Sing Sing prison. Eighteen hundred prisoners 'enjoyed a respite from the dull monotony of their existence' on 12 February, when

. . . the film was shown to the prisoners in the new audiorium, and the Warden, his little daughter, Joan, and the members of Mr. Chaplin's party sat in a box . . . After the showing Mr. Chaplin made a brief talk to the prisoners in which he expressed happiness at being able to bring a little enjoyment into their lives and told of his pleasure at seeing them respond so appreciatively to his comedy. Warden Lawes described the evening's entertainment as 'the biggest hit we've had.'

One wonders if Preston Sturges, then a not very successful playwright, had this screening in mind when he devised the scene of the laughing prisoners in his 1941 movie *Sullivan's Travels* . . .

The following night, Chaplin sailed on the *Mauretania*, with his entourage – his secretary, Carlyle Robinson, valet and 'Man Friday' Kono, and his friend Ralph Barton. He told the newsmen,

The chief aim of my trip abroad is England. I am looking forward to seeing once more the haunts of my boyhood and finding out if the hot saveloy and crumpet man is still going around ringing his bell . . . I want to see if the tripe dresser of Birdcage Walk, Bethnal Green, the stalls on Saturday night in the Mile End Road and the fakers who sell painted sparrows for canaries in Middlesex Street, known as the 'Spank' . . . are still there Sunday mornings . . .

Ten years on from his first trip, Chaplin's fame had increased exponentially, and the crowds mobbed him from the moment the ship docked at Plymouth, as the London *Times* proceeded to describe:

For another hour the observation-car which the Great Western Railway Company had placed at the comedian's disposal on the boat-train to Paddington was surrounded with hero-worshippers, and during that time nobody with the courage to thrust a head into the carriage was sent empty away. Some were for autographs, and Mr. Chaplin scribbled away indefatigably; some for assurances that their good wishes were reciprocated, and the assurances were given with unflagging gaiety. The comedian's responsiveness to the mood of the crowd was complete. He was as exuberant as any of his admirers, a gushing spring of enthusiasm. But as the train drew out of the station and the sound of the cheering died away his mood died with it. It was a wholly different man who plunged with anything but an easy optimism into a discussion of economics. From its dismal throes he was abruptly rescued by the arrival of a tin of Devonshire cream, a long-promised 'treat' to which he addressed himself with the eagerness of a schoolboy . . .

At Paddington station, the adulation-addict had another fix, *The Times* noting:

Dickens knew something of popular enthusiasm, but could he have beheld the press of people gathered . . . in honour of Mr. Chaplin, he might have rubbed his eyes in astonishment. Dispassionate onlookers – if any such there were – might have observed that Mr. Chaplin's own excitement at once attained without apparent effort to precisely the same pitch as that of the crowd's. An escort of police somehow contrived to propel him through the crowd to the door of a waiting motor-car. He promptly scrambled on the roof of the car, and, waving his hat and returning the shouts of the crowd, he was borne in slow triumph out of the station.

At the Carlton Hotel in London, Chaplin was 'a virtual prisoner . . . in the face of a crowd of admirers', and his plan to wander about his old cockney haunts seemed unlikely to happen given the plaudits as were trumpeted by the popular papers, such as the *News-Chronicle*: 'The names of great statesmen, Generals and preachers may become household words, perhaps, in more continents than one. But how faint is their image upon the human mind in comparison with that of the incomparably vivid figure which Charles Chaplin has created and made?'
Instead of meeting the saveloy and crumpet man and the tripe dresser of Birdcage Walk, Chaplin was quickly meeting George Bernard Shaw at the home of Viscountess Astor on 25 February, following which he 'rushed off for dinner at the country home of Winston Churchill'. He visited the House of Commons, had tea with

Sir Philip Sassoon, and had a dinner in his honour graced by Prime Minister Ramsay MacDonald, former PM David Lloyd George and 'others from all parties'. On 5 March he visited Eton College, took tea in a 'sock shop' and made a speech to the boys.

In his subsequent series in the *Woman's Home Companion*, Chaplin wrote that he had grabbed an early taxi ride down to his old place in Kennington, taking a quick look at a woman and a child in the park, then rushing back to the Carlton Hotel in time for breakfast. He expatiated at greater length on his meeting with Shaw, whom he liked, but whose reputation disturbed him, and whose intellect daunted him–

. . . wasn't he quoted as saying that all art should be propaganda? To me, such a premise would restrict art. I prefer to think the object of art is to intensify feeling, color or sound – if object it has – for this gives a fuller range to the artist in expressing life, in spite of the moral aspect of it. I would like to broach him on the subject, but I know that in such a controversy his intellect would win out.

In front of the parliamentarians, however, he had no such cavils, and eagerly lectured them about 'what we would do if we had the power of a Mussolini to help England in her present crisis'. As he wrote of himself, 'fools shout where angels fear to whisper, and so I started.' Chaplin's formula, which he had clearly worked out, was to 'reduce the government. The world is suffering from too much government and the expense of it.' Government should, however, own the banks and revise the banking laws and the Stock Exchange, controlling prices, interest and profit. England's colonies should be amalgamated into an economic unity. 'My policy would stand for internationalism, world cooperation of trade, the abolition of the gold standard and world inflation of money . . . I would endeavour to raise the standard of living, preferably internationally, otherwise throughout the British Domain.' Labour hours should be reduced and a minimum wage applied.

Lloyd George and company clearly gave this the polite reception appropriate to a comedian. Churchill, on the other hand, preferred to talk about show business, having read that Chaplin was thinking of producing a film about Napoleon. 'You must do it,' he told Chaplin, 'Napoleon in his bath-tub arguing with his imperious brother who's all dressed up . . . it is action and fun.' In a section cut from the published account of his argument with the members of parliament,

Chaplin replies to comments about Gandhi being a menace to the Far East with the remark that 'the Gandhis or Lenins do not start revolutions. They are forced up by the masses and usually voice the want of a people,' at which Churchill laughs and says: 'You should go into parliament.' Chaplin demurs, but voices his belief in 'evolution to avoid revolution . . . there's every evidence that the world needs a drastic change.' This was obviously too hot for the good lady readers of *Woman's Home Companion*, but remains in the archive draft of the text.

Chaplin had discovered the polite embrace of the ruling class in his first trip of 1921, but was he not emphatically one of them now? He described another brief wander down Lambeth at night, remembering old songs and dreaming of fish and chips, but: 'I'd love to buy a penny-worth, but I haven't the courage. One of the customers recognises me, so I steal away in the darkness.'

Another attempt to revisit the past proved to be a sombre experience: a drive to west London with Ralph Barton to look for the old workhouse where Sydney and he had passed their harshest times. The current head of the school had found some old records of the two brothers: 'Sydney Chaplin handed back to mother, March 10, 1896. Charles, ditto.' Ralph comments to him: 'You see? You're just a ditto.' The regime now was freer, Chaplin found, and the children were gathered to be told by their headmaster that the school was to be 'presented with a motion picture machine. We are to have a gala night with motion pictures, and sweets and oranges will be served.'

Chaplin might have remembered the story he told Benjamin de Casseres in the *New York Times* in 1920, about the apple he had picked out for his Christmas present, only to be denied it because he told the other boys 'pirate stories'. Interestingly, Chaplin's downbeat description of his visit to Hanwell contrasts with a more positive version in the *Daily Mail* (relayed by the *New York Times* on 29 March) where Chaplin was said to have

. . . performed his famous antics of the films before 400 wildly delighted boys and girls. He visited the infirmary and spoke to every one of the children in bed . . . Mr. Pace, the headmaster, told me: 'I did not know that Mr. Chaplin was coming. When he arrived the children were in their classes and he had a cup of tea with me while waiting for them to gather . . . He climbed to the platform and made a little speech. He performed his famous little walk, took off his hat and jumped into the air.'

The *Daily Mail* reporter also claimed to have followed Chaplin in a cab as he whizzed off to the Kennington Road and then continued to a Balham market, where he got out and

. . . stood there alone – a short, smartly dressed figure in neat hard-felt hat with velvety gray overcoat and dark blue suit. He laughed to see once more the hawkers in cap and muffler . . . he laughed at the children. He laughed at the cries of confusion. He was home – and oh! So happy . . . And there I lost sight of him among the cabbages and potatoes and fish and shoes and stockings and sausages. And I was glad – because I felt that he ought to be alone, really alone.

So perhaps Chaplin did get to see the tripe dresser and the saveloy and crumpet man after all. But he did not linger. At the end of his own account of his second London homecoming Chaplin writes: 'I have been besieged by all sorts of invitations and requests, and letters are piling up . . . One cannot find time to see all one's friends . . . If I do not wish to offend them I must pack up and leave. I suddenly make up my mind to visit Germany . . .'

Or not so suddenly, as the press reported he was heading for the premiere of *City Lights* in Berlin. Once again, crowds mobbed him at Liverpool Street station as he boarded the Hook of Holland express train. When he arrived, at the Friedrichstrasse station, he was 'affectionately welcomed by some thousands of people who awaited him in the snow' and 'several hundreds who were waiting at his hotel in Unter den Linden'. *The New York Times* wrote: 'The film comedian was escorted down from the platform to a waiting automobile amid wild choruses of "hochs" and enthusiastic whistling – youthful Berliners were uncertain if handclapping was approved in Hollywood and compromised on whistling as the loudest and most unmistakable form of greeting.'

Chaplin spent only a week in Berlin, the highlight being his visit to Professor Albert Einstein's home. Einstein had first met Chaplin in Hollywood, together with Lita, and the two men had hit it off from the start. Now it was Einstein's fifty-second birthday. Mrs Einstein, according to Chaplin's own account, made some 'delicious home-baked tarts', and during the conversation Einstein's son 'remarked on the psychology of the popularity of Einstein and myself. "You are popular", he said, "because you are understood by the masses. On the other hand, the Professor's popularity with the masses is because he is not understood."' The two luminaries discussed neither science nor movies, but Chaplin's new bugbears: business, economics and the gold standard. Einstein professed himself uninterested in 'business mathematics', but agreed with Chaplin that 'every man should be clothed and fed, with a roof over his head, for there is enough for all.'

Before leaving the two exchanged photographs: 'One had been taken of the Professor and myself in California which he signed as follows: "To Charlie, the Economist." I autographed one in return, and for the life of me I couldn't think what to say. The Professor came to my rescue. "Why not 'et tu, Brute,'" he smiled.'

Chaplin found time to meet Marlene Dietrich and to sample Berlin's famous night life, with men dressed as women and women dressed as men, but the sight of 'two effeminate youths' dancing together seemed to horrify him, 'so [we] hurriedly drank our ginger ale and fled out into the night.' Nevertheless, there were opportunities to flirt with a lady called 'G', before rushing off to Vienna, the sad 'city of yesterdays'. Here a Hungarian woman in a cabaret toppled him over with her enthusiasm when she tried to kiss his hand, and he visited the famous Workmen's Apartments, the ex-king's palace and the Museum. Then off to northern Italy.

Chaplin was obviously in no hurry to return to America, though he was galloping back and forth in Europe. In Venice, he was hoisted shoulder high by a young man who carried him alone from the railway station to the hotel. A few days after marvelling at the canals he was back in Paris, to be awarded the Legion of Honour and meet Foreign Minister Briand and other members of the French cabinet. Then he left for the country estate of the Duke of Westminster, who took him on a wild-boar hunt which takes up two full pages of the *Woman's Home Companion*, episode three.

Brother Sydney was staying in Nice, and Chaplin could discover the Riviera. He met Sir Philip Sassoon again, who seemed to be everywhere, the Duke of Connaught, writers Maurice Maeterlinck (author of the 1909 play *The Blue Bird*) and Emil Ludwig (biographer of Goethe, Napoleon and Bismarck, among others), and the Prince of Monaco. Chaplin expressed his literary limitations to Ludwig, who, he imagined, had read everything from the early Greeks to the modern day, while 'the foundations of my literary education would take in the Bible, Shakespeare, Plutarch's *Lives of the Great*, Burton's *Anatomy of*

Melancholy and Boswell's *Life of Johnson*, with a few philosophers thrown in such as Nietzsche, Emerson, Schopenhauer and Robert Ingersoll, the latter the first to arouse my interest in philosophy.' Not bad for a Lambeth-bred kid. (Robert Ingersoll was the noted late nineteenth-century apostle of the freethinkers, humanists and agnostics.)

The latest book to arouse his interest, Chaplin told Ludwig, was Sadakichi Hartmann's *The Last Thirty Days of Christ*, which showed Christ as both mystic and philosopher, 'a lone figure, misunderstood even by his disciples'. An appropriate theme perhaps for Chaplin's innermost thoughts . . .

After Nice, Chaplin took a boat to Algiers, another winter resort at that time for wealthy Europeans, and here too 'thousands were lined along the road all the way to the hotel'. An Arab guide took him through the famous Casbah and its threaded alleys and souks. Then it was back to France, to stay with an old acquaintance, Frank Harris. Harris had by now published his infamous *My Life and Loves*, but Chaplin offers us no views of this project, noting only that this meeting came only six months before Harris's death.

On the journey went: from Biarritz, where he met Edward, the Prince of Wales, into Spain to San Sebastian for a visit to a bullfight with the Marquis de Sorreana. Chaplin witnessed 'a dramatic killing . . . a large arena, the silence of thirty thousand people and standing in the bleak sunshine a man and a bull facing each other, the bull in the throes of death. The beast had been courageous and given a wonderful performance – a perfect foil for the artistry of the matador . . .' One might imagine Charlie peeking out of Chaplin's eyes. The bullfight in San Sebastian, however, is reliably dated by the press record to 9 August, so presumably Chaplin condensed his long Riviera stay for his magazine series. One of the reasons, perhaps the main one, for Chaplin's lingering was a new affair, with a Czech dancer, Mizzi Muller, otherwise known as May Reeves, whom Chaplin met through his brother Sydney.

After Spain Chaplin returned to England, where, in September, he had another notable encounter, this time with India's dissident leader, Mahatma Gandhi. Chaplin attended Gandhi along with more fervent admirers at the modest home of a Dr Katial in Beckton Road, Canning Town. Chaplin records that 'it all seems like a revival meeting':

Chaplin in London with Mahatma Gandhi, 1932.

The Mahatma is arriving. The whole street is in a cheer. I look out of the window. Below is a limousine. The police are endeavouring to make a way to the house. Someone struggles to open the car door. Smiling and serenely cool, Ghandi [*sic*] gathers his calico around him and steps out of the machine. From the window a Hindu lady showers him with flowers. 'Here, you throw some, too.' 'Oh, no,' I answer. 'I never make demonstrations.'

Chaplin challenged Gandhi on his views on machinery, and Gandhi – the only person Chaplin met who had seen none of his films – explained that conditions in India were different from those in the west. Indian people could do without machines because 'our climate, our mode of living, make this possible. I wish to make our people independent of industry which weapon the western world holds over us . . . We must learn agriculture, to grow our own rice and spin our own cotton . . .'

Chaplin comes away 'wondering whether this was the man destined to guide the lives of over three hundred million people', and then comments: 'The following day I had tea at Lady Ottoline Morrell's. Lytton Strachey, Aldous Huxley, Augustus John and several others were there. I told them of my visit with Ghandi . . .'

He was now living in a rarefied world in which, as he was acutely aware, the Tramp would have been booted out by the first hotel major-domo, though not, perhaps, from Gandhi's presence. He had left the 'little fellow' frozen in his moment of hope by the flower girl and was clearly at a total loss as to what to do next in movies. When in Algiers he was said to be planning a film as a sheikh, although Ben Turpin had already made that parody. In December 1931 the *New York Times* announced that he was going to produce a talking film at the British-Dominion Studio starring the great Russian singer, Feodor Chaliapin: 'The story will be of an opera singer in pre-war Russia and will take Chaliapin through the war and the Russian Revolution.' But nothing more was heard of this either. The film on Napoleon was constantly being mooted, and had been a gleam in the eye since 1926, as a follow-up to *A Woman of Paris*, but it never got off the ground. There was another vague shadow, that was to take shape later as a synopsis of a film about a woman taking ship for Shanghai, and this lay dormant until, three decades later, it emerged as *A Countess from Hong Kong*.

In October, Chaplin witnessed the general election which gave the National Coalition government a majority that enabled Ramsay MacDonald, who had been expelled from the Labour Party for forming the coalition with the Tories, to form a National Coalition Cabinet that lasted until 1935. It seemed that politics were not playing out in the direction Chaplin and like-minded friends might have wished for. In December, he became embroiled in a court case brought by a Miss May Shepherd, secretary and publicity agent, who claimed £100 for services rendered. For some reason Chaplin decided to dispute this, but once in court he agreed to settle in full. It seemed England was becoming mundane.

Chaplin decided to return to America, but by the most circuitous route he could find. Taking Sydney with him, he travelled east, through Switzerland, aiming to take ship from Naples through the Suez Canal, and on to the Far East, stopping at Ceylon, Singapore, Indonesia (then the Dutch East Indies) and Japan. In Rome a meeting with Mussolini was suggested, but the Duce, thankfully, could not find the time. In March, Chaplin sailed to the Orient.

This phase of his travels was presented as a holiday, but its influence on Chaplin's thought was profound. Perhaps Gandhi's comments on the machine-less East whetted his appetite for these exotic destinations. As a mime, he could not fail to be fascinated by the various traditional dances and acts that he observed along the way. In Ceylon, there were jugglers 'twirling cans of fire attached to a rope which they spin like a baton'. Devil dancers, the warm, sultry air, the constant sound of insects, swayed him. He saw Buddhism in action in the temples, people handing out grain to mendicants. In Singapore he had to be treated for 'a slight attack of fever', but he soon moved on to Java, and to Bali, the island 'untouched by civilization', where 'one doesn't worry about depression. The problem of living is easy. And the women are beautiful.' Chaplin was entranced by the lush green landscape and the ten-year-old dancing girls, whose sinuous dance was 'appreciated without comment . . . Those dancers had practised assiduously, striving for perfection without any consideration for personal gain.'

The Tramp was discovering an art that was organic to its culture, ways of life in which ghosts and spirits were as real as any daylight sights. He saw a traditional 'barong play', relating an episode in the life of the ancient King Erlangga, in which 'a wicked witch, a widow, with her pupils, brought all manner of ill-luck to the flourishing king-dom'. The actor playing the witch became so immersed in his role that he 'lost control and rushed madly through the crowd and into the jungle, shrieking in a state of hysteria'. A pig was killed, and then the actor's mask was placed in a box and carried off by the players.

From Bali Chaplin returned to Singapore and saw a traditional Chinese drama that played over several nights: 'My brother and I would sit of an evening trying to guess the different symbols that the actors used during the play.' This eastern style of emblematic acting may well have reminded him of his own comedy equivalent. These acts too had their wandering heroes, their villainous Eric Campbells, their gormless Albert Austins and their looming Mack Swains. He would have felt vindicated in his instinctive belief in the universal lan-guage of gesture, even though this was no mime. Travelling on to Japan, Chaplin was delighted that the kabuki season 'was in full swing, so we got tickets for all the performances'. The acute styliza-tion seized his interest and he paid minute attention to the structure and mechanics of the plays: 'The actors sometimes enter and exit from a runway that extends on out through the audience to the back of the theatre. A revolving stage facilitates the rapid change of scenery. These devices they have used for hundreds of years.'

From being an innocent abroad, Chaplin was realizing the deep sediment of art in other cultures, the techniques which resonated to him first in their exoticism, and then in recognition. He noted that the essence of this art was nevertheless being 'undermined by western influence. The beautiful school of some of the old masters – Harunobu, Hokusai, Utamoro, Hiroshige – is entirely neglected, and in place of it are hybrid entrepreneurs whose work is neither Japanese nor European.' The ancient tea ceremony impressed him too with its simplicity and beauty, applied to the commonplace. But another ancient human ceremony, neither simple nor beautiful, was also playing itself out during his visit. On the very day after his arrival in Tokyo on 14 May 1932, to the accolade of the usual cheering crowds throwing their hats into the air, a group of young Japanese army and navy officers broke into Prime Minister Tsuyoshi Inukai's official residence and shot him dead, after which they turned themselves in to the police. Other zealots of the 'Young Officers of the Army and Navy and Farmer's Deathband' also attacked the Bank of Japan and a power station, but held back on some projected targets, among them the assassination of Charlie Chaplin. The young son of Premier Inukai was apparently meeting Chaplin at the very moment his father was gunned down.

Chaplin had coincidentally reached Japan at a time of crisis between the Japanese military command – who had launched a ferocious invasion of China in Manchuria – and the civilian government, which was largely opposed to this naked aggression: the first volley in what would be the Second World War seven years later. Having been spared a handshake with the founder of Fascism, Benito Mussolini, in Italy, Chaplin brushed against its growth in Japan, and was soon to find out, together with the rest of the world, the dangers it was to pose in the heart of Europe, in Germany.

Small wonder that he concentrated on the kabuki and *cha-o-nu*, and then loaded up on a consignment of live prawns for tempura to take with him on the good steamship *Hikawa Maru*, bound on 2 June for Seattle.

24

Making a Living

Or: *Tramp Tramp Tramp Keep on a-Trampin'* . . .

Chaplin returned to America, if not quite ready to drive the money-lenders from the temple, still resolved to scourge its crushing machines. Hollywood, as ever, existed at a tangent to the affairs of ordinary people in the world at large, but even here, the Great Depression had bit hard. Studio staff had been laid off, executives axed, and more people than Chaplin were asking how it was that in the richest country in the world five million people were out of work. Some movie people were in full employment: the talking comics – the Marx Brothers, W. C. Fields, Mae West – were about to flourish. Tough movies were being churned out by studios like Warner Brothers, built on the foundations of scripts by playwrights and journalists like Ben Hecht, Charles Lederer, Charles MacArthur, Gene Fowler et al., imported to fuel the talkie age.

Would Chaplin at long last have to speak, if he was eager to have his say?

When in Rome, however, do as the Romans, and as one of Hollywood's rich, Chaplin could afford to dally in LA's eternal sun. In fact, Chaplin was disclosed as being 'filmdom's wealthiest celebrity', according to the County Tax Assessor, who nailed him as possessing 'taxable stocks and bonds valued at $7,687,570', well ahead of the next grandee, Douglas Fairbanks, who had a mere $689,000. Chaplin immediately filed a protest with the tax authorities, claiming his securities were only worth $1,657,316. This story would run and run.

Meanwhile, in the department of affairs of the heart, old flames continued dying down. Georgia Hale, who had stayed close until his foreign trip, was not happy to be left in the lurch for fifteen months, and peeled off to go her own way. Lita got into another conflict with her ex-husband, this time over her plans for their sons, Charles and Sydney, aged seven and six, to appear with her in a movie entitled *The Little Teacher*, which was supposed to co-star Shirley Temple. Chaplin sued to prevent his children working in films, claiming they were being exploited and recalling, somewhat ingenuously, his own hard times as a child actor. (No such film, in the end, was made.) But Chaplin soon found a new flame: on a party aboard United Artists' president Joseph Schenck's yacht, he was introduced to a vivacious young actress, Paulette Goddard. Goddard had been married to a rich playboy when she was sixteen. When Chaplin met her she had long divorced the playboy, advanced on Hollywood and got bit parts in several films, including *The Kid From Spain*, with Eddie Cantor. When Chaplin met her, she was twenty-one, well past the safety range. The press soon got wind of this new dalliance with Chaplin's 'mysterious blonde', but it was not till 1933 when the pundits began speculating about a possible marriage. Stargazer Edwin Schallert, predicting the nuptials, nevertheless declared this would not happen before the completion of his next picture.

Early that year, however, Chaplin was still not ready with a film project, and was still fixated on the fall-out from his foreign tour and his stimulating meetings with prominent thinkers. In Japan, he had bent the ear of anyone he could grab on his economic plan to save the world from its doldrums, which involved a world currency with the value of gold that would be used to pay off the reparations that the Great War's victors required from the losers. Although this plan was utopian and impractical, he had been encouraged on the social front by the campaign for recovery waged by the Democratic presidential candidate, Franklin D. Roosevelt. When Roosevelt won the November 1932 election, and began, in 1933, to deploy his radical New Deal policies, Chaplin, in line with most Hollywoodians, was an enthusiastic supporter. (The most prominent dissident in town was W. C. Fields, who became a Republican in protest against Roosevelt's plan to tax high-earning actors.) In celebration, Chaplin bought a new yacht, a thirty-eight-foot cruiser with luxury fittings, named the *Panacea*, where he could wine and woo Paulette in peace.

Finally settling down, Chaplin spent several months writing up his serial for the *Woman's Home Companion*, which ran in draft manuscript to over 280 pages. Then he could set his mind to the task of the next film, which would derive from his renewed conviction that Charlie should speak his mind to the world. Copious notes were scribbled, scripts began to take shape, and in September 1933 production began on the movie that would become *Modern Times*.

In the beginning, it had the title *Commonwealth*, and then was named *The Masses*, aka 'Production No. 5'. Chaplin told *New York*

Times reporter Karl Kitchen, in March 1935, that it would be 'a satire on certain phases of our industrial life', but 'it does not, he told me, contain any political inferences. As it is designed to amuse Hottentots in Africa as well as filmgoers in London, Patagonia and Siam, its humor is decidedly obvious.' Kitchen visited the set, noting the vast engine room, 'built to resemble the interior of a huge power plant', with 'moving machinery, made of wood and rubber but painted to look like steel, fully a block long and several stories high'. Chaplin had already sunk one million dollars of his own money in the preparation and shooting, but, Kitchen wrote, 'as "City Lights," his last picture, grossed over $5,000,000, there is little doubt that Charlie will get his million back and a handsome profit in addition.'

Unlike *City Lights*, or previous Chaplin Tramp films, the general shape and structure of the story was established at an early stage. The notes on the start of *City Lights* supplied the opening montage for the new film: 'Crowds entering office buildings . . . Cattle driven into slaughter house,' in place of which we have a cluster of sheep, and then the rushing human mass. This time Chaplin was determined not to get caught in a repeat of the dilemma of *City Lights*, when one crucial scene that set the tone for the picture had to be got right or the entire project was doomed. He opted therefore for an episodic structure that would take his protagonist from scene to scene in a succession of social settings. When in doubt, always return to the tried and true – the Keystone formula, but with a far richer brew.

The early script of *The Masses* opens directly with a 'FACTORY LANDSCAPE – CHIMNEY STACKS SMOKING . . . HUGE FURNACES INTO WHICH IRON ORE IS BEING DUMPED . . .' dissolving then into the 'cattle herded out of pens' and 'passengers being belched up from subways'. The great dynamo set then dissolves to the President's office, 'showing boss leaning back with comic paper'. The boss's face is 'hidden by the comic paper, on the back of which is "The Katzenjammer Kids."' The rest of the sequence remained unchanged through all subsequent drafts, into the final picture. The scene dissolves into the bench set, where the Tramp, now a worker, is 'screwing nuts . . . He has a mallet and a piece of steel pipe, which he places over nuts and with a mallet hits the pipe . . . A bee enters the scene. It hovers about his face and disconcerts him . . .'

In fact, the protagonist of *The Masses/Modern Times* is not quite the old Tramp at all. The itinerant life, when it engulfs him, is as a result of the series of mishaps that has exiled him from his conveyor-belt labour. Had he not been a victim of the Depression he might have stayed on at the Electro Steel Corp. all his life, tightening endless bolts, or perhaps even gaining promotion to the engine room, where sweaty hunks rushed from lever to lever, pulling switches and turning the wheels. Or perhaps, as the early working scenes suggest, he would have been driven mad to end his life in the asylum . . .

Chaplin's early notes defined the movie's central relationship between Charlie and the 'Gamin' as 'the only two live spirits in a world of automatons . . . Two joyous spirits living by their wits.' But he is perhaps more closely akin in this movie to the original Tramp who must have scrawled that 'IWW' on Mack Sennett's shed door. The one eulogized in Joe Hill's song:

> If you all will shut your trap,
> I will tell you 'bout a chap,
> That was broke and up against it, too, for fair.
> He was not the kind that shirk,
> He was looking hard for work,
> But he heard the same old story everywhere:
>
> Tramp, tramp, tramp, keep on a-tramping,
> Nothing doing here for you,
> If I catch you round again,
> You will wear the ball and chain,
> Keep on tramping, that's the best thing you can do!

In his score, Chaplin used another song, Woody Guthrie's 'Hallelujah, I'm a Bum', the hobo's anthem:

> Hallelujah, I'm a bum,
> Hallelujah, bum again,
> Hallelujah, give us a handout
> To revive us again . . .

This runs in the background of the scene in which Charlie, having left the hospital after his 'nervous breakdown', gets caught up in a demonstration when he picks up the red warning flag that falls from a truck. The script instructions for this scene run as follows:

While he is looking, distant voices are heard singing: 'Hallelujah I'm a bum.' He turns around looking dejected. As he does so, a wagon passes with a red flag tied to the end of two large telegraph poles. Thru the jolting of the truck, the flag flies off in the center of the road. The Tramp sees this and runs to pick it up then waves it after the truck, which continues on. The Tramp in the center of the road, calls after the truck, holding the flag high and waving it to attract the driver's attention. The truck stops. The Tramp half runs then walks towards it, keeping in the center of the road. From around the corner, a parade of the unemployed comes into view. The Tramp, walking in the direction of the truck, is unconscious that he is leading the parade and waving a red flag at the head of it. Suddenly from the camera, comes a concerted charge of policemen on horseback and on foot and the crowds scatter. The Tramp is lost in the midst of them as he rushes towards the curb. Before he gets there, somebody knocks him down and we show an INSERT of feet stepping over him as he is crawling between the skirmish . . .

One can see that Chaplin's script of *Modern Times* was far more constructed in advance than that of any of his previous films, despite the fact that, yet again, it was going to be a 'speechless' picture, with only the boss, or a machine, actually speaking, until Charlie's gibberish song. On film, the entire red flag sequence, from Charlie wandering in the street until the police find him trying to hide in a manhole, lasts a mere forty-five seconds.

The world of *Modern Times* is no longer a dreamscape, a place of magical encounters with flower girls or mad millionaires. Chaplin's Electro Steel Corp., with its echoes of Fritz Lang's *Metropolis* and its precocious television, later satirized again in *A King in New York*, may be quasi-science fiction, but it also echoes with the brutal truth of Capital's would-be-benevolent airs. As our friend the mechanical salesman pitches its 'practical device which automatically feeds your men while at work', it urges the boss: 'Don't stop for lunch. Be ahead of your competitor . . . Increase your production, and decrease your overhead.' It all makes sense, but Charlie, and his workmates, are lucky that it spectacularly fails. In the explosion of its manic collapse, whacking him repeatedly in the face, Charlie becomes a cartoon character, caught in reality's cartoon world.

In *Modern Times*, the Tramp, frozen in his *City Lights* dream, has finally woken up, as a cog in society's war with itself. Instead of Victoria Cherrill's angelic flower girl, he has found a strong-willed urban waif – Paulette – to partner him. As the 'Gamin', the word for a homeless street urchin (though Chaplin should have used the feminine 'Gamine'), she is a grown-up Jackie Coogan, extremely grown-up in fact, and clearly too old and too well fed for the role. What she lacked in authenticity, however, she made up with the energy she contributed to her double act with Charlie as society's cast-aways. Charlie, though, still maintaining his mythic distance from the world, keeps any hint of adult intimacy to a dream: their rural idyll, where an orange tree is in arm's reach out the window and the cow ambles in to be milked. The imp of Keystone, with his aggressive snarl, has long become a would-be bourgeois.

What one recalls from *Modern Times* is its steady drum roll of episodes satirizing what a stream of radicals up to the present day would call 'The System'. Charlie as automaton, getting literally caught in the machine – an image used far beyond the realm of Chaplin or movies. The feeding machine. Charlie berserk with an oil can. The red flag – here more than perhaps elsewhere Chaplin's idea of Charlie as a fallen English gentleman peeks through, as who else might try to

Modern Times – in the machine.

restore a dropped rag from a lorry? The prison scene, with its hulking cell mate trying to thread a needle, and the dope scene, with his table-mate at the mess hall hiding his stash of white powder in the salt cellar. Charlie becoming more and more excited, smearing white stuff on his nose and grabbing back his slab of bread from the hulk: an unexpected gag to find in a picture made during the white heat of the Hays Code, the renewed censorship rules that tightened up the chains upon the talkies.

The new code came into effect as part of the Industrial Recovery Act introduced by President Roosevelt in June 1933. In terms of the movie business, it brought production, distribution and exhibition together under one set of rules. Censorship, which had always been the produc-ers' bugbear, had been codified on a voluntary basis by Hollywood studios since the appointment of Will Hays in 1921 in the wake of the Fatty Arbuckle scandal. When talkies began, the code was further tightened after studios tried brazenly to argue that its provisions did not apply to dialogue, as the spoken word was not mentioned specifi-cally. Following the spate of bold pictures made in what is mislead-ingly called the 'pre-Hays Code' period of 1931–3, mainly flirting with sex in movies starring Barbara Stanwyck, Marlene Dietrich, Jean Harlow and Mae West, Catholic newspapers led demands for a boy-cott of 'immoral motion pictures'. A 'Legion of Decency' was formed to push this campaign. The Code itself was drafted by such Catholic luminaries as Martin Quigley, Father Daniel Lord and Joseph Breen, who became the code's high inquisitor.

The depiction of any kind of drug-taking was banned outright, but somehow Chaplin slipped it through. Perhaps the censors had read an earlier draft of his picture, in which he had inserted an ending that called for the 'Gamin' to become a nun. The nervous breakdown scene was placed late in the film, and the recovered Charlie is told he has a visitor in the hospital's reception room. When he gets to the reception, 'To his surprise, he finds the Gamin, attired as a nun. She is standing, and beside her is a Mother Superior.'

Chaplin had obviously been following the code's progress, and he was most likely aware of the intense battle over Mae West's film in progress, *It Ain't No Sin* (released in 1934 as *Belle of the Nineties*), as well as other transgressive titles. In Chaplin's discarded version, Charlie walks off alone, while the Gamin-nun stands watching, and 'out of herself the ghost of the Gamin appears and runs rampant down the hospital steps, dancing and bounding after him'. But then 'she is awakened from her revery by a light touch, the hand of the Mother Superior. She starts, then turns and smiles wistfully at the kindly old face and together they depart into the portals of the hospital again.'

Chaplin clearly couldn't fool even himself with this nonsense, and he proceeded as most Hollywood producers did at this time, with caution and a fair dose of low cunning. In the event, when the film was ready for the censor's viewing in January 1936, there were a mere handful of cuts proposed, involving the 'pansy' in the cell, Charlie's hulking cell mate, who had been more effeminately shown in the scene, the word 'dope' in the intertitle, a close-up of the fantasy cow's udders, the 'brassiere gag in the department store', and the scene of stomach-rumbling in the prison warden's office when Charlie and the minister's wife take tea. The latter point was ignored by Chaplin, and Joseph Breen held his peace. One might speculate that the censor's office was so obsessed with double entendres and sexual and other allusions in spoken dialogue that Chaplin's silent apotheosis was considered light relief.

Chaplin had been as usual disingenuous when he told reporters like the *New York Times*'s Karl Kitchen that his film would contain no 'political inferences'. But politics apart, the film was also peppered with nostalgic citations of the old silent comedies. The most prominent was the appearance of the veteran Keystoner Chester Conklin as the chief fixer of the great engine-room turbine. When he is caught in the cogs after the lunch hour stops the machine, Chaplin feeds his partner's protruding head, using a roast chicken as a funnel to pour coffee into his mouth. To every problem there is a solution, mad as it may be – an old Keystone principle. Apart from stock Chaplin actors Allan Garcia (the Company Boss) and Henry Bergman (Café Owner), Chaplin used old Keystone Kop Hank Mann as a burglar and also resurrected 'Tiny' Sandford, the iconic cop who stands by noting the outrages of Laurel and Hardy and Jimmy Finlayson as they demolish each other's house and car in 1929's classic *Big Business*. Sandford played the factory foreman who, as one of the unemployed, becomes a burglar whom Charlie confronts during his stint as a night watchman in the department store.

In the store scene, Charlie gives an echo of *The Rink*, skating blindfold to impress Paulette on the edge of a drop over the floor below. Later, when he is hired in the cafe, a lengthy sequence reprises every

waiter gag that he had ever pulled in *The Rink*, and other episodes
going back to *Caught in a Cabaret*. The addition of sound, however,
does enable Chaplin to give the cafe dining-and-dance-hall routines
that extra vigour as the roar of the crowd combined with the band
closes in on poor Charlie trying to deliver a duck to an irascible diner.
The noise and the baying of the drunken football players who use the
duck as their ball set up the scene in which Charlie, having thrown off
the white cuffs on which he has written the words of his song as
he skims on to the dance floor, has to resort to his own invented
Italo-French lines to the echoes of Leo Daniderff's tune 'Titine':

> *La spinach o la busho,*
> *Cigaretto porto bello,*
> *Ce rakish spagoletto,*
> *Ce la tula tula tois!*

It is a startling moment in the Tramp's saga, when a sacred principle is
breached, only to be subverted by nonsense. In all that he might have
said, after Chaplin's long circumnavigation from New York to Tokyo
and back, he remained nevertheless faithful to the expectations of his
global base. Charlie still belonged to the world, and the world was still
refracted through Charlie.

Instead of words, Chaplin once again orchestrated, with his music
arrangers David Raksin and Edward Powell, the synchronized score
for the picture, interweaving his lush chords, with echoes of Gershwin
and Puccini, together with the hobo theme and the popular tones of
the old music-hall days. His scores would be echoed, one generation
on, in the themes that composer Nino Rota supplied for so many
Fellini films. In essence, Chaplin still had no choice, if he wanted to
keep his character timeless, but to deny him meaningful speech and an
accent that would at last tie him down.

In the world outside, comedy had surged forward, despite the
censorship chains, and had already passed through the best repartee of
the Marx Brothers, W. C. Fields, Laurel and Hardy and Mae West, as
well as embracing the new voices of social comedy, with Frank Capra's
It Happened One Night, starring Clark Gable and Claudette Colbert.
Capra had been criticizing American mores since *American Madness*
in 1931, with Walter Huston as a banker who throws Wall Street into
confusion by lending to poor people without collateral, and *The
Miracle Woman* of 1932, in which Barbara Stanwyck played a fake

evangelist clearly based on the moral crusader Aimee Semple McPherson. In 1936 Capra released *Mr. Deeds Goes to Town*, with Gary Cooper, another satire on money-grubbing versus simpleton honesty. If Charlie could speak properly, he might have been Longfellow Deeds, the 'Cinderella Man' who inherits a fortune and is besieged by crooks and city slickers, or at least a close relative. But Chaplin's contemporary America was still Any Place, a universal dystopia, with the lingering echoes of Fred Karno's speechless war against the State and its authorizers: the police, prison warders, and the men in white coats, who are always ready to pounce and take away those who fail to fit in.

Against the machine world and the scourge of the Depression Charlie can only offer dreams, and the open road towards the rolling hills of California at sunrise, a proper American pioneer vision at last. Here he could sing, with Walt Whitman:

> Afoot and light hearted, I take to the open road,
> Healthy, free, the world before me,
> The long brown path before me, leading wherever I choose.

> Hence I ask not good fortune – I myself am good fortune,
> Henceforth I whimper no more, postpone no more, need nothing,
> Strong and content, I travel the open road . . .

And he could end, with the poet:

> I give you my love, more precious than money,
> I give you myself, before preaching or law;
> Will you give me yourself? Will you come travel with me?
> Shall we stick by each other as long as we live?

There cannot have been anyone who had heard or read the merest morsel about the life behind the screen of Mr Charles Chaplin who did not know that the real life of Hollywood's richest inhabitant did not follow the dictums of America's troubadours of freedom, nor the simple society of Henry David Thoreau, which seems to peep over the parapet in *Sunnyside* and in *Modern Times*'s rural dream scene. But they also knew that Charlie, the Tramp, was indeed a free spirit, independent of the man behind the mask. Chaplin had survived the assault of Lita Grey's formal divorce petition, with its intimation of sex crimes including underage intercourse that could have sunk almost anyone else, as he would survive the gossip columnists and the further attacks on his morals that would be mounted a few years later on – because his audiences embraced the mask before the man. Even when he was bombarded with the denunciations of the right-wing press, and the career-killers of the House Un-American Activities Committee, his fans never abandoned him, even when he had already discarded 'the little fellow' and morphed him first in his doppelganger act into Adolf Hitler, and then nakedly into the petit-bourgeois murderer Verdoux, the serial killer of serial wives. It was the State, in the end, that wielded the rubber stamp of Immigration controls to chase the miscreant out, to excommunicate the heretic and lock him outside the gates of paradise. Perhaps they understood, these stern officials, that, as Whitman had sung:

> I and mine do not convince by arguments, similes, rhymes;
> We convince by our presence.

But there was yet a way to walk before this blow was struck . . .

25

The Great Dictator
Or: 'Flat-footed but Noble'

In January 1935, Dr Joseph Goebbels, Germany's Minister of Propaganda, issued an order banning *The Gold Rush*. The film, according to an official statement, 'does not coincide with [the] world philosophy of the present day in Germany'. The *New York Times*, reporting this, wrote that 'the absence in recent years of any new Chaplin film has spared the National Socialist government the embarrassment of deciding whether it should ban the film star's pictures from the German screen because he is Jewish'.

Chaplin's 'Jewishness' appeared to obsess the Nazis, and they included him in a book of photographs of their favourite villains entitled *The Eternal Jew*, published in 1937. It consisted of 265 images with captions that portrayed Germany as beset by these evil enemies of the Aryan race both from within and without. The picture of Chaplin was from *The Kid*, showing him and little Jackie Coogan, with the caption:

Charlie Chaplin and Jackie Coogan. The Galician Charlie Chaplin (whose mother was born Thornstein) emigrated to America. Along with Jackie Coogan, who also came from the East (Jacob Cohen), their tear-jerking comedy makes poverty both pitiable and laughable, reaching the tear ducts of the innocent viewers. The slapstick gang of this flat-footed, clumsy, impoverished yet eternally generous man with the huge shoes was a sensation for the non-Jews. Flat-footed but noble – that is Charlie Chaplin's formula.

Other pictures in this literary compendium portrayed the artist Jacob Epstein, described as 'a pregnant idiot', standing beside his 'Neanderthalic' sculpture. 'In sculpture even more than painting,' said the caption, 'Jews display their absolute lack of talent. To get the attention that their vanity demands, they turn primitive.' Other pictures showed 'The Jew in his element: With blacks in a Parisian night club – the Jews bring people the glittering world of perversion as a way of unnerving and enslaving them. He seems to worry as little about it as the rats worry about the plague they carry.'

The tone and title of this book were replicated in the 1940 'documentary' hate film *Der Ewige Jude* (*The Eternal Jew*), which also
featured Chaplin along with 'the Jew Ernst Lubitsch . . . the Jew Emil
Ludwig-Cohn' et al., showing archive footage of Chaplin's 1931 trip.
'The Jew Chaplin was welcomed by an enraptured mob when he
visited Berlin,' rants the narrator, who keeps up a stream of invective
throughout the picture. 'It cannot be denied that at that time a portion
of the German public applauded unsuspectingly the foreign Jew, the
deathly enemy of their race. How was that possible? A mendacious
dogma of human equality had dimmed the healthy instinct of the
people.'

Needless to say, Chaplin was not Jewish. His grandmother on his
father's side appears to have been a gypsy girl named Ellen Elizabeth
Smith, as David Robinson confirms the oral history presented in *My
Autobiography*: 'Grandma was half gypsy. This fact was the skeleton
in our family cupboard . . . I remember her as a bright little old lady
who always greeted me effusively with baby talk. She died before I
was six.' This is as far from straightforward English Christianity as the
family tree reaches. Chaplin clearly recalls his mother Hannah's turn
to religion, her attendance of Christ Church in the Westminster Bridge
Road: 'Every Sunday I was made to sit through Bach's organ music
and to listen with aching impatience to the Reverend F. B. Meyer's
fervent and dramatic voice.' She would talk to him of Jesus and his
calvary, and may well have been the font of the pantomime tale of
David and Goliath that Charlie relates as a fake minister in *The
Pilgrim*. Chaplin Senior's faith wavered between the church and pub,
with the pub winning hands down. Chaplin's son, Charles Junior,
related that his father declared himself an agnostic, rather than an
atheist: 'Some scientists say that if the world were to stop revolving
we'd all disintegrate. But the world keeps on going. Something must
be holding us in place – some Supreme Force. But what it is I couldn't
tell you.'

Chaplin's comment about the Jewish 'genius', in his encounter with
the little girl aboard ship in *My Trip Abroad*, showed his admiration
for the very traits that anti-Semites hated in Jews: their universalism
and abjuring of boundaries – characteristic, if the generalization holds
at all, only of secular, rather than orthodox Jews. It was clear to
Chaplin that when the Nazis attacked him as a Jew, they were attack-
ing the very qualities that he embraced as central to his beliefs and his

art. Their fictional identification of his origin as 'Galician', i.e. stemming from eastern Poland, may well have sparked some ideas about the character Charlie might inhabit in his next outing. A similar source was another Nazi book his British friend Ivor Montagu sent him, *Juden Sehen Dich An* (*Jews Are Looking at You*) which described Chaplin as 'the little Jewish tumbler, as disgusting as he is boring'.

Being accused of being a Jew by a racist dictatorship, Chaplin's natural tendency would have been to say: Why not? As he had countered with questions about Bolshevism back in 1921: 'I am interested in life. Bolshevism is a new phase of life. I must be interested in it.'

Indeed, Chaplin was not the only one in Hollywood to be interested in the Communist revolution in Russia and in universalist ideals. Among those who looked with keen interest to the east were Harpo Marx, who went off to Moscow in 1933, and no less than Cecil B. DeMille, who took his wife on a long tour down the Volga in 1932. DeMille noted the many signs of dire poverty he saw along the way, but also stated on his return to Los Angeles that 'Russia is the most interesting place in the world . . . The theatres are packed to the doors, and they are ahead of us in using pictures as one of their principle educational mediums in the schools . . .'

Closer to home, screenwriters like John Howard Lawson, Sidney Buchman, Budd Schulberg, Albert Maltz and Ring Lardner Junior went so far as to join the Communist Party itself, and this party presence was to become a major factor in the hunt for subversives launched by the House Un-American Activities Committee after (and in some cases before) the Second World War. The involvement of the Party members and their instigation of anti-fascist activities in the mid-1930s came to haunt a whole host of dissenters and liberals who joined such organizations as the Anti-Nazi League, which was formed in 1936. The more broadly based 'popular front' in Hollywood embraced all those whose concern with the domestic effects of the Depression, the Nazi takeover in Germany, Italy's genocidal war in Abyssinia (Ethiopia) and the Civil War in Spain led them to sign their names to many petitions, pack political meetings and donate to various funds. These donors stretched far and wide to include Groucho Marx, James Cagney, John Ford, Melvyn Douglas, Edward G. Robinson, Fredric March, William Wyler, Ernst Lubitsch and many others, some of whom would flip-flop politically in due course. As well as Lubitsch, who had come to Hollywood to make movies and money ten years earlier, there were many foreigners in town, German Jews and gentiles, who were exiles from the Nazi regime: Peter Lorre, Max Steiner, Erich Korngold, Fritz Lang, Otto Preminger, Wilhelm Dieterle, Billy Wilder and Bertolt Brecht, to name but a few. Their most distinguished member, Nobel Prize-winner Thomas Mann, reached Los Angeles in 1938.

All these would be exactly the sort of people Charles Chaplin cherished and saw as the vanguard of artists, and other professionals, scientists, etc., who represented the best of human endeavour, his soul mates, whatever their creed. Unlike many, however, he was an inveterate non-joiner, perhaps the original of Groucho Marx's famous dictum that 'I would never be the member of a club that would have me as a member.' This basic individualism would be his defence against the many attacks and accusations hurled at him in later years. His economic views hardly marked him as a socialist, let alone a Communist, and he was acutely aware of the distance his wealth placed between himself and ordinary people. When Chaplin wanted to know what ordinary people thought, he sent Charlie, the mask, among them.

We might note, however, that in their definitive chronicle of the Hollywood left, *The Inquisition in Hollywood* (1979), authors Larry Ceplair and Steven Englund counted Chaplin among the radicals rather than the liberals, along with Edward Dmytryk, Dashiell Hammett, Lillian Hellman, Dorothy Parker, Robert Rossen and the Party members – but this was in the context of his wartime activities during 1940–45, not in the 1930s. Some more genuine radicals at that time, in fact, chastised him for portraying in *Modern Times* not the Working-Class Hero of Labour, but the little man who runs away from the fight. Charlie carrying the red flag because he mistakes a symbol of defiance and mutiny for a discarded rag is the true imp of Chaplin's individualistic perversity.

This little man was once again to be resurrected on screen. But in what form? The Tramp had been cloned, as in the Sorcerer's Apprentice, into a vast army of the destitute and the unemployed. He had disappeared into the mass. Who could replace him? In the aftermath of *Modern Times*, Chaplin had dabbled with other projects. There was, once again, the 'Napoleon' script, entitled *Napoleon's Return from St Helena*, which seemed to consist of boring speeches about uniting

Europe into one state. Then there was *Regency*, set in early-nineteenth-century England, about a young woman who falls in love with an outlaw. This too was soon dropped. Chaplin's attentions were also taken up by trying to help Paulette Goddard get the part of Scarlett O'Hara in the film of the decade, *Gone With the Wind*. Immediately after the premiere of *Modern Times* Chaplin and Paulette had set off on another 'world tour', reaching Shanghai on 9 March 1936, where Paulette announced their engagement to the press. They then set off on a cruise around the Malay archipelago, from Singapore, aboard a 'bridal yacht', the *Sea Belle*. On 23 March they flew in to Java, and then continued to Japan, where Chaplin could indulge in tempura again. In April they were in Annam, French Indo-China. In Canton, China, they were at last discreetly married. On their return to California the pursuit of Scarlett O'Hara continued. But, as we know, Paulette did not get the part. Chaplin continued to dabble in writing, publishing, in *Rob Wagner's Script Magazine* ('A Weekly of Comment and Fun' printed in Beverly Hills) in January 1938 a short story called 'Rhythm', about an execution in the Spanish Civil War. To quote briefly:

Only the dawn moved in the stillness of that small Spanish prison yard – the dawn ushering in death, as the young Loyalist stood facing the death squad . . . Up to the last, the rebels had hoped that a reprieve would come from headquarters, for although the condemned man was an enemy to their cause, in the past he had been a popular figure in Spain, a brilliant writer of humor, who had contributed much to the enjoyment of his fellow countrymen.

The officer in charge of the firing squad knew him personally. Before the Civil War they had been friends. Together they had been graduated from the university in Madrid . . .

But, about to give the order to fire, the officer stops, his mind a blank:

The scene in the prison yard had no meaning. He saw only objectively – a man with his back to the wall facing six others. And the group there on the side, how foolish they looked, like rows of clocks that had suddenly stopped ticking. No one moved. No one made sense. Something was wrong. It must all be a dream, and he must snap out of it . . . 'Stop!' he screamed frantically at the firing squad.

Six men stood poised with rifles. Six men were caught in rhythm. Six men when they heard the scream to stop – fired.

This did not inaugurate a new Chaplin career, though it expressed some of the thoughts that were to feed into his next film, ideas of the inevitable slide of mankind into a moral abyss of violence: the next stage of *Modern Times*'s human automata.

The seeds of this next project were already planted, as reports of the 'Jewish Charlie Chaplin' in Germany kept reaching him from various sources. Another nudge came from a script treatment by the radical writer Konrad Bercovici, whose Red Revolution novel, *The Volga Boatman*, had been filmed by Cecil B. DeMille in 1926. Bercovici's treatment became the object of a later court case, as the author claimed Chaplin had taken his idea without attribution and that *The Great Dictator* was essentially his own original story. In Bercovici's treatment, Charlie would be a little Jewish peddler, or perhaps a barber, who is mistaken for Hitler. (The case was eventually settled out of court, after Chaplin testified that he had never read Bercovici's text.)

Whatever the sequence of events, or the many influences that fed into Chaplin's magpie mind, the decision to split Charlie into two opposing characters, a Jekyll and Hyde, was soon made. There were some startling parallels between Chaplin and the Führer, apart from the moustache, which Charlie had adopted at the time when poor Corporal Adolf was pinned down in the German trenches. They had been born within days of each other, Chaplin's 16 April 1889 as against Hitler's 20 April. Hitler too had tasted poverty, when as a failed art-school entrant he had walked the streets of Vienna, taking refuge in a poorhouse. There was the deliberate creation of a persona – the Tramp and the Dictator.

Close observation of newsreels showed Chaplin how Hitler built his repertoire of facial tics and gestures. The voice, more than anything, to a non-German speaker, seemed to ape the grotesque screeching of the bourgeois celebrants of 'Peace and Prosperity' in *City Lights*. There was something inescapably comic about the posing of fascist leaders, and Chaplin found his perfect Mussolini in the avuncular Jack Oakie (who had partnered W. C. Fields in *Million Dollar Legs*, playing an American brush salesman). Of course, the dictators were no laughing matter, but if one did not laugh at the dictators, what could one laugh at in an increasingly dangerous and darkening world?

Early drafts of *The Great Dictator* reveal again how Chaplin could best imagine his work-in-progress on paper primarily in the shape of a play. Dated 10 November 1938, the script is headed in his habitual fashion thus:

A DRAMATIC COMPOSITION IN FIVE ACTS AND
AN EPILOGUE

THE DICTATOR

by Charles Spencer Chaplin of Great Britain,

Domiciled in the United States at Los Angeles, California.

THE DICTATOR – A story of a little fish in a shark-infested ocean . . .

Characters:

Charlie
Hinkle
Mussemup
Moses Goldstein

Act 1.
Note: For all acts one of the stage boxes will be outfitted like a radio station. In it will sit the Commentator who bridges the action as it flows from scene to scene, and from year to year. His voice will be heard coming over a loudspeaker at the rear of the balcony.

Scene: Somewhere on a European battlefront. Center stage a large cannon pointed off right. Stage left an anti-aircraft gun. Stage right a sand-bagged trench. Piles of shells lie near the cannons, as well as boxes of food and stacks of hand grenades.

COMMENTATOR: The year 1912 [sic]. Europe flames with war along a thousand mile battlefront. Ptomania single-handed is battling the overwhelming armies of the Allies . . . How long can she hold her lines? Her men fight bravely – nay, desperately. On the tenth day of September . . .
(the curtain parts to reveal a scene of violent action. A gun crew is shoving a projectile into Big Bertha. Among them is Charlie . . . from near and far the sounds of a great battle . . .)
(they fire)
CHARLIE: All we hit was a chicken. And a small chicken at that! What a business!

As in the finished film, the shell fired out of Big Bertha falls flat and then chases the soldiers around. But then Armistice is declared, and we meet

Charlie in the next scene as a demobbed soldier, in a flophouse filled with various 'peddlers and panhandlers'. There is a German street band, an organ grinder with his monkey, a pretzel vendor and a flea-circus proprietor. Chaplin was still determined to get his flea-circus scene done by hook or by crook. The conversation proceeds accordingly:

SOLDIER: Why don't I end it all? We've lost the war. Our Fatherland is being trampled on by the Allies. What have I got to live for? Oh, it's disgraceful. It's a shame.
2ND SOLDIER: Shut up!
FLEA-CIRCUS OWNER: My fleas! Somebody stole my fleas! (he sees the monkey attempting to hide guiltily) You – I'll get even with you – you Irishman! (he wanders about the room calling softly to his performers) Adolph! Nanette! Terence!

The familiar not-to-be-filmed-yet routine ensues: Charlie extracts fleas from a man with a beard, mayhem results, et cetera. In the following scene, Charlie is back in the city, among the Jews, being harassed by supporters of the new dictator, Hinkle. In the Hinkle scenes, the dictator is married and henpecked, and his non-Jewish-made suit doesn't fit. While his fellow dictator Mussemup visits, Charlie and his friends Abie and Moses have been rounded up and are in the concentration camp, 'draining a swamp, or maybe it's just building fences to keep us in jail with'. They plan to escape, and manage to dash out only a few miles from the border with neighbouring Ostrich, dressed in Ptomanian uniforms. At this point army officers catch up with them and, mistaking Charlie for Hinkle, take them off to inspect a 'Synthetic Factory'. Meanwhile Hinkle, found bathing without his uniform, is captured by mistake as an escaped prisoner. Charlie marches up the streets with the Ptomanian officers, saluting the crowds, into the factory, where Charlie absent-mindedly continues saluting rows of sausages. After this, Charlie and his friends, still mistaken for Hinkle and his retinue, arrive at Vanilla, the Royal Palace of Ostrich, where he is harassed by Mrs Hinkle, and told by General Herring that he is expected to make his great speech. In a plot element absent from the final film, Charlie is also harassed by various Conspirators, who 'reach out from everywhere . . . hands come from all sides, from bouquets of flowers, from table legs . . .' Charlie responds: 'I wonder how they do it! Smart people, these Vanillaneze . . . but I'm getting hungry. Hey, bring me some icecream.'

Charlie makes his big speech to the crowd, while 'in a box sits an assassin smoking a cigarette, a rifle slung over his knees . . .'

CHARLIE'S SPEECH: I don't want to conquer anybody. I want to do good by everybody. Because – this is a big world, and there's plenty of room for all of us in it. Yes, even for dictators. Even for Hinkle! Hinkle. He wants to do right. He's just full of hate and bitterness, that's all. But we shouldn't hate. We shouldn't feel bitter because we're all one family – white man, black man, yellow man – men and women of all races and all nations – we are all one. One with the sun, one with the trees, the flowers and the sunshine!

MEN IN UNIFORM (CONFUSED BUT LOYAL): Hail, Furor. Three cheers for Fascism!

CHARLIE: No, three cheers for humanity!
(now he smiles)
All of you – what are you so tense for? I'm not going to hurt you! Why don't you relax? . . .

OFFICER: At ease!

CHARLIE: Don't shout like that! You're not talking to your wife. Just tell them to sit down quietly.
(the soldiers sit down wondering)
Now I'm going to ask you all to eat a nice cold ice cream cone. You've been standing there since dawn many of you. Help yourself and don't worry. Hinkle's paying the bill!

HERRING (JUMPING TO THE MICROPHONE): I ask you all to leave. The Furor's sick. He doesn't know what he's saying!

CROWD: Let him talk! Don't touch our Furor!
(Ice cream vendors pass across the stage and through the audience. The great rank and file enjoy their treat. Only the captains eat with apathy.)

CHARLIE: Now! Play, bands! And you people dance! Right here in the street! Dance!
(from everywhere comes the music of old Vanilla – the beautiful waltzes of Strauss. The people get to their feet, singing and laughing)

COMMENTATOR: Are you listening, China? Are you listening, Spain? Do you hear what's going on? Can you hear the music? Vanilla's going crazy! Storm troopers are dancing with Jews. They're going into kosher restaurants and ordering Gefullte fish! The conspirators have thrown down their guns! The captains no longer patrol their men! Prisoners are being let out of prisons. And everywhere, music! Music!

Epilogue: Through the music comes the playing of a bugle call. The scene shifts back to the concentration camp. Charlie wakes up with a smile as a storm-trooper enters. Charlie smiles at him. The storm-trooper starts to smile back, then ashamed at his softness, he bellows: 'Get up, Jew! Where the hell do you think you are?'

What might be surprising is not the difference between this 1938 draft and the movie that opened on 15 October 1940 but how close it is to the tone and satire of the final work – including the final speech, which some histories state mistakenly was added at a much later stage. Although the fleas, the flophouse and the Nazis rushing to eat gefilte fish have been excised, as well as Mrs Hinkle, much of the broad, even 'camp' nature of some of the shot scenes remains in principle the same. What is salutary, also, is the fine tuning that made scenes that would appear stilted and even inept on paper resonate when played on the screen.

In essence, the early draft resembles – though as ever with Chaplin, the whole project was presented as *sui generis* – a kind of film that was not new in Hollywood, if one recalls the 'Ruritanian' comic fantasies of W. C. Fields in 1932's *Million Dollar Legs*, or the Marx Brothers' more famous *Duck Soup*. In Fields's film, in which he plays the President of Klopstokia, who can arm-wrestle any opponent, he is constantly spied on by Ben Turpin, present through the picture in hidden doors, fireplaces, and even inside a portrait. The President enters blowing his own horn and banging his own drum, demanding 'the usual oath of allegiance to me, and no stalling!' The Fields movie was directed by Eddie Cline from an original story by Joseph L. Mankiewicz, brother of Henry, the future writer of *Citizen Kane*. The Marx Brothers' version, directed by Leo McCarey in a film 'supervised' by Henry Mankiewicz, presented the vision of two warring states, Freedonia and Sylvania, with President Ruphus T. Firefly obsessed with money rather than racial purity or lethal inventions. Groucho's rant that he paid a month's rent on the battlefield would however have been perfect for Hynkel.

Rather than drawing just a comic grotesque, Chaplin wanted to get into Hitler's personality, noting the enormous self-absorption and vanity that the Führer displayed in newsreels, particularly in his 'performance' at the Nuremberg rally in 1935, which featured in Leni Riefenstahl's *Triumph of the Will*, and was shown in America in a version cut, odd to relate, by Luis Buñuel. These observations were fleshed out in a subsequent script of 29 June 1939, in a scene designated 'Third Palace Sequence':

The Great Dictator.

Hinkle at the piano. The scene is Hinkle's private suite. He is sitting at the piano dramatically playing Mendelsohn's Spring Song or Afternoon of a Faun, when out of the corner of his eye he catches sight of his reflection in the mirror on the music rack. He is pleased with his dramatic pose. Still playing with his right hand he admires it, and tries one or two more poses. Now he elevates his eyebrows and looks pathetic. Falling in love with himself, he slowly drops his chin and becomes coy, looking at his reflection under his lashes. He now gets sensuous about it all, breathing deeply. He smiles coyly, scowls for contrast, then smiles again. A shade of anxiety crosses his face. He slaps his breast pockets. Nothing there! He frowns, rises, opens two drawers. No luck! His anxiety increases as he searches under a pile of books. He goes to the waste basket, stirs its depths, then a pleased expression comes over his face. He pulls out a cigarette butt, cocks his foot, strikes a match, lights his cigarette and goes to lie down on the divan.

Fanny (Hinkle's wife?) enters as Hinkle lies on the couch . . .

FANNY: I'm worried. Something is going to happen. I've been having awful dreams lately . . .
HINKLE: Dreams? What about?

F: Blimps. I dreamed I was chased by one . . . and just as it caught up to me, you came along with your sword and went aaanh! And the blimp went blaanh!

HINKLE: What nonsense!

FANNY: It means war. I know it . . . This persecution in the ghetto. This thirst for power. It frightens me. It's all so desperate.

HINKLE: These are dramatic days. We are going to invade Ostrich!

FANNY: No, no, don't! You mustn't! It will plunge us into war!

HINKLE: What of it?

FANNY: Don't you realize? It will be the end of everything!

HINKLE: That's my affair! Not yours!

In the event, Chaplin came up with the ideal metaphor for Hitler's vanity in his dance with a great world-balloon, that is finally pricked, leaving him forlorn. This gag, Kevin Brownlow and David Gill revealed, was first played by Chaplin in a home movie, as he prances with guests, dressed in an ancient Greek-style dress, in 1928. Kevin Brownlow and Michael Kloft's 2003 documentary, *The Tramp and the Dictator*, reveals that just such a globe was present in Albert Speer's monumentally built Berlin Chancellery, whose pictures were studied for Chaplin's movie design at the time. (Eerily, newsreels of the same building in ruins toured by Russian officers shows the globe as almost the only piece of furniture left standing.)

The scene that follows, in the script, has Hinkle reviewing an inventor, Professor Spittenkopf, who has 'the most wonderful invention of the age – the Monoblimp – derives its power from splitting the atom . . . the works no larger than a watch . . .' The Professor takes off and soars around the room, inflating and deflating, as General Herring explains: 'It goes solely on atoms.' 'How many miles to the atom?' asks Hinkle. Herring replies: 'We haven't gone into that yet.' Hinkle dons the contraption and soars through to the grand hall, but the inflation doesn't last. In the film, the device the inventor tries is a parachute hat, which fails to open, off screen, as he plummets out the window. 'Herring, why do you waste my time like this?' Hinkle asks wearily.

Chaplin's final script for *The Great Dictator* was a massive three-hundred-page affair. As we can see from the above, for the first time it set down in writing precise details of action and gesture, rather than these being worked out during the shoot. Production lasted a total of

559 days, with an early Schedule of Shooting giving a glimpse of the general atmosphere on the set:

Since it has not been found possible to arrange these weekly schedules with any brilliant accuracy, perhaps it would be better simply to list the <u>probable order</u> in which the next scenes and sequences will be shot. It must be remembered, however, that even though the schedule is thus qualified it is <u>still subject to change</u> on short notice. That's the way life is, citizens!

INFORMATION DEPARTMENT: CHRISTMAS WILL FALL, AS USUAL, ON OR ABOUT THE TWENTY-FIFTH OF THE MONTH. GUESTS WILL PLEASE KEEP THEIR DOGS AT LEAST THIRTY FEET FROM THE CHRISTMAS TREES. QED.

As shooting proceeded through the New Year into 1940, another notice, posted on Tuesday 2 January, proclaimed: 'Please throw all broken New Year's resolutions in receptacles located at strategic spots . . .' Chaplin's resolution, however, remained unbroken. In the time that had elapsed between the 1938 draft and completion, the war in Europe had broken out, Poland was invaded and her cities bombed, the Germans had marched into Belgium, Holland, Luxembourg and France, and Paris was occupied on 13 June 1940. The blitz on British cities began with a massive thousand-plane raid on 15 August. In September Germany, Italy and Japan formed their Axis pact, and Chaplin's alliance between Hynkel and Jack Oakie's Benzino Napaloni was sealed in real blood.

Americans, however, were not yet certain as to their role in this second World War. President Roosevelt himself had signed a 'Neutrality Act' in 1937 which barred loans to warring powers and restricted trade with belligerent countries. This was amended in November 1939 in response to the threat to US allies, France and Britain, and allowed arms to be sold 'cash and carry'. A vast $2.5 billion appropriation was presented to Congress in May 1940, to expand the US Army and Navy. In September Congress passed the Selective Service Act to register all men aged between twenty-one and thirty-six. It was clear that Roosevelt favoured intervention, but many influential Americans were still in favour of staying out of the European battlefield. Pearl Harbor was over a year in the future.

Chaplin's *The Great Dictator* was therefore an unintended battle cry, as Hollywood pussyfooted around the subject of anti-fascist commitment. The Hays Code itself prohibited movies from insulting or offending other countries, as the Marx Brothers discovered when the line 'You can't Mussolini all of us' was banned from *A Night at the Opera* in 1935. This was policed as sternly in the case of Nazi Germany as any other regime the United States was not in conflict with. Despite the Jewishness of most of Hollywood's studio leaders, the overwhelming feeling as late as 1936, as recorded by Neal Gabler in his book on Hollywood's Jewish moguls, *An Empire of Their Own*, was that 'Jews should not stick their necks out'. Very few openly anti-fascist films were produced. (Anatole Litvak's 1939 *Confessions of a Nazi Spy* and Frank Borzage's *The Mortal Storm* of 1940 were among the few examples.) Even after the war began in Europe, Gabler recounts, the US ambassador to Britain, Joseph P. Kennedy, spoke to Jewish executives in Hollywood, telling them, as related by Douglas Fairbanks, that 'although he did not think that Britain would lose the war, still, she had not won it yet. He repeated very forcefully that there was no reason for our ever becoming involved in any way.' Kennedy told the executives that 'the Jews were on the spot, and they should stop making anti-Nazi pictures or using the film medium to promote or show sympathy to the cause of the "democracies" versus the "dictators." He said that anti-Semitism was growing in Britain and that the Jews were being blamed for the war.' Ben Hecht later wrote that, because of this kind of pressure from powerful people, 'all of Hollywood's top Jews went around with their grief hidden like a Jewish fox under their gentile vests.'

Chaplin's independence, however, and precisely his non-Jewishness, made all the difference in his ability to cut through this knot. There were, nevertheless, momentary wobbles, as Chaplin wondered if his comic-book Nazism was being overtaken by events that were unsatirizable. These doubts were laid to rest, his assistant Dan James later related, by a direct message from President Roosevelt, relayed by his close advisor, Harry Hopkins, that he should ignore the dissuaders and press ahead. Roosevelt was well aware that an anti-Nazi message from America's most popular film-maker, Tramp or not, would bolster the case that he was eventually to make in December 1940, when he pledged US military aid to Great Britain in his 'arsenal of democracy' speech.

The strange case of *The Great Dictator*, however, is that it resonates, not so much with an effective call to arms against tyranny, but with an unequivocal cry for justice and peace.

Chaplin's own initial battle cry, in the film, might well have been The Tramp is Dead – Long Live the Tramp, as he is reborn as the Other Side of Adenoid Hynkel, the Jewish barber, drafted into the First World War. A blood brother of the doughboy of *Shoulder Arms*, he is ready and eager to do his bit for his country. Chaplin condensed the Great War of 1914–18 into a series of bravura scenes, moving from the near-documentary shots of trench warfare to the company of klutzes who man Big Bertha, the giant gun that is intended to shell Paris but instead blows up a latrine. All is chaos and futility, as soldier Charlie loses a grenade in his pants, finds himself with the wrong army in the fog and nevertheless manages to rescue a wounded airman, Schultz, his ultimate benefactor.

Flying inadvertantly upside down, with the camera upended so that we experience this from Charlie's point of view, his hair standing up and water pouring up into the sky, is just one of many scenes in which Chaplin veers wildly between reality and fabulation. From an early stage, copious designs were made of spectacular sets for the Dictator's realm in Tomania, from the grand interior halls to the great arch upon which Hynkel cradles a clock – an image that rates only one shot in the movie! In contrast, the Jewish ghetto, constructed on Chaplin's lot, was a small-town dream of street markets and court-yards, with signs written in the international language, Esperanto, invented in 1887 in Warsaw by Dr Lazarus Ludwig Zamenhof. Zamenhof's dream of a universally spoken tongue with a simplified grammar never quite took off, though it still has adherents to our day. Perhaps Chaplin thought that Yiddish, which is written in Hebrew characters, would alienate audiences from his Jews. As it is, they are a stereotypically argumentative lot of worthy citizens, patriotic to a fault, but prone to yearning for a halcyon past, as in the words of the young waif, Hannah: 'Wouldn't it be wonderful if they'd just let us live and be happy again?'

Charlie, having crashed in the plane with Schultz, has been a hospitalized amnesiac throughout the years in which Tomania fell to the Dictator, Hynkel. Imagining that only a few weeks have passed, he returns to his old barber shop, wipes away the cobwebs, and gives Chester Conklin – unrecognizable without his trademark moustache – a rapid shave as the radio plays Brahms's 'Hungarian Dance Number Five'. Once again, Chaplin's instinct in returning to the essence of mime is impeccable: the whole scene with its flourishes of the razor and twirls to the beat plays in one medium-long shot, lasting just under two minutes.

As Hannah – whom he first tries to lather with shaving cream when nudged to make his old shop a beauty parlour – Chaplin cast Paulette Goddard again, her consolation prize perhaps for losing out to Vivien Leigh in *Gone With the Wind*. Behind the scenes, however, their ardour was already cooling. Once again, her miscasting is mitigated by energy and enthusiasm. A strange characteristic of *The Great Dictator*, indeed, is how decisions on tone, decor, mood and settings often lie on the edge of the mawkish, or the misjudged, or the sentimental, but are vindicated by the overall structure of the piece. Stormtroopers who are bullying figures of fear, pelting Hannah with stolen tomatoes, are then brought to heel by her knocking them out with a frying pan from her window – surely one of the oldest comedy gags in the movies.

In a significant change from the Tramp, the barber's instinct is to stand and fight for his rights, rather than run away. In this situation, Chaplin knows, there is no golden sunset to escape to, and Hannah's flight to a rural idyll in Osterlich is broken by Hynkel's invasion. The route of escape from the concentration camp to which both he and Schultz – who finally stands up to Hynkel's tyranny – have been sent is a road that leads straight into the arms of Hynkel's minions. The 'Fooey', advised to pull a fast one on his rival dictator, Napaloni, by going duck-hunting incognito as a ruse to cover his own plans of invasion, falls into the lake as he tries to shoot down his duck and is mistaken for one of the escaped convicts, while Charlie, marching beside Schultz in Tomanian army uniform, is mistaken for the leader who is due to make his great speech announcing his plans for world domination.

All of this could easily fail its transition from a problematic script, full of potential pitfalls in its switch from tragedy to farce and back again, to a screen presentation in which Chaplin triumphs over adversity, were it not for the workings of fate that logically drive the narrative forward. All the barber's denials of the sheer malice of the forces that are closing on the Jews to destroy them lead him inexorably to the moment when he has to become Hynkel, his other self. Tongue in cheek, Chaplin placed a title in the credits of the film: 'Any resemblance between Hynkel the Dictator and the Jewish barber is purely coincidental.'

Studying the monumental architecture of the Nuremberg rally as portrayed in Leni Riefenstahl's film, Chaplin and his designers came up with a simple great slab, inscribed 'LIBERTY', alongside which Hynkel/Charlie ascends to the podium. Even at this solemn moment, when all the tensions between laughter and fear are heading for some necessary resolution, Chaplin inserts some purely slapstick business of confusion with folding chairs. Minister Goebbels/Garbitsch makes his speech, announcing the death of the defunct ideas of democracy and equality, and then Schultz nudges Charlie. 'You must speak.' 'I can't,' Charlie whispers back. But he must mount the podium.

Chaplin laboured for many weeks on the final speech, reworking, changing lines around, adding, subtracting, rewriting. Countless drafts bit the dust before he decided that he should eschew all thought of keeping close to the simple characterization of the barber, and speak directly as Charlie Chaplin. This was his moment. It would never come again. As the old Jewish saying proclaimed: If I am not for me, who is for me? And if only I am for me, who am I? And if not now, when? And so Chaplin gave forth:

I'm sorry, but I don't want to be an Emperor, that's not my business. I don't want to rule or conquer anyone. I should like to help everyone if possible – Jew, gentile, black man, white. We all want to help one another. Human beings are like that. We all want to live by each other's happiness – not by each other's misery. We don't want to hate and despise one another. In this world there's room for everyone and the good earth is rich and can provide for everyone. The way of life can be free and beautiful, but we have lost the way. Greed has poisoned men's souls – has barricaded the world with hate – has goose-stepped us into misery and bloodshed. We have developed speed, but we have shut ourselves in. Machinery that gives abundance has left us in want. Our knowledge has made us cynical; our cleverness, hard and unkind. We think too much and feel too little. More than machinery we need humanity. More than cleverness, we need kindness and gentleness. Without these qualities, life will be violent and all will be lost.

The aeroplane and the radio have brought us closer together. The very nature of these inventions cries out for the goodness in man – cries for universal brotherhood – for the unity of us all. Even now my voice is reaching millions throughout the world – millions of despairing men, women, and little children – victims of a system that makes men torture and imprison innocent people. To those who can hear me, I say: 'Do not despair.' The misery that is now upon us is but the passing of greed – the bitterness of men who fear the way of human progress. The hate of men will pass, and dictators die, and the power they took from the people will return to the people. And so long as men die, liberty will never perish.

Soldiers! Don't give yourselves to brutes – men who despise you and enslave you – who regiment your lives – tell you what to do – what to think and what to feel! Who drill you – diet you – treat you like cattle, use you as cannon fodder. Don't give yourselves to these unnatural men – machine men with machine minds and machine hearts! You are not machines! You are not cattle! You are men! You have the love of humanity in your hearts. You don't hate, only the unloved hate – the unloved and the unnatural!

Soldiers! Don't fight for slavery! Fight for liberty! In the seventeenth chapter of St Luke, it is written the kingdom of God is within man, not one man nor a group of men, but in all men! In you! You, the people, have the power – the power to create machines. The power to create happiness! You, the people, have the power to make this life free and beautiful – to make this life a wonderful adventure. Then in the name of democracy – let us use that power – let us all unite. Let us fight for a new world – a decent world that will give men a chance to work – that will give youth a future and old age a security.

By the promise of these things, brutes have risen to power. But they lie! They do not fulfil that promise. They never will! Dictators free themselves but they enslave the people. Now let us fight to fulfil that promise! Let us fight to free the world – to do away with national barriers – to do away with greed, with hate and intolerance. Let us fight for a world of reason – a world where science and progress will lead to all men's happiness. Soldiers, in the name of democracy, let us unite!

Indeed, Chaplin's text had come a long way from the mawkish cry of its 1938 draft calling for ice cream for all on Hynkel's tab. In the shooting, however, he still tried to cleave to its original aftermath, and filmed a sequence in which the Tomanian soldiers broke into happy dancing. Even as he shot it, he knew it could not be used, and it survives as part of the unique colour production footage of the shoot that was unearthed much later by the archivists. Instead, the film cut to Hannah, in conquered Osterlich, marvelling at the voice that comes out of the sky, speaking directly to her:

Hannah, can you hear me? Wherever you are, look up Hannah. The clouds are lifting! The sun is breaking through! We are coming out of the darkness into the light. We are coming into a new world – a kindlier world, where men will rise above their hate, their greed and their brutality. Look up, Hannah! The soul of man has been given wings and at last he is beginning to fly. He is flying into the rainbow – into the light of hope, into the future, the glorious future that belongs to you, to me, and to all of us. Look up, Hannah . . . look up!

Speaking from the heart, Chaplin revealed his essence, and his aware-ness of the flaws as well as the strengths that had led him to this moment, the movie clown addressing the world from the Dictator's podium. The podium was as much Hollywood as Hynkel, the power of box office that invested Chaplin with his celluloid robes of empire. The speech revealed how strongly Chaplin had been affected by two of the prominent men he had met in his trajectory of trips among the famous and the outstanding: Einstein and Gandhi. Einstein had shown him that science and humanity were not incompatible. Gandhi had shown him, despite his initial scepticism, that the machine was not the be all and end all, and that the apparently slightest person could wield a moral example as a sword. Socialism had, at most, provided him with the rhetoric of unity, which he tried to apply in his wartime activities against the Axis powers. At this moment, however, as Chaplinologists have pointed out, Nazi Germany and Soviet Russia were still linked by the non-aggression pact they had signed in August 1939, which freed Germany to attack Poland, while the Soviets also invaded, from the east, on 17 September. Communist parties through-out the West, particularly those in which Jews were prominent, fell into disarray and confusion. Chaplin's speech, however, gives no com-fort or evidence to those who sought to tar him with the pro-Soviet brush at this time. The only significant fact about Communism in *The Great Dictator* is that it is never mentioned.

At the core, Chaplin's view of his own call to sacrifice was expressed much better in a scene in the ghetto in which Schultz, who is being sheltered by the Jews after a previous escape from the concentration camp, proposes to them that they draw lots, in the form of a tray of puddings one of which contains a coin, to choose which one of them will assassinate Hynkel at the cost of his own life. Hannah, who makes the pies, puts a coin in every pudding, but each candidate, igno-rant of this, tries to pass what he believes to be the fatal coin to the other. Charlie ends up swallowing three coins, which clink tellingly in his stomach. It is a replay of an old story, a familiar chestnut in the comedy of resistance: laughter in the face of sheer terror. Chaplin's originality lay in his knack of reproducing tried ideas that were ever as true as the artist's ability to imbue them with a fresh energy, and a meaning that spoke directly to people's immediate concerns.

26

Dough and Dynamite
Or: 'I Fear Nothing, Only the Truth.'

From the *New York Times*, 16 October 1942:

Famous Mustache to Be First Casualty as Charlie Chaplin Becomes
'Lady Killer.'

Charles Chaplin, famous film comedian, director and author, announced
yesterday on arriving here from Hollywood that he would discard his traditional mustache, baggy trousers and wabbly [*sic*] walking stick when he starts
work on his new picture, 'Lady Killer.'

The mustache that helped make him famous will disappear to make way
for a silly, pretty mustache of a French variety . . . He reported that the
picture would be a satire on the Bluebeard theme, the principle character
having been suggested by the career of the French multiple murderer, Henri
Landru . . .

Mr. Chaplin, in his suite at the Waldorf-Astoria, was dressed in a blue suit
with a blue tie and shirt to match. His hair, which appears black and curly in
the movies, was white. The comedian said he was tired and that he had been
caught in the rain.

When asked why he went out, he said, 'I wanted to get a feed of clams and
caviar . . .' Mr. Chaplin, who is to be the principle speaker at the Artists Front
to Win the War rally at Carnegie Hall tonight, said that he had no set speech
in mind and would talk on generalities. He might choose economics or
anything that might come to his mind, he declared, adding:

'I'm not a politician, I belong to an honored profession, that of a clown.

'I will say what is on my mind. I have arrived at the delightful age where I
fear nothing, only the truth.'

Mr. Chaplin remarked that he was 53 years old, still a Britisher, and 'a
citizen of the world.'

'I am here under the hospitality of the United States, you might say a
paying guest, to the extent of $10,000,000,' he went on. 'I feel it a privilege
and a pleasure. I feel as much an American as any other American.'

The grand premiere of *The Great Dictator*, held at the Astor
and Capitol Theatres in New York, was an evening of glitz and glitter
in the midst of deepening gloom for anyone observing the dire fate

of Europe. Movies being movies, 'thousands of excited admirers surged . . . and klieg lights penciled the darkness above Times Square' as Chaplin arrived at the Astor with Paulette, and 'forced his way into the theatre while a detail of thirty patrolmen and mounted police tried to hold back the crowd'. To the lobby crowded with newsmen Chaplin waved and called out, 'I hope you like it!' and then sped off to the Capitol with a police escort, where 'the throngs again pressed against the pair so heavily that Mr. Chaplin was momentarily thrown to his knees'.

Bosley Crowther, reviewing for the *Times*, praised the event to the skies:

. . . no picture ever made has promised more momentous consequences . . . and the happy report this morning is that it comes off magnificently. 'The Great Dictator' may not be the finest picture ever made – in fact, it possesses several disappointing shortcomings. But, despite them, it turns out to be a truly superb accomplishment by a truly great artist – and, from one point of view, perhaps the most significant film ever produced.

While lauding the satire, Crowther listed, on the debit side: 'The picture is overlong, it is inclined to be repetitious and the speech with which it ended – the appeal for reason and kindness – is completely out of joint with that which has gone before.' Along with many other critics, Crowther pointed out that, when Chaplin stepped 'out of character' and addressed his heart to the audience,

. . . the effect is bewildering, and what should be the climax becomes flat and seemingly maudlin. But the sincerity with which Chaplin voices his appeal and the expression of tragedy which is clear in his face are strangely overpowering. Suddenly one perceives in bald relief the things which make 'The Great Dictator' great – the courage and faith and surpassing love for mankind which are in the heart of Charlie Chaplin.

This speech from the heart, Crowther realized, in an article published a few days later, was something extremely dangerous for an actor, whose entire rapport with the public was based on the mask he had so carefully nurtured –

. . . the meek and inarticulate little man who could not conceivably unburden himself of such expressions . . . It is bad construction – confusing, banal and embarrassing . . . as though Chaplin were revealing, in an unguarded moment, the details of his most intimate grief . . . During that tragic outburst, we weren't listening much to the words, which really do not add up. We were listening rather to a voice which was coming from the soul of Charlie Chaplin, the little fellow we have known and loved for many years, finally speaking out bravely and defiantly against the brutal forces loose in this sad world.

Perhaps it was part of Chaplin's tragedy, despite the break he could always take for a feed of clams and caviar, that even his admirers could fail to pay attention to the core of what he wanted to say. Having laboured for weeks over the words of his final monologue, to be told that they 'do not add up' was a frustrating rebuff. Every word had in fact been carefully weighed, before being uttered. But Chaplin knew, as a clown, that he would only be judged as a clown. Robert Payne, writer of more than one hundred books running the gamut from Greta Garbo to Lenin, Dostoevsky, Albert Schweitzer and Mao Tse-tung, who portrayed Charlie as 'the Great God Pan' ('the high and presiding genius of sensuality who is also the mocker of sensuality'), also compared him to Joseph Grimaldi, the primal English clown of the early nineteenth century. In his book, *The Great Charlie*, Payne recounts the old tale of Grimaldi, melancholic and depressed, seeing a doctor, who advises him to cheer himself up by seeing the great comedian Grimaldi, whereupon the patient tells him: 'Doctor, I am Grimaldi.'

The clown, even in a gilded cage, cannot escape, though Chaplin did try, following his call for anti-fascist unity with personal appearances, including one for the Daughters of the American Revolution in January 1941, in which he reprised and expanded his speech. But this was not intended as a prelude to any major political activity on his part. In March the *New York Times* ran a story about Chaplin announcing plans to come to New York to make 'a new picture about a bibulous refugee in a full-dress suit, lost in the big city'. Paulette would co-star – despite rumours of their imminent divorce (or separation) – and 'the picture will have the view-point of two human beings trying to function in these chaotic times with no future – just living for the moment . . . I'll be the refugee, but I won't be a tramp. I'll play most of the role in a full-dress suit.' Another putative project was a movie of a drama of Irish life, *Shadow and Substance*, based on the play by Paul Vincent Carroll, but the origin of that project was to become part of Chaplin's next, explosive personal tangle.

On 22 June 1941, however, the war in Europe escalated dramatically, when Nazi Germany invaded Russia. The German armies advanced along a two-thousand-mile front, and within a month had conquered huge swathes of territory. In October Great Britain and the United States entered into a formal agreement to supply materials for the Russian war effort. The Soviet Union and America had become allies. On 7 December, the Japanese attacked Pearl Harbor. The war was now truly global.

The record shows that it took several months for Charlie the clown to add his voice, through Charles Chaplin, to the cause of Russian War Relief. The political agenda for this activity was the call for the Allies to open a 'second front' in the east, to relieve the Russians, who were taking a massive pounding by Hitler's divisions and whose civilian population were perishing in vast numbers by starvation and massacre. Chaplin first spoke at the San Francisco Civic Center on 18 May 1942, as a substitute for the former US ambassador to the Soviet Union, Joseph E. Davies, who had lost his voice that day. He addressed the audience as 'Comrades!' and urged the allies to commit those forces that were idle to help the Russians, who 'alone are facing about two hundred divisions of Nazis'.

Rather than Communist fervour, it was clear to anyone who followed events in Europe, as Chaplin did, that the Second World War would be won or lost in Russia. Chaplin was hardly straining at the bit, as he had spent the previous period preparing his silent film, *The Gold Rush*, for a re-release, with a new soundtrack featuring his own commentary on the action.

Napoleon Bonaparte is credited with the saying that 'from the sublime to the ridiculous there is but one step'. (Perhaps Chaplin should have played the French Emperor after all . . .) Chaplin's private affairs were about to precipitate him into his most spectacular brush to date with the press, the courts, and American public opinion over his personal, rather than his artistic qualities.

As life with Paulette soured, Chaplin had begun 'dating' other actresses: Carole Landis and Hedy Lamarr were mentioned. In May 1941 he also met a twenty-two-year old aspiring actress, born in Detroit, called Joan Barry. One of the many thousands of girls attracted to the magnet of Hollywood's rags-to-riches Neverland, she had previously had a dalliance with the millionaire J. Paul Getty, and clearly knew how to get to know famous people. A young socialite friend of Chaplin's, Tim Durant, apparently introduced her to him. What happened next was to become the stuff of endless gossip, allegations, charge and counter-charge and eventually an indictment that fuelled newspaper headlines for the next four years.

The explosion did not occur until June 1943. In the preceding two years Chaplin, apart from his public speeches about the war, spent most of his time working on ideas for the next project of the Chaplin studios. He had purchased the Paul Vincent Carroll play and prepared a script of *Shadow and Substance*. The play focused on the tale of an Irish girl, Brigid, who has visions of her namesake, St Brigid, which sets off a conflict of faith among priests. This was clearly a strange choice for Chaplin, and like other unsuitable projects was destined to be discarded. Chaplin had not lost that Mutual-era uncertainty which led him to veer off in wrong directions. Sudden enthusiasms could derail him in art and in politics, as his speeches on Russian War Relief escalated to excessive rhetoric about Stalin's Russia that was recorded in FBI files. Biographer Kenneth Lynn quotes a file report that Chaplin had told a dinner at the Hotel Pennsylvania in New York on 3 December 1942 that people ought to understand the Soviet purges as a rooting out of Russia's own quislings, stating outright: 'I am not a Communist but I am proud to say that I feel pretty pro-Communist.' All this was being taken down for later use.

In the realm of art and love, or lust, as subsequent court records showed, Chaplin told Joan Barry that he was thinking of her for the leading role of Brigid. He gave her some personal acting tuition, and paid her fees at the Max Reinhardt drama school. In the autumn of 1942, however, a complication ensued when he met Oona O'Neill, the seventeen-year-old daughter of playwright Eugene O'Neill. Having been anointed Debutante of the Year that spring, she had arrived in Hollywood to test for the movies. In October Chaplin offered her a contract, to avoid her signing with Fox studios.

Trouble was inevitable. Chaplin was losing interest in *Shadow and Substance*, and as the *New York Times* report of 16 October showed, had already veered towards the Bluebeard idea, based on the French serial killer Landru. On the night of 23 December 1942, Joan Barry climbed up a ladder to break into Chaplin's house on Summit Drive, produced a gun, and threatened to commit suicide. Chaplin's two sons, Charles Junior and Sydney, were witnesses to this event. She left in the morning, but returned later, and Chaplin called the police, who arrested her on a vagrancy charge. She returned again in May, six months pregnant. On 3 June 1943, her mother, Gertrude E. Barry, filed a suit on behalf of her daughter's unborn child, naming Chaplin as the father. Conception, it was claimed, had taken place the night Joan Barry had broken into his home.

In June 1943, US forces were engaged in fierce fighting with the Japanese over a wide swathe of the south Pacific. Allied armies had captured Tunis in North Africa and begun the planning that would lead in July to the invasion of Sicily. All over the lands occupied by Nazi Germany, partisan resistance continued long and costly campaigns. In the death camps of Hitler's war against the Jews, gypsies, homosexuals and others, Adenoid Hynkel's absurd plans were played out in real mass murders in the murk and fog of war. But the editors of America's newspapers found copious space in their wartime paper allocation for the Chaplin–Barry case. (Note that press and FBI records consistently spelled her name as 'Berry'.)

CHAPLIN PROTÉGÉ READY TO DENY VAGRANCY PLEA:

Lawyer Due to Make 'Emotionally Distraught' Appeal in Beverly Hills Court Tomorrow.

Joan Berry, titian-haired erstwhile protégé of Charlie Chaplin, who claims the comedian is the father of her child-to-come, is scheduled to appear in Beverly Hills City Court tomorrow at 2 p.m., when her counsel will seek to vacate her plea of guilty to vagrancy last January . . .

CHAPLIN CASE GIRL CLEARED

Vagrancy Charge Against Joan Berry Dismissed by Court . . .

PATERNITY TANGLE FIGURE'S PLEA PREVAILS . . .

GIRL ACCUSER OF CHAPLIN PREPARES FOR STORK VISIT . . .

JOAN BERRY TELLS JURY OF 'LIFE WITH CHAPLIN'
(*Los Angeles Times*, 21 January 1944)

Little more than two years ago, while visiting friends in Mexico, she met Tim Durant, motion-picture producer and friend of Chaplin. Durant later introduced her to the comedian in Hollywood.

Then followed a contract with Chaplin as a 'dramatic student' – she as pupil and he as mentor, with a tempting star role in one of his productions dangled before her. During this association, she said, the role of pupil and teacher was forgotten and they became intimate. As a result, she charges, Chaplin fathered the child. While under contract to him, she asserts, they quarreled and Chaplin cut her salary from $100 to $25 a week. Shortly after

Christmas, 1942, she said they quarrelled while driving and that Chaplin drove up to the Beverly Hills City Jail and said:

'Get out! This is where you belong!'

She said she left the car, went into the police station and demanded to be booked on 'any charge' but the officers told her to go home.

Two nights later she was taken to the receiving hospital as a result of a suicide attempt and later booked for vagrancy.

'I didn't really want to kill myself. I just painted my lips with iodine so Mr. Chaplin would know how I felt,' she related to investigators . . .

The vagrancy charge was a result of her residing outside the limits of Beverly Hills, a convenient get-out for rich denizens wishing to control their lower-class visitors. In a 1952 account by Hedda Hopper, the Hollywood gossip queen related that she had coached the distraught Joan in how to get the most out of her attachment to Charlie by bringing her mother down from New York and confronting Chaplin with her unborn child. By then, it was also known that Chaplin was living with Oona O'Neill, and he would be doubly disposed to pay out. In the event, Chaplin hurried to wed Oona in Santa Barbara on 16 June, barely two weeks after Ma Barry's paternity suit. Joan Barry's child, named Carol Ann, was born on 2 October 1943.

Meanwhile, Federal authorities, getting in on the act, organized a case against Chaplin under the Mann Act, otherwise known as the 'White Slavery' Act, which banned prostitution across state lines. The argument was that Chaplin had 'feloniously transported' Joan Barry from Los Angeles to New York 'with the intent and purpose of engaging in illicit sex relations'. Chaplin was also charged with others with conspiring to deprive Barry of her civil rights by the drummed-up vagrancy charge in Beverly Hills. A Federal Grand Jury indicted him on 10 February 1944.

On 22 January 1944, Allied forces landed at Anzio. By February large parts of southern Italy were freed by Allied troops. In the Pacific, US troops invaded the Marshall Islands and fierce battles were being fought on the Admiralty Islands and New Guinea during February and March. But on 31 March American newspapers were full of detailed reports of Charlie Chaplin's appearance in court to start his defence against his Mann Act indictment:

Q. – The record here has been developed beyond dispute, Mr. Chaplin, that Miss Berry and her mother left Los Angeles Oct. 2, 1942 . . . Did you have any discussions or arrangements with her in Beverly Hills or in any part of

California that she should go back to New York so she should be there when you got there so you could have her near you for immoral purposes or any other purpose?

A. – I did not.

Q. – Did you go to New York for any purpose other than making a talk at Carnegie Hall on Oct. 16, 1942, after your acceptance there?

A. – I did not . . .

Q. – Did you have a secret thought in your mind for immoral purposes with Joan Berry in New York?

A. – I did not.

Q. – Or anyone else?

A. – I did not.

The night that Joan Barry had threatened to kill herself was pawed over in great detail, as was every other jot and tittle of Chaplin's relationship with her, his promises, his disbursements, his intentions. It was a scandal made in heaven, a perfect distraction for readers in their third year of the gruesome despatches of an apparently unending war:

Q. – That night in your home, did you have intimate relations in your bedroom with Miss Berry, before which she laid the gun down and afterwards picked it up again?

A. – I did not.

The jury in the Mann Act case found Chaplin not guilty, but the case of Joan Barry's paternity suit was yet to be heard. Outside the courts the war dragged on, through the D-Day landing of 6 June, and slowly turning the tide. On 25 August the Allies liberated Paris. In September they first entered Germany. In October Allied troops entered Greece and the Soviets broke through in Yugoslavia. In November US bombers began a massive offensive against mainland Japan. On 16 December the Germans began their last-ditch defence in the Ardennes, known as the Battle of the Bulge. The Barry–Chaplin paternity case resumed on 13 December, although three separate blood tests had established by February 1944 that Chaplin was not the father of Miss Barry's child. On 1 August, Oona had given birth to her first child, a baby girl, Geraldine. Chaplin's two grown-up sons were now both in the army. But the intrusive spotlight would not shift:

JOAN BERRY ASKS JURORS TO NAME CHAPLIN FATHER:

Actress Calls Herself 'Forgotten Woman' in Tearful Plea to Decide Paternity of Child–

For the first time yesterday Chaplin took a long, intense look at the chubby, red-haired baby – 'Exhibit A' in the case – whose paternity he denies.

The gurgling youngster was seated directly behind the 54-year-old actor, cuddled on the lap of her maternal grandmother . . . The child was squealing and chuckling, finally causing Chaplin to turn around and peer intently at her. The baby was looking in the other direction.

Chaplin was accused by the prosecution of acting up on the witness stand, getting excitable and pounding his fists on the stand, although his defence attorney, Jerry Giesler, later wrote that for most of the time Chaplin was 'merely sitting there, lonely and forlorn, at a far end of the counsel table. He is so small that only the toes of his shoes touched the floor.' The blood tests' evidence, however, was not admissible in Californian courts at the time. The atmosphere in the court was implacable. Joseph Scott, counsel for the plaintiff, 'recited passages from the Bible, quoted "Bluebeard," told the story of Mary Magdalene, and finally wound up with the tale of Svengali and Trilby . . . Referring to Chaplin, Mr. Scott shouted such epithets as "master mechanic in the art of seduction," "cheap cockney cad" and "gray-haired old buzzard."' Miss 'Berry' was described as 'a wretched girl, aflame with the glamour of Hollywood' and 'a girl of limited intelligence, who could not have concocted her story'.

Chaplin took the witness stand on 12 April 1945, testifying that he had resisted Joan's demands for $150,000, even though:

'I knew 95 per cent of the press was against me and had been ever since I dared to demand a second front on behalf of Russia . . . I told her I was not the father of the child . . . I said, 'You know I have had nothing to do with you for over a year.' She told me then, 'all the papers are against you and will blast you out of the country.'

The Superior Court Jury held, on 17 April 1945, by an eleven-to-one verdict, that Joan Barry's claim of Chaplin's paternity was proved. (A previous jury, three months before, had been deadlocked in Chaplin's favour, seven to five.) The second jury comprised eleven women and only one man, the foreman. The only holdout was a Mrs Mary H. James, housewife, who said: 'I came into court wanting to uphold American womanhood, but after hearing the evidence here, I changed my mind . . . I'd hate to have it on my conscience that I perhaps named an innocent man.' The rest of the jurors clearly wanted to punish Chaplin for his moral turpitude with a woman, however disturbed, who was vastly his inferior in wealth, social standing and power.

The case of Joan Barry versus Chaplin had almost outlasted the war in Europe, the verdict coming thirteen days before Adolf Hitler committed suicide in his bunker as the Russians occupied Berlin. Adenoid Hynkel's shadow was finally lifted, and 8 May marked Victory in Europe Day for the Allies. The war in the Pacific raged on until its nuclear cataclysm in August. The inventors had finally found their lethal atomic weapon, the Allies' scientists, in the event, having been ahead of Hynkel's.

Chaplin, exhausted by the long process, bitterly disappointed in the outcome, but comforted by the new family life he had found with Oona, could now turn back to the 'Landru' picture he had confidently announced to the *New York Times* three years earlier.

Joan Barry married a Pittsburgh businessman a year later and bore two more children, enabling Hedda Hopper to claim, in September 1952, that she had helped to rehabilitate her life. In typical Hopper style, she wrote that 'Charlie had his revenge. When he married Oona O'Neill he gave Louella Parsons the story and special photographs of his elopement to Santa Barbara . . . The front pages of the *Los Angeles Examiner* were splashed with wedding pictures. *The Los Angeles Times* got none.' Hollywood is, as ever, as Hollywood does.

Joan Barry still bore her scars. By 1953 she had separated from her husband, and travelled alone from Mexico to Torrance, California, where she was picked up 'in a dazed state' and committed to a mental state hospital, diagnosed as schizophrenic. Thereafter she disappears from all searches, scans and traces, a forgotten victim, both of Chaplin's irresponsible use of his power, and of a State that had seized ruthlessly and pitilessly on her predicament to try to bring him down.

27

Monsieur Verdoux
A Comedy of Murders

Whither the Tramp? Having merged with the Jewish barber, who then became Hynkel, who then spoke peace-in-our-time unto mankind, he faded away, shrinking from the colossal podium. One can imagine him, one with the millions of refugees, survivors of holocausts, trekking on foot or piled in trucks, heading for a home that might be nothing but rubble. This was a world in which he could not raise many laughs by a desperate tussle with a cop, or a soldier, over a rare plate of sausages, or fall in love with a blank innocent face. Withered, the Tramp would be a horrific rather than a pitiable figure clinging to the barbed wire of a liberated camp, if he were not one of the dreadful emaciated remains shovelled by bulldozers into a mass grave.

Having dared to laugh at terror, Chaplin could only admit that terror had prevailed, even if there was something called 'Victory' at the end. And what could be the feelings of the Tramp's creator, as he sat, the toes of his shoes hardly touching the floor, in a Los Angeles courtroom, humiliated in a modern version of the medieval stocks, put up for the jeers and disapproval of the mob? If his sins were real, what were they judged against those of his accusers, not to speak of the mass crimes carried out all over the world, as he was asked to respond, on oath, about the secret thoughts in his mind?

As was ever Chaplin's fate, and luck, if not his genius, human, all too human as it was, he found a way to respond through his art. And if this response emerged by trial and error, and by apparently discon-nected circumstances, it was none the less his response, available to us to be evaluated, praised, criticized, or denounced. Out of the mud and muck of war, hypocrisy, mass slaughter and lies, and a searing urge both to confess and to explain human transgressions, the Tramp crawled back out of the shadows, slipped into the dressing room of Chaplin's studios, raided the costume and make-up closets, and emerged in a completely new guise.

Thus was born Monsieur Verdoux, unemployed bank clerk, prim French bourgeois, moralist and murderer.

As a movie project, this had its own set of complex sources.

Once upon a time, Orson Welles, visiting Charles Chaplin at his Summit Drive home, mentioned an idea about a film based on the real-life antics of Henri Landru, a French serial killer of the First World War period, who married women and then murdered them for their money, disposing of their bodies in an oven he had specially built in his garden. Some time later, Chaplin telephoned Welles and suggested he could buy the idea for $5,000, to avoid future fights and recriminations about plagiarism and credits.

According to Welles, he had written an initial script about Landru and shown it to Chaplin in the summer of 1941. Chaplin, who at first agreed to act with Welles directing, then changed his mind and asked to buy the story outright. In the event the film contains a credit, 'Based on an Idea by Orson Welles.' As we have seen from the *New York Times* report of October 1942, Chaplin had by that date adopted *The Lady Killer* – Welles's original title – as his next film. By then the studio-butchered version of Welles's *The Magnificent Ambersons* had been released, and Welles had hied to Brazil to shoot endless footage of festivities and fishing.

Few drafts of the script of the film survive, so we do not know to what extent, if any, Chaplin made use of a Welles script. Chaplin, as ever, conducted his own research, including books on Landru, one typescript of which, 'Landru, the Bluebeard of France, by William le Queux', is in the Chaplin archive. There was, in fact, a previous film titled *Landru, Der Blaubart von Paris*, a German film made in 1922 fairly soon after Landru's execution, but though it was reviewed in *Variety* in 1923 ('the production work is excellent and nasty'), there is no evidence that Chaplin ever saw it.

Whatever the sources, there were many distractions, combined with the usual hesitation and uncertainty, before the film could go ahead. It began production in April 1946, was shot till September, and was ready for its premiere in April 1947.

Few films have had such leaps of reputation as *Monsieur Verdoux*, which opened to general puzzlement and a fair amount of hostility, even at the New York premiere itself. For the first time in his life, Chaplin was booed and hissed, and he did not even stay to the end of the show. A press conference the next day, 12 April, at the Gotham Hotel, was murderous. Questions started with the expected 'Are you a Communist sympathizer?' and escalated to a full inquisition by a

Catholic pressman, James W. Fay, who challenged Chaplin's patriotism and homed in on his 'pro-Russian' war activities. His main defender, and a passionate one, was the critic James Agee, who lambasted those people who harped on freedom but then attacked a man's political views and his citizenship. Nevertheless, attacks on Chaplin escalated, and moves were made to boycott the movie in several states. One such proposal, in early May 1947, was by 325 'Theater Owners of Ohio', who 'denounced the former comedian for "again attempting to reach into the pockets of American movie-goers" although he has no use for this nation's citizenship.' They suggested that 'screen time be withheld from the new Chaplin picture "until he proves he is worthy of the support of American movie-goers."'

The most cutting part of the above may well have been the description of Chaplin as 'the former comedian'. Chaplin persuaded United Artists to use the criticism of the picture, and of himself, as part of its publicity, presenting *Monsieur Verdoux* as 'the picture that couldn't be stopped!' This lifted the film from its initial poor run to the status of a minor hit, so that *Variety* headlined: 'Chaplin Should Heckle Congress More!' But this was a short-lived triumph, and the film soon faded, not to be resurrected properly until a re-release in 1972. James Agee's rave reviews of the picture may have helped the screenplay to be nominated for the 1947 Academy Awards, but the award made on 20 March 1948 went to Sidney Sheldon for *The Bachelor and the Bobby Soxer*. (The scripts for Vittorio de Sica's *Shoeshine* and Abraham Polonsky's *Body and Soul* were also nominated that year.) Agee had his own reasons for cheering on Chaplin, as he had written a script he was trying to get Chaplin to read, of which more later . . .

Chaplin's baiting of his critics was courageous or foolhardy, depending on one's point of view, as the movie came out in the run-up to the House Un-American Activities Committee's full-blown hearings in Washington in October into subversion in the movie business. In Hollywood, the anti-Red forces had been organizing since February 1944, when a Motion Picture Alliance was formed with Sam Wood, director of two of the Marx Brothers' films (among much else) as its president, and featuring Walt Disney, Clarence Brown, Fred Niblo, to be joined later by John Wayne, Gary Cooper, Hedda Hopper and Adolphe Menjou, to name but a few. Apart from Communists, trades unions were targeted in a ferocious crusade by Cecil B. DeMille against the closed shop. The combination of left-wing screenwriters and militant union crews inspired the defenders of the faith to such declamations as DeMille's to the Boy Scouts of America that 'If we value liberty for ourselves and our children, we must fight our enemies in the schools, the churches, industries and labor unions.' Which amounted to a pretty clean sweep . . .

In all this, the cultural outrage of *Monsieur Verdoux*, following Chaplin's alleged ravaging of Joan Barry, was a red rag to the bulls. Rather than diminish the onslaught, the film was a proof that the patriots' suspicions of Mr Charles Chaplin, British citizen but resident of Los Angeles, were now completely borne out.

From its opening in a quiet French graveyard, to its final shot in the death march towards the guillotine, Chaplin's assault on society, marriage, money and even God was unprecedented in the American cinema. Compared to the experimentalism of Orson Welles, for instance, it seemed to be formally conservative, with no bravura effects, no expressionist lighting, no startling camera angles, and a progression of mostly middle-to-long shots. Chaplin, as some of his detractors were quick to point out, was in some senses a cinematic primitive, whose *mise-en-scène* had not moved on from silent days, and who was not in fact concerned with new developments. It was only later that, as the moral storm faded, critics and viewers were able to appreciate the fine tuning of the film, the careful, story-boarded compositions, fitted to meticulously designed sets that provided Chaplin the director with exactly the right staging in each shot that Chaplin as actor required.

In terms of the main character, the film had no equivalent. Hitchcock had cast the urbane and soft-spoken William Holden as his suspected murderer in 1943's *Shadow of a Doubt*, subverting the cosy image of small-town America. But Hitchock's film is not seen from the point of view of the suspected 'Uncle Charlie'. Henri Verdoux is charming, ruthless, amoral, utterly businesslike and convinced of the inescapable logic of his multiple lies as well as his multiple murders. Some of Chaplin's early notes on the film revealed his basic thinking on Verdoux:

When all the world turns against a man he becomes holy . . .
Where there are no facts, sentiments prevail . . .
Virtues are less acquired than vices . . .
Good is in everything – even in evil . . .

Chaplin as Bluebeard – *Monsieur Verdoux*.

In the last analysis there is no reason for anything . . .
Violence is patience's last resort . . .
A reputation is the concern of cooks and butlers . . .

As his own narration elegantly announces, over the shot of his grave-stone, 'Henri Verdoux – 1880–1937':

Good evening. As you can see, my real name is Henri Verdoux, and for thirty years I was an honest bank clerk, until the Depression of 1930, at which year I found myself unemployed. It was then I became occupied in liquidating members of the opposite sex. This I did as a strictly business enterprise, to support a home and family. But let me assure you that the career of a Bluebeard is by no means profitable. Only a person with undaunted optimism would embark on such a venture. Unfortunately, I did. What follows is history . . .

The film explores the fastidious and increasingly desperate attempts by Verdoux to impose order on the chaos he himself has caused. We first see him clipping the roses in his garden, in smock and beret, picking a caterpillar he is about to step on out of his path, while behind him the oven spews out black smoke. Preceding this, we have been introduced to the squabbling Couvais family, wine merchants, a ménage of wives, brothers and sisters, each less attractive than the other, arguing about the fate of their missing sibling, Thelma, who married a stranger, withdrew all the money in her bank account and then disappeared. They have a picture, which introduces us to Verdoux: 'Funny-looking bird, isn't he?' but it gets thrown in the fire, as we find out later.

Verdoux's ventures proceed with a kind of clockwork precision, moved from location to location by the quick whirr and clack of rushing train wheels. Verdoux comes in from the garden, the flowers go in a vase, he checks himself in the mirror, the doorbell rings, alarming him. The postman brings a registered letter that must be signed by his wife, he rushes upstairs and carries out a charade of a conversation by a shut door, pretending to have secured the signature, dismissing the postman, opening the letter with its sixty thousand francs cash. Counting the money, the professional bank clerk's quick riffle through the notes. Phoning the stock exchange, requesting 'five hundred shares of Consolidated Gas, five hundred shares of Consolidated Copper . . .' et cetera, the money to be wired in the morning.

In the morning another potential victim, Mme Grosnay, arrives promptly to view the house, which the widowed gentleman has placed on the market. Verdoux proceeds to woo her immediately, but becomes too ardent too soon, and she rushes off with her estate agent in panic. Verdoux, however, will find her again.

As was the case with the real Landru, Verdoux keeps several households, women who wait for him at home while he supposedly builds bridges in Indochina, or serves as captain of a merchant ship, or is away on business, which is his ploy with his primary family, the wheelchair-bound Mme Verdoux and their small son, to whom he comments, seeing him torment the cat: 'Peter, don't pull the cat's tail! You have a cruel streak! I don't know where you get it.'

Chaplin's script is an unexpectedly elegant and acute concoction of Verdoux's acts as the foundation of his philosophy, expounded as the film proceeds to a variety of subsidiaries, the wife, the street-girl he almost murders but then helps instead, and, in the end, to judge and jury, pressman and priest. Some subtle solutions anticipated censorship problems which the film could not avoid, and which the writing found ways to allay or evade. The first murder is the best example: rushing from the first off-screen disposal, in the garden scene, and the unsuccessful wooing of Mme Grosnay, Verdoux finds he requires fifty thousand francs by the next morning to avoid a heavy stock-market loss. The train wheels whisk him towards Lydia, neglected, ageing and furious at being left alone for over three months. A smooth rigmarole about an imminent general bank failure persuades her reluctantly to withdraw all her money in cash in the afternoon. Then the mood darkens as her husband follows her upstairs to the bedroom, by an open window through which the full moon shines. 'How beautiful, this pale Endymion hour,' sighs Verdoux, explaining to his irritated wife, already off screen in the bedroom, 'Endymion, my dear, a beautiful youth possessed by the moon . . .' 'Well, forget about him and get to bed,' she snaps. Chaplin moves off screen into the bedroom, as the music alone signals what is to follow. The camera remains on the corridor, with the night changing to morning light in the window.

The censor Joseph Breen's detailed objections to the original script had insisted, in this scene, that the original phrase 'indecent moon' be altered, thus giving us the obscure 'Endymion', and that the original 'Forget him and come to bed' was forfeit because it hinted at carnal relations.

Breen had initially rejected the screenplay entirely for containing 'a false enunciation of moral values', but this was a standard ploy of the censor's board, and his long letter to Chaplin of 15 March 1946 was a familiar example of the lists that had to be dealt with by countless 'transgressive' Hollywood films, as comedians like W. C. Fields and Mae West and their producers could readily testify. There is no rancour in the letter, which, Breen notes, is written in confirmation of agreements reached on 12 March, 'in a very pleasant conference between yourself and Messrs Breen, Lynch and Vizzard of our offices, regarding certain problems raised by your story A COMEDY OF MURDERS'. These 'understandings' were set out as follows:

1. (a) There will be no comedy interruptions of the trial.
   (b) Revisions shall be made in Verdoux's final speeches to avoid confusing the issue of Verdoux's guilt, as well as to avoid what might be construed as an unjust attack on society . . .
2. With regard to Verdoux's attitude towards the Priest, it was agreed that this important scene would be subject to rewriting, to achieve the effect of giving the Priest his proper dignity and importance.
3. 'The Girl' will be changed from a street-walker to a derelict . . .
4. We advised you that censor boards would delete any references to specific chemical poisonings . . . The same is to be said with regard to chloroform . . .

In other points, on page 3: 'Pierre's expression "thank God" could not be approved, since it is not used reverently. So also the exclamation ". . . for God's sake" on page 139; as well as the phrase "My God" on page 147A . . .' Page 16: 'The business of Verdoux giving Mme. G.'s rear view the once-over, is unacceptable . . .' Page 25: 'There will be no vulgar emphasis on the "outlandish curves, both in front and behind," of the middle-aged woman . . .' Pages 36 and 37: points about Lydia's 'come to bed' line, and so forth. Page 48: 'The cruelty of the child, Peter, towards the cat, is unacceptable . . .' Page 59: 'The entire final dialogue of Verdoux on this page, and the accompanying action are unacceptably sensuous and will need to be substantially modified . . .' Details of 'all crimes that are easily imitable' must be omitted. Page 99: 'The joke about "scraping her bottom" is unacceptable.' Pages 101–6: 'This sequence between Verdoux and Annabella is unacceptably sex suggestive as presently written, and will need to be revised to get away from the suggestion that they are about to indulge in marital privileges.' Page 136: 'There should be no showing of, or suggestion of toilets in the bathroom.'

All these directives were par for the course, and in fact Chaplin easily got around or ignored them. The focus of the State Censor Boards that Breen was required to appease was invariably on sex, and there was in fact very little of that in *Monsieur Verdoux*. Chaplin had cast his wives, apart from the saintly and crippled Mme Verdoux, as either pompous matrons or shrewish harridans, and he knew well that not only his male audiences would find themselves sympathizing, against their own moral judgements, with the assassin. He is, in any case, the classic example of the 'little man' seizing power by his embrace of all-out criminality, a deliberate extension of Europe's many 'little men' – and women – who willed and voted Fascism into power.

For 'comic relief' – since Verdoux's own comic antics were more sinister than funny, rushing through doors and vaulting over windows to avoid disclosure, falling out of the window while wooing Mme Grosnay – Chaplin cast the comedienne Martha Raye as the wife of 'Captain Bonheur'. Literally a vaudeville baby, born to actor parents, she had foghorned her way through several comedies and musicals including the madcap 1941 *Hellzapoppin'*. With her gale of a voice and vulgar antics, she manages to be an indestructible force that Verdoux cannot poison or drown in the lake.

Verdoux's undoing, in the end, is not a failed murder, as he manages even to poison the policeman who comes to arrest him, but his one act of mercy: sparing the Girl he meets in a Paris street (whom Breen forbade to be a prostitute) and lures to his home in the hope of testing a poison on her, but changes his mind when she tells him she would have killed for her now deceased war-wounded husband. When Verdoux loses his money, in a great mid-Depression crash heralded by iconic headlines – STOCKS CRASH, PANIC FOLLOWS – BANKS FAIL, RIOTS ENSUE – CRISIS IN EUROPE – NAZIS BOMB SPANISH LOYALISTS – he meets her again in the street when she calls him over to her cab: her fortunes have turned since she met him and she has hooked up with a munitions manufacturer. (Verdoux: 'That's the business I should have been in.') As they sit in a cafe, one of the old Couvais family enters coincidentally and spots him, setting off the moment when he allows himself to be captured by the police. As the Girl has said to him: 'You seem to have lost your zest for bitterness.' Tired of his long trajectory which has ended in bankruptcy by blind economic forces, Verdoux sees the Girl off in her cab and returns through the swing doors of the cafe – reminiscent of the swing doors of *The Cure* – to be eventually discovered and seized.

Chaplin cuts directly to the outcome of Verdoux's trial (whizzing train wheels mix to VERDOUX TRIAL NEARING END). There is no need to argue over guilt or innocence. Verdoux's argument is a Nietzschean one, with a Marxist twist: there is no individual Good or Evil in the faceless clash of modern politics. When the prosecutor calls out: 'Gentlemen of the jury, you have before you a cruel and sinister monster!' Verdoux turns in the dock to look round for whom this epithet might be aimed at – a wicked moment that savours of Chaplin's demonization in the Joan Barry case. Called to make his statement, he comes to his feet, and declaims a very different creed to that propounded by Charlie-as-Hynkel. Explaining to the jury that he had tried to use his brains honestly for thirty-five years till he was forced to go into business for himself, he continues:

As for being a mass killer, does not the world encourage it? Is it not building weapons of destruction for the sole purpose of mass killing? Has it not blown unsuspecting women and small children to pieces – and done it very scientifically? As a mass killer, I am an amateur by comparison. However, I do not wish to lose my temper, because very shortly I shall lose my head. Nevertheless, upon leaving this spark of earthly existence, I have this to say: I shall see you all, very soon.

The 'Verdoux defence' echoes down the decades from the shadow of Hiroshima to our own day. Chaplin knew that when the Jew/Hynkel had spoken on the podium of *The Great Dictator* he was not speaking for Charlie the Tramp, but for himself. The final bitter and terrible legacy of the Tramp in modern times, in the age of the Bomb and of Auschwitz, looking into the bleak future of the Cold War and the strong possibility of Mutually Assured Destruction, was voiced by Verdoux in court, and then in the death-cell where he awaits his execution by the guillotine – as he converses with the reporter who, we are told, has followed all the off-screen days of his trial:

REPORTER: Well, well, Verdoux, you have to admit crime doesn't pay.
VERDOUX: No, sir, not in a small way.
REPORTER: What do you mean?
VERDOUX: To be successful in anything one must be well organized . . .
REPORTER: What's all this talk about Good and Evil?
VERDOUX: Arbitrary forces my good fellow – too much of either one would destroy us all . . .
REPORTER: Give me a break. Give me a story with a moral to it. You, the tragic example of a life of crime.

VERDOUX: I don't see how anyone can be an example in these criminal times.
REPORTER: Well, you certainly are, robbing and murdering people.
VERDOUX: That's business.
REPORTER: Well, other people don't do business that way.
VERDOUX: That's the history of many a big business – wars, conflict, it's all business. One murder makes a villain, millions, a hero. Numbers sanctify, my good fellow.

The reporter walks away, baffled. Then the priest enters, to tell the condemned man:

PRIEST: I've come to ask you to make your peace with God.
VERDOUX: I am at peace with God, my conflict is with man.
PRIEST: Have you no remorse for your sin?
VERDOUX: Who knows what sin is, born as it was from Heaven, from God's Fallen Angel. Who knows the ultimate destiny it serves? After all, what would you be doing without sin?
PRIEST: May the Lord have mercy on your soul . . .
VERDOUX: Why not? After all, it belongs to him.

Verdoux's final walk towards the guillotine was unusually filmed by Chaplin right at the start of the production. This decision might have served a dual purpose: symbolically to seal the fact that all that transpired in the story was destined to come to this moment, and to lift a burden from the actor, whose performance might be subtly altered by concern about the nature of the character's end. By putting it emotionally out of the way first, Chaplin cleared himself to be the Verdoux he required of himself: the vainglorious and even cheerful sinner, who had no thought for consequences. In his own way, Verdoux was not just Charlie's alter ego, he was, in fact, the very automaton that Charlie in *Modern Times* struggled with all his heart to avoid becoming. In that true sense, Verdoux is heartless, and Chaplin plays him that way, with only a few flashes of self-realization that are, in the plot, his weakness, that fault in the machine-human that will inevitably cause it to fail.

As Verdoux, who has finally become Charlie again, is offered a last swig of rum, and, after a hesitation, says, 'I've never tasted rum,' and takes it, throws out his chest and breathes deep the fetid air of the execution chamber – the only air he has left – he recapitulates, for the last time, the Tramp's walk into the sunset. But there is no sunset, merely the vaulted grille of the death chamber, with the axe, unseen, waiting.

It is a strangely triumphant walk, as the music swells, to the very temporary, technically obligatory but misleading fade and title of THE END.

NEW YORK HERALD TRIBUNE

Cartoon Cited by President to Ridicule Senate Inquiry

Berryman cartoon which appeared yesterday in "*The Evening Star,*" of *Washington,* and to whi attention was called by President Roosevelt in reply to a question concerning Senate inquiry into ti film industry

'Now what could I possibly tell those past-masters about comedy?'

28

Limelight

Or: The Passion of Vaudeville Part 1

Chaplin did not testify at the House Un-American Activities Committee in Washington, despite news reports that he was expected to be the star witness. He had to wait to film the experience as a fictional moment in *A King in New York*. Many zealous patriots demanded that he be investigated for a whole raft of past and present activities, from his pro-Russian statements to a cable of support sent to the 'noted French artist and Communist' Pablo Picasso. As early as April 1947 newspapers called for him to be barred from the US, calling him a 'moral nonentity' and accusing him of 'joining the ranks of subversives who have the overthrow of the American way of life as their avowed objective'. As he had mounted so articulate a defence of the core anti-values of Henri Verdoux on screen, HUAC may well have been wary of providing him a platform for yet more articulate responses, and may well have calculated that there was still a reservoir of popular support for the 'little fellow', however tarnished. Similar thoughts probably prevented them calling Groucho Marx, another comic with an FBI file.

Comedians apart, the committee sent out forty-three subpoenas in September for Hollywood witnesses to attend at Washington in October. Nineteen 'unfriendly' witnesses were called, screenwriters and directors, all men, ten of them Jews. All, apart from Bertolt Brecht, were American citizens. Their defence strategy was mainly to invoke the Fifth Amendment, which ensured that a citizen could not give self-incriminating evidence, rather than the First Amendment, which ensured free speech. This strategy was not successful, and the evasive answers to the Committee's standard question, 'Are you now or have you ever been a member of the Communist Party?' alienated public opinion. While 'friendly' witnesses like Walt Disney, Jack Warner, Louis B. Mayer, Adolphe Menjou, Ronald Reagan and Gary Cooper rushed to denounce Communists in the movie ranks, ten of the 'unfriendlys', eight writers and two directors (Herbert Biberman and Edward Dmytryk), were sentenced to jail for defying the committee. Various appeals delayed their imprisonment until mid-1950. Blacklisting of movie people who refused to co-operate or give names to the committee followed.

While agitation to deport Chaplin was embryonic, a more immediate threat hung over his good friend the composer Hanns Eisler, whose pro-Soviet brother, Gerhart, had been imprisoned on Ellis Island for passport fraud. Hanns was accused by HUAC of perjury and deportation proceedings were begun against him in September 1947. Chaplin's vocal support of Eisler won him more attention and hostility from the zealots, despite the fact that both Albert Einstein and Thomas Mann were also among Eisler's defenders.

Political problems apart, Chaplin had had to contend with a measure of conflict with his colleagues too during the filming of *Monsieur Verdoux*. Chaplin had first employed his half-brother, Wheeler Dryden, as an assistant on *The Great Dictator*, but when he put together Dryden and writer-director Robert Florey for *Verdoux* conflict ensued, as Florey claimed he was under the impression that Chaplin had considered offering him the post of director, after praising his copious notes on the script. Florey had written a booklet in French about Chaplin as far back as 1927, and was to pen another, *Monsieur Chaplin ou le rire dans la nuit* (with Maurice Bessy) in 1952, as well as a detailed account of his work on Verdoux in his 1948 book, *Hollywood d'hier et d'aujourd'hui*. His portrait of Chaplin was far from flattering. He wrote:

Charlie . . . has two distinct personalities . . . Charlie that the whole world adores, the Charlie who wants to please, to amuse, to seduce. And the tyrannical, wounding, authoritarian, mean, despotic man, imbued with himself. One could attribute to him . . . the verse of Corneille, in the tragedy of *Medea*, 'Me, me alone, and that's enough.'

Chaplin seemed to have a habit of enraging Frenchmen, as he had also alienated a previous assistant, Henri d'Abbadie d'Arrast, who nursed his resentments till he could gloat over the failure of Chaplin's *A Countess from Hong Kong* of 1967. Among Chaplin's sins, according to Florey, were his ignorance of 'the technical side of motion pictures', his general disdain for advice, his moodiness –

Often, Charlie gets into great rages which often last only a few moments . . . His film is ruined, destroyed, it's a real conspiracy. He has to do it all over, that's going to cost him an arm and a leg . . . And then the storm passes, he films a scene that pleases him, everything is better, he smiles, he is content, he is gracious . . .

He had the chance of giving Edna Purviance a late blooming as one of Verdoux's wives, but turned away from that. Henry Bergman, now seventy-three, wanted to be one of the judges at the trial, but Chaplin denied him a last cameo, out of spite. Florey's ire was directed mostly at the fact that, despite Chaplin's barracking of Wheeler Dryden as an ignoramus, he favoured him in the credits over Florey, who got second place.

All this might surprise no one who has some knowledge of how films are directed, or of the intensity on a set, or who fails to figure that, playing Monsieur Verdoux for several months, the character might seep into the director, just as studio footage of the filming of *The Great Dictator* shows the uniformed director in Hynkel-like moments. Clearly Chaplin was a boss, rather than a father figure, to his assistants. The director who is convinced of his own infallibility, like Cecil B. DeMille, is no stranger in film history, and it would be a foolhardy crew member who did not accept that a Chaplin film was a Chaplin film, to the hilt.

Nevertheless, it was no boon to Chaplin that he was accumulating enemies, his political foes becoming more and more fervent. Following the HUAC hearings and their aftermath, lists were being drawn up of Un-Americans who sponsored events such as the World Peace Conference of March 1949, or the 'hundreds named as Red Appeasers' in June 1949, which, apart from Chaplin, included Pearl Buck, Lillian Hellman, Katharine Hepburn, Dashiell Hammett, Danny Kaye, Gene Kelly, Thomas Mann, Clifford Odets, Gregory Peck, Paul Robeson, Edward G. Robinson, Frank Sinatra and Orson Welles, as well as the usual suspects like Ring Lardner Junior, Lester Cole and John Garfield. Counter-measures proposed by the California State Senate Committee on Un-American Activities included: 'Legislation to control and prevent subversive activity . . . Continuous investigation and exposure of subversive activity' and 'Adoption of a broad, community-wide approach to a "clear understanding of the American heritage in contrast with the brutal, inhumane and treacherous doctrines of Marxism-Leninism-Stalinism."'

In August, the State Department warned that an 'American Continental Congress for Peace' in Mexico City, supported by Charles

Chaplin, W. E. B. Dubois, Dr Linus Pauling and Paul Robeson would be 'Moscow directed'. At the meeting, Paul Robeson's wife excoriated 'violence that for many years has been directed in my country against Negroes, Jews and labor unions'. Chaplin sent a cable from Hollywood saying: 'In this era of the atomic bomb the only defense against war is peace among all the nations of the earth regardless of their ideology.'

The FBI was growing its dossier on Chaplin, which included a long interview taken by the Immigration and Naturalization Service on 17 April 1948, when Chaplin had applied for a re-entry permit in context of a plan to visit Europe with Oona to research his new movie project, then titled *Footlights*. In the event, though the visa was issued, he postponed the trip. Chaplinologist Charles Maland published the interview transcript in *Cineaste* magazine in 1986. Responding to an array of questions about his contacts, membership of or contributions to Communist Party 'front organizations', Chaplin said:

I am liberal and I am interested in peace, but by no means am I interested in Communism. I have always made that statement. As I said, I never need any front or any other name. I have always used my own name throughout my whole life . . . I have never belonged to any political organization other than the things I have to belong to in accordance with my work.

Chaplin reiterated his support for Russia as a war ally, stating:

During the war everybody was more or less a Communist sympathiser. By that I mean the Communists of Russia . . . I never read a book about Communism. I don't know anything about it. I never read Karl Marx or anything like that. My interpretation of Communist was Russia . . . I naturally felt they put up a very good cause. I have always felt grateful because they helped us to get ready and prepare our own way of life . . .

The interrogation proceeded in great detail into Chaplin's contacts and communications, and quizzed him about the Soviet takeover of Czechoslovakia, which he naïvely defended – 'No soldiers were there. There was no bloodshed . . . I frankly believe the press is trying to create a war with Russia, and I wholeheartedly disapprove of it, and I am sure that I am not a Communist . . . I have $30,000,000 worth of business – what am I talking about Communism for?'

About his citizenship Chaplin said:

From the time I was nineteen I have always had a sense of internationalism and I feel that it is coming closer every day, for the United Nations and the

One World . . . I consider myself as much a citizen of America as anyone else and my great love has always been here in this country. I have been here thirty, thirty-five years. My children and everybody are as much a part of my – at the same time I don't feel that I am allied to any one particular country. I feel that I am a citizen of the world. I feel that when the day comes and we have the barriers down and so forth so the people come and go all around the world and be a part of any country, and I have always felt that about citizenship . . . I don't like war and I don't like revolution . . . I just want to see things function in harmony. I want to see everybody pretty well, happy and satisfied.

In retrospect, with the hindsight of history, Chaplin's choices, as were those of thousands of peace-oriented liberals in America and western Europe at the time, were deeply flawed. When one reads the histories of American Communists such as Paul Robeson one can sense the false hope of the embrace of a supposedly anti-racialist, anti-capitalist social alternative in the world shaped by the Depression and Fascism, but one cannot fail to cringe at his whole-hearted support of Stalin's regime. It is not enough to say that the well-meaning were fooled, for the facts were available for those who took the trouble to find out. As an intellectual, one has to make an effort to be fooled, as well as to avoid foolishness. Chaplin's willed ignorance was one with all those who wished to see, and were encouraged to make a clear-cut distinction between Good and Evil. What may be interesting to reflect upon is that the Tramp and Monsieur Verdoux, the scamp and the assassin, knew that this distinction is blurred, uneasy, and stands on the edge of an abyss.

Now that the Tramp had been guillotined, the question arose what Chaplin the artist could achieve next. Chaplin the man had at last achieved an equilibrium in his family life, and the press pundits waited in vain for his latest marriage to fail. It held, and Oona provided the stability he had always craved. On 28 March 1949 their second daughter, Josephine Hannah, was born. By then, Chaplin had been working for just over a year on his new script. This replaced the project he had mentioned to some newspapers during 1947, a film 'to revive the old Charlie with his baggy clothes and funny boots' as 'a displaced person from Europe who lands in the United States, becomes a nine-day wonder, tires of pomp and circumstance, and sails again for Europe, waving good-bye to the Statue of Liberty. What makes the little man famous is the fact that a shock has brought memories of a former life to his mind and he speaks Sanskrit.' This peculiar prospect was reported by the British *Manchester Guardian* on 7 July, but there is no trace of it in the annals. Instead, work proceeded eventually on his 'story of the stage, showing some of those Biblical people of the theatre, the simple, trusting children of God in a wild world'.

This early wide brief is reflected in an undated set of handwritten notes, headed 'The Passion of Vaudeville', which sets out roughly the tale of 'a vaudeville couple [who] are very much in love with each other. The girl is very young but the man is many years her senior. He has looked after the girl ever since she was a baby, she having been left to him by his old friend, who was his partner and who was a drunkard . . .' The tale followed this lopsided but clearly familiar alliance through love, marriage and disillusion, with a show of various music-hall acts featuring in the course of the tale: the family of acrobats, the jugglers, the hypnotist, the 'vaudeville team starting their first tour'. Despite these early notes, however, the focus of the tale inevitably came down to 'Me, me . . . and that's enough.'

The first extensive version of this story was, unlike the play-scripts of previous movies, an almost full-fledged novel of ninety-three pages, entitled *Footlights*. Obviously, it was never intended for publication, but Chaplin felt he needed to flesh out his characters in much more detail than he had hitherto found necessary. From the start, it was clear that he was working with ideas that were autobiographical, dealing with his own roots in vaudeville, but that in fact ran even deeper.

The 'novel' took pains to recount the 'back story' both of the main character, Calvero, and of the young girl, Terry, whom he rescues from a suicide attempt in the opening sequence of the eventual film. The narrative tells us that –

Terry Ambrose is different from other children, in the fact that she was introspective and had developed a sense of inferiority, much too early in her life. She was the youngest member of a family of six that consisted of herself, her father and mother and three sisters – two of whom died within a year.

The novel recounts that Terry's father had been a rover, the son of impecunious gentry (in the film she describes him as the fourth son of a lord), who ran away to sea, married a poorer woman and his family cut him off. Her mother was the daughter of a labour leader, 'who had been one of the chief instigators in the East India Dock strike'.

She became a dressmaker whose customers included prostitutes whom Terry saw passing in and out of the house. As a girl she used to run to the pub to buy them gin. Both her parents died before she was fourteen, but she managed to get a job as a dancer. Struck by rheumatic fever, she couldn't dance any more and got work in a stationery shop, Sardou & Co. Here the narrative catches up with the eventual movie, with the tale of the poor musician, Mr Neville, to whom she gives extra music sheets and extra change, till she is discovered by the shop owner and discharged. The novel goes into great detail on the details of her subsequent misfortunes, when she takes work at 'Northrup's Pickle Factory':

Her hands become stained yellow with the pickle and at weekends she wears black gloves to hide them. One Saturday night she walks into a room over a Soho pub where a 'Mr John' is rehearsing some dancers. He is a brutish looking man with a broken nose, a large ugly mouth and a voice low and woolly that sounded like the drawing of a bow over a loose, bass string of violin.

Mr John auditions Terry as a dancer, but she collapses, and spends eighteen weeks in the hospital.

On the clown, Calvero, the 'novel' expounds:

In his youth he yearned to be a musician but could not afford an instrument . . . another longing was to be a romantic actor, but he was too small and his diction too uncultured. Nevertheless, he believed himself to be the greatest actor living. Necessity made him turn to comedy, which he loathed, because it demanded of him an intimacy with his audience which he did not feel and which never came natural to him. Calvero was not gregarious. He was shy and reserved and difficult to know. At times strange, melancholy and austere . . . That's why he would have to get half drunk before he could face an audience . . .

He had married Eva Norton, the daughter of an old flame of his 'who, in his youth, caused him to suffer much unrequited love . . .' This old flame had left with a rival to South Africa, and bore a daughter, Eva, who was twenty-five years younger than Calvero. The narrative describes their life together in small-time vaudeville: 'His make up was ridiculous; a small toothbrush moustache, a small derby hat, and a tight-fitting swallow tail coat, baggy pants and a large pair of old shoes . . .'

The 'novel' enabled Chaplin to etch out, at an ocean's distance from the London of his youth, the whole milieu of turn-of-the-century

English music hall. What emerges clearly is an amalgam: both of Charlie the Tramp – the toothbrush moustache, the shoes – and, more evidently, his father, Charles Chaplin Senior, and his mother, the early Hannah, whose youthful struggles are imagined in the tale. The man of song, dance and patter, brought down by the booze, was unmistakable.

The central point of *Footlights*, and the movie, *Limelight*, that emerged from its cocoon, was that it was a tale of failure. The clown was not only going to die, nakedly, upon the stage, but he was to be shown in the bleak fade of the spotlights that are turned off, leaving him in darkness. This Chaplin had to explore in the light of his imagination – since he had never failed. Despite the hard road of his early childhood, much drawn on in his familiar curriculum vitae, from the moment he began clog-dancing as one of the Eight Lancashire Lads he almost never looked back, only forward. Even Chaplin Senior had not failed as spectacularly as Calvero, but only faded from the position of a moderately successful jobbing variety act to the status of unreliable lush.

Chaplin wanted to use Calvero as a mouthpiece for his own thoughts about the nature of the comedian's psyche, the vital necessity of rapport with the audience, and the eternal fear, experienced by every comic since Grimaldi and before, of losing the connection, the existential terror of ceasing, one day, to be funny.

In one of the scripts, which emerged from the 'novel' but never made it into the movie, Chaplin inserted a lengthy scene of an interview Calvero gives to a reporter, in which he muses on this deep anxiety (script deletions in square brackets):

CALVERO: I wonder – if I'm funny. Sometimes I think perhaps it's the audience that can't laugh any more. Although, there's really very little to laugh at. [When I was young, I used to think there was. There used to be a great deal to laugh at. As I grow older, it doesn't tickle my funny bone any more.]
REPORTER: Perhaps you take things too seriously.
CALVERO: I wonder. Maybe the audience are taking it too seriously. [Yes, that's what's frightening.] What a horrible thing if the audience could never laugh again . . . I'm funny, but the audience don't know it.
REPORTER: The audience haven't known it for a long time, Calvero.
CALVERO: Do you think I'm funny?
REPORTER: That's [an unfair question] difficult to answer. I know you.

CALVERO: [You've no need to go any further.] No one's funny, when you
know them. White paint and red noses don't fool anybody. A comedian is
not appreciated in his own home. Sometimes I wonder whether it's the
audience that I hate, or myself . . . Many a time, they've been friendly and
appreciated and when I've come on, given me a tremendous ovation, which
for some reason, I've resented – like lovers sulking after a quarrel, when
one tries to make up with the other. I've resented their warmth, their friendliness, because of its challenge to live up to what they expect of me.

REPORTER: I think you hate yourself.

CALVERO: Do you think I have an inferiority complex?

REPORTER: That's funny – Calvero with an inferiority complex. No . . . I
shouldn't think so. I think it's fear. You're afraid that they won't laugh . . .
What's funny? What constitutes a joke? We know that the element of
surprise has a great deal to do with every comic situation. Also the sense
of the incongruous and the ridiculous, which you undoubtedly have.
And which a philosopher like Bergson has also. But why is it? – You're
funny . . . and he isn't.

One telling script deletion has Calvero musing: 'If only the young and
the old could all be the same age . . .' In another scene, in the
Queenshead Saloon, the regulars are discussing Calvero, in another
unfilmed sequence:

– Never any good. Pig-headed. He's high strung and emotional. Suffers with
terrific anxiety before he comes on. Never must be conflicting, or of the
same type act as his. It must never be something funny, otherwise he's self-
conscious that he's competing. He's exacting on the position and place he
fills on the bill. He prefers dancers, acrobats, but never strong personalities
or other comedians to follow, or precede him. He will not work on the bill
with another comedian because he's afraid that they might be funnier than
he is. Not because he's jealous, but that he knows he will be self-conscious
and won't do his best.
– Calvero has suffered from extreme poverty as a child. Now that he is a
success, he takes delight in revenging himself on society for his childhood.
– He is an instinctive artist, therefore highly strung. Emotional, intolerant,
egotistical; yet with it all, generous and kindly to those who are not
competing in his world. (someone says: 'That's why he likes Claudius, the
armless wonder – because he doesn't compete with him')
– He loathes the philistine and their superficial hero worship – their basking
in other people's sunlight . . . their rank materialism, their hypocrisy, their
vulgarity and bad taste.
– He is accused of having a swollen head.

Chaplin's examination of the comedian's fear is all the more telling for the context of the period in which he worked on the script. As HUAC continued the hunt for Hollywood Communists, and the press continued to bay for the suspects' blood, the Cold War intensified both on the foreign and domestic front: July 1948 saw the beginning of the Berlin Blockade, when Soviet forces in Germany closed off the capital to contact over land and the western powers began an airlift. In February 1949, Mao Tse-tung completed the Communist takeover of China, setting off a furious 'who lost China?' argument in the US. In September 1949 the Soviets tested their first atomic bomb. In June 1950 North Korea invaded the south, and China soon committed its Red Army to this war. In the US, in January 1950, a State Department official, Alger Hiss, was convicted of perjury for denying that he had passed state secrets to ex-Communist and now right-winger Whittaker Chambers. In March, Klaus Fuchs, a German-born physicist, was convicted in England of passing hydrogen bomb secrets to the Soviet Union. On 17 July, Julius Rosenberg, a small-time engineer and trade-union activist in New York, was arrested and accused of being part of Fuchs's spy ring. His wife Ethel was arrested in August. Their case would be a famous cause célèbre.

Within the film community, controversy raged in October 1950 over a 'loyalty oath' passed by a vote of the Screen Directors' Guild while their president, Joseph L. Mankiewicz, was abroad. On his return, Guild members lined up in a crucial meeting that cast the union-bashing Cecil B. DeMille, with Clarence Brown, Frank Capra, Henry King, Leo McCarey and others, against the assorted liberals, with John Ford unexpectedly casting the crucial verbal stone at DeMille.

Apart from the brimstone and sulphur, there were also severe financial problems at United Artists, whose distributing company was being taken over by a syndicate headed by Paul V. McNutt, former Governor of Indiana. Most of the company stock held by Mary Pickford and Chaplin was transferred to the syndicate, which put $3,500,000 into the depleted company funds. The Artists were no longer running the crucial distribution end of their films.

Despite the climate of fear and angst, Chaplin soldiered on, finalizing his script and casting for the film. This was going to be to a great extent a family show: son Sydney Chaplin was to play the composer Neville, half-brother Wheeler Dryden would be wheeled in as a dry old doctor, and Oona's kids, Geraldine, Josephine and the youngest, Michael, were to appear in cameo. For Terry, the young ballerina, Chaplin cast twenty-year-old Claire Bloom, who had made her first major West End stage appearance in 1949 in *The Lady's Not for Burning* alongside Richard Burton. Her first film role had been in a 1948 British film, *The Blind Goddess*. Chaplin flew her over with her mother as chaperone (mindful of his fearful reputation with young actresses) and rehearsed her to a successful screen test. In the crew, there was a raft of new faces, including Eugene Lourie as art director and Robert Aldrich as associate director. Karl Struss, who had co-photographed *The Great Dictator*, replaced Rollie Totheroh, who got a credit as 'Photographic Consultant'. In November 1951, more than three years after the first drafts of the story had been formulated, the cameras were ready to roll . . .

29

Limelight
Or: The Passion of Vaudeville Part 2

LIMELIGHT

ORIGINAL STORY AND SCREENPLAY BY CHARLES CHAPLIN . . .

> The glamour of limelight,
> from which age must pass as youth enters.
> The story of a ballerina and a clown . . .
> London, a late afternoon in the summer of 1914.

From the opening sequence, in which Calvero staggers home, drunk, to his rooms in Mrs Alsop's apartment house, smells gas, and after examining his own breath and his shoes breaks into the ground-floor flat and rescues Terry from her attempted suicide, we are made aware with absolute clarity that this film is not a comedy. Despite its comedic tics and twitches, comedy remains simply the métier, the job, the business of Calvero, while the characters are driven by their deeply thwarted desires, and, in Calvero's case, an innate, subterranean need to find justification in life, to find the energy to go on.

In the opening shot a London street is not presented as particularly poor, and certainly nowhere near the destitution of nineteenth-century Lambeth. A barrel organ churns. A series of tracking shots lead us to a door, through the hallways to an inner door, towards the girl who lies in bed, a small jar of pills in her hand. Track past the open gas stove to a cloth shutting the space under the door. Outside, as Calvero approaches, three small kids, Chaplin and Oona's Geraldine, Josephine and Michael, watch his clumsy attempts to open the front door, calling out to him that the landlady is not home. He finally makes his way in, smells the gas . . . Breaking Terry's door down, he carries her out, places her on the steps, and rushes out to the nearby dispensary to fetch a doctor. Together they bring her up two floors to his room.

The picture that both Calvero and the doctor assume is bleak. A young girl adrift, probably a woman of the streets. If she is taken to the hospital her attempted suicide will be reported. She would go to

Limelight – Calvero unmasked.

jail. As an act of ordinary charity she must stay in Chaplin's rooms. When the landlady returns, in any case, she repossesses her room, as the girl has not paid her rent. To keep up the respectability of the house, Chaplin must pretend the sick girl is his wife. When she awakes, he continues his assumption of her plight: a prostitute, with a sexual disease. All is hinted at as broadly as might pass the censor's habitual restriction of any mention of such harsh realities of life. Eventually, Terry gives Calvero a quick run-down on how she reached her desperate moment, a sharply condensed version of the first chapters of Chaplin's original *Footlights* narrative.

Before this, Calvero's first dialogue with Terry, the moment she awakes and asks 'Why didn't you let me die?' sets up his basic philosophy, as, stewed to the gills, he lectures her about the importance of life – 'billions of years it's taken to evolve human consciousness and you want to wipe it out . . . wipe out the miracle of all existence, more important than anything in the universe. What can the stars do? Nothing, but sit on their axes . . . And the sun, shooting flames two hundred and eighty miles high. So what?'

Having flimflammed the landlady, and brought in some groceries, Calvero goes to sleep under a poster of 'Calvero – Tramp Comedian' and two portraits of himself in stage costume, while three street musicians strike up outside the pub. The camera closes in on Calvero and his first dream flashback of his theatrical heyday – the chance, at long last, to present on screen the flea-circus sketch that Chaplin had baulked at since 1919.

Just over fifteen minutes of the film have passed to this point, and the whole has been suffused with a deep melancholy that will remain throughout the work. Calvero the drunk has presented himself as emphatically different from Charlie the Tramp's alter ego, the Drunk of 'Mumming Birds'. The old Drunk's progress on stage and screen was always the motivation for a stream of gags, up to the spectacular house-of-tricks of One A.M. Calvero is just a drunk, the most he can muster a set of ogling grimaces cast at the landlady, Mrs Alsop, who clearly has a soft spot for him, and whom we will see later on in the narrative as drunk as any trooper.

Nothing in Chaplin's previous oeuvre, in all his seventy shorts and eight features to date, prepares one for Limelight, yet they are all in some way a preparation for what Chaplin himself privately told friends would be his greatest and his last film. In his embrace of Karl Struss's high-contrast lighting and anxious tracking shots it was a break from all past efforts, and a rebuke to those who dismissed him as a cinematic primitive.

And yet Limelight, in a curious sense, is a completely private communication between Charlie Chaplin and his own audience, not necessarily just fans or admirers, but all those who were touched in some way by those three-and-a-half decades of film-making, by the Tramp's progress from the aggressive world of Mack Sennett to the presumption of The Great Dictator and Monsieur Verdoux. For those for whom Chaplin means little, or nothing, or who never 'got it', Limelight is unlikely to inspire a conversion. Its broad melodrama, drawing from the world of Victorian sentiment, risks alienating rather than appealing to audiences. The lush score, welling up like some great musical whale breaking the waves, rising to crescendo as Terry, turning the tables on Calvero's own despair when his first comeback show proves disastrous, lambasts him and then, finding herself on her feet for the first time, cries out: 'Calvero, I'm walking!', risks breasting a crest of mawkish overload. But it is all of a piece with the central purpose of the work: to reach deep down into the core of the clown, that legendary moment of confession: 'Doctor, I am Grimaldi.'

Very consciously and overtly, Chaplin drew even deeper, referencing the world of the old *commedia dell'arte* in the warp and weft of the piece. The theme is made plain in the internal ballet in which Calvero is employed as a clown, with Terry cast as a dying Columbine. Traditionally, there was a host of stock characters in the *commedia*, the merchant Pantaloon, a maidservant, Columbine (sometimes his daughter), Harlequin, a disobedient servant and then lover, a comic doctor, a captain, the hook-nosed Pulcinella – who became the English Punch – another servant type, Pedrolino, who morphed into the French Pierrot, and various other low-lifes in masque.

When Joseph Grimaldi began his series of satirical sketches in the early 1800s, drawing on the traditional types to pastiche favourite narratives, such as Don Quixote or Baron Munchausen, or to score political points off the Emperor Napoleon or English power-players up to and including the much lampooned Prince Regent, he foregrounded Harlequin, the bad servant, as his main representative. In Pierre Louis Duchartre's book *The Italian Comedy*, Harlequin is described as

. . . of all the traditional characters . . . the most strongly individualized and yet the most enigmatic . . . a paradoxical figure . . . both sluggish and full of bounce . . . Only rubber could do him justice in effigy, only rubber could receive the impress of his subtle spirit, created by the gods in a moment of uncontrollable fantasy and bred by men of bold imagination . . . now delicate, now offensive, comic or melancholy, and sometimes lashed into a frenzy of madness. He is the unwitting and unrecognized creator of a new form of poetry, essentially muscular, accented by gestures . . . enriched with philosophic reflexions and incongruous noises.

Chaplin, like his contemporaries, Laurel, Keaton, Lloyd and later the quintessential twentieth-century Pulcinella-Pantaloon W. C. Fields, knew the background of his art and his trade very well. In the *Limelight* ballet, Columbine is dying, while her lover Harlequin weeps, and the clowns try in vain to cheer her up. She dies, and Harlequin wields his magic wand by her grave to try to resurrect her.

But the nymphs, with Columbine, dance in to show she is in fact immortal.

This is *Limelight* in embryo: the composer Neville is a particularly withdrawn Harlequin, with whom Calvero prophesies she will fall in love. Calvero is the old clown, whom the impresario, Postant (a figure drawing on the old British music-hall impresario and theatre owner Oswald Stoll), wants to sack till he discovers his identity and sets up the final benefit show for him. The chorus of clowns is present outside and in the bar, joined by Calvero when he leaves Terry to jolt her into fulfilling her proper destiny. One of his fellow players is a pretty unrecognizable Snub Pollard, yet another survivor from silent days. In the crowning moment of the benefit show, Chaplin famously brings in Buster Keaton, practically forgotten and lost in the post-war period, to partner him in the last great comic act we will see from Chaplin-Harlequin, Calvero's farewell. In its peroration, Calvero falls into the orchestra drum and suffers his fatal heart attack, while Terry, youth exemplified, dances on into eternity.

Calvero and Terry's love story, the holdout from the first 'Passion of Vaudeville' notes, is, despite its Victorian-Edwardian cadences, a fake, as Calvero knows well. Terry's gushing love combines gratitude with pity, as Calvero tells her it's 'wasted on an old man', and her denial of her love for the composer Neville is an act of sheer masochism and submission, which Calvero cannot accept. 'In my last years,' he cries out, 'I must have truth!' The line is so corny, and yet Chaplin's passion is profound. Despite the deployment of old traditional themes, the underlying fault-lines of *Limelight* are resolutely modern, imbued with post-Freudian anxieties about the loss of personality, meaning and the fragility of not only the ego, but the id. Calvero's constant exclamations about life and energy are invocations to himself to rise above adversity, his own rack of follies, and old age, the inevitable dying of the light.

More than in any other Chaplin film, the camera is used to move in closely to these crucial moments of terrible self-realization. When Terry auditions for Postant, and re-encounters Neville, the pianist and now successful composer, Calvero is left behind sitting among props on the stage as they saunter out. The spotlights are switched off, one by one, leaving a pool of light on his eyes, invoking the terror of a small boy left in the dark. Another scene is set in the dressing room, after his failed one-night comeback at the Middlesex Theatre: Calvero has 'died' on the stage, the audience asleep in their seats, his jokes falling like dry husks, until a voice mercilessly cuts him loose with the call, 'All right, old boy, let's all go home!' Left alone before the mirror, the clown removes his make-up, wiping off the cream as the camera moves in, again, to those eyes, those genetic jewels that can identify Chaplin offspring at a glance. They seemed to be saying, these remorseless tracks in to close-up: I was content to present the mask, to this moment, but now I will strip it off, and be revealed without mercy, in the fallibility of my humiliation.

Even the comedy segments, Calvero's vintage acts, or perhaps most of all the comedy segments, are imbued with melancholy, vibrating with a faded passion. Finally, Chaplin has got the flea act in, though the glorious company of Professor Bosco's box of minuscule performers has shrunk to a little capsule containing the two survivors, Phyllis and Henry, bobbing invisibly from one of Calvero's fists to the other. The jolly song 'I'm an Animal Trainer, a Circus Entertainer', that precedes the flea act could be another incarnation of Groucho Marx's Captain Spaulding:

> Why should I hunt for animals,
> And through the jungle roam,
> Oh when there's local talent
> To be found right here at home!

But when Calvero returns to the stage for applause, the theatre is empty, returning us to the dreamer, awakening in the shadow of his old glory.

Chaplin revived the comic songs and patter of old vaudeville with close attention to the defunct accents and cadences of time gone by, particularly in his dream flirtation with a dancing Terry, after his happy song of Spring: 'It's love, it's love, it's love love love love love . . .' But here, too, he is returned to the present, giving her an explanation as good for the elder Chaplin as Calvero: 'As a man gets on in years, he wants to live deeply. A feeling of sad dignity comes upon him, and that's fatal for a comic.' Using part of the dialogue from the initial draft of his scene with the reporter, he muses about the crowd that could thrill him with its roar of laughter, but which can also be 'a monster without a head, that never knows which way it's going to turn, it can be prodded in any direction' – bringing us up to date with HUAC's America.

The *pièce de résistance*, of course, remains the sketch with Keaton, as two musicians – the manic violinist and the lugubrious pianist – which returns again to a tradition older than music hall. The sketch is pure mime, a piece devoid of slapstick, the only violence being done to the instruments, the piano denuded of its wires and the violin crushed under Keaton's shoe. As Keaton struggles endlessly with his cascading music sheets, Chaplin paces impatiently, nonplussed by the disappearance of his own feet up his baggy pants. The players are caught in an obsessive state of their inability to perform, due to the forces of cosmic madness, until Chaplin whips out a spare violin from his pants and launches into the gypsy extravaganza that will hurl him towards his death in the drum. In the final aftermath, played in a lengthy, static long shot, the clown lies on a sofa, dying before us, surrounded by those people of the theatre who have been his staff and his bane in life. Terry departs before the final moment, in her tear-smudged make-up, to dance on the adjoining stage, as the cloth is drawn up over the corpse.

Unlike previous Chaplin films, *Limelight* was shot quite quickly, and wrapped by the end of January 1952. For the first time, Chaplin invited press people to observe him at work on the set. There was certainly no need for the excessive secrecy that marked the shoot of *The Great Dictator*, and of *Monsieur Verdoux*. After all, this was an innocent film, devoid of politics. Or so Chaplin might have dreamed. The *New York Times*'s Hollywood correspondent Thomas M. Pryor reported:

On the first of three visits to the set of *Limelight*, the writer asked Chaplin to characterize the film for him. 'It's a funny picture,' he said quickly and a little defensively. He added diffidently: 'I hope.' When Chaplin began work, however, the diffidence vanished and the visitor found himself in the presence of a charged personality. This was exemplified when Eglevsky [as Harlequin] did his dance at the grave of Columbine and Chaplin was directing . . . After making certain that the camera was properly set up and the lighting regulated he signalled for a rehearsal of the action. The orchestra in the pit went into the motions of performing as previously recorded music welled from a loudspeaker and Eglevsky made his entrance . . .

Chaplin, standing a little to the rear of the camera, became tense, his eyes riveted on the stage. But the music and the dance aroused him. His feet moved and his body swayed. Abruptly, he went close to the camera, almost as though he were charging it, and he peered through the finder . . . Again he swayed to the music. The mood lasted less than a minute. He turned quickly and raced to the back of the orchestra to get a distant perspective of the action. Suddenly he dropped into a chair, legs outstretched like a man in a state of complete exhaustion . . .

Everything about his pictures – good or bad – is his own. He acts every role for his performers, including the smallest gestures of a bit player. Nothing escapes his critical eye. At the same time, Chaplin seems to have little regard for established procedures . . . He simply has an innate contempt for anything he believes to be interfering with his complete freedom of expression . . . At one point in the ballet scene his assistant director, Robert Aldrich, called to an aide before the cameras started to turn: 'If anything goes wrong technically give me a signal.' To which Chaplin promptly appended: 'We'll stop if anything goes *esthetically* wrong.' Chaplin later told his visitor that 'if the audience is so intent on watching technique that people become disturbed if you come into the scene from the left in one shot and from the right in the next, then you are not entertaining them. If the picture is good enough they should be too absorbed in the story to notice.'

But when Chaplin's absorption in his own production was ended, there were some things he had to notice himself. The HUAC hearings had resumed in 1951, the latest phenomenon being recantations and the naming of names by previous victims, like Larry Parks, Edward Dmytryk, Sterling Hayden and Elia Kazan. One of the Hollywood Ten, Albert Maltz, wrote to his fellow-prisoner Herbert Biberman, after both had been released from their sentences: 'The new Hollywood business is very grim, very savage . . . Oh, the moral horror of this parade of stoolpigeons, what a sickness it spreads over the whole land . . .' The informers resumed their Hollywood careers; others, the named, managed a car park or worked in a warehouse. Still there were those who resisted the committee, 'took the fifth' or avoided their subpoenas. Many went into hiding till the ill wind might pass. Civil society groups supporting the committee's work took up whatever slack was left in the crusade, groups like the Wage Earners' Committee, American Business Consultants, the American Legion and the Jewish Anti-Defamation League of B'nai B'rith. These established – beside the 'blacklist' – a 'gray list' of those who could be offered a way back into favour by aiding the anti-Red cause in some way. These groups, and others, would provide clearance for those who volunteered to co-operate.

Chaplin's circle of acquaintances shrank as the right's onslaught on him continued unabated throughout the making of *Limelight*. In May

1949 the aptly named Republican Senator Cain of Washington demanded that Chaplin be deported over his support of Hanns Eisler and his 'treasonous' message to Pablo Picasso, 'self-admitted French Communist', asking him to head a committee of French artists against the Eisler deportation proceedings. In July 1950 Hedda Hopper wrote in the *Los Angeles Times* that 'the Commie Daily People's World advertised that Charlie Chaplin's picture "The Circus" is being shown here for their benefit. While our boys die in Korea Chaplin's picture is making money for the loyal Commie opposition.' Chaplin's lawyers hurried to make it known that he had no knowledge of such a benefit showing and opposed it, but this cut very little ice.

Chaplin decided that he would hold the premiere of *Limelight* in England, since the film was about his London roots. He would combine the launch with a family holiday so that Oona and their kids could see his home country, the soil from which Charlie had grown. In their last days in New York they spent time with close friends and dined the night before their sailing with Lillian Ross and James Agee and his wife Mia. Agee had become close to Chaplin after his strong support for *Monsieur Verdoux* and had been invited to watch the *Limelight* shoot. He was even trusted enough to write some suggestions on editing, on the flea-circus sequence and some scenes with Claire Bloom. He had managed at last to get Chaplin to read his script, tentatively titled *The Tramp's New World*, which was received politely, though Chaplin had no intention of taking it on.

Agee's script is intriguing, and is the subject of a book by John Wranovics (*Chaplin and Agee: The Untold Story of the Tramp, the Writer, and the Lost Screenplay*, published in 2005). The complete typed manuscript (included in the book) is clearly unfilmable as it is, containing a vast amount of exposition and speechifying by characters called the Voice of Time, the Voice of Individualist, and a Grand Old Man, who pontificates about Americanism for several long pages. The idea of the script derived from Agee's shocked reaction at the atomic bombs dropped on Japan, and his reading of John Hersey's searing witness report and book, *Hiroshima*. The film was to be an apocalyptic fable, in which,

Without warning, a super-atomic bomb is dropped, which outdoes the grandest expectations of those who set it off. All life on the planet, human and subhuman, is instantly exterminated . . . But there is one survivor, the Tramp. In a long solo he wanders the absolute desolation of New York (or some huge 'internationalized' metropolis), examining civilization as it looked in the fraction of a second before it ceased to live.

In echoes of *The Kid*, Agee gave the Last Tramp on Earth a last girl, and a baby, and together they begin the post-apocalypse life, and of course there are other survivors. The main conflict pits the rag-bag of pacifists against the scientists, who have survived in their underground laboratories, and are eager to rebuild their weapons arsenal.

Agee, enthusiastic as he was about the Tramp, may not have realized, or did but soldiered on with his text, that Chaplin had done with the Tramp, and had no thoughts of his resurrection, even as a symbol of resurgent Mankind. However much Calvero reflected the senior Chaplin, everyone who watches the end of *Limelight* experiences the death of Charlie, Charlot, as the primal strands of his persona from Karno to Keystone and beyond are drawn together to the final moment of extinction. Agee's basic ideas, on which he based his narrative, were also at a tangent to Chaplin's philosophy. The propositions which Agee outlined were: 'That it is exceedingly hard under the best of circumstances, to exist and develop as a full human being; but not impossible. That it is impossible, for most people, under contemporary civilization. That contemporary civilization is doomed, by that fact, more surely than by any other.'

Agee's propositions were those of the frustrated American liberal, whose core belief in the values of individual and social liberty had been so harshly curtailed by the incessant witch-hunts. But this was not what Chaplin believed. His synthesis of American and European ideas, with a soupçon of pantheism and Gandhi-esque thoughts, derived, more than he might admit, from the nineteenth-century emphasis of nature, not nurture, on the essential character of any man or woman, and on the belief in the primacy of the life-force itself that Calvero impresses on Terry. Agee's ideas were born of ideological disappointment, Chaplin's of the creative processes of his art. The artist and the journalist could never quite meet. 'The heart and the mind,' Calvero muses to Terry, 'what an enigma . . .'

Chaplin sailed with Oona and the children on 17 September 1952 aboard the liner *Queen Elizabeth*, dodging a subpoena which he was warned had been issued against United Artists as part of the ongoing shenanigans over the company's management transfer. Two days later, as the ship was in mid-Atlantic, his public enemies struck their most effective blow. As the *New York Times* announced on the 20th:

WASHINGTON, September 19 – Charles Chaplin, who has made generations laugh, may be banished from the United States as a result of accusations that he has subversive tendencies.

Attorney General James P. McGranery said tonight that he had ordered authorities of the Immigration and Naturalization Service to determine whether the famous comedian should be readmitted . . . News of the action was confined to the terse, cryptic announcement of the Attorney General. From other Justice Department sources it was learned, however, that when the comedian sought to return – his home is in Beverly Hills, Calif. – he would have to meet the requirements of law imposed on any new immigrant.

Although Mr. Chaplin came to the United States in 1910, he will have to satisfy the authorities that he is of good health, sound mind and good morals.

The essence of the sudden attack was based, the sources said, on Section 137, Paragraph (c) of Title 8, 'Aliens and Citizenship', aimed at 'persons who advocate the overthrow of the government'. The case was brought as a result of 'an investigation made over a considerable period of time by investigators of the Immigration and Naturalization service', and presented in the context of McGranery's post as a 'new broom' to sweep out racketeering and corruption. Later revelations from FBI files revealed that McGranery and J. Edgar Hoover had met to review the multi-volume files on Chaplin's politics and his 'moral conduct' as shown by the Joan Barry case. McGranery, a strongly Catholic opponent of abortion and defender of 'the high state of womanhood', brought a religious zeal to his new office. Lumping Chaplin together with '100 underworld big shots and other undesirable characters' he was rounding up to deport from the US, he declared:

Chaplin will be required to show, as does every alien seeking original entry, that he is admissible under our immigration laws . . . He has been here 40-odd years. He has enjoyed the hospitality and all the opportunities that this country offers . . . There have been public charges that Chaplin was a member of the Communist Party, grave moral charges, and the making of statements that would indicate a leering, sneering attitude toward a country whose hospitality has enriched him. No harm can come from a fair hearing, and if he can meet the standard of our laws, he will be readmitted.

The Attorney General was also responding to the vitriolic campaigns directed against Chaplin both by Hedda Hopper and by right-wing columnist Westbrook Pegler, who had been inveighing against all things liberal and radical – in particular Franklin and Eleanor Roosevelt – since the 1930s and whose motto was 'I claim authority to speak for the rabble because I am a member of the rabble in good standing.' Pegler's two-fisted take-no-prisoners rant, familiar as that of his present-day counterparts, took in the defence of a Californian lynching, the hygienic state of writers, uppity women and union leaders. Pegler called Chaplin 'a repulsive . . . rotten little rake . . . flouting our ideals, degrading our moral standards – a man to whom we gave asylum in two world wars'. Hedda Hopper continued her high-minded defence of Joan Barry, and declared that she had discovered that 'Charlie Chaplin received his visa to go abroad, but not through the Immigration Department . . . I had a very close check on that for months.' Thus prodding McGranery on to the battlefield.

While en route, Chaplin could only respond to this broadside by radio, declaring mildly, 'Through the proper procedure I applied for a re-entry permit, which I was given in good faith and which I accepted in good faith. Therefore I assume that the United States Government will recognise its validity.'

But good faith was nowhere in sight, from the west Atlantic, and Chaplin had to make do with another rapturous welcome in England. Once again, as in 1931, crowds mobbed him at Waterloo station and at the Savoy Hotel. The London *Times*, covering his arrival, ignored the American hoo-hah completely in its report of 24 September:

For the triumph of Charlie Chaplin, the world-famous cinema actor, Mr Charles Chaplin is now reaping the reward, and paying the penalty. The reward is . . . the adulation, in part, perhaps, nostalgic, of thousands. The penalty is to be mobbed, to move through Press conferences like the queen bee in the midst of a swarming hive, to have not breath enough nor time enough to answer a tenth of the questions, grave or footling, which the emissaries of the Press long to put to him.

In Mr. Chaplin, face to face, one looks, of course, for signs of his tragi-comic screen creation. One sees instead a small friendly man, white-haired, his complexion pinker than usual from the lighting of the little stage from which he addresses the hungry journalists through a microphone . . .

No man can be accused of being vain who forgets his first step to success, and Charlie Chaplin cannot remember which was his first film. It may have been *Making a Living*, or it may have been *A Day at the Races*. What he did remember was something of the exacting requirements of the old music-hall in which he started. Compared with the rough and ready justice of, say, a Glasgow music-hall audience in the days when Mr. Chaplin had to face it as a young and unknown performer, the modern American music-hall is 'much more polite.' One had hoped to see him on the stage of a British music-hall, which many a lesser film celebrity has trodden, but . . . Mr. Chaplin was careful to hold out no hope of this. 'You have to be in constant practice,' he said. And the fact that one reminded him of the pleasure it would give and how inconceivable it was that a music-hall actor should ever lose his sense of craft could not persuade him to change his mind.

On general subjects . . . Mr. Chaplin was on happier ground. He talked of his pleasure in coming back to London after 21 years – to launch his new film, *Limelight* . . . and of the mingled familiarity and strangeness of the City. 'It was rather a shock,' he said, 'when I saw Waterloo Bridge to-day. I am not a modernist, and I was looking for that old noble structure. Then I looked east – I think I mean 'west' – to Big Ben, and that was a beautiful sight.

It was all strangely moving, with the rose-lit little figure trying so gallantly, as Michael Arlen would have said, to be all things to all journalists simultaneously, and being for each of them perhaps a little less than he had bargained for. Certainly no one who spoke to him yesterday or merely watched him open-eyed would ever forget him. And that is less a testimony to Mr. Chaplin's 'dynamic' personality than to the intensity of our wish, irrational and even childish as it is, to perceive in him the lineaments of his unique creation . . .

Back in America, the furore raged on, the press reporting on his comments in France, where his ship had docked before its last stop in England. At Cherbourg, Chaplin had told reporters: 'I am not political. I have never been political . . .' 'I don't want to create a revolution. I only want to make some more films. I shall probably be in pictures till I drop dead.' 'Today is not the day of great artists. Today is the day of politicians. People are only too willing to make issues about anything . . .' Asked yet again about his citizenship he said, 'Super-patriotism leads to Hitlerism. I assume that in a democracy one can have a private opinion.'

Everyone had an opinion about Chaplin, however, as the affair rumbled on past the simultaneous premieres of *Limelight* in London and New York in October. Chaplin's supporters rallied round, Bosley Crowther noting in the *New York Times*: 'The main thing that comes through in the film [is] an appreciation of the courage and the gallantry of an ageing man. There is no social issue in "Limelight," no basic conflict to compare with . . . the "little man" against a mechanical world.

The fate that confronts the ageing comic is a natural inevitability.' It was not 'a great film', Crowther wrote, but 'a genial and tender entertainment and a display of audacity and pride'. In the last analysis, ' "Limelight" is a very moving film . . . Mr. Chaplin has turned out a movie that should do anybody good to see.'

This was not, however, the view of the zealots on the warpath, as the American Legion, whose Californian branch had given a plaque to Attorney General McGranery, threatened to picket movie theatres that scheduled *Limelight*. McGranery had praised the Legion because it had 'sounded the bell of liberty and prepared the spiritual armor needed by all against the godless serfs of the Soviets'.

An anonymous document in FBI files set out a 'Fact Sheet Containing Pertinent Material on the Communist Affiliations and Activities of Charles Chaplin', quoting an alleged issue of *Pravda* of 12 January 1923, which stated:

Charlie Chaplin is an old member of the Socialist Party of America. According to the latest information he has joined the American communists . . . When we decide to build a 'factory of laughter' (of course it will be a cinema factory) the President of the Comintern will have to consider the request of a group of Communist workers 'for the transfer of Comrade Charlie Chaplin from America to the RSFSR* as a matter of party discipline . . .

Russian Socialist Federation of Soviet Republics

Writer Victor Lasky set out the case against Chaplin in a somewhat more measured form in the *American Legion Magazine* of December 1952 (aforementioned in our prologue). He reminded his readers of 'a remarkably candid moment' in which Chaplin had set himself out as 'a disciple of the French philosopher Anatole France, who, said Chaplin, "philosophically knows nothing of good or bad, much the same as myself. As for ideals, they are dangerous playthings, barren of results, and for the most part, false." ' If he had just stuck to such cynical views, wrote Lasky, all might have been well, but Chaplin instead 'became a fellow-traveler of communism'.

Lasky set out all Chaplin's sins, his defence of Russia, his support of Hanns Eisler, his Carnegie Hall speech, his cries of 'Comrades!', his salute to the Soviet armies 'which closed with the words, "Russia, the future is yours!" ' Lasky had to admit there was no evidence Chaplin was a Communist Party member: 'It would be difficult even to imagine this supreme egotist submitting to the de-personalized, rigid discipline which party members are forced to accept.' But he noted Chaplin's weaselling out of a condemnation of Stalin as a dictator and his implication that 'in this country anti-communism was leading to nazism, a theory better expressed in the pages of the Daily Worker'. Lasky even quoted a passage from Hedda Hopper's book *From Under My Hat*, which claimed he had refused to contribute to funds to arm Jewish fighters in Palestine (this referred to anti-British militants dubbed terrorists by the British government) just before America entered the war. As Hedda Hopper wrote: 'During the fund-raising, which I started with a donation, Charlie was called upon. He got up in a white heat of hate and said, "I am not a Jew; I am not a citizen of America; I am a citizen of the world, I will give nothing to this cause. I deplore the whole thing."'

Trying to tar him as anti-Jewish may have been the nadir of his detractors' efforts, but it was clear that his utter lack of remorse at supporting Russia during the war, and his implacable internationalism and refusal to pander to flag-waving pressure, doomed Chaplin to his exile.

In April 1953, the new US Attorney General, Herbert Brownell Junior, announced that Chaplin 'had surrendered his re-entry permit to State Department officials in Geneva, Switzerland'. Immigration officials clarified that this 'can be construed as surrender of his domicile in the United States'. Chaplin had decided to give up his short-lived fight against McGranery's order and remain in Europe. In the interim, the United States had seen the election, in November 1952, of Dwight D. Eisenhower as President, running against the Democrat Adlai Stevenson. McGranery was replaced, but America was still in the grip of the witch-hunts spearheaded by Senator Joseph McCarthy, whose Republican Party was now in government.

Chaplin had settled, with Oona and their children, in a villa at Corsier-sur-Vevey, with grounds covering thirty-seven acres of gardens and parkland. This promised a physical refuge for himself and his family and a financial refuge for his money. On a trip to London in mid-April he made a formal statement, denouncing his persecutors:

It is not easy to uproot myself and my family from a country where I have lived for forty years without a feeling of sadness. But since the end of the last World War, I have been the object of lies and vicious propaganda by powerful reactionary groups who by their influence and by the aid of America's yellow press have created an unhealthy atmosphere in which liberal minded individuals can be singled out and persecuted.

Under these conditions I find it virtually impossible to continue my motion picture work and I have therefore given up my residence in the United States.

In September, Chaplin sold his movie studio in Los Angeles to a New York real estate firm, Webb & Knapp. The *New York Times* reported that 'they might raze the studio to make way for an office building or department store'. Chaplin had already sold his house in Beverly Hills and 'is reported to have no other property in the United States'.

In February, Oona Chaplin revealed that she had renounced her US citizenship and had become a British subject. In December the press announced that her father, Eugene O'Neill, who died in a Boston hotel, had excluded both his daughter Oona and his son Shane and their issue from his will, leaving his third wife, Carlotta, as his sole beneficiary. As the *New York Times* put it, 'the holder of the Nobel and Pulitzer Prizes had been unable to write in recent years because of illness'.

Calvero's exit may have been as painful, but the legacy he left was more generous.

30

A King in Vevey, a Ghost in New York

Our tale is almost done, though Charles Chaplin lived another twenty-four years, and died in Vevey, surrounded by his family, on Christmas Day of 1977. W. C. Fields, too, had died of a Christmas, in 1946; it seemed to be a mortal day for clowns.

The Tramp, however, had departed some time earlier, if not decisively beheaded, visibly faded out in the twilight of Calvero. Many of his peers wrote to Chaplin in appreciation of what appeared to be the final stand in *Limelight*, among them Vittorio de Sica, cabling from Italy to thank him for the film – 'I CANNOT THINK OF ANYTHING ELSE AND AS DAYS GO BY YOUR FILM ENTERS DEEPER AND DEEPER INTO MY MIND AND HEART' – and from Chicago, Studs Terkel, who wrote to him on 20 June 1953:

Dear Mr. Chaplin:
    Your reply to my letter was most heartwarming.
    Even during these dismal days, the Chaplin wit and tenderness comes through. Jesting on the square, you advise me to keep my admiration to myself: A whimsical thought to which I cannot agree . . . You write that at the moment the name of Chaplin is an anathema in the States. Yes, it is . . . with the vociferous men of small mind and little faith. No, it is not . . . with the quiet ones, confused, bewildered, frightened. These, the latter, are groping for gentleness and warmth and good humor in their daily lives. I've a hunch they far, far outnumber the Neanderthal Boys . . .
    In any event, writing to you and hearing from you has been a rich experience for me . . . In this Era of Mediocrity it is doubly gratifying to communicate with one of the most sensitive and civilized artists of our day. Perhaps, too, your stubborn sense of individuality has impressed me. As a boy I was bitten by Thoreau: 'I will breathe after my own fashion.'
    Warmly, Studs Terkel.

Chaplin, of course, continued to do so, enjoying his family life, continuing to cock a snook at American political taboos by such events as a much publicized dinner with the Prime Minister of Communist China, Chou En-Lai, in July 1954, prompting the *Saturday Evening Post* to bemoan the fact that he had 'openly joined our enemy, the Soviet slave masters'. He had also accepted an award from the World Peace Council, an undoubted Soviet front, and had, worst of all, sent a telegram of support to a Salute to Paul Robeson, which had taken place in New York in May, with such subversive luminaries present as Thelonius Monk and Pete Seeger.

In October, he announced his plans for a new movie, his first project to be shot outside the United States. As the *New York Times* put it:

CHAPLIN PLANS FILM; Comedian is Working on Script That Will Spoof US . . .

It will 'not be bitter but very funny,' the comedian said. He added that the film would be 'the story of a little man from Europe who goes to America expecting to find everything wonderful, and then . . .' Mr. Chaplin said the little man would have a small black moustache and a cane but 'he will be very respectably dressed and will have plenty of money.' He added that he had not yet finished the script.

This embryonic resurrection sounded close to the idea Chaplin had broached to the *Manchester Guardian* back in 1947, except that the 'rich tramp' would not be speaking Sanskrit. Back in Los Angeles, writer Louis Berg, hearing of the new Chaplin project, penned a two-part political sermon in the *Los Angeles Times,* under the heading 'The Strange Case of Charlie Chaplin', printed on 5 December 1954. Berg's thesis, expounded at length, was that the millions who worshipped Chaplin were unaware that 'their beloved "Charlie" – the wistful tramp in the baggy pants – is dead, killed by the man who created him.' Berg continued:

It was deliberate murder, long contemplated. For Charles Spencer Chaplin – this is the first of a number of astonishing facts – hated 'Charlie' from the beginning. The wonderful tramp was an unwanted child. 'There are days,' he told Benjamin de Casseres, a well-known writer in 1920, 'when I am filled with disgust at the character that circumstances forced me to create.' 'That dreadful suit of clothes,' he added with a shudder.

Galloping swiftly from Keystone to Verdoux, Berg pointed out that Chaplin's original stage character, with Karno, was a toff, albeit drunk, and his shabby garb was merely a by-product of Mack Sennett's plebeian needs. The 'supposedly soft side' of Chaplin's nature, as expressed in the Tramp, was only a deception, masking a far more ruthless, cynical outlook. Berg offered his own testimony, from his meeting with Chaplin when working for United Artists:

I found him cold, haughty and completely indifferent to his associates there, from the top executives down. He smiled rarely and sourly, and seemed in every way the complete opposite of his screen impersonation. His reputation was that of a tough and unyielding executive. People were unquestionably afraid of him. And his 'no' was the coldest and sharpest I have ever heard in my life.

Berg went on to comment on Chaplin's love life, on the 'cruel streak [that] has been revealed in his relations with women'. His preference for very young girls suggested that 'when he later tangled with the McCarran Act, he feared examination of his morals more than an investigation into his political activities'. Proceeding to catalogue the familiar list of Chaplin's pro-Communist activities, Berg's subhead asked, 'Why did this former idol turn from us and befriend our enemies?' Berg suggested that the trauma and loneliness of Chaplin's early life embittered him and toughened him for his future career, and the disappointment of his first teenage London love was played out in all his later affairs. He concluded that:

Europe is beginning to discover what many people in this country have known for some time: that Chaplin is not as amiable, as modest, as warm as the little fellow on the screen. And that is the tragedy. No man living has given so much pleasure to so many millions. But, by the same token, no artist in his lifetime has been so much appreciated or so highly rewarded and is so ungrateful . . .

The real symbol of Chaplin's downfall lies in his repudiation of 'Charlie,' the little fellow who made him great. If posterity remembers and cherishes him it will be for 'The Kid,' for 'The Gold Rush,' for 'City Lights.' Never for 'Monsieur Verdoux,' nor even 'Limelight.'

Not for the picture he is reportedly making in Switzerland, with hatred in his heart.

This pre-emptive strike, delivered in the Hollywood heartland, may have reflected an unease that Studs Terkel's 'quiet . . . confused, bewildered' citizens were still rooting for the anti-patriot Chaplin. By the end of 1954, Senator Joe McCarthy had fallen, discredited by his extremism and uniquely censured by the Senate. The Cold War was now a cold fear, domestically warmed by the cosy glow of 'I Like Ike' America, the 'cool' medium of television and the fifties consumer boom. It would take a long time, though, for the many blacklisted movie felons to claw their way back to professional life. And the attack on Chaplin would, with or without Hedda Hopper or Louis Berg, be resumed as a result of his new film.

But the work proceeded, across the Atlantic, from draft to draft of the script. In one of its earliest forms it was simply called 'Mr. X', bearing the contours of *A King in New York* to be, but in a more didactic form. Having been deposed from his kingdom by a popular revolution ('one of the minor annoyances of our modern life'), the unnamed ex-King is visited by his minister, 'Mr. Gypont', when he arrives at his American exile. Gypont's wiles to re-assert his control of the King reflect Chaplin's bitter experiences with the bespoke press (including deleted material in square brackets):

KING: Well, what do you want?

GYPONT: I'm here on a patriotic mission in the cause of my country . . . Your country needs you.

KING: You mean, you need me.

GYPONT: Your Majesty, liberty no longer exists. [They are taking away our civil liberties.] Those freedoms which were so dear to your Majesty's heart, [which you guarded with your life and honour] are being trampled upon. Communism has taken over. The nationalization of our whole country is taking place. Free speech no longer exists and our newspapers have already been suppressed.

KING: Your newspapers?

GYPONT: Yes, your Majesty.

KING: So after your newspapers have kick [*sic*] me out of the country you want my support to get them back?

GYPONT: Your Majesty, I must speak frankly. When the people's happiness is at stake, the destiny even of a King should not be considered. I love my country and will make every sacrifice for it, even the esteem of my best friends.

KING (sardonically): Yes, I think you would. So you're also in the newspaper business? . . . Will you kindly tell me what you don't own?

GYPONT: Your Majesty, in all seriousness, the country is in dire circumstances . . . They're fed up with this socialization . . .

KING: But tell me, how d'you expect to get me back?

GYPONT: It's simple. Good public relations. New editorials every day about your character, your generosity, your charity, your genius as a politician – showing the contrast between your regime and the present one.

KING: But if they've confiscated all your newspapers, how do you expect to do all this?

GYPONT: I still own the radical ones . . . which, of course, is confidential.

KING: You swine – to think you've been fooling the public all these years, playing Jack against Jill and all the time it was you owned the newspapers which started the revolution against me. That's the kind of patriot you are.

In an alternative version, Gypont details his promises (the King is named 'Gustoff' in this version):

GYPONT: We'll start a campaign. Build you up as a hero – 'Gustoff the Martyr' – the man who sacrificed himself for his country. Gave up his throne in the interests of the country. Every radio in the country will build you up, show your charity work abroad, your mode of living – living in your sorrow.

KING: You own the radio too?

GYPONT: No, I don't have to, I control it with my advertising.

KING: Listen, I was a good King, I did everything conscientiously for my country until your newspapers started tearing me apart and within 6 months I was known as a tyrant . . . a dictator . . . a monster.

GYPONT: We can cure all that in two weeks.

KING: How do you expect the public to swallow all this?

GYPONT: It's up to you, just give the word and within a month you'll be the biggest hero. The whole nation will be lined up to welcome you.

KING: No, you can keep it.

GYPONT: You'll be free of assassins, your life will be out of danger and you'll go down in history as the greatest monarch that ever lived.

(The King makes a speech on why he doesn't want to go back. Why he doesn't want to subject himself to this rule of hidden power and to be the servant of all the designing rascals like Gypont. He tells him that life is greater than ruling people – being able to rule himself. At last he's found himself, all his life he's wanted to be an actor etc. etc. etc.)

As we might expect, Chaplin boiled all this down in the final version to a more economical scene, excising the lengthy point-scoring. He had decided that his political argument would be much better served literally out of the mouth of babes: spoken by his son, Michael, as Rupert Macabee. The choice of the name Macabee was curious, as in the Jewish canon the Macabees were the freedom fighters who wrested their first post-Biblical independence from Greek rule in Palestine in the second century BC. It was not an uncommon Jewish name, but in the context of the HUAC hearings and the persecution of young Rupert's parents it could not have been accidental. (The King refers to him in the movie as 'a Scot'.)

Chaplin knew he would be questioned about the casting of Rupert, with its obvious allusions and implications. Wary of being misquoted by the press, he prepared meticulous answers in advance. Notes from June 1957, even before the film opened, show him working hard on his spontaneity:

I have been asked why I put my son in the role of the precocious American school boy. For one reason it was difficult to find an American boy to play the part, and would have involved many problems. Michael Chaplin, having been born in America – and being the right age, presented no difficulties. The problem was, could he act? This question I put to him. 'I may have difficulty in memorizing the lines, but I can act it easily,' he said confidentially.

There were many words he could not pronounce or understand. About a month before we went into production, his nurse went over the lines with him. And by the time I was ready to rehearse with him, he was word perfect, in fact he corrected me several times when I slipped up in my own lines . . .

I must say he was a courageous little chap, and never once would forget that he was a boy.

One day he came to me and said: 'I think I know the secret of it: you got to be natural.'

When he saw the complete picture, his reaction was very strange. He never said he liked the picture or himself – his only comment was to his nurse, that I look young. I think he had quite another idea of himself.

Notes show him also working on answers to yet unasked questions about making his first film in England:

3 July 57:
It was with trepidation and uncertainty that I ventured onto the stages at Shepperton Studios: I felt like an old horse in a different stable. Everybody was so English and slightly diffident . . . I felt I was the only vulgarian . . . The atmosphere was quite different to American studios – at least, to my own studio in Hollywood. There the environment was like a family; and there I was treated like a spoiled child. There I was reassured by everybody – the property man, the carpenters, the electricians, the camera man . . . reassuring, confident, 'you'll get through, we're all behind you' attitude. Naturally, I am nervous when starting a picture – and irritable. Something I want – a prop is missing, I almost weep, 'where's my gloves, my hat!' I am panicky. Five people run in all directions to stitch on a button . . . I am treated like a patient in a mental hospital . . .

Other notes mentioned the problem of 'red tape' union rules –

... for example the termination of work at the hour of six when perhaps a Company is in the middle of a scene ... If you want to make good films and compete with other countries for foreign films to be made here, the flexibility of time is essential. I do not think that this would weaken our Union's position if a producer is willing to pay whatever overtime the Union demands of him. I believe both would profit ... I speak as a Union man, maybe it is to our advantage and if it isn't, then we must adjust accordingly ...

In November, after the film had been released in Britain and he was preparing its release in the US by long distance, he rehearsed himself for the most inevitable question of all: 'Is your film anti-American? Is it political and controversial?'

ANSWER: All comedy is controversial ... whether it be a clown on a trapeze or a buffoon in a circus, their laughter is derived from criticizing, either of themselves or of the behaviour of society in general ... Whatever subject I touch upon is for the purpose of creating laughter and entertainment. It is essentially a comedy on modern life ...

Q: Are there any serious moments in the picture?

A: Yes, and very moving, I hope, but there are no arch-villains or great heroes, everyone is to a degree more or less kindness and humanity ...

Q: What would you say is the overall theme of 'A King in New York'?

A: Its theme is self-esteem (and individuality, personified in a child of 10). In this modern world of hysteria and unrest, where all ideologies seem directed towards regimentation, uniformity and rubber-stamp thinking, we must endeavour to maintain that which is indispensable in humanity's pursuit of happiness ... the dignity and nobility of man.

Finally, in *A King in New York*, the mask and the man had meshed completely: the maker knew that his creation would be judged solely as an expression of his own 'real-life' personality and opinions, not as fiction, not as art. King Shahdov was Charlie Chaplin, and Charlie Chaplin was Shahdov. But Chaplin knew that he could not present Shahdov as his mouthpiece, since kings, by their nature, are amoral, feral beasts, obsessed with survival at all costs. As Shahdov says when his ambassador, Jaume (played by Oliver Johnston), greets him after his escape: 'We fooled them!' When Shahdov takes in Rupert, it is not from some innately democratic impulse, but from *noblesse oblige*, the prerogative of a superior whom pure circumstance has landed with a human challenge. This decency is the value Chaplin presents as the definition of a common humanity, from kings to proletarians to fools, and particularly to fools, who do not make considered judgements but leap in where sentiment leads. This is, too, the definition of the Tramp, Charlie, for whom Shahdov was the last disguise. In his impish rejection of conventional rules, the King is as much Charlie as Verdoux, who took his foolishness to extremes in a world that worshipped mass violence but punished its individual use, unsanctioned by society. As Verdoux states: 'Numbers sanctify.' In this sense, Calvero was not Charlie – he was the spirit of the social responsibility of a previous age, before the red flag of 'Socialism' divided the proper use of human solidarity into pros and cons, depending on which side of the barricades you stood. In *Limelight*, Charlie forgave his father. For someone pilloried as a Godless atheist, or a self-denying Jew, it was an act of perfect Christian charity, if, as ever, peculiarly defined.

Shahdov's self-esteem, his dignity, stands in contrast to the puerile and grotesque shadowplay of American consumer madness, wrapping round Shahdov and Jaume as they descend into a Dantesque New York. Tranced youth cavort in the aisle of a cinema before the series of bizarre trailers ('Man or Woman'; the cold-blooded killer who will 'creep into your heart') that will culminate in a neck-bending Cinemascope shootout before the two foreigners look for shelter at a restaurant where the jazz band wheels round to blast their ears. It is a curiously conservative apocalypse, in which Chaplin shows his distaste not just for commercial excesses, but for the escape routes of the modern world. People are either insane or mendacious – the jazz girl ('she bit me!') or the society woman-cum-journalist Ann (played by Dawn Addams) who inveigles him into a society dinner in which he is tricked into appearing to endorse products and filmed by a TV camera hidden in the wall. Persuaded that this might be a way to survive when he finds his loot purloined by his prime minister, Shahdov submits to an ordeal of plastic surgery to make himself look younger for his nationwide whisky ads: 'Royal Crown Whisky I Always Enjoy!' But the face-lift unravels in a nightclub, when a most unlikely but totally appropriate workman-and-patsy act, a reprise of the clowns' slapstick in *The Circus*, makes him laugh and loosen the stitches.

A King in New York, once one counts its grand counter-attack on the blacklisters of the House Un-American Activities Committee, and their final dousing by the royal witness who arrives entangled in his fire hose, boils down to a bitter farewell to the long history of

Charlie/Chaplin's struggle on behalf of the common individual and against dehumanization by big business, the military war machine, the massive intimidation by nationalist zealots, the crushing of creativity by cultural guardians and executioners. His own collection of slogans, once called out to the world from the giant podium of Charlie/Hynkel, his great *cri de cœur*, has been reduced to the angry ranting of a ten-year-old boy: 'And free speech! Does that exist? And free enterprise – today it's all monopolies! Today the whole world will blow up because of too much power!' But in the end Rupert is defeated, crushed by the witch-hunters who have induced him to name his parents' friends in order to save them, to capitulate to that very power. Power – destructive, remorseless, shameless – uses the child to break the adults, just as Charlie may have recalled it attempting to do to himself and Sydney at the twilight of the previous century.

In his last *deus ex machina*, after that symbolic hosing, the newspapers announce that King Shahdov has been designated a Friendly Witness and cleared of Communism, a conceptual *reductio ad absurdum*. Shahdov flies out of New York, leaving his fingerprint records behind, to a new and more comfortable exile in Paris.

Charlie had blown his razberry, and then retreated to his mansion by the lake. When his film opened, in September 1957, the American press noted with some satisfaction that even the British critics were generally disappointed. The *Daily Mail* called it 'a lumpish mixture of subtle slapstick and clumsy political satire'. The *Daily Telegraph* said it was 'the work of a very bitter man'. The *News Chronicle*, on the other hand, wrote that it 'nails more genuine lies in its 105-minute duration than any 105 pictures I have seen in the past year'. Reporting this, the *New York Times* added that 'there are no arrangements at present for it to be shown in the United States'.

The London *Times*'s review of the film, however, was less damning than its New York counterpart suggested, as 'Our Film Critic' wrote on 11 September:

Modern Times was a satire aimed at the monstrous power of industry, a power which is opposed to and oppresses all that is natural and wayward in man . . . In *The Great Dictator*, Mr. Chaplin, while aiming at the general concept of dictatorship, narrowed his sights to focus them on Hitler and Mussolini. A *King in New York* combines the two processes. It is an attack on many facets of modern life that are apparent everywhere: noise, the tactics and success of the more vulgar forms of advertising, the credulity of the public, the swing away from the habit of independent thought to a mass entertainment medium such as commercial television . . . to seek its target in America and the American way of life, with special reference, as in so totally contrasting a film as *Les Sorcières de Salem*, to the phenomenon known as McCarthyism.

The question of personal motives is one that it is now seldom held proper to discuss, and satire has come too often to mean parody with a disarming, good-natured grin on its face. Swift, however, had personal motives to spare, and Mr. Chaplin may not be too disconcerted by the charge that here his own brand of visual satire is not without its own dash of malice . . .

The reviewer was critical, however, of the somewhat 'pedestrian' nature of the story, enlivened by hilarious 'fits and starts'. *A King in New York*, wrote the reviewer, 'may prove to be that rare thing, a film which seems better at a second viewing than the first'.

Indeed, the issue here might well be another of Chaplin's many paradoxes, from the world's richest actor playing a vagrant to the necessities of an exiled director filming the dynamic life of New York in a British studio, with wary union crews watching the clock for any hint of unwanted overtime. This final paradox is that despite Chaplin's much-vaunted 'anti-Americanism', he had best flourished in the grand and generous setting of American movie-making. Despite the universalism – and Englishness – of his iconic character (and for once the oft-used 'icon' word is proper), his works were the epitome of the American movie: brash, action-packed, vastly sentimental, brimming with incidental life, anarchic, glittering with the high technical qualities that Hollywood could so amply provide.

We have seen that Chaplin's films, from the early Mutuals and Essanays through *The Kid* and *A Woman of Paris* and *The Gold Rush* et al., are precise and machine-tooled, cut to the exact measurements required by the clown. Up to the deceptive formal simplicities of *Monsieur Verdoux*, and the lucid light of *Limelight*, Hollywood's craft served Charlie Chaplin well. In contrast, *A King in New York* is work-manlike, but no more, in its settings, its *mise-en-scène*, its compositions and lighting, even the acting, in which the only truly memorable contributions are from the Chaplins, father and son. In his American films, one had Chester Conklin, the Scot Eric Campbell, Mack Swain, Henry Bergman, Edna Purviance and a host of performers who could encapsulate their slice of screen life in one scene, sometimes in one glance. Chaplin's great films could not have been made anywhere else, with the level of freedom ensured the director by the massive box-office loyalty of his domestic as well as his worldwide fans. The machine of global distribution, ruthlessly managed by the American movie business, as much as his own qualities, undoubtedly made him what he was.

At the centre of the storm, however, Chaplin remains, whatever his setbacks and sins in life, triumphant in art. As he noted in one of his advance-written answers to questions not yet asked, in April 1957:

Personally, I have no axe to grind. I am no pamphleteer or propagandist. In writing for the screen, I can only do what I can do, that is, I can only choose those situations that can challenge and arouse my enthusiasm. For all creative work can only be done in the heat of enthusiasm – something that one can get excited about . . .

I like to go contrariwise to accepted formulas – it may be egotistical, nevertheless it is my modus operandi. I like to think that I am doing something new, novel, daring and original, 'even if I deceive myself,' and that can only be accomplished by not 'playing safe,' but by taking up the so-called controversial theme.

In these touchy, easily scary days, controversial subjects are given a wide birth [sic]. For this reason, I like to take up the challenge and enjoy making fun of them. That is my stimulation.

I have no brief, no preconceived ideas, either political or moral, whether pro or con. My one object as an artist, is to create comedy and drama, and if it is advantageous to use a controversial theme to heighten these phases, then I have no compunction in doing so . . .

Humour is that quality which is many sided; it is a faculty to see the fallacy in what appears to be normal – to pick out the unsuspecting inanities and insanities of what we take for granted as being sane. Humour is that faculty to see the wrong in the accepted right, to see the sane in the insane, to see the ridiculous in the sublime, the inconsequential in the important, the tragedy in comedy, the weakness in power and the strength in weakness. Humour is an ally of truth and truth is by no means one-sided.

EPILOGUE

The King in Repose

A King in New York was not shown in New York until 1973. Between its British and American releases winds of change swirled through so many old certainties, unfinished business of the great world war: unrest in the Soviet satellite countries, a revolution in Cuba and fomenting rebellion in other Latin American countries, the ceding of colonial territories to independent forces, the looming disaster of Vietnam, the student heirs of King Shahdov's drugged youngsters rising from their stupor to shake campuses, fuelling rebellious movements from San Francisco to Paris. The eclipse of Ike, the rise of John Fitzgerald Kennedy and his striking down, the new realpolitik world of Richard Nixon and Henry Kissinger, recurring wars in the Middle East.

Through all this the exile floated in his bubble in Vevey. Groucho Marx tried to home in on the new hippie anarchism of love and acid, appearing as a character called 'God' in Otto Preminger's bizarre *Skidoo*, in 1968. By that time Chaplin had made yet another film, his last, *A Countess from Hong Kong*, in 1966. But this was an echo from another world.

In 1958, Chaplin was still not forgiven in America, as, symbolically, a citizen's group in Hicksville, Long Island, campaigned successfully to stop a retrospective of four of his films by the Hicksville Public Library. The offending films were *The Cure*, *The Fireman*, *The Pawnshop* and *The Floorwalker*, which had been rented from Brandon Films Inc. of New York for $22.50. Mrs Emil Szendy, president of the Friends of the Library, said that Mr Chaplin 'was not worthy of being honored by us since any film that is shown would be promoting him', and he had shown 'neither gratitude nor loyalty' to the United States. There were, of course, counter-petitions to allow the films, but the point had been made. Chaplin's films, which had made millions not only for himself but for so many theatre owners, produced by one of the nation's most successful and famous figures, were not even worth showing.

In 1959 he celebrated his seventieth birthday, in his Elysian retreat. He gave interviews about his views on the atomic bomb, on peace and war, and about his marriage to Oona, who told the news crews: 'I am married to a young man.' The Chaplin children grew up in an atmosphere in which the child and the man were often intermingled, with variable results. Michael the Macabee became the family rebel, an actor, a pop musician, a doper, a husband, and unemployed, signing on for the British 'National Assistance'. The man-child, on the other hand, kept up his creative juices by writing his memoirs, the great book of his life, *My Autobiography*, published in 1964. Chaplin, who was never as good with words as with gestures, surprised everybody by his vivacity and observation. The opening chapters, inaccurate in detail as most reminiscences are by nature, portrayed the early struggles of his life with Sydney and their mother Hannah in end-of-nineteenth-century London with a powerful hand and fairly pitiless eye. Of his teenage years he wrote:

I was a worshipper of the foolhardy and the melodramatic, a dreamer and a moper, raging at life and loving it, a mind in chrysalis yet erupting with sudden bursts of maturity. In this labyrinth of distorting mirrors I dallied, my ambition growing in spurts. The word 'art' never entered my head or my vocabulary. The theatre meant a livelihood and nothing more.

In every memoir of this kind that is honestly written, there is the shadow of the writer's present mood over the recollections of the past. The description was not a bad one of Chaplin's state of mind in his retirement, a concept that he never embraced. Having completed the book, he moved on to plan the next Chaplin film, no longer presented, as *Limelight* once had been, as his last. There would be no last acts for Chaplin, no last walks into the sunset, no sad little kick, and then Sayonara, down memory lane. There was a pause, when his brother Sydney died, in Nice, on 16 April 1965, at the age of eighty. He had spent his final years between his home there with his wife and Charlie's family, as the jovial uncle. The other Sydney, Charlie's second son, would co-star in the new movie, alongside Marlon Brando and Sophia Loren.

Full of enthusiasm, Chaplin began shooting in January 1966. This would be his first film in colour and Cinemascope. Its origins lay in one of Chaplin's oldest abandoned scripts, at one time named 'Stowaway' or 'Shanghai'. This was the only project that had derived directly from Chaplin's trips to the Far East in 1931 and then in 1936, on his cruise via Honolulu with Paulette Goddard, which saw them married in Canton. Along the way he is known to have stayed at the Astor Hotel in Shanghai, which still advertises Room 404 as the room in which Charlie Chaplin slept. In its early forms, the script was suffused with social background. As one draft sets forth:

By the Whangpoo River is the city of Shanghai, a Chinese international settlement, where merchants, fortune hunters, political refugees, fugitives from justice and adventurers ply their trade.

It is a city of seething masses of humanity – struggling and fighting in a ruthless, competitive world, where the loser falls by the wayside, or is left to starve or die on the Deltic refuse by the Whangpoo River.

In this cauldron of activity, are the dregs of human enterprises – the night clubs, the opium dens and the brothels – in this shadow underworld, are the half tones of human tragedy, men and women in a foreign land, where they have no national standing . . . outcasts whose status is even lower than that of a coolie. They are the White Russians of Shanghai . . .

This draft was clearly written by 1937, which was the year in which Japan invaded the Chinese mainland and laid siege to the foreign concessions in Shanghai. Chaplin's image of China was hazy and derivative, as he had spent barely a few days in Shanghai, and his description of the White Russians as lower than the 'coolies' was absurd. He probably felt that he could not get a proper handle on the subject and discarded it, swept up by the more urgent task of dealing with Adenoid Hynkel. When he revisited the idea in the 1960s, China had changed dramatically, and despite dinner with Chou En-Lai, Chaplin could not seriously hope to return to check out Shanghai. The locale switched to Hong Kong, the harsh social background faded apart from a brief opening shot, and the work became a light comedy set among the escort women of the cosmopolitan city, one of whom, the Russian refugee Natascha Alexandroff, latches on to American millionaire Ogden Mears, and stows away aboard his luxury liner when he departs. All that remains of the original story is Natascha's explanation to Ogden that she had fled to Shanghai as a child and become a gangster's moll at the age of fourteen.

Chaplin at the helm again! It was an exciting prospect, but several things doomed the enterprise from the start. He had never worked before with recognized stars and his relationship with Marlon Brando became disastrous on the set. Brando's method acting was a complete puzzle to Chaplin, who deployed his standard mode of acting out all the parts and requiring his actors to follow his lead. This Brando could not do, and his growing truculence became almost open hostility. Brando wrote in his own 1994 memoirs that Chaplin was 'fearsomely cruel', 'an egotistical tyrant' and 'probably the most sadistic man I'd ever met'. He noted Chaplin's scornful treatment of his son, Sydney, bullying him when things did not go exactly as he wished. We have heard this kind of witness before, from Robert Florey, another crew member with an axe to grind, but here Chaplin was obviously out of his depth. Clearly, he could not abide the thought that anyone else but himself might legitimately have a star-sized ego on the set. Sophia Loren, on the other hand, got along with him fine, as her romance aboard ship with Ogden danced through its pretty paces.

As comedy, however, the film misfired on all cylinders. Watching Brando one becomes aware that he is supposed to play the part as Chaplin might play it, in his 'King in New York' mode. Everything that might have been wily and wry charm, however, is reduced to a stoic, glowering pique. Consequently, we have no reason to empathize with this bilious oil millionaire and his predicament with the beautiful stowaway due to his appointment as the American ambassador to Saudi Arabia, even though at the end, of course, love triumphs over politics. Simply telling Brando to 'do it my way' palpably did not work. It may have been intended as satire but nothing gels properly in the frenetic opening and closing of bathroom doors. There are some ribald moments with Patrick Cargill as Ogden's valet Hudson, obliged to marry Natascha to provide her with an American passport, but little to raise chuckles besides. British cinematographer Arthur Ibbetson provided a bright and rich colour background, but this could not lift the suffusing gloom.

As in A Woman of Paris, Chaplin appeared only in a cameo role, as an old steward who peeks around the cabin door. It was all too brief a farewell. A Countess from Hong Kong opened in January 1967, in London, to a murmur of lugubrious reviews. There was evident mourning among Chaplin fans and some glee from his long-term enemies. Chaplin was combative, claiming that the film was 'the best thing I've done . . . The critics now are terrified of being old-fashioned, but this picture is ten years ahead of its time . . .' But this was 1967, the cusp of major social changes and new types of films, both in old-fashioned Hollywood and in the nouvelle vague

anti-narratives of Europe. In Paris, of course, where they worship
Jerry Lewis, and Charlot was still an icon, the picture was much better received. In the US, however, where it opened in March, it rapidly
sank out of view. To this day, nevertheless, the film has its defenders.
The loyal memories of 'Charlie' go a long way.

Chaplin spoke of one other film he was planning to make, a story
called *The Freak*, about a young girl who grows wings. This was
intended as a vehicle for his daughter, Victoria, born in 1951. But two
years later, Victoria left home with a young French actor who wanted
to start his own circus, and *The Freak* was abandoned. The irony of
Charlie Chaplin's daughter running away to join a circus might have
amused him, many years before, but not now.

In all Oona and Charles produced five daughters and three sons:
Geraldine, Michael, Josephine, Victoria, Eugene, Jane, Annette and
Christopher, to add to Charles Junior and Sydney. (Charles Junior
died in 1968.) Much has been written about Chaplin's relationship
with his great gaggle of children, some by them (Charles Junior's *My
Father, Charlie Chaplin*, Michael's *I Couldn't Smoke the Grass on My
Father's Lawn*), much by others analysing an old man's power-play
with such a late-blooming field. Home movies show him cavorting
with much glee in his gardens, being Charlie, competing with them for
the loot of vast chocolate boxes. In *My Autobiography*, he had written
about his life with Oona:

Schopenhauer said happiness is a negative state – but I disagree. For the last
twenty years I have known what happiness means. I have the good fortune to
be married to a wonderful wife. I wish I could write more about this, but it
involves love, and perfect love is the most beautiful of all frustrations because
it is more than I can express . . .

With such happiness, I sometimes sit out on our terrace at sunset and look
over a vast green lawn to the lake in the distance, and beyond the lake to the
reassuring mountains, and in this mood think of nothing and enjoy their
magnificent serenity.

This, surely, is the Tramp's nirvana, his imagined paradise with Edna
Purviance or Paulette Goddard in *Modern Times*. But the Tramp could
not rest completely, as he was tugged by the consequences of his creator, Chaplin's earthly cords and bonds. He was bestowed with
awards: co-recipient, with Ingmar Bergman, of the Dutch Erasmus
Prize in 1965, given to institutions or individuals who have made

notable contributions to European culture, society or social sciences. Special Award at the twenty-fifth Cannes Film Festival in 1971, and Commander of the Legion of Honour in the same year. Then, in 1972, the great American recantation, as he was invited to Los Angeles to be awarded an Honorary Oscar by the Academy of Motion Picture Arts and Sciences. On arrival in New York, on 2 April, he was whisked away to a gala performance at the Philharmonic Hall. For the first time since the 1940s, Chaplin could re-engage with an American audience, with some old faces, and many of a new generation, who knew him only as a symbol, not a man. Looking down at Los Angeles from the plane bearing him there, he remarked, according to Candice Bergen, who was writing about his trip for *Life* magazine: 'Oh well . . . it wasn't so bad. After all, I met Oona there.'

And so an old man, choked with emotion, blinks on the stage of Hollywood's great celebration of itself, its innate goodness, its ebullient self-congratulation at discovering and nurturing so much talent. No one, in those days, used that platform for anything but the tearful Thank Yous, the preening in the golden mirror of Narcissus resurgent. Nevertheless, he could still connect to reality, as he murmured to Groucho Marx, himself eighty-two years old, at the post-Oscar dinner, 'Stay warm, Groucho, you're next.'

Still, there was no complete retirement, as from 1970 on he got to work reviving his old films, preparing a new musical soundtrack for *The Circus*, *The Kid* and *The Idle Class*. After the Oscar boost, he began to work on another book, *My Life in Pictures*, for which he wrote the captions, the last page showing him at his study in Vevey with the heading: 'In my study at Vevey, reading my latest film script, *The Freak*. It's about a girl who was born with wings. I wrote it for my daughter Victoria and we began to rehearse it – then she left home to get married. But I mean to make it one day' The entry does not end with a full stop.

His last work was the composition of a proper score for *A Woman of Paris*, which included themes from his other movie scores as well as new elements. David Robinson, who met him during his recording sessions in England, asked him if this had been a long job, to which Chaplin replied: 'Not long – inspiration mostly.' Then he returned to Vevey. His last outing from his home, Robinson records, was to a nearby circus, in October 1977. In the early hours of Christmas Day 1977 he died at home, after Santa Claus had made his annual visit to distribute the children's presents.

He was buried at Vevey. On 2 March 1978, a strange epilogue was written when Chaplin's remains were dug up and his coffin stolen from his grave. The thieves, two eastern European auto-mechanics, tried to extort money from the family but were eventually nabbed by the cops at a call-box in Lausanne.

It was, of course, necessary that Chaplin's life, and death, should have a Keystone coda. Mack Sennett would have fully approved.

And then?

The world's most written-about film-maker, Chaplin remains an enigma. When Stan Laurel, then simply Stanley Jefferson, a relatively fresh Karno jobbing actor, joined Chaplin in their 1910 American tour, Charles Chaplin was already a modest success in the English music hall, but far from a star. When, in 1915, Chaplin became a worldwide phenomenon, a new force in American comedy, Stan may well have asked: Why him, and not me? After all, in the fullness of time, Stan Laurel was recognized as a screen phenomenon himself, the brains of the Laurel and Hardy duo, an abiding comic master, with an even larger following that has endured to this day. But in February 1915, having eked out a dismal year in small-time vaudeville, Stan was reduced to one third of the 'Keystone Trio', a stage Chaplin imitator, with partners who imitated, respectively, Chester Conklin and Mabel Normand. He was, in fact, the first in a line of professional Chaplin imitators, which led to the prolific Billy West, who imitated Chaplin on screen for many years – some of his films co-starring Oliver Hardy in the Eric Campbell role.

Stan Laurel's problem, of course, which lasted for years, was his uncertainty about the character that he might wish to be on the screen. His abiding wish, following Chaplin, was to be a solo act, a brash young man about town, perhaps like Harold Lloyd, but more manic, in the Karno style. This gave him a minor star status, until the merry-go-round of Hal Roach studios teamed him with Hardy, and the rest is history.

But as we have seen, the Tramp made Chaplin, despite all his hesitations and efforts to shuck him off, twist him in different directions, explore his alter egos, or retreat behind the camera and allow Adolphe Menjou to shine.

One goes round in circles. He was famous because he was famous. The Tramp caught on, as a universal figure. Attempts to psychoanalyse entire populations might follow. In the beginning, as we have seen, the tramp was a familiar, everyday figure in the American street, a by-product of boom-and-bust business cycles coupled with the modern mobility of the cross-country trains. A Joe Hill hobo, he scrawled the sign of the IWW wherever he went. He was a true American radical, the immigrant who didn't fit in. But as time passed, after the First World War, the old vagrant was largely replaced by the army veteran, the 'Forgotten Man' of soup-kitchen lines, as celebrated in Mervyn LeRoy's *Gold Diggers of 1933*.

By *The Gold Rush*, when Charlie was at his most famous, the tramp himself was an anachronism. Perhaps, because he was no longer a figure of fear – in the rising curve of a consumer society – he could better be a figure of love: the 'little fellow'. As an Everyman, he may have appeared as a symbol, but he was also very precisely located in the spectrum of classes: a petit bourgeois who has fallen on hard times. The hat, the cane, pointed towards this, Chaplin's genteel Englishman reduced temporarily, until the mountain of gold can be found. In 1948, the radical psychiatrist Wilhelm Reich published a book addressed to just such a person: *Listen, Little Man*, in which he portrayed this generic character as the most vulnerable to authoritarian and fascist ideas:

Listen, Little Man: Your heritage is a burning diamond in your hand.

See yourself as you really are. Listen to what none of your leaders and representatives dares tell you: You are a 'little, common man.' Understand the double meaning of these words: 'little' and 'common.'

You are afflicted with the emotional plague. You are sick, very sick, Little Man. It is not your fault. But it is your responsibility to rid yourself of this sickness . . .

To Reich, this 'Little Man', with his fear of free speech and the abnormal, had begun to play 'a governing role on this earth' through his ceding to 'impotent people with evil intentions the power to represent you . . . You must come to realize that you make your little men your own oppressors, and that you make martyrs out of your truly great men.'

This type of 'Little Man' was portrayed by Chaplin as Hynkel, the Jewish barber's and Charlie's evil alter ego. Reich's 'Little Man' was by definition sexually repressed and conformist, the small family man par excellence. Chaplin, of course, meant his 'little fellow' as the citizen unleashed from repressive and repressed convention. His poverty, painful as it may be, was also a freedom from material chains.

The 'little fellow', then, was always a more complex character than his creator Chaplin intended when, in the jumble of Keystone's prop department, he picked out the accoutrements which would have been familiar to him from a host of predecessors. When, in 1922, he tried to sue a US imitator who used the name 'Charlie Aplin' in his films, the producing company pointed out that

. . . a moustache similar to Charlie Chaplin's was worn by George Bevan in the character of a French waiter in Chicago in 1889, that Chaplin's hat appeared on the music-hall stage on the head of Chris Larex in 1898, that Harry Morris first made a stage hit with what is now known as the 'Charlie Chaplin walk' in 1892 . . . The 'Mobee Brothers' first introduced Chaplin's cane, Shermann Morrissey his shoes . . . The complete combination of moustache, tight-fitting coat, baggy trousers, large boots, and cane was used for many years in the music-halls by a certain Billy Riche [*sic*, for Ritchie].

And this without counting the commonly known borrowing from Fred Kitchen, George Robey and Will Murray.

So if the tramp comedian was commonplace, why was Charlie not? Many forests' worth of books, magazine articles and newspaper essays have been expended debating this point. As one writer, Philip G. Rosen, put it: 'Any artist, but particularly a giant like Chaplin, becomes property of the scholars as soon as his artistry is generally acknowledged; he must expect to have every aspect of his life examined thoroughly.' A somewhat daunting, if not terrifying prospect. Not only scholars, but commercial forces have latched on to the popularity of the 'little fellow' to sell their products: the 'merchandising' of Chaplin was the first major example of such an enterprise from the cusp of 1915, and he fought tirelessly, as we have seen above, to keep his own image under his control. In the present day, 'exploitation of the image' has become a highly controversial issue, as computerization enables advertisers to make Fred Astaire dance with a vacuum cleaner or Gene Kelly dance in the rain for a car.

Once in the hands of the scholars, every contradiction in Chaplin's self-expressed thoughts and ideas can be spun off to suit preconceptions. Rosen, in his 1969 article in *Cinema Journal*, 'The Chaplin World-View', analysed Chaplin as 'something of a romantic, at least in his distrust of the intellect relative to the intuition'. We have seen, however, that he derived economic and social ideas both from his reading and from many intellectual luminaries like Einstein and Emil Ludwig. At the core, Rosen argued, Chaplin manifested both a nostalgia for his childhood, harsh as it was, together with 'a profound aversion to the idea of poverty'. Chaplin put just such a sentiment in the mouth of his son, Sydney, in *A Countess from Hong Kong*, as he looks through binoculars at the Chinese city: 'Look at them, packed together like sardines. That's what I dislike about the poor. They have no taste. They indulge in squalor. They pick the worst neighborhoods to live in, eat the worst kind of food and dress atrociously.'

The comment is meant as a joke to perk up Ogden Mears, the multi-millionaire, but it falls somewhat flat, while evoking George Bernard Shaw's tongue-in-cheek and possibly apocryphal aphorisms such as: 'The world is populated in the main by people who should not exist.' But this was said, I hope, before Hitler.

Chaplin indulged in his position as a self-made millionaire, and we might remember the scene in *Easy Street* in which he scatters feed to the poor family's children as to so many chickens in a coop. Since he had spent his early years climbing out of Lambeth destitution by sheer will-power and a precocious talent, he worshipped the sense of individual freedom that human beings can deploy to save themselves. Big business, nationalist strictures, state power and the machines of war became his bugbear. Rosen quotes a passage from the book *Naked Truth*, by the sculptor Clare Sheridan, in which Chaplin, in a Whitmanesque mood, expounded to her:

There must be no dreams of posterity – no desire for admiration – for these are not worth anything. You must make something because it means something for you. You work because you have a superabundance of vital energy . . . In the end it is you – your work, your thought, yours the conception and the happiness, yours alone the satisfaction. Be brave enough to face the veil that hides the world, to lift it and see and know that within yourself is the world.

This was a strange dictum from Chaplin, who thrived on admiration, although, in the fullness of time, he would have to accept exile from the place where he had been adored most, and from which admiration had been withdrawn.

One of the unique things about Chaplin, almost alone among the major film-makers, was his ability, from the Mutual period onwards, to take time to make his pictures, to set aside schedules, and to think. In researching the life of Cecil B. DeMille, for example, I found a dynamo of industrial output, fifty silent feature films produced and directed from 1914 to 1929, twenty subsequent talkies till 1956, and a batch of pictures directed by others. He worked non-stop for four decades. Others who achieved less, like Erich von Stroheim, were constrained by external forces, battling constantly against the studio odds. Laurel and Hardy appeared, separately and together, in over 460 films (mostly, of course, short). Chaplin buzzed through thirty-five Keystones, fourteen Essanays and twelve Mutuals before settling down to a more sedate pace with his eight First National pictures (including *The Kid*) and then his ten subsequent features. In the interim, from 1918, there was ample time to reflect. And those reflections inevitably leached into his films, and into the Tramp himself.

In the main, he was in search of simplicity, believing that the complexities of life begat confusion, despair and conflict. In *My Autobiography*, he deplored 'the kinetic invasion of the twentieth century', in which the individual was hemmed in by 'gigantic institutions that threaten from all sides . . . We are becoming the victims of soul-conditioning, of sanctions and permits . . . We have gone blindly into ugliness and congestion and have lost our appreciation of the aesthetics.'

In this, Chaplin, a man born of the nineteenth century, still cherished what we now consider an old-fashioned belief in the pursuit of beauty in art. In movies, however, one could not avoid the 'kinetic invasion of the twentieth century', implicit as it was in the technique of the camera, as well as the instantaneous distribution of many copies of the work across the entire world. Chaplin's fame and fortune was the direct result of this process. Throughout the globe, his image proliferated, into the nooks and crannies of cultures that were granted only the leftovers of western consumption along with the blunt end of western power. All over Asia and Africa one could find local entertainers with a cane, a funny hat, big shoes and a strange walk. In Cambodia, popular comedians with a small moustache and cane carry on to our day. According to web writer Darryl Leon Collins, 'his pervasive presence is also found in the Lakhaon Bassac folkloric theatre where young Cambodian performing arts students learn to apply the same make-up to recreate his facial character.' Half-way across the world, in Turkey, he appeared as a character in a modern shadow-puppet play, *Karagoz in Ankara*, written by one Ismail Hakki Baltacioglu in 1940 (discussed in an article in *Asian Theatre Journal* in 2006, by Serdar Ozturk). Karagoz is the traditional fool raised to power. 'Once Karagoz has power, situations arise, either from the acts of Karagoz himself or from other characters, which opens up the normal societal controls on sex and violence.'

Charlie Chaplin appears as a character in the play, which was written to show the superiority of the Turkish Republican modernists. According to Ozturk's translation it goes:

CHARLIE CHAPLIN: I want to produce a film and there must be a stupid, supine, gullible clown in it.

KARAGOZ: Would you like to have this slap? (He slaps Charlie Chaplin) . . .

CHARLIE CHAPLIN: Maybe, but we Americans don't love the *karagoz* art so much.

KARAGOZ: Bandy-legged, look and listen how much we understand this art. We had our *karagoz* for ages before you had your cinema. You memorize and then play, whereas we play in improvisation. You play with the help of electricity, but we do it by candlelight . . . You are dependent on machinery, while we perform live . . .

Despite Charlie being presented as the western invader, perhaps the writer implied he was a true *karagoz* fool himself. As Ozturk explains: 'After overcoming Charlie Chaplin, Karagoz meets Tarzan, and . . . is upset because Tarzan is naked . . .' After which the Turkish hero meets Greta Garbo, and insists that Turkish women are more beautiful. The whole piece ends in a nationalist paroxysm – 'Long live the Republic of Turkey!'

Charlie was so malleable, he could appear anywhere. This was apparent from the early 1920s in Europe, and before, when he became a poster boy for the Dadaists, and a set of cubes for Léger. We have traced his influence in France and Spain, Russia and Germany. He became a Christ on the cross for Erwin Blumenfeld, a ribald icon of fun and booze for Rudolf Ausleger, an anti-dictatorship figure for Czech cartoonists. When the surrealists came to Paris, he was generally lionized as a figure of licence and freedom, though later, in the 1930s, Salvador Dalí demoted him in contrast to Buster Keaton, whose 'great stone face' signified nothing, and even to Harpo Marx, whom Dalí decided he adored. Harpo's face was of 'persuasive and triumphant madness,' whereas Chaplin's look at the end of *City Lights* was 'infinitely prosaic . . . a look of sweet go-getting that knows no equal other than the alleged look of revolting blind men or that of the smug and springlike, phenomenal and smelly, legless cripple.'

Dalí called this 'pseudo-transcendentalism'. I think he meant Chaplin's intense humanism, which the surrealists, especially the Spanish ones, were vowed to spit on and revile as the antithesis of the grand destruction of all conventions that surrealism was expected to achieve. In the end, of course, Dalí became as rich as Chaplin, selling to the same moneyed aesthetes that the surrealists hated like the plague.

In fact, Dalí included Chaplin in a drawing for one of his never-made film projects, *Les Mystères surréalistes de New York* (1935), at the right hand of a panel showing figures in a paroxysm of violence involving guns, knives, breaking glass and an explosion catching the Charlie figure in the street. But Art for Art's Sake ever was a difficult pose to maintain, if any degree of earthly success beckoned. Both Dalí and Chaplin became commercial enterprises, industries unto themselves.

Chaplin himself became a mini Electro Steel Corporation, complete with TV screens and whirring cogs and wheels. No wonder some of the crew on his slow-moving conveyor belt saw him as the boss barking orders rather than the prole on the assembly line. If the Communists taught him anything, it was the maxim about control of the means of production, which he pursued single-mindedly, knowing that if this faltered, all was lost. He could have slid, as Keaton had, down the commercial waste chute towards a jobsworth's oblivion.

His relationship with the socialists and with socialism has, of course, been widely debated, no less in these pages. Retrieved FBI files show that he was the subject of official files as early as 1922, logging his association with such radicals as Max Eastman and, no doubt, reflecting his comments on Bolshevism in *My Trip Abroad*. In 1923 the Justice Department's investigators found the aforementioned article in the Soviet newspaper *Pravda* that appeared to claim he had 'joined the American Communists'. (The source was an article by Nikolai Lebedev, *Theatre and Music: Charlie Chaplin*, dated 12 January 1923.)

From 1942 onwards, the files proliferate, trying to link Chaplin with both the Communist Party itself and a host of 'fronts' like Russian War Relief, the National Council of American-Soviet Friendship, the Artists' Front to Win the War and the Joint Anti-Fascist Refugee Committee. (David Robinson found that Chaplin's FBI file ran to over

1900 pages.) Chaplin's refusal to repudiate or denounce his acquaintances was seen as proof of his guilt. Biographer Kenneth Lynn has sternly judged him culpable of condoning Soviet repression in Stalin's show trials and the takeover of Soviet-sphere Europe after the Second World War. Friends like Ivor Montagu and the Eislers, Hanns and Gerhart, have been found wanting, tarred as Soviet stooges. His silence on the anti-Soviet failed revolution in Hungary in 1956 was deafening, at a time when many loyal Communists found this to be their last straw.

Hindsight is, of course, easy. Today, throughout eastern Europe and Russia herself, nobody has ever been a Communist, apart from those Russian organizations which have morphed into nationalist Stalin-nostalgists and wave the red flag still at Red Square. But the history of world Communism is full of the tales of idealistic people who believed, agitated, protested, joined, followed the Party line religiously, sacrificed, lost futures, jobs, lives – not counting those like Chaplin, who never joined, but nevertheless gave the benefit of the doubt to the only movement that seemed to them capable, at a certain moment in history, of confronting the vast, pitiless forces that appeared to be taking millions of people into the Moloch-mouth of economic ruin and war. The slogan 'Socialism or Barbarism' echoed down the mid-decades of the twentieth century.

Now that the great edifice has crumbled, and one can sift through the ruins, old delusions can be easily spotted, particularly by those who are reluctant to examine their own contemporary certitudes and beliefs. Who shall cast the first stone? Clearly, a very large number. To those, like myself, who have known an older generation that was touched by, or joined the Party, the easy demonization taken up by right-wing America seems to be a blindfold, rather than a lantern picking out the good from the bad.

In America, the Communist Party was prey to a unique delusion: that when the Day finally dawned, and Capitalism was dethroned, the American branch of the Party would be in charge of the world's most powerful economic force, to use it for Good, rather than Evil means. The ideological war in America was one of matched Manicheans. But the war was lopsided: American communists never got within a million miles of power, and their demonizers held all the cards in the game.

The FBI, however, was convinced, from an early stage, that Hollywood in particular was rife with subversion, full of dedicated

secret agents of Moscow following orders to place ideological mes-
sages in American movies. Cecil B. DeMille's brother William was
a candidate, having made films in 1915 and 1916 highlighting the
plight of factory workers and their strikes. Like their present
inheritors, the zealous investigators perceived every incidence of liber-
alism as potential subversion, however strange the notion might be of
such ultra-capitalists as Adolph Zukor or Louis B. Mayer presiding
over left-wing nests. The driving force in this was, as ever, J. Edgar
Hoover, who tagged Groucho and Harpo Marx as early samples of
dangerous Reds.

Charlie the Tramp was so obviously a subversive that investigation
was self-evidently required. He indulged in squalor, picked the worst
neighbourhoods to live in, ate terrible food and dressed atrociously. On
occasion, having struck it lucky, he masqueraded as a millionaire. He
presented America as misery-ridden, unjust, violent and ultimately
absurd. His creator, Chaplin, was even worse, since he was a foreigner,
who did not avail himself of the golden gift that America held out for
newcomers, citizenship of the United States. And the crowning insult –
Charlie was amazingly popular, as Richard B. Hood, Los Angeles FBI
Special Agent, wrote to Hoover in March 1944, enclosing an article
from *Rob Wagner's Script* that claimed that 'there are men and women
in the far corners of the world who have never heard of Jesus Christ;
yet they know and love Charlie Chaplin.'

Crucify him! Chaplin's calvary was a gentle one, delivered by government fiat, rather than hammer and nails, but, in its political impact,
almost as counter-productive as the original model. Chaplin did not
found a new religion, but his image took on a new lustre everywhere
except in America, sealing his status as that extremely rare creature –
a persecuted white American artist. The Englishness that he had
always prized was bolstered, despite his choice of the Swiss lakes as his
abode, and his universalism was re-affirmed. Beyond the status of
fame, which had been his since 1915, he achieved a central signifi-
cance in the twentieth century's struggle of the avant-garde against
convention. Uniquely, he had achieved this by mastering the century's
industrial art form, the cinema, working in a conventional mode, in
the realm of mass commerce. The only other American artist to
achieve this, equally paradoxically, is Walt Disney. But Disney capitu-
lated to the demands of convention, and embraced the State, while
Chaplin remained implacably free.

Was Chaplin, with all this, the Nietzschean Superman that critic Heywood Broun identified, whimsically as it may have been, in the aggressive skater of *The Rink*, as early as 1916? A proponent of the 'master morality', and the 'will to power'? The joke may carry some truth if we look at the philosopher's book entitled *Human, All Too Human*, a short volume of aphorisms subtitled 'A Book for Free Spirits'. One of Nietzsche's little homilies is headed: 'The illogical necessary' –

Among the things that can drive a thinker to despair is the knowledge that the illogical is necessary for man and that much good comes from it. It is so firmly lodged in the passions, in speech, in art, in religion, and generally in everything which endows life with value, that one cannot extricate it without doing irreparable harm to these beautiful things. Only the very naïve are capable of thinking that the nature of man can be transformed into a purely logical one; but, if there were degrees of approximation to this goal, how much would not have to vanish along this path! Even the most rational man needs nature again from time to time, that is, his *illogical basic attitude to all things*.

In the end, we remain with personal responses: Charlie Chaplin and me. No semiotic icon, no theme of academic study, no artistic giant, just an old companion on the road. Like many, I remember from the beginning no specific titles, not even narratives, but just an image of the 'little fellow' who was essentially alone in the world. It was this aloneness that resonated. Not the romances, not the yearning, not the social comment, although the confrontation with Eric Campbell in what was obviously *Easy Street* stuck forcefully in the mind. For a boy growing up in the 1950s, in the pretty provincial State of Israel at that time, it was David and Goliath.

I remember the immigrant ship yawing from side to side as the steerage passengers grab their spoonfuls of soup from the sliding plates. Again, I remember Eric Campbell, and the fallen coin in the cafe. And then I remember *The Gold Rush*, the desperation of hunger, Chaplin as chicken, the teetering cabin, and the meal of the shoes. These are just elements of existence, of growing up, of awareness of fantasy in the world.

Existence, of course, is the teetering cabin, poised in a blizzard over the cliff. Aware of something amiss, inside the cabin, Charlie and Mack Swain try jumping up and down, to figure out whether it's just the stomach cramps, or external reality. When both walk to the wrong side, reality swiftly tips over, held by a rope caught in a cleft. Every child knows this feeling, that derives from nature, not nurture. It is the human condition, that Chaplin understood instinctively, derived no doubt from his own childhood, but also, and perhaps more so, from the very fact of being alive, of being vulnerable in a void filled by the self and perception, and which becomes a sharper dilemma as we grow older, and realize our temporary sojourn on earth.

We may try a kick and a shrug, and a cane twiddle, and a walk off down a pathway towards some destination, on the other side of the fade-out, but, unlike the film-maker, we can never be sure of another movie, waiting to fade in, at a familiar theatre.

The Sufi mystics, following the ancient Persian Mazdaist myths, conceived of an invisible world, inhabited by ideal forms, which can be accessed by the adept in a mirror, by the contemplation of the divine. Secular mysticism does not incorporate ideal forms, but allows for the contemplation of the intangible by imagination: this was very much the surrealist realm. Luis Buñuel wrote that he stopped worrying about divine moral imperatives once he had accepted the reality of imagination. 'My form of atheism', he wrote, 'leads inevitably to an acceptance of the inexplicable.'

He could well have been speaking for Chaplin. There he sits, on his director's chair, surrounded by the machines of creation, camera, lights, cables, sets, props, costumes, film crew and actors, trying to conjure, out of this chaos – something. He knows not what it is. Unlike other movie masters, he does not have the film in his head, fully formed. It will emerge out of the mulch of experience, out of the process of this communal art which is also so intensely personal. An assistant is poised with that dreaded instrument of time wasted, the clapperboard:

Slate number 4,655!

Will this brief flurry of action produce the imaginary moment that Chaplin knows exists, yet unformed?

It will. It did. It is.

Chaplin's farewell.

Acknowledgements

Once again, thanks to all the usual suspects on my 'frequent archives' ticket: The British Film Institute in London and its diligent staff, and the staff at the New York Public Library Film and Theatre section, which has finally brought the full glories of the Robinson Locke Scrapbook collection's volume on Chaplin, with its multitude of ancient clippings in font previously readable only through an electron microscope, into an easily accessible format. The main Chaplin archive now resides in Bologna, Italy, and my heartfelt thanks to Cecilia Cenciarelli and staff at the Chaplin Research Centre at the Cineteca di Bologna Library for making this vast collection available for researchers. The collection is a boon for the burgeoning industry of Chaplinology, enabled by the generosity of the Chaplin Association and the many archivists and film historians who have mined these nuggets for years: chief among them David Robinson, Kevin Brownlow and Patrick Stanbury (and David Gill, alas deceased), whose *Unknown Chaplin* film project is a treasure trove of insights into Chaplin's work. I am grateful for the work done by many other archives, in Britain and elsewhere, in restoring the long and short Chaplin films, in particular the ongoing and painstaking work of restoring the Keystone shorts out of the shadowy glimmer that we have all had to endure for decades. Seeing the films as they were seen and known in their first releases is an indispensable precondition for appreciating the art of any film artist, none more so than Chaplin, whose skill as both actor and director is apparent in small details and gestures. For insight into these restorations I am primarily indebted to Clyde Jeavons, who opened my eyes and propped my eyelids with matchsticks when I showed signs of flagging at the sheer bulk of newly restored cinema. Thanks as well to Joel Finler, Walter Donohue and the movie loyalists of Faber and Faber, to Mairi, who suffers the slings and arrows with endless patience, and to all those who laid the foundations for the study and appreciation of the cinema's pioneers.

Illustration Credits

Notes on Sources

Abbreviations

BFI: British Film Institute Library & Archive
CAB: Chaplin Archive, Bologna
LAT: *Los Angeles Times*
NYPL: New York Public Library, Film and Theatre
NYPL-RL: New York Public Library, Robinson Locke Scrapbooks
NYT: *New York Times*

Quotations of script text unlisted below are from onscreen segments of the individual Chaplin movies.

Prologue

xii 'LONDON, Sept. 10 – Charles Chaplin was here today . . .' NYT
     11 Sept. 1957.
xiii 'ordered authorities . . .' etc., NYT 20 Sept. 1952.
xiv 'While you are preparing your engraved subpoena . . .' David
     Robinson, *Chaplin: His Life and Art*, William Collins Sons & Co.,
     1985, Paladin Grafton Books, 1986, p. 545.
xviii 'He wonders why he's being "persecuted" . . .' *American Legion
     Magazine*, Dec. 1952, NYPL.
xviii 'he never paid a visit to the Hollywood Canteen . . .' etc., ibid.

1 Caught in a Cabaret

5 'An entertainment of the People . . .' W. MacQueen Pope, *The Melodies
   Linger On: The Story of Music Hall*, W. H. Allen, 1951, p. 3.
6 'an era of prosperity . . .' ibid.
6 'Let there be merriment by all means . . .' James Harding, *George
   Robey and the Music Hall*, Hodder and Stoughton, 1990, p. 35.
8 'Being the faithful recital of a romantic career . . .' *Charlie Chaplin's
   Own Story*, Bobbs-Merrill, 1916, reprinted ed. Harry M. Geduld,
   Indiana University Press, 1985.
9 'I do not know my mother's real name . . .' ibid., p. 2.
9 'when my mother came in . . .' ibid., p. 3.

9 'My father was a great, dark, handsome man . . .' ibid., p. 2.

10 'He who is without sin among you . . .' Charles Chaplin, *My Autobiography*, Simon and Schuster, 1964, Pocket Books, 1966, p. 15.

10 'Dryden entered her lodgings . . .' Robinson, p. 15.

11 'There's nothing worth talking about . . .' *Photoplay*, Feb. 1915, NYPL-RL.

11 'I came to New York with my brother Sidney . . .' ibid.

12 'America! I am coming to conquer you . . .' John McCabe, *Mr. Laurel and Mr. Hardy*, Signet, New York, 1968, p. 27.

12 'When I asked Mr. Chaplin . . .' *Motion Picture*, Mar. 1915, NYPL-RL.

2 The Kid

13 'Whilst we have been building our churches . . .' *The Bitter Cry of Outcast London*, W. T. Stead. www.attackingthedevil.co.uk.

14 'The child-misery that one beholds . . .' ibid.

14 'A child seven years old . . .' ibid.

15 'beautiful in those days . . .' etc. Chaplin, *My Autobiography*, p.20.

15 'The story of Lambeth in the last ten years . . .' 'Notes on Walks with Policemen', Charles Booth archive, http://booth.lse.ac.uk.

16 'It was a cold wet evening . . .' *Charlie Chaplin's Own Story*, p. 36.

16 'My brother Syd was four years old . . .' *Photoplay*, July 1915, NYPL-RL.

16 'The very first thing I can remember . . .' ibid.

17 'My early life was far from humorous . . .' *San Francisco Chronicle*, July 1915, NYPL-RL.

17 'She was one of the greatest pantomime artists . . .' *American*, Nov. 1918, NYPL.

17 'Music, even in my poorhouse days . . .' *Photoplay*, July 1915, NYPL-RL.

18 'HIS EARLIEST RECOLLECTION . . .' ibid.

18 'History, poetry and science . . .' *My Autobiography*, p. 33.

20 'A mischievous boy, always up to monkey tricks . . .' A. J. Marriot, *Chaplin, Stage by Stage*, Marriot Publishing, 2005, p. 3.

20 'I don't remember when I began regularly as a professional . . .' *Photoplay*, July 1915, NYPL-RL.

20 'One day I was giving an exhibition . . .' Robinson, p. 28, quote from *Glasgow Weekly Herald*, 9 Oct. 1921.

22 'I lived in terror of him . . .' *Charlie Chaplin's Own Story*, p. 12.

22 'In the evenings we were marched out . . .' ibid., p. 12.

22 'A splendid promenade . . .' D. F. Cheshire, *Music Hall in Britain*, Associated University Presses, 1974, p. 29.

23 'Hamlet by Bransby Williams . . .' quoted in Marriot,, p. 6.

23 'They said old England was worked out . . .' *The Era*, 9 June 1900.

3 The Face on the Bar-room Floor

26 'Master Charles Chaplin . . .' etc., quoted in Robinson, p. 47.

26 'a clever example of the low comedy . . .' *Southern Daily Echo*, 20 March 1906, quoted in Marriot, p. 69.

26 'a slapstick affair about a jury . . .' *My Autobiography*, p. 95.

26 'a deaf-mute, a drunk . . .' etc., Robinson, p. 69.

27 'three flights of narrow stairs . . .' etc., ibid., p. 38.

27 'worked as a barber's boy . . .' ibid., p. 39.

27 'The foreman put me to work . . .' *San Francisco Chronicle*, July 1915, NYPL-RL.

28 'In Mr. Pink's sketch there are . . .' *Referee*, 5 May 1906, quoted in Marriot, p. 71.

29 'Nobody seemed to have any broken windows . . .' J. P. Gallagher, *Fred Karno, Master of Mirth and Tears*, Robert Hale, 1971.

29 'a humorous donkey . . .' *The Era*, 9 Jan. 1897.

30 'caught the very essence . . .' etc., ibid., 10 Jan. 1903.

31 'Broad English humor is very broad . . .' Clipping, 21 Mar. 1911, NYPL.

31 'I have discovered . . .' *New York Telegraph*, 14 Sept. 1906, NYPL.

31 'FRED KARNO, ONE OF LONDON'S . . .' *New York Morning Telegraph*, 7 Oct. 1906, NYPL.

4 A Night in the Show

35 'At last came an opportunity . . .' *San Francisco Chronicle*, July 1915, NYPL.

36 'In spite of Mr. Karno's name . . .' Lord Chamberlain's Manuscripts, British Library, London, 'Mumming Birds' ms.

37 'ARCHIE: Can you put me up for the night . . .' ibid, 'Skating' ms.

38 'It may have been a childish infatuation . . .' 'A Comedian Sees the World', *Woman's Home Companion*, Sept. 1933, BFI.

39 'bejewelled Indian princes . . .' etc., *My Autobiography*, pp. 110, 111.

40 'He told me my society was superfluous . . .' Harding, p. 36.

42 'LYDIA: Did you sleep well last night . . .' etc., Lord Chamberlain's Manuscripts, 'Wow Wows' ms.

42 'Chaplin will do all right for America . . .' *Variety*, 8 Oct. 1910, NYPL.

5 The Tramp

46 'All persons who rove about from place to place . . .' Sidney L. Harring, 'Class Conflict and the Suppression of Tramps in Buffalo, 1892–1894', *Law & Society Review*, vol. 11, no. 5, 1977, p. 909.

46 'It was fair-time . . .' Jack London, *The Road*, The Macmillan Co., New York, 1907.

47 'In those depression years . . .' etc., Harring, p. 873.

48 'our distaste for the real tramp . . .' John D. Seelye, 'The American Tramp: A Vision of the Picaresque', *American Quarterly*, vol. 15, no. 4, 1963, p. 535.

48 'such as being a beggar is almost unknown . . .' ibid.

48 'There is much unclear thinking . . .' O. F. Lewis, 'The Tramp Problem', *Annals of the American Academy of Political & Social Science*, March 1912, p. 217.

49 'In the first decade of the 1900's . . .' etc., Douglas Gilbert, *American Vaudeville*, Whittlesey House, McGraw-Hill Co., 1940, p. 269.

49 'Clothes – old, torn, loose and unclean . . .' *Black and White Budget*, London, 16 Mar. 1901, British Library Newspaper Collection.

49 'I stood where Sennett could see me . . .' *My Autobiography*, p. 148.

50 'His first costume didn't suit him . . .' *Photoplay*, July 1915, NYPL-RL.

50 'Oh' Sid I can see you . . .' Robinson, p. 97.

6 The Fatal Mallet

54 'He had only arrived here the day before . . .' *Philadelphia Record*, April 1913, NYPL.

55 'He builds his plots around . . .' *Toledo News Bee*, May 1913.

55 'Chaplin's methods of getting laughs . . .' *Saturday Evening Post*, Sept. 1916, NYPL.

55 'I left New York for California . . .' *Chicago Herald*, 18 July 1915, NYPL-RL.

56 'His first days at Keystone were anything but happy . . .' *Photoplay*, ibid., NYPL.

58 'He is a mischievous child . . .' Robinson, p. 118.

58 'At this point drunk comes along . . .' Script, 10 Jan. 1915, Mack Sennett Collection, Academy of Motion Picture Arts & Sciences, Los Angeles.

7 A Film Johnny

62 'A glare of light and heat . . .' *Charlie Chaplin's Own Story*, p. 118.

63 'Seeker of Information . . .' *Toledo Daily Blade*, 23 Jan. 1917, NYPL-RL.

72 'The comic spirit is entirely too deep . . .' *Montgomery Journal*, 31 Jan. 1915, NYPL.

72 'Well, Sid, I have made good . . .' etc., Robinson, pp. 131–2.

8 His New Job

74 'It is unwise to call this . . .' *New York Dramatic Mirror*, 6 May 1914, NYPL.

74 'In one year as a motion picture comedian . . .' etc., *Chicago Herald*, 10 Jan. 1915, NYPL.

75 'Mulligan stew was my daily bread . . .' etc., interview with Neil M. Clark, 'The First Fifty Years were the Hardest for Ben Turpin', *The American*, Nov. 1934.

76 ' "Ben," somebody said to me . . .' Quoted in *Slapstick*, issue 2, courtesy Steve Rydzewski.

76 'I know now why my comedy is good . . .' *Motion Picture*, Mar. 1915, NYPL-RL.

77 'I endeavor to put nothing . . .' *Picture-Play Weekly*, 24 Apr. 1915, NYPL-RL.

78 'For some time past rumors . . .' ibid., 4 Apr. 1915, NYPL-RL.

79 'Man Who Has Made Millions Laugh . . .' etc., *New Jersey Evening News*, Apr. 1915, NYPL.

81 'also decorated the New York Public Library . . .' *New York Telegraph*, 25 May 1915, NYPL.

81 'The management of Luna Park . . .' *Cleveland Plain Dealer*, 9 June 1915, NYPL.

82 'HAVE YOU THE CHAPLINOIA? . . .' *Kansas City Star*, 3 Sept. 1915, NYPL-RL.

82 'Next to reading . . .' *Chicago Herald*, 25 July 1915, NYPL-RL.

83 'I am sore in body and in mind . . .' ibid., 1 Aug. 1915, NYPL-RL.

83 'It is the general impression . . .' etc., ibid.

83 ' "Ah!" he said, *sotto voce* . . .' *Motion Picture*, Aug. 1915, NYPL-RL.

9 The Champion

89 'The Plumber, the Paperhanger . . .' *Referee*, 5 May 1906, from Marriot, p. 71.

91 'the divine prince of knaves and liars . . .' Robert Payne, *The Great Charlie*, Andre Deutsch, 1952, Pan Books, 1957, p. 20.

91 'In a sense . . .' ibid., p. 32.

10 Easy Street

98 'SIGNING CONTRACT FOR HIGHEST SALARY . . .' *Louisville Post*, 3 Mar. 1916, NYPL-RL.

98 'standing hat in hand . . .' *Kansas City Star*, 6 Mar. 1916, NYPL-RL.

99 'Next to the war in Europe . . .' *Los Angeles Enquirer*, 15 Mar. 1916, NYPL-RL.

99 'have been tumbling by thousands . . .' NYT, 19 Jan. 1916.

99 'Charlie Chaplin! Charlie Chaplin . . .' NYT, 6 Mar. 1916.

100 'Charlie Chaplin's the funniest freak . . .' Clipping, 1916, NYPL-RL.

100 'Poor little Charlie Chaplin . . .' ibid., NYPL-RL.

103 'He didn't have a script at the time . . .' *Film Culture*, Spring 1972, BFI.

106 'For the first time . . .' Clipping, 1 July 1916, NYPL-RL.

106 'chief hobby is found in his violin . . .' *Star Eagle*, 31 May 1916, NYPL-RL.

11 The Adventurer

111 'It is one a.m. . . .' *Motion Picture*, Oct. 1916, NYPL-RL.

112 'the new caretaker – Charlie . . .' ibid.

112 'Making fun is a serious business . . .' *New York Telegraph*, 5 Nov. 1916, NYPL-RL.

114 'his ruling passion . . .' Robinson, p. 176.

115 'I'll tell you one important reason . . .' *New York Telegraph*, 5 Nov. 1916, NYPL-RL.

115 'an old character they called "Rummy" Binks . . .' ibid.

116 'gruesome jollity of English poverty . . .' *The Era*, 10 Jan. 1903.

12 Shoulder Arms!

120 'As an actor who only gets drunk . . .' Clipping, Nov.? 1916, NYPL-RL.

120 'to which Minneapolis teachers . . .' *Minneapolis Tribune*, 13 Mar. 1917, NYPL-RL.

121 'preacher at the noonday services . . .' etc., *Detroit News*, 17 Apr. 1916, NYPL-RL.

121 'Say, you don't mean to tell me . . .' Undated clipping, NYPL-RL.

122 'Ah, ze Caruso of ze cinema . . .' Clipping, Apr. 1916, NYPL-RL.

122 'lock horns in Cleveland this week . . .' *Cleveland Leader*, 12 Apr. 1917, NYPL-RL.

123 'They say that poor little Charlie . . .' Clipping, July 1916, NYPL-RL.

125 'summer camp . . . situated between the rugged mountains . . .' *Motion Picture*, Nov. 1917, NYPL-RL.

126 'When a thing don't go your way . . .' Clipping, 1917, NYPL-RL.

128 'Field Headquarters, American Expeditionary Forces . . .' *Chicago News*, 9 Nov. 1917, NYPL-RL.

13 His Trysting Place

129 'NIETZSCHE HAS GRIP ON CHAPLIN . . .' quoted in Robinson, p. 178.

130 'one of the funniest films . . .' *Hartford Courant*, 30 Dec. 1915, NYPL-RL.

132 'To raise the Jester . . .' Clipping, 1919, NYPL-RL.

132 'by means of "vibrations" . . .' Clipping, 1919, NYPL-RL.

132 'The first time I met Charlie Chaplin . . .' etc., LAT, 18 Aug. 1918.

133 'a very good looking, ascetic . . .' *Buffalo Enquirer*, 1 Aug. 1916, NYPL-RL.

133 'was carried away . . .' Robinson, p. 237.

133 'We were all trying to appear modest . . .' LAT, 18 Aug. 1918.

134 'one of the charms of Charlie . . .' etc., ibid.

134 'I have never been so rich . . .' etc., ibid.

135 'Your charming personality is evident . . .' Robinson, p. 275.

14 Those Love Pangs

141 'I have never seen in my life . . .' *Photoplay*, Sept. 1919, NYPL-RL.

143 'He climbs in by the right hand door . . .' Frederick Lewis Allen, *Only Yesterday: An Informal History of the Nineteen-Twenties*, Bantam Books, New York, 1946, p. 21.

144 'When traveling, his secretary . . .' etc., *Ladies' Home Journal*, Aug. 1918, NYPL-RL.

144 'The Chaplin home is gorgeous . . .' *Detroit Journal*, 31 Jan. 1920, NYPL-RL.

145 'A couple of years ago . . .' etc., *Theatre*, June 1919, NYPL-RL.

145 'world travelers have told us . . .' *New York Telegraph*, 5 Nov. 1916, NYPL-RL.

146 'Chaplin isn't a great artist . . .' *Theatre*, June 1919, NYPL-RL.

146 'My clowning, as the world calls it . . .' NYT, 12 Dec. 1920.

148 'in the depressed period . . .' Robinson, p. 252.

15 The Bond

153 'A Letter to a Genius . . .' etc., *Photoplay*, Apr. 1920, NYPL-RL.

154 'she had no sense of reality . . .' etc., *My Autobiography*, pp. 248, 257.

162 'Midmost in this his mortal life . . .' etc., NYT, 12 Dec. 1920.

16 The Idle Class

166 'on her arrival in New York . . .' Robinson, p. 271.

167 'Mr Chaplin, why are you going to Europe . . .' etc., Charles Chaplin, *My Trip Abroad*, Harper & Brothers, 1922, p. 4.

167 'Are you a Bolshevik?' etc., ibid., p. 8.

167 'Charlie Chaplin thinks short skirts . . .' NYT, 30 Aug. 1921.

168 'my radical ideas have been much misunderstood . . .' NYT, 18 Sept. 1921.

168 'I felt proud . . .' etc., *My Trip Abroad*, ibid., pp. 10, 11.

168 'Why did you come over . . .' ibid., p. 37.

169 'I am in England . . .' etc., ibid., p. 43.

169 'Thousands are outside . . .' ibid., p. 47.

169 'I last saw him when he was . . .' *The Times*, 1 Sept. 1921.

170 'Soon after Chaplin had arrived . . .' etc., ibid., 12 Sept. 1921.

170 'special performance . . .' ibid., 16 Sept. 1921.

170 'the same old blind man . . .' *My Trip Abroad*, ibid., p. 53.

170 'I just walk down Chester Street . . .' etc., ibid., pp. 56, 57.

171 'very much like an American . . .' ibid., p. 99.

171 'not much interested in people . . .' Thomas Burke, *City of Encounters*, 1932, quoted in Kenneth S. Lynn, *Charlie Chaplin and His Times*, Aurum Press, 1998, p. 259.

171 'Germany belies the war . . .' *My Trip Abroad*, p. 114.

172 'Offered a drink . . .' ibid., p. 117.

172 'Oh, Mr. Chaplin . . .' ibid., p. 145.

17 Pay Day

175 'Men rough with women . . .' CAB, quoted in Robinson, p. 296.

178 'funny little guy . . .' Fernand Léger, Exhibition Catalogue, Acquavella Galleries, 1987 (www.acquavellagalleries.com).

179 'Poor Charlot! People love him . . .' NYT, 19 Mar. 1922.

180 'it was the first of the silent pictures . . .' *My Autobiography*, p. 322.

180 'an insult to every American . . .' quoted in Arthur Lennig, *Stroheim*, University Press of Kentucky, 2000, p. 145.

18 A Woman of Paris – A Man of Los Angeles

182 'Time and Destiny . . .' Script notes, *A Woman of Paris*, CAB.

183 'There is something refined . . .' *My Trip Abroad*, p. 125.

183 'The consciousness of our misery . . .' etc., script notes, *A Woman of Paris*, CAB.

189 'News broken to boy's mother . . .' ibid.

191 '35-year-old oil operative . . .' Clipping, 1 Feb. 1924, NYPL.

192 'Recently it was whispered . . .' NYT, 29 July 1923.

192 'Mr. Chaplin is a charming fellow . . .' ibid.

192 'she disposed of. ... as completely . . .' *Los Angeles Examiner*, 28 July 1923.

192 'In my first serious drama . . .' Script notes, *A Woman of Paris*, CAB.

193 'there is more real genius . . .' *New York Herald*, quoted in Robinson p. 320.

193 'Chaplin . . . straying far from his haunts . . .' *Variety*, 27 Sept. 1923, BFI.

193 'this film lives . . .' NYT, 2 Oct. 1923, NYPL.

19 The Gold Rush

194 'Scene: The interior of a miner's cabin . . .' Script versions, *The Gold Rush*, CAB.

195 'realism that will portray emotions . . .' NYT, 7 Oct. 1923.

196 'This was a wonderful theme . . .' *My Autobiography*, p. 327.

197 'trudged through the heavy snows . . .' Souvenir programme, *The Gold Rush*, 1925, CAB.

201 'We must laugh in the face . . .' *My Autobiography*, p. 327.

201 'something of the comedian's early life . . .' NYT, 17 Aug. 1925.

201 'To my mind, the underlying motif . . .' NYT, 9 Aug. 1925.

20 The Masquerader

205 'Not Harvard's, but the original Gold Coast . . .' NYT, 5 July 1925.

206 'Charlie Chaplin rules the risible muscles . . .' NYT, 25 Apr. 1920.

207 'Chaplin is unable to provide . . .' Sabine Hake, 'Chaplin's Reception in Weimar Germany', *New German Critique* no. 51, Autumn 1990, p. 92.

207 'other people have an ego consciousness . . .' ibid., p. 93.

207 'representatives of the German . . .' etc, NYT, 19 Feb. 1926.

208 'a human being without surface . . .' Hake, p. 93.

208 'No, no! Chaplin is anything but a convinced . . .' *Mersus*, 1931, quoted ibid., p. 95.

208 'In his films, Chaplin has turned . . .' ibid., p. 95.

208 'Charlot is the genius of our age . . .' Ivan Goll, '*Apologie des Charlot*', quoted in Sherwin Simmons, 'Chaplin Smiles on the Wall: Berlin Dada and the Wish-Images of Popular Culture', *New German Critique*, no. 64, 2001, p. 33.

209 'Why have we failed time and time again . . .' etc., Vsevolod Meyerhold, 'Chaplin and Chaplinism', 1936, in *Tulane Drama Review*, vol. 11, no. 1, Autumn 1966, pp. 190–1.

209 'the Soviet State's motion picture monopoly . . .' NYT, 18 Jan. 1926.

210 'Yours is the kindest sense of comedy . . .' Clipping, 20 Sept. 1925, CAB.

210 'the war removed Max Linder . . .' quoted in C. Brian Morris, 'Charlie Chaplin's Tryst with Spain', *Journal of Contemporary History*, vol. 18, no. 3, July 1983, p. 519.

210 'My hat, my cuffs . . .' ibid., p. 527.

211 'Chaplin is a tramp who has lost his way . . .' ibid., p. 521.

211 'Chaplin eats no meat . . .' ibid., p. 522.

212 'In his oceanic bowler . . .' quoted in Clare Cavanagh, 'Rereading the Poet's Ending: Mandelstam, Chaplin and Stalin', *PMLA* vol. 109, no. 1, 1994, p. 76.

212 'Charlie Chaplin / Left the movie house . . .' ibid., p. 80.

21 The Circus

215 'Under the archway of a bridge . . .' Script notes, *The Circus*, CAB.

216 'on a high place troubled . . .' quoted in Robinson, p. 360.

218 'Charlie's eyes . . .' etc., Lita Grey Chaplin (with Morton Cooper), *My Life with Chaplin: an Intimate Memoir*, Bernard Geis Associates, New York, 1966, p. 88.

218 'hodgepodge of English . . .' ibid., p. 90.

218 'a bottle of cologne . . .' etc., ibid., pp. 92, 93, 95.

219 'Lovemaking is a sublime art . . .' ibid., p. 98.

219 'I'm sure that Dr. Einstein . . .' ibid., p. 220.

219 'Charlie's movies reflected him . . .' ibid., p. 228.

220 'Plaintiff alleges with regard . . .' ibid., p. 253.

220 'the act of sex perversion . . .' ibid., p. 254.

220 'going for millions . . .' ibid., p. 256.

220 'WIFE QUITS CHARLIE CHAPLIN . . .' NYT, 2 Dec. 1926.

220 'SPLIT PERMANENT . . .' NYT, 3 Dec. 1926.

220 'PARTY ROW SPLIT CHAPLINS . . .' etc, *New York Daily News*, 3 Dec. 1926–15 Jan. 1927.

221 'Charlie Chaplin has had a nervous breakdown . . .' etc., NYT, 16 Jan. 1927.

223 'A pretty looking girl is appearing . . .' NYT, 15 July 1928.

22 City Lights

226 'I don't think the talking moving picture . . .' *Film Daily*, 4 Mar. 1927.

226 'It is obvious that the talking picture . . .' *Film Daily*, 31 Dec. 1928.

226 'Talking pictures will never displace . . .' *Motion Picture News*, 14 July 1928.

227 'I shall never speak in a film . . .' *Theatre Arts Monthly*, Nov. 1930, p. 908.

227 'By far the finest . . .' Chaplin, 'The Best Interview Ever Written about the Comic Genius of the Screen', *Book-sided*, Dec. 1929, BFI.

229 'Dream – Awakening – Wandering . . .' Script notes, *City Lights*, CAB.

229 'Exterior of Theatre. Night.' etc., ibid.

230 'Sequence of Charlie walking with girl . . .' etc., ibid.

233 'And now we want to see the film run off . . .' etc., NYT, 18 August 1929.

235 'I remember the first time . . .' Luis Buñuel, *My Last Breath*, Jonathan Cape, 1984, p. 134.

237 'enough to shrivel the heart . . .' James Agee, 'Comedy's Greatest Era', *Life*, 5 Sept. 1949.

23 His Regeneration

243 'The disillusion of love . . .' 'A Comedian Sees the World', Part 1, *Woman's Home Companion*, Sept. 1933, BFI.

243 'He said that the little tramp . . .' NYT, 5 Feb. 1931.

244 'enjoyed a respite . . .' ibid., 13 Feb. 1931.

244 'The chief aim of my trip abroad . . .' ibid., 14 Feb. 1931.

245 'For another hour the observation-car . . .' ibid., 20 Feb. 1931.

245 'The names of great statesmen . . .' quoted in ibid., 20 Feb. 1931.

245 'rushed off for dinner . . .' ibid., 26 Feb. 1931.

246 'wasn't he quoted as saying . . .' etc., 'A Comedian Sees the World', Part 1, BFI.

246 'My policy would stand for . . .' ibid.

247 'I'd love to buy a penny-worth . . .' etc., ibid.

247 'performed his famous antics . . .' NYT, 29 Mar. 1931.

248 'I have been besieged . . .' 'A Comedian Sees the World', draft text, CAB.

248 'The film comedian was escorted down from the platform . . .' NYT, 10 Mar. 1931.

248 'delicious home-baked tarts . . .' etc., 'A Comedian Sees the World', Part 2, BFI.

249 'two effeminate youths . . .' etc., ibid.

249 'the foundations of my literary education . . .' etc., 'A Comedian Sees the World', Part 3, BFI.

250 'a dramatic killing . . .' 'A Comedian Sees the World', Part 4.

250 'it all seems like a revival meeting . . .' 'A Comedian Sees the World', draft text, CAB. This section was omitted from the published *Woman's Home Companion* article.

252 'The story will be of an opera singer . . .' NYT, 24 Dec. 1931.

253 'twirling cans of fire . . .' etc., 'A Comedian Sees the World', Part 4.

253 'untouched by civilization . . .' etc., 'A Comedian Sees the World', Part 5, BFI.

253 'My brother and I would sit of an evening . . .' ibid.

254 'undermined by western influence . . .' etc., ibid.

24 Making a Living

255 'filmdom's wealthiest celebrity . . .' NYT, 8 July 1932.

257 'a satire on certain phases . . .' NYT, 17 Mar. 1935.

257 'Crowds entering office buildings . . .' Script notes, *Modern Times*, CAB.

257 'FACTORY LANDSCAPE . . .' etc., Script, *The Masses*, CAB.

258 'the only two live spirits . . .' Notes, *Modern Times*, CAB.

258 'If you all will shut your trap . . .' Joe Hill, 1913, IWW *Little Red Song Book*.

258 'Hallelujah, I'm a bum . . .' Folk song, Harry McClintock, ?1897, IWW circa 1908.

258 'While he is looking . . .' Notes, *Modern Times*, CAB.

261 'To his surprise, he finds the Gamin . . .' quoted in Robinson, p. 463.

261 'out of herself the ghost . . .' ibid.

264 'Afoot and light hearted . . .' Walt Whitman, 'Song of the Open Road', *Leaves of Grass*, 1856.

25 The Great Dictator

266 'does not coincide with . . .' NYT, 9 Jan. 1935.

266 'Charlie Chaplin and Jackie Coogan . . .' *Der Ewige Jude*, Munich, 1937, quoted in www.calvin.edu/academic/cas/gpa/diebow.htm.

266 'In sculpture even more than painting . . .' ibid.

267 'the Jew Ernst Lubitsch . . .' translated text of narration, *Der Ewige Jude*, Imperial War Museum, London.

267 'Grandma was half gypsy . . .' *My Autobiography*, p. 8.

267 'Every Sunday I was made to sit through Bach . . .' ibid., p. 12.

267 'Some scientists say that . . .' Charles Chaplin Jr, *My Father, Charlie Chaplin*, Longman's Green, 1960, p. 240.

268 'the little Jewish tumbler . . .' quoted in Lynn, p. 395.

268 'Russia is the most interesting . . .' quoted in Simon Louvish, *Cecil B. DeMille and the Golden Calf*, Faber and Faber, 2007, p. 307.

270 'Only the dawn moved . . .' etc., *Rob Wagner's Script Magazine*, Jan. 1938, CAB.

272 'A DRAMATIC COMPOSITION . . .' Script, *The Great Dictator*, CAB.

273 'SOLDIER: Why don't I end it all . . .' ibid.

273 'reach out from everywhere . . .' ibid.

274 'CHARLIE'S SPEECH . . .' Early draft, *The Great Dictator*, CAB.

276 'Hinkle at the piano . . .' Script, *The Great Dictator*, CAB.

277 'the most wonderful invention . . .' ibid.

278 'Since it has not been found possible . . .' Schedule notes, *The Great Dictator*, CAB.

278 'Please throw all broken New Year's . . .' ibid.

279 'Jews should not stick their necks out . . .' Neal Gabler, *An Empire of Their Own: How the Jews Invented Hollywood*, Anchor Books, 1989, p. 342.

279 'although he did not think . . .' etc., ibid., p. 344.

282 'I'm sorry, but I don't want to be an Emperor . . .' etc., onscreen dialogue, *The Great Dictator*.

26 Dough and Dynamite

285 'Famous Mustache to Be First Casualty . . .' NYT, 16 Oct. 1942.

286 'thousands of excited admirers . . .' ibid., 16 Oct. 1940.

286 'no picture ever made has promised . . .' etc., ibid.

286 'the meek and inarticulate little man . . .' ibid., 20 Oct. 1940.

287 'a new picture about a bibulous refugee . . .' ibid., 6 Mar. 1941.

289 'I am not a Communist but . . .' Lynn, p. 422.

290 'CHAPLIN PROTÉGÉ READY TO DENY . . .' LAT, 10 June 1943.

290 'CHAPLIN CASE GIRL CLEARED . . .' ibid., 12 June 1943.

290 'PATERNITY TANGLE . . .' ibid.

290 'GIRL ACCUSER . . .' ibid., 17 Sept. 1943.

290 'JOAN BERRY TELLS JURY . . .' ibid., 21 Jan. 1944.

291 'Q. – The record here has been developed . . .' etc., ibid., 31 Mar. 1944.

292 'JOAN BERRY ASKS JURORS . . .' ibid., 21 Dec. 1944.

293 'merely sitting there . . .' Robinson, p. 524.

293 'recited passages from the Bible . . .' NYT, 30 Dec. 1944.

293 'I knew 95 per cent . . .' ibid., 13 Apr. 1945.

293 'I came into court . . .' LAT, 18 Apr. 1945.

294 'Charlie had his revenge . . .' LAT, 17 Sept. 1952, NYPL.

27 Monsieur Verdoux

297 'Theater Owners of Ohio . . .' NYT, 8 May 1947.

298 'If we value liberty for ourselves and our children . . .' *Los Angeles Citizen-News*, 6 June 1947, quoted in Louvish, *Cecil B. DeMille*, p. 382.

298 'When all the world turns . . .' Script notes, *Monsieur Verdoux*, CAB.

302 '1. (a) There will be no comedy interruptions . . .' etc., Breen letter, 15 Mar. 1946, MPPDA (Motion Picture Producers & Distributors of America) files, Academy of Motion Picture Arts & Sciences, Los Angeles.

28 Limelight (Part 1)

307 'joining the ranks of subversives . . .' *Los Angeles Herald Express*, 15 Apr. 1947.

308 'Charlie . . . has two distinct personalities . . .' Quoted in Brian Taves, 'Charlie Dearest', *Film Comment*, Mar./Apr. 1988, BFI.

308 'Often, Charlie gets into great rages . . .' ibid.

309 'Legislation to control and prevent . . .' NYT, 9 June 1949.

310 'violence that for many years . . .' ibid., 12 Sept. 1949.

310 'I am liberal and I am interested in peace . . .' etc., *Cineaste*, vol. 14 no. 4, May 1986, BFI.

311 'to revive the old Charlie . . .' *Manchester Guardian*, 7 July 1947, BFI.

312 'a vaudeville couple . . .' Notes, *Limelight*, CAB.

312 'Terry Ambrose is different . . .' *Footlights* text, *Limelight*, CAB.

312 'who had been one of the chief instigators . . .' etc., ibid.

313 'In his youth he yearned . . .' etc., ibid.

314 'CALVERO: I wonder . . .' Script, *Limelight*, CAB.

315 'Never any good . . .' ibid.

29 Limelight (Part 2)

321 'of all the traditional characters . . .' Pierre Louis Duchartre, *The Italian Comedy*, Dover, 1966, quoted in David Madden, 'Harlequin's Stick, Charlie's Cane', *Film Quarterly*, vol. 22, no. 1, Autumn 1968, p. 14.

324 'On the first of three visits . . .' NYT, 17 Feb. 1952.

325 'The new Hollywood business . . .' Larry Ceplair and Steven Englund, *The Inquisition in Hollywood, Politics in the Film Community 1930–1960*, p. 376.

326 'the Commie Daily People's World . . .' LAT, 30 July 1950.

326 'Without warning, a super-atomic bomb . . .' John Wranovics, *Chaplin and Agee: The Untold Story of the Tramp, the Writer, and the Lost Screenplay*, Palgrave Macmillan, New York, 2005, p. 159.

327 'That it is exceedingly hard . . .' ibid., p. 162.

328 'WASHINGTON, September 19 – Charles Chaplin . . .' etc., NYT, 20 Sept. 1952.

328 '100 underworld big shots . . .' etc., LAT, 3 Oct. 1952.

329 'a repulsive . . . rotten little rake . . .' *Sunday Graphic*, New York, 21 Sept. 1952, BFI.

329 'Charlie Chaplin received his visa . . .' *Chicago Tribune*, 20 Sept. 1952, NYPL.

329 'Through the proper procedure . . .' *Observer*, London, Sept. 1952, BFI.

329 'For the triumph of Charlie Chaplin . . .' *The Times*, 24 Sept. 1952.

330 'I am not political . . .' etc., *New York Herald Tribune*, 23 Sept. 1953.

330 'The main thing that comes through . . .' NYT, 24 Oct. 1952.

331 'sounded the bell of liberty . . .' NYT, 29 Oct. 1952.

331 'a remarkably candid moment . . .' etc., Victor Lasky, 'Whose Little Man?', *American Legion Magazine*, Dec. 1952, NYPL.

332 'During the fund-raising . . .' *Chicago Tribune*, 3 June 1943, NYPL.

332 'had surrendered his re-entry permit . . .' NYT, 16 Apr. 1953.

332 'It is not easy to uproot myself . . .' NYT, 28 Apr. 1953.

333 'they might raze the studio . . .' NYT, 1 Oct. 1953.

333 'the holder of the Nobel . . .' NYT, 25 Dec. 1953.

30 A King in Vevey, a Ghost in New York

334 'I CANNOT THINK OF ANYTHING . . .' Correspondence, CAB.

334 'Dear Mr. Chaplin, Your reply . . .' Correspondence, CAB.

335 'openly joined our enemy . . .' *Saturday Evening Post*, 4 Sept. 1954.

335 'CHAPLIN PLANS FILM . . .' NYT, 16 Oct. 1954.

335 'It was deliberate murder . . .' Louis Berg, 'The Strange Case of Charlie Chaplin', LAT, 5 Dec. 1954.

336 'I found him cold, haughty . . .' etc., ibid.

336 'Europe is beginning to . . .' ibid.

337 'KING: Well, what do you want?.. .' Script, *A King in New York*, CAB.

338 'GYPONT: We'll start a campaign . . .' ibid.

339 'I have been asked why I put my son . . .' Notes, *A King in New York*, CAB.

339 'It was with trepidation . . .' ibid.

340 'ANSWER: All comedy is controversial . . .' ibid.

342 '*Modern Times* was a satire . . .' *The Times*, 11 Sept. 1957.

344 'Personally, I have no axe to grind . . .' Notes, *A King in New York*, CAB.

Epilogue

347 'was not worthy . . .' NYT, 12 Nov. 1958.

348 'I was a worshipper of the foolhardy . . .' *My Autobiography*, p. 91.

349 'By the Whangpoo River . . .' Script notes, *A Countess from Hong Kong*, CAB.

350 'fearsomely cruel . . .' Marlon Brando, with Robert Lindsey, *Songs my Mother Never Taught Me*, Random House, 1994, p. 316.

350 'the best thing I've done . . .' *Sunday Times*, quoted in Robinson, p. 616.

351 'Schopenhauer said happiness . . .' *My Autobiography*, p. 538.

352 'In my study at Vevey . . .' Charles Chaplin, *My Life in Pictures*, Grosset & Dunlap, New York, 1975.

354 'Listen, Little Man . . .' Wilhelm Reich, *Listen, Little Man*, Farrar Straus & Giroux, 1948, quoted at www.orgone.org.

355 'a moustache similar to Charlie Chaplin's . . .' *The Times*, 3 Apr. 1922.

355 'Any artist, but particularly . . .' etc., Philip G. Rosen, 'The Chaplin World-View', *Cinema Journal*, vol. 9, no. 1, p. 3.

356 'There must be no dreams of posterity . . .' ibid., p. 7.

357 'the kinetic invasion . . .' *My Autobiography*, p. 507.

357 'his pervasive presence . . .' www.north-by-north-east.com/articles/
11_04_2.asp.

358 'Once Karagoz has power . . .' Serdar Ozturk, 'Turkish Shadow Theatre
of the Early Republic (1923–1945)', in http://muse.jhu.edu/journals/asian_
theatre_journal?vo23/23.2ozturk.html.

358 'persuasive and triumphant madness . . .' *Dalí & Film*, Tate Publishing,
2007, p. 142.

362 'Among the things that can drive a thinker to despair . . .' Friedrich
Nietzsche, *Human, All Too Human*, trans. Marion Faber, chapter on
'First and Last Things', segment 31.

363 'My form of atheism . . .' Luis Buñuel, ibid., p. 174.

Filmography

The following is a basic summary; full filmographies can be found in David Robinson, Chaplin filmography books, and online at imdb.com.

At Keystone – January–December 1914

(Charles Chaplin starring in all titles except 'The Knockout')

Making a Living
Henry Lehrman, Virginia Kirtley, Alice Davenport, Chester Conklin, Minta Durfee.

Mabel's Strange Predicament
Mabel Normand, Chester Conklin, Alice Davenport, Henry Lehrman, Harry McCoy, Al St John, Hank Mann.

Kid Auto Races at Venice
Henry Lehrman, Frank Williams, Thelma Salter.

Between Showers
Ford Sterling, Chester Conklin, Emma Clifton, Sadie Lampe.

A Film Johnny
Mabel Normand, Roscoe 'Fatty' Arbuckle, Minta Durfee, Ford Sterling, Mack Sennett, Virginia Kirtley.

Tango Tangles
Ford Sterling, Fatty Arbuckle, Chester Conklin, Minta Durfee.

His Favorite Pastime
Fatty Arbuckle, Peggy Pearce.

Cruel, Cruel Love
Chester Conklin, Minta Durfee, Alice Davenport.

The Star Boarder
Edgar Kennedy, Minta Durfee, Alice Davenport, Gordon Griffith.

Mabel at the Wheel
Mabel Normand, Chester Conklin, Harry McCoy, Mack Sennett, Al St John, Fred Mace, Mack Swain.

Twenty Minutes of Love
Minta Durfee, Edgar Kennedy, Chester Conklin, Hank Mann, Joseph Swickard, Gordon Griffith.

Caught in a Cabaret
Mabel Normand, Harry McCoy, Chester Conklin, Edgar Kennedy, Minta Durfee, Alice Davenport, Hank Mann.

Caught in the Rain
Mack Swain, Alice Davenport, Alice Howell.

A Busy Day
Mack Swain, Phyllis Allen.

The Fatal Mallet
Mabel Normand, Mack Swain, Mack Sennett.

Her Friend the Bandit
Mabel Normand, Charles Murray.

The Knockout
Fatty Arbuckle, Minta Durfee, Edgar Kennedy, Al St John, Hank Mann, Mack Swain, Mack Sennett, Charles Parrott (later Charley Chase), Eddie Cline. (Chaplin in bit part as the Referee.)

Mabel's Busy Day
Mabel Normand, Chester Conklin, Slim Summerville, Harry McCoy, Wallace MacDonald, Edgar Kennedy, Al St John, Mack Sennett, Charles Parrott.

Mabel's Married Life
Mabel Normand, Mack Swain, Alice Howell, Harry McCoy, Hank Mann, Al St John, Wallace MacDonald.

Laughing Gas
Fritz Schade, Alice Howell, Joseph Sutherland, Slim Summerville, Mack Swain, Joseph Swickard.

The Property Man
Fritz Schade, Phyllis Allen, Alice Davenport, Mack Sennett, Charles Bennett, Norma Nichols, Harry McCoy.

The Face on the Bar-room Floor
Fritz Schade, Cecile Arnold, Chester Conklin, Vivian Edwards, Hank Mann, Wallace MacDonald.

Recreation
Norma Nichols, ?Charles Murray.

The Masquerader
Fatty Arbuckle, Chester Conklin, Fritz Schade, Minta Durfee, Charles Murray, Cecile Arnold, Harry McCoy, Charles Parrott.

His New Profession
Minta Durfee, Fritz Schade, Cecile Arnold, Harry McCoy, Charles Parrott.

The Rounders
Fatty Arbuckle, Minta Durfee, Phyllis Allen, Al St John, Wallace MacDonald, Charles Parrott.

The New Janitor
Fritz Schade, Minta Durfee, Jack Dillon, Al St John.

Those Love Pangs
Chester Conklin, Cecile Arnold, Vivian Edwards, Edgar Kennedy, Harry McCoy, Norma Nichols.

Dough and Dynamite
Chester Conklin, Fritz Schade, Norma Nichols, Cecile Arnold, Vivian Edwards, Edgar Kennedy, Slim Summerville, Charles Parrott.

Gentlemen of Nerve
Mabel Normand, Mack Swain, Chester Conklin, Phyllis Allen, Edgar Kennedy, Charles Parrott, Alice Davenport.

His Musical Career
Mack Swain, Charles Parrott, Fritz Schade, Alice Howell, Joe Bordeaux, Normal Nichols.

His Trysting Place
Mabel Normand, Mack Swain, Phyllis Allen.

Tillie's Punctured Romance
Directed by Mack Sennett. Scenario by Mack Sennett from the play *Tillie's Nightmare*.

With Marie Dressler as Tillie, Charles Chaplin as City Slicker, Mabel Normand, Mack Swain, Charles Bennett, Charles Parrott, Charles Murray, Edgar Kennedy, Harry McCoy, Minta Durfee, Phyllis Allen, Alice Davenport, Al St John, Slim Summerville, Wallace MacDonald, Joe Bordeaux, G. G. Ligon, Gordon Griffith.

Getting Acquainted
Mabel Normand, Mack Swain, Phyllis Allen, Edgar Kennedy, Harry McCoy, Cecile Arnold.

His Prehistoric Past
Mack Swain, Gene Marsh, Cecile Arnold, Al St John, Fritz Schade.

At Essanay – February 1915–May 1916

(Charles Chaplin starring in and directing all titles)

His New Job
Ben Turpin, Charlotte Mineau, Charles Insley, Leo White, Bud Jamison, Gloria Swanson, Frank Coleman, Agnes Ayres, Billy Armstrong.

A Night Out
Ben Turpin, Bud Jamison, Edna Purviance, Leo White, Fred Goodwins.

The Champion
Edna Purviance, Lloyd Bacon, Leo White, Bud Jamison, Billy Armstrong, Carl Stockdale, Paddy McGuire, 'Broncho Billy' Anderson.

In the Park
Edna Purviance, Leo White, Margie Reiger, Lloyd Bacon, Bud Jamison, Billy Armstrong, Ernest Van Pelt.

A Jitney Elopement
Edna Purviance, Fred Goodwins, Leo White, Lloyd Bacon, Paddy McGuire, Carl Stockdale, Bud Jamison, Ernest Van Pelt.

The Tramp
Edna Purviance, Fred Goodwins, Lloyd Bacon, Paddy McGuire, Leo White, Billy Armstorng, Ernest Van Pelt.

By the Sea
Billy Armstrong, Margie Reiger, Bud Jamison, Edna Purviance, Carl Stockdale, Paddy McGuire.

Work
Charles Insley, Edna Purviance, Paddy McGuire, Billy Armstrong, Marta Golden, Leo White.

A Woman
Edna Purviance, Marta Golden, Charles Insley, Billy Armstrong, Margie Reiger, Leo White.

The Bank
Edna Purviance, Charles Insley, Carl Stockdale, Billy Armstrong, John Rand, Leo White, Fred Goodwins, Bud Jamison, Lloyd Bacon, Wesley Ruggles, Paddy McGuire.

Shanghaied
Edna Purviance, Wesley Ruggles, John Rand, Bud Jamison, Billy Armstrong, Paddy McGuire, Lawrence A. Bowes, Fred Goodwins, Leo White.

A Night in the Show
Edna Purviance, Charlotte Mineau, Dee Lampton, Leo White, Wesley Ruggles, John Rand, James T. Kelley, Paddy McGuire, May White, Phyllis Allen, Bud Jamison, Fred Goodwins, Charles Insley, Carrie Clark Ward.

Charlie Chaplin's Burlesque on Carmen
Edna Purviance as Carmen, Ben Turpin as Don Remendado, Leo White as Officer of the Guard, John Rand as Escamillo, May White as Frasquita, Bud Jamison, Wesley Ruggles, Frank J. Coleman, Lawrence A. Bowes.

Police
Edna Purviance, Wesley Ruggles, James T. Kelley, Leo White, John Rand, Fred Goodwins, Bud Jamison, Billy Armstrong.

At Mutual – May 1916 – October 1917

(Charles Chaplin starring in and directing all titles)

The Floorwalker
Eric Campbell as the Store Manager, Edna Purviance, Lloyd Bacon, Albert Austin as Shop Assistant, Leo White, Charlotte Mineau, James T. Kelley.

The Fireman
Edna Purviance, Lloyd Bacon as Her Father, Eric Campbell as the Fire Chief, Albert Austin, John Rand, James T. Kelley and Frank J. Coleman as Firemen, Leo White as Owner of Burning House.

The Vagabond
Edna Purviance, Stolen by Gypsies; Eric Campbell as Gypsy Chief, Leo White as Old Gypsy Woman and Old Jew; Lloyd Bacon as the Artist, Charlotte Mineau as Mother, Albert Austin and John Rand as Musicians, James T. Kelley and Frank J. Coleman as Musicians and Gypsies.

One A.M.
Albert Austin as Cab Driver.

The Count
Edna Purviance as the Heiress; Eric Campbell as the Tailor; Leo White as the Count; Charlotte Mineau as Mrs Moneybags; May White, Albert Austin, John Rand, James T. Kelley, Stanley Sandford, Frank J. Coleman.

The Pawnshop
Henry Bergman as the Pawnbroker; Edna Purviance as his Daughter; John Rand, Assistant; Albert Austin, Alarm Clock Customer; Wesley Ruggles, Customer with ring; Eric Campbell as the Burglar, Frank J. Coleman as Policeman; James T. Kelley as Lady with goldfish and Old Bum.

Behind the Screen
Eric Campbell, Property Man; Edna Purviance, Henry Bergman, Lloyd Bacon, Albert Austin, John Rand, Frank J. Coleman, Leo White, James T. Kelley, Charlotte Mineau, Wesley Ruggles, Tom Wood, Leota Bryan.

The Rink
Edna Purviance, the Society Girl; James T. Kelley as her Father; Eric Campbell as Mr Stout; Henry Bergman as Mrs Stout and Angry Diner; Lloyd Bacon, Albert Austin, Frank J. Coleman, John Rand, Charlotte Mineau, Leota Bryan.

Easy Street
Edna Purviance, the Missionary Girl; Eric Campbell, the Scourge; Albert Austin, Policeman and Clergyman; Henry Bergman, Anarchist, Lloyd Bacon as the Drug Addict, Charlotte Mineau, Loyal Underwood, Janet Miller Sully, Frank J. Coleman, John Rand, Tom Wood as Chief of Police.

The Cure
Edna Purviance, Eric Campbell as Guest with Gout; Henry Bergman as the Masseur; Albert Austin, John Rand, Frank J. Coleman, Leota Bryan, Tom Wood, Janet Miller Sully, Loyal Underwood, James T. Kelley as Ancient Bellboy.

The Immigrant
Edna Purviance, Kitty Bradbury as her Mother; Albert Austin, Henry Bergman as Woman Refugee and the Artist; Eric Campbell as the Head Waiter; Stanley Sandford, John Rand, James T. Kelley, Frank J. Coleman, Tom Harrington as the Registrar.

The Adventurer
Edna Purviance, Henry Bergman, Marta Golden, Eric Campbell as the Suitor; Albert Austin as Butler; Toraichi Kono as himself (the Chauffeur), John Rand, Frank J. Coleman, Loyal Underwood, Monta Bell, May White, Janet Miller Sully.

The First National Films – January 1918–July 1922

A Dog's Life
Charles Chaplin, the Tramp; Edna Purviance, Bar Singer; Mutt the dog, Scraps; Sydney Chaplin, Lunch Wagon Vendor; Albert Austin, Crook; Henry Bergman, Employment Agency Man and Fat Lady in Dancehall; Charles Reisner, Clerk and Drummer; Tom Wilson, Policeman; etc.

The Bond
Charles Chaplin, Edna Purviance, Sydney Chaplin as the Kaiser, Henry Bergman as John Bull, Dorothy Rosher as Cupid.

Shoulder Arms

Edna Purviance, Sydney Chaplin as the Sergeant and Kaiser; Henry Bergman as Fat German Sergeant and Field Marshal von Hindenburg; Albert Austin as American Soldier, German Soldier and the Kaiser's Chauffeur; Tom Wilson, John Rand, Park Jones, Loyal Underwood etc.

Sunnyside

Edna Purviance, Tom Wilson as the Boss; Tom Terriss as the Young Man from the City; Henry Bergman as Villager and Edna's Father; Tom Wood as Fat Boy; Loyal Underwood as Fat Boy's Dad; Helen Kohn, Olive Burton, Willie Mae Carson and Olive Acorn as Nymphs, etc.

A Day's Pleasure

Charles Chaplin as Father; Edna Purviance as Mother; Marion Feducha and Bob Kelly as Boys; Jackie Coogan as Smallest Boy; Tom Wilson as Husband; Babe London as his Seasick Wife; Henry Bergman as Captain and Man in Car, Loyal Underwood, Albert Austin, Jessie Van Trump.

The Kid

Charles Chaplin as the Tramp; Jackie Coogan as the Kid; Edna Purviance as the Mother; Baby Hathaway as Kid as baby; Carl Miller as the Artist; Henry Bergman as Night Shelter Keeper; Charles Reisner as the Bully; Lillita McMurray (Lita Grey) as the Flirtatious Angel; Jack Coogan Sr as Pickpocket/Guest/Devil; with Granville Redmond, Raymond Lee, Tom Wilson, Mae White, Edith Wilson, Nellie Bly Baker, Albert Austin, etc.
Released 9 February 1921.

The Idle Class

Charles Chaplin as the Tramp and the Husband; Edna Purviance as the Neglected Wife; Mack Swain as her Father; Henry Bergman as Hobo; Allan Garcia as Hobo and Guest; John Rand as Golfer and Guest, Lillita McMurray as Maid; with Lillian McMurray, Rex Storey, Loyal Underwood, Edward Knoblock, Granville Redmond, et al.
Released 25 September 1921.

Pay Day

Charles Chaplin as the Worker; Phyllis Allen as his Wife; Mack Swain as the Foreman; Edna Purviance as his Daughter; Sydney Chaplin as Charlie's Mate and Lunch Wagon Man; Albert Austin, John Rand and Loyal Underwood as Workmen; Henry Bergman and Allan Garcia as Drinking Companions.
Released 2 April 1922.

The Pilgrim

Charles Chaplin as the Escaped Convict; Edna Purviance as the Girl; Mack Swain as the Deacon, Kitty Bradbury as Edna's Mother; Loyal Underwood as

Elder; Charles Reisner as the Thief; Dinky Dean Reisner as Horrid Child; Sydney Chaplin as Child's Father; May Wells as the Mother; Henry Bergman as Sheriff on train; Tom Murray as Local Sheriff; Monta Bell as Policeman; with Raymond Lee, Phyllis Allen, Frank Antunez, Joe Van Meter, et al.

Released 29 February 1923.

(**The Professor** – Charles Chaplin as Professor Bosco, filmed September–October 1919.)

United Artists features

A Woman of Paris

Produced, directed and written by Charles Chaplin. Photography: Roland Totheroh with Jack Wilson. Assistant director: Edward Sutherland. Art director: Arthur Stibolt. Researchers: Jean de Limur and Henri d'Abbadie d'Arrast.

Edna Purviance as Marie St Clair; Adolphe Menjou as Pierre Revel; Carl Miller as Jean Millet; Lydia Knot as Jean's Mother; Charles French as Jean's Father; Clarence Geldert as Marie's Father; Betty Morrissey as Fifi; Malvina Polo as Paulette; Henry Bergman as Head Waiter; Nellie Bly Baker as Masseuse; Harry Northrup as Man About Town; Charles Chaplin cameo as Porter at station.

Released October 1923.

The Gold Rush

Produced, directed and written by Charles Chaplin. Photography: Roland Totheroh. Operators: Jack Wilson, Mike Marlatt. Art director: Charles D. Hall. Assistant directors: Charles Reisner, Henri d'Abbadie d'Arrast, Eddie Sutherland. Production manager: Alf Reeves.

Charles Chaplin as the Lone Prospector; Georgia Hale as Georgia; Mack Swain as Big Jim McKay; Tom Murray as Black Larsen; Malcolm Waite as Jack Cameron; Henry Bergman as Hank Curtis; John Rand, Albert Austin, Heinie Conklin, Allan Garcia and Tom Wood as Prospectors; Betty Morrissey, Kay Deslys and Joan Lowell as Georgia's friends; with Stanley Sandford, Barbara Pierce, Fred Karno Jr, et al.

Released June 1925.

The Circus

Produced, directed, written and edited by Charles Chaplin. Photography: Roland Totheroh. Operators: Jack Wilson, Mark Marlatt. Assistant Director: Harry Crocker. Art director Charles D. Hall.

Charles Chaplin as the Tramp; Merna Kennedy as Equestrienne; Allan Garcia as Ringmaster/Proprietor; Harry Crocker as Rex; Henry Bergman, John Rand and Armand Triller as Clowns; Stanley 'Tiny' Sandford as Property

Man; George Davis as the Magician; Betty Morrissey as Vanishing Lady; Steve Murphy as Pickpocket; Bill Knight as Cop; Jack Pierce as Circus Rope Operator; with H. L. Kyle, Eugene Barry, et al. 'Bobby', 'Josephine' and 'Jimmy' the Monkeys, and Numi the Lion.

Released January 1928.

City Lights

Produced, directed, written and edited by Charles Chaplin. Photography: Roland Totheroh. Operators: Mark Marlatt, Gordon Pollock. Assistant directors: Harry Crocker, Henry Bergman, Albert Austin. Art director: Charles D. Hall. Music by Charles Chaplin arranged by Arthur Johnson. Music director: Alfred Newman.

Charles Chaplin as the Tramp; Virginia Cherrill as the Blind Flower Girl; Florence Lee as her Grandmother; Harry Myers as the Millionaire; Hank Mann as Boxer; Eddie Baker as Referee; Tom Dempsey, Willie Keeler, Victor Alexander, Toby Stabeman and Eddie McAuliffe as Boxers; Emmet Wagner as the Second; Allan Garcia as the Butler; Henry Bergman as Mayor and Janitor; Albert Austin as Burglar and Street-sweeper; with John Rand, Spike Robinson, Tiny Ward, James Donnelly, Mrs Hyams, Harry Ayers et al.

Released January 1931.

Modern Times

Produced, directed and written by Charles Chaplin. Photography: Roland Totheroh, Ira Morgan. Assistant directors: Carter de Haven, Henry Bergman. Art directors: Charles D. Hall, Russell Spencer. Music by Charles Chaplin arranged by Edward Powell and David Raksin. Musical director: Alfred Newman.

Charles Chaplin as Worker; Paulette Goddard as the Gamin; Allan Garcia as the Boss; Chester Conklin as the Mechanic; Stanley J. Sandford as Big Bill; Henry Bergman as Café Owner; with Hank Mann, Louis Natheaux, Stanley Blystone, Sam Stein, Juana Sutton, Jack Low, Walter James, Dick Alexander, Dr Cecil Reynolds, Myra McKinney, Lloyd Ingraham, Heinie Conklin, John Rand et al.

Released February 1936.

The Great Dictator

Produced, directed and written by Charles Chaplin. Photography: Karl Struss, Roland Totheroh. Assistant directors: Dan James, Robert Meltzer, Wheeler Dryden. Art director: J. Russell Spencer. Editor: Willard Nico. Music by Charles Chaplin, with 'paraphrases of Wagner and Brahms'. Musical director: Meredith Wilson. Sound: Percy Townsend, Glenn Rominger. 'Co-ordinator': Henry Bergman.

Charles Chaplin as the Barber and Adenoid Hynkel; Paulette Goddard as Hannah; Jack Oakie as Benzino Napaloni; Henry Daniell as Garbitsch; Billy

Gilbert as Herring; Reginald Gardiner as Schultz; Grace Hayle as Mme Napaloni; Maurice Moskovich as Mr Jaeckel; Emma Dunn as Mrs Jaeckel; Chester Conklin as Barber's Customer; Leo White as Hynkel's Barber; Carter de Haven as Ambassador; Hank Mann and Eddie Gribbon as Stormtroopers; with Richard Alexander, Bernard Gorcey, Paul Weigel, et al.

Released October 1940.

Monsieur Verdoux

Produced, directed and written by Charles Chaplin. Photography: Curt Courant, Roland Totheroh. Cameraman: Wallace Chewning. Associate directors: Robert Florey, Wheeler Dryden. Assistant director: Rex Bailey. Art director: John Beckman. Costumes: Drew Tetrick. Make-up: William Knight. Hair-stylist: Hedvig M. Jornd. Editor: Willard Nico. Music by Charles Chaplin. Musical director: Rudolph Schrager. Sound: James T. Corrigan.

Charles Chaplin as Henri Verdoux; Martha Raye as Annabella Bonheur; Isobel Elsom as Marie Grosnay; Marilyn Nash as the Girl; Mady Correl as Madame Verdoux; Allison Roddan as Peter Verdoux; Margaret Hoffman as Lydia Floray; with Audrey Betz, Ada-May, Marjorie Bennett, Helen High, Irving Bacon, Edwin Mills, Virginia Brissac, Almira Sessions, Eula Morgan, Bernard J. Nedell, Charles Evans, Arthur Hohl, Fritz Lieber as the Priest, Fred Karno Jr, et al.

Released April 1947.

Limelight

Produced, directed and written by Charles Chaplin. Photography: Karl Struss. Photographic consultant: Roland Totheroh. Assistant producers: Wheeler Dryden, Jerome Epstein. Associate director: Robert Aldrich. Art director: Eugene Lourie. Editor: Joseph Engel. Music by Charles Chaplin. Musical director: Ray Rasch. Songs by Charles Chaplin and Ray Rasch. Choreography: Charles Chaplin, Andre Eglevsky, Melissa Hayden.

Charles Chaplin as Calvero; Claire Bloom as Terry; Sydney Chaplin as Neville; Nigel Bruce as Postant; Marjorie Bennett as Mrs Alsop; Wheeler Dryden as Doctor and Clown; Leonard Mudie as Doctor, Norman Lloyd as Bodalink; Barry Bernard as Redfern; Buster Keaton as the Pianist; with Snub Pollard, Loyal Underwood, Julian Ludwig, Andre Eglevsky, Melissa Hayden, Charles Chaplin Jr, Geraldine Chaplin, Michael Chaplin and Josephine Chaplin, et al.

Released October 1952.

Produced by Attica-Archway

A King in New York

Produced, directed and written by Charles Chaplin. Photography: George Perinal. Camera operator: Jeff Seaholme. Assistant producer: Jerome Epstein.

Assistant director: Rene Dupont. Art director: Allan Harris. Editor: John Seabourne. Music by Charles Chaplin, arranged by Boris Sarbek. Sound recording: Bert Ross, Bob Jones. Sound editor: Spencer Reeve. Special effects: Wally Veevers. Continuity: Barbara Cole. Shot at Shepperton Studios.

Charles Chaplin as King Shahdov; Oliver Johnston as Jaume; Dawn Addams as Ann Kay; Maxine Audley as Queen Irene; Jerry Desmonde as Prime Minister Voudel; Michael Chaplin as Rupert Macabee. Sidney James as Johnson the TV adman; with Joan Ingrams, John McLaren, Phil Brown, Harry Green, George Woodbridge, Clifford Buckton, Vincent Lawson, et al.

Released September 1957.

Produced by Universal

A Countess from Hong Kong

Produced by Jerome Epstein. Directed and Written by Charles Chaplin. Photography: Arthur Ibbetson. Assistant director: Jack Causey. Production designer: Don Ashton. Art director: Robert Cartwright. Editor: Gordon Hales. Music by Charles Chaplin. Musical director: Lambert Williamson. Musical associate: Eric James. Sound by Michael Hopkins, Bill Daniels, Ken Barker. Production supervisor: Denis Johnson. Technicolor, CinemaScope.

Marlon Brando as Ogden Mears; Sophia Loren as Countess Natascha Alexandroff; Sydney Chaplin as Harvey Crothers; Patrick Cargill as Hudson; Tippi Hedren as Martha Mears; Margaret Rutherford as Miss Gaulswallow; Michael Medwin as John Felix; with Oliver Johnston, John Paul, Angela Scoular, Peter Bartlett, Bill Nagy, Maureen Russell, Geraldine Chaplin, Josephine Chaplin, Victoria Chaplin et al., and Charles Chaplin as an Old Steward.

Released January 1967.

Select Bibliography

Some books on Charles Chaplin:

Chaplin, Charles, *My Trip Abroad*, Harper & Brothers, 1922.

Chaplin, Charles, *My Autobiography*, Simon and Schuster, New York, 1964.

Chaplin, Charles, *My Life in Pictures*, Grosset & Dunlap, New York, 1975.

'*Charlie Chaplin's Own Story*', as told to Rose Wilder Lane, Bobbs-Merrill, 1916. Reprinted with editorial comments by Harry M. Geduld, Indiana University Press, 1985.

Chaplin Jr, Charles, *My Father, Charlie Chaplin*, Longman's Green, 1960.

Chaplin, Lita Grey, with Morton Cooper, *My Life with Chaplin: an Intimate Memoir*, Bernard Geis Associates, New York, 1966.

Chaplin, Michael, *I Couldn't Smoke the Grass on My Father's Lawn*, G. P. Putnam's Sons, 1966.

Geduld, Harry M., *Chapliniana: A Commentary on Charlie Chaplin's 81 Movies: The Keystone Films*, Indiana University Press, 1987.

Huff, Theodore, *Charlie Chaplin, a Biography*, Pyramid Books, 1964.

Lynn, Kenneth S., *Charlie Chaplin and His Times*, Aurum Press, London, 1998.

Maland, Charles J., *Chaplin and American Culture, the Evolution of a Star Image*, Princeton University Press, 1989.

Marriot, A. J., *Chaplin, Stage by Stage*, Marriot Publishing, 2005 (obtainable from Marriot Publishing, 20 Oughton Close, Hitchin, Herts SG5 2QY, UK).

McDonald, Gerald D., Conway, Michael, and Ricci, Mark (eds), *The Films of Charlie Chaplin*, The Citadel Press, New Jersey, 1965, 1977.

Mellen, Joan, *Modern Times*, BFI Film Classics, 2006.

Niebaur, James L., *Chaplin at Essanay, A Film Artist in Transition, 1915–1916*, McFarland & Company, 2008.

Payne, Robert, *The Great Charlie*, Andre Deutsch, 1952; Pan Books, 1957.

Robinson, David, *Chaplin: His Life and Art*, William Collins Sons & Co., London, 1985; revised and updated, Penguin Books, 2001.

Vance, Jeffrey, *Chaplin, Genius of the Cinema*, Harry N. Abrams, 2003.

Wranovics, John, *Chaplin and Agee: The Untold Story of the Tramp, the Writer, and the Lost Screenplay*, Palgrave Macmillan, New York, 2005.

Books on American cinema history, the silent period, social history, and comedy

History of the American Cinema Series, University of California Press:

Balio, Tino, *Grand Design, Hollywood as a Modern Business Enterprise, 1930–1939* (Volume 5), 1993.

Bowser, Eileen, *The Transformation of Cinema, 1907–1915* (Volume 2), 1990.

Crafton, Donald, *The Talkies, American Cinema's Transition to Sound, 1926–1931* (Volume 4), 1997.

Koszarski, Richard, *An Evening's Entertainment, The Age of the Silent Feature Picture, 1915–1928* (Volume 3), 1990.

Musser, Charles, *The Emergence of Cinema, the American Screen to 1907* (Volume 1), 1990.

Allen, Frederick Lewis, *Only Yesterday, the Fabulous Twenties*, Bantam Books, New York, 1946.

Bergman, Andrew, *We're In the Money, Depression America and Its Films*, Elephant Paperbacks, Ivan R. Dee Publisher, Chicago, 1992.

Brownlow, Kevin, *Behind the Mask of Innocence*, Jonathan Cape, London, 1990.

Ceplair, Larry, and Englund, Steven, *The Inquisition in Hollywood, Politics in the Film Community 1930–1960*, University of Illinois Press, 2003.

Dmytryk, Edward, *Odd Man Out: A Memoir of the Hollywood Ten*, Southern Illinois University Press, 1996.

Doherty, Thomas, *Pre-Code Hollywood: Sex, Immorality and Insurrection in American Cinema 1930–1934*, Columbia University Press, New York, 1999.

Finler, Joel L., *The Hollywood Story*, Wallflower Press, London, 2003.

Gabler, Neal, *An Empire of Their Own, How the Jews Invented Hollywood*, Crown Publishers Inc., New York, 1988.

Gilbert, Douglas, *American Vaudeville, Its Life and Times*, Whittlesey House, McGraw-Hill, New York, London, 1940.

Horne, Gerald, *The Final Victim of the Blacklist: John Howard Lawson, Dean of the Hollywood Ten*, University of California Press, 2006.

Kerr, Walter, *The Silent Clowns*, Alfred A. Knopf, New York, 1975, London; Thomas Yoseloff Ltd, 1971.

Kiehn, David, *Broncho Billy and the Essanay Film Company*, Farwell Books, 2003.

Lahue, Kalton C., *World of Laughter, the Motion Picture Comedy Short, 1910–1930*, University of Oklahoma Press, 1966.

Lahue, Kalton C., *Mack Sennett's Keystone, the Man, the Myth and the Comedies*, South Brunswick & New York, A. S. Barnes and Company; London: Thomas Yoseloff Ltd, 1972.

Lahue, Kalton C., and Brewer, Terry, *Kops and Custards, The Legend of Keystone Films*, University of Oklahoma Press, 1968.

Lahue, Kalton C., and Gill, Samuel, *Clown Princes and Court Jesters*, South Brunswick & New York, A. S. Barnes and Company; London: Thomas Yoseloff Ltd, 1970.

Leff, Leonard J., and Simmons, Jerold L., *The Dame in the Kimono, Hollywood, Censorship and the Production Code from the 1920's to the 1960's*, Anchor Books, Doubleday, 1990.

Louvish, Simon, *Stan and Ollie, the Roots of Comedy, the Double Life of Laurel and Hardy*, Faber and Faber, London, 2001.

Louvish, Simon, *Keystone, The Life and Clowns of Mack Sennett*, Faber and Faber, London, 2001.

Mitchell, Glenn, *The Chaplin Encyclopedia*, B.T. Batsford Ltd, London, 1997.

Mitchell, Glenn, *A–Z of Silent Film Comedy*, B.T. Batsford Ltd, London, 1998.

Robinson, David, *The Great Funnies, a History of Film Comedy*, Studio Vista, 1969.

Robinson, David, *From Peepshow to Palace, the Birth of American Film*, Columbia University Press, New York, 1997.

Sennett, Mack, as told to Cameron Shipp, *King of Comedy*, Doubleday & Co, New York, 1954; Mercury House Inc., San Francisco, 1990.

Sklar, Robert, *Movie-Made America, A Cultural History of American Movies*, Vintage Books, New York, 1994.

Sloan, Kay, *The Loud Silents, Origins of the Social Problem Film*, University of Illinois Press, Urbana and Chicago, 1988.

Yallop, David, *The Day the Laughter Stopped, the True Story of Fatty Arbuckle*, St Martin's Press, New York, 1976.

A Fictional Curiosity

Coover, Robert, *Charlie in the House of Rue*, Penmaen Press, 1980.

Index